RELIGION AND NOTHINGNESS

The translator and the University of California Press wish to express their thanks to the Japanese Ministry of Education for making this book possible through the award of a Grant in Aid for the Publication of Scientific Research Results.

Nanzan Studies in Religion and Culture

James W. Heisig, General Editor

Hans Waldenfels, *Absolute Nothingness: Foundations for a Buddhist-Christian Dialogue*. 1980.

Frederick Franck, ed., *The Buddha Eye: An Anthology of the Kyoto School*. 1982.

Keiji Nishitani, *Religion and Nothingness*. 1982.

Religion and Nothingness

Keiji Nishitani

Translated, with an Introduction by
Jan Van Bragt

Foreword by Winston L. King

UNIVERSITY OF CALIFORNIA PRESS
Berkeley • *Los Angeles* • *London*

University of California Press
Berkeley and Los Angeles, California

University of California Press, Ltd.
London, England

COPYRIGHT © 1982 by Nishitani Keiji
First Paperback Printing 1983

Library of Congress Cataloging in Publication Data

Nishitani, Keiji, 1900–
  Religion and nothingness.

  (Nanzan studies in religion and culture; 2)
  Includes bibliographical references and index.
  1. Religion—Philosophy—Addresses, essays, lectures.
  2. Sunyata—Addresses, essays, lectures. I. Title.
  II. Series.
  BL51.N625   200'.1   81-4084
  ISBN: 0-520-04946-2   AACR2

PRINTED IN THE UNITED STATES OF AMERICA

3   4   5   6   7   8   9

CONTENTS

FOREWORD

Despite Rudyard Kipling's firm assurance three-quarters of a century ago that East and West could never meet, they have met hundreds of times and ways in this century. The East has reached out to the West or has been forced to accept technology, political and economic control, and occasionally philosophies and a crust of cultural forms. The West has reached out to the East for raw materials, cheap labor, exotic products, ideas, and lately to Japan for improved Western technology. But Kipling may still be correct in that a genuine, sympathetic, essence-to-essence encounter has not yet occurred because of the diverse natures of the two cultural streams.

In this volume we have something of an anomaly. Instead of the Western scholar, or spiritual pilgrim, going eastward in search of ancient philosophies of enlightenment, an Eastern Buddhist philosopher is coming westward to make his case, equipped with a considerable knowledge of Christian and Western thought. Indeed, anyone who reads the following pages will soon become aware of the extraordinary openness of Keiji Nishitani to the West, of the width and intelligence of his reading in Western literature, and of the sympathy which he displays for Western philosophy and religion. This is something quite different from the usual Zen-Western encounter, in which there is on the one side the Eastern Sage who deliberately mystifies the Westerner with an array of *kōan* which must be either appropriated in the esoteric Zen manner or altogether left alone, and on the other side the Westerner who registers frustrated or devout bemusement.

Of course it must be further said that the desire, herein evident, to communicate with Western thought, no matter how earnestly and knowledgeably expressed, does not automatically assure the Easterner an intelligent, let alone sympathetic, hearing in the West. Nishitani's effort is both encouraging as conversation and intensely interesting as critique. The respective ways of thinking and feeling, however, the total cultural resonances of the East and the West, have been too long and too far separated for mutual acceptance and intelligibility to come readily.

I

A basic difficulty that stares us in the face immediately, as noted in the translator's introduction, is the differing relation of philosophy and religion in East and West. And it is very important to keep this in mind from the beginning. For us in the West, religion and philosophy have been two ever since the time of the Greek philosophers. For though the Catholic theological tradition incorporated Aristotle into its theology and Platonism into its experience, philosophy never lost its independence, even in the Middle Ages. In the early modern period it asserted its independence anew under the impulse of humanism and the new empirical sciences. By the time of the Enlightenment it had come to qualify and question the basic foundations and assumptions of the Christian faith and ended up, as at present, occasionally in rational support of religious verities (always on the basis of its own rational foundations), more often in outright hostility toward all religion, but in any event always completely separate. And this separation has been institutionalized in the faculty structures of many universities, especially in the United States.

In the millennia-long traditions of the Hindu and Buddhist East, philosophy and religion have in effect and intent been branches of the same enterprise, that of seeking man's salvation. In India it is not uncommon for the professor of philosophy to spend the years of his retirement in personal religious quest, that is, in fully existentializing his intellectualism. In Japan since the Meiji Restoration, the Western pattern of separating the public (national and prefectural) universities from the religiously founded and supported ones has been faithfully followed, but the interchange of professors between the two systems and the similar content of the philosophico-religious courses taught in both bring them closer. After all, the Western pattern has been present in university learning for only a century, while the Buddhist cultural pattern has been dominant in all Japanese learning for fifteen centuries. Thus it is no anomaly in Japan that Nishitani should concurrently teach philosophy in Kyoto University (national) and religion in Ōtani University (a Jōdo Shinshū Buddhist institution). A Japanese friend says flatly that there would have been no difference in content between the way in which Nishitani would have taught a given course in the "philosophy" faculty of Kyoto University and in the department of "religion" in Ōtani University.

One must add to this another factor that confirms the above disparity and compounds the difficulty of East-West exchange, namely the Japanese cultural context whose influence Nishitani's thought reflects. Every historian of Japanese culture has remarked on the ease with which Buddhism adapted itself to the somewhat amorphous Shinto patterns of early Japanese times, and on the symbiotic relationship of the two thereafter. The Japanese cultural sensibility, to which Shinto ritual gives formal expression and which is so congruous in spirit to Zen Buddhism, can be characterized by two terms: organic-totalistic, and existential-aesthetic. Its organic-totalistic apprehension of human life in the world admirably fitted it to subtly "infiltrate" Zen. For Shinto (and the Japanese) do not sharply separate mind-body, inner-outer, man-nature, and religious-secular, but experience them as continua. The *kami* (gods) were within everything—the ocean, the pine tree, the steel of the swordmaker, and man himself, especially the hero and genius, good *or* evil—as innate power and quality. Matter is thus spiritualized and spirit materialized, so to speak.

This organic totalism of the Shinto-Japanese sense of life applied also to the religious organization of life. Between them Buddhist and Shinto ceremonies dealt with almost everything from the building of a house, the planting of a crop, and the making of a sword to birth, marriage, and death. Government and religion, whether Buddhist or Shinto, mutually supported each other, one with material benefits and the other with prayers and ritual. Political and religious personnel frequently were interchanged—princes, emperors, and *daimyō* entering the monastery for political or personal reasons, and returning from it to secular life for the same reasons. In any event the "wall of separation" between the sacred and secular in general, and church and state in particular, was totally unknown to Japanese culture until the American military authority disestablished Shinto as a state religion and dedivinized the emperor in this mid-century.

Equally or more important is the aesthetic-existential component of

Japanese culture, "aesthetic" here signifying the sensed and emotionally appropriated, and "existential" that which affects the very roots of
one's personal being and identity. Aesthetic form and feeling in many
situations are taken to be more important in Japan than practice or
substance. Ethical values and such virtues as righteousness and goodness, as well as the ultimate realities, are more often intuited and
emotionally sensed than rationally defined.

Correlative with this, and a not unimportant factor, is the character
of the Japanese language. It is of a loosely related, agglomerative nature,
admirably suited to the expression of ambiguous, infinitely suggestive
nuances of feeling-tone, and frustratingly indeterminate to a Westerner. Contrast this with German, for example, with its ordered gram-
matical structures in which each word is strictly held in its proper place
in a sentence so that it may deliver its bit of meaning clearly and
accurately to its hearer! Is it any wonder that the ontological proof of
God's existence and present day symbolic logic developed in the West
and not in Japan? Or that Eastern Buddhist philosophy, when filtered
through the Japanese cultural milieu, may have difficulty in communi-
cating with Western philosophies, even though one, such as Professor
Nishitani, has taken particular pains to seek out congruences or contact
points between the two?

There is yet another factor, Buddhist in general and Zen in particular, which is fully as central to the difficulty of East-West communica-
tion as any of the above: the differing East-West views of the universe
and man's place in it. A comparison of the two by means of somewhat
stereotypical models may illustrate this fundamental difference of cultural stance. The Western traditional model of the universe may be said
to be a mechanical one, not too unlike an intricate piece of clockwork
with the greater and lesser wheels and their movements meticulously
geared to one another. The whole tends to be a more or less definite and
limited system, both in time and space. The parts may be closely
related to one another, but much of the causality is conceived in a
somewhat mechanical single-line mode, item to item. (I recognize that
modern physical theory greatly qualifies this picture; but this does not
alter the general validity of the comparison here.) Relationships therein
are genuine and important but tend to be discreet and external; there is
no confusion of the being or individuality of any one part with that of
any other.

Conjoint with this underlying conceptual model, part and parcel of
the same cultural philosophical mode of awareness, are the basic build-

ing blocks of the Western thought structure—culturally inevitable, one
might say. In Western religious thought there is God (prime mover,
"watch" creator) who is transcendent of his creation, including man.
(Judaism and all its derivates have been strongly averse to humanizing
God or divinizing man.) But since man is more Godlike than any other
creature, he in turn transcends them all, the little lord of creation under
its Great Lord. The ultimate purpose of this subcreation, according to
Christianity, is to serve man and in the end to be conducive to his
eternal bliss. In post-Christian philosophy man as subject remains
rather lordly in his relation to objects. Mind, soul, or consciousness
alone "within" the citadel of individual selfhood looks "out" at everything else, whether human or nonhuman, as "other." As Nishitani
often insists, this Cartesian division of reality into immaterial, invisible,
subjective consciousness and material, visible objectivity is the epitome
of Western thought, the creator of its cultures and civilization. Out of
this climate has arisen the Western dichotomous type of logical assertion that A is *not*, *can*not be B. Nurtured in this atmosphere, deeply
conditioned by the Christian world view, there has arisen the dualistic
ethic of (absolute) good versus (absolute) evil, right versus wrong,
selfishness versus unselfishness and similar sharp distinctions. On this
same subject-object foundation, the human intellect, deliberately ab-
stracting itself from all emotion and aesthetic sensibility (except perhaps the beauty of systematic order), can dispassionately and logically
consider and analyze any *other*, be it man, animal, plant, rock, star, or
component thereof, and thus create an immense and all-pervasive
structure called science.

By contrast the Eastern and Buddhist model for conceiving the
universe can be termed a biological-organic one. The East speaks of the
interdependency of part upon part and of part and whole, of the
internal relations of one entity to another within the organism that is the
universe. There is here the amorphous unity of nondistinction, of the
Taoist Great Primordial Nothingness (which is prior, perhaps temporally, certainly structurally, to all individual being in the universe)
out of which beings flow in their diverse forms and to whose oceanlike
womb they return upon dissolution. Hua Yen Buddhism's philosophy
of totality placed all beings in what Van Bragt, using a Christian term
for the interrelations within the Trinity, calls "circuminsessional interpenetration" of one another. Fa Tsang illustrated it by his hall of
mirrors in which each mirror (individual being) reflects (or "contains")
the central Buddha image as well as every other mirror in the hall (the

universe). Thus the whole can be said to be *in* the part as truly as the part is *in* the whole. These and many similar figures clearly suggest a living body rather than an intricate machine.

It is then inevitable that a philosophy (Zen Buddhist) which had its origins and nourishment in this thought complex will characteristically portray the universe in a way radically different from the Western manner. In place of one-on-one causal sequences there will be wholistic, contextual-causal interpretations. In place of a straight-line historical-causal "progress" of events to a climax of some sort in a limited time-span there will be a historical "process" wherein time is cyclical and infinite, and "purpose," "drive," and "direction" much less obvious and important. Individual entities, including man, will not be seen as so substantially separable from other entities as in Western thought, but rather as a single flowing event in which the interdependent relationships are as real as, or even more real than the related entities themselves. And man will have none of that proud, unique difference and lordship over creation which the Christian West has given him—and which he retains in post-Christian secularized form. In Eastern thought he is part and parcel of the universe in which his existence is set, one little wavelet in a vast ocean of being/non-being. And quite obviously his visceral values, existential concerns, and intuitional awareness will be fully as important in relating to and understanding the universe as his sheerly rational knowledge—if not more so.

II

What happens now when a Buddhist philosopher (Nishitani) working from his own Eastern Buddhist basis seeks to relate his perceptions of the universe to the Western corpus of Christian faith and philosophical thought? Philosophical-religious unity and an organic view of the universe will encounter a divided philosophical and religious thought structure and a generally mechanistic universe; strongly intuitive-existential thought tries to deal with rational-logical thought. Thus a brief sketch of what has already happened in Nishitani's use of European philosophical and religious motifs and ideas may perhaps open the way to a projection of some probabilities in a fresh encounter with more specifically American philosophical and religious thought. As we shall see, the latter encounter is yet to begin.

It is evident at once in reading the following pages that Nishitani perceives the long-dominant Christian and Greek rationalist traditions as irretrievably undermined by their own inherent logic and by the modern scientific world view. They have been devoured by their own progeny, the consequences of their own intrinsic qualities. What is left? An underlying nihility, a spiritual vacuity, and a pervasive sense of meaninglessness, coming explicitly to the surface in the philosophies of Nietzsche, Sartre, and Heidegger. Second, the West—and all those cultures affected by Western influences—present the spectacle of a massive superstructure of brilliant, scientific achievement strung precariously over a chasm of meaninglessness, and are apparently incapable of building themselves new foundations from within their own traditional resources. Hence they are in desperate need of a more enduring foundation unassailable even by scientific and philosophical skepticism.

Viewing European philosophy and religion in this context, Nishitani has a rating scale of sorts for various types of Western thought. At the bottom of the scale is the area in which East and West are most at variance with each other, where the East makes least or only negative contact with Western thought and values. Here stand Christian theism and Cartesian subject-object dualism. Aside even from its dubious proofs of God's existence and evidences of his operation in historical events, theism is inherently unsatisfactory to Nishitani because of a chasm at the root of being, that between God and his creation, between God and man especially. This fundamental cleavage at the very base of man's being and of his religious awareness, which Christianity indeed holds to be the *true* character of that awareness, is directly antithetical to the Taoist-Buddhist principle of harmonic, organic oneness at the core of all being and of *true* human awareness. And in the philosophical area the all-pervasive Cartesian subject-object duality must be viewed as totally and perniciously divisive of man's intellect from his existence. It is even more subtle in its perversion than the religious duality in that it egoistically perverts efforts to escape its self-imprisonment by ever more rarefied, yet genuine, forms of subject-object consciousness. Thus theism and subject-object consciousness are Westernness encapsulated and essentialized. They have opened a Pandora's box of good and evil: on the one hand, science and self-aware humanism; on the other hand, meaninglessness, intellect cut off from its existential rootage, and technology out of control.

In the middle range for Eastern appreciation are those philosophers who have been more or less aware of the failing health and insecure foundations of the dominant European world-view and have tried to remedy the situation. Immanuel Kant, for example, shocked out of his complacent Christian rationalism by Hume, strictly limited the scope of Reason in its apprehension of ultimate realities, but compensated by rationally structuring the basic forms under which that reality appears to us, and immensely deepening human subjective awareness. Yet for Nishitani Kant remains the prisoner still of subjective intellectual abstractions. Very significantly for our understanding of Nishitani, he finds in Nietzsche, Sartre, and Heidegger (with whom he studied for three years) the philosophers with whom he is most in consonance. And, of equal significance for his thought's encounter with typically optimistic American thought, is the reason for this: they all, Nietzsche most particularly, speak out of the depths of a rational-religious despair, self-consciously despairing among the ruins of Greek-Christian thought and belief structures. Basing themselves squarely on the nihility that now threatens—existence in a no-God, no-meaning world wherein all human values come to naught in death—they propose a new set of "meanings" fabricated solely out of "nothingness" and the courage of desparation, so to speak. But, argues Nishitani from his basis of Absolute Emptiness (*śūnyatā*), even they are still within the Western dualistic trap, caught in a subtle form of Cartesian selfhood—Nietzsche in his Superman's Will and Sartre in his absurd and irrational proclamation of the self's freedom from all but self. Yet of all Europe's philosophers, they are nearest to the kingdom of *śūnyatā*.

A few (by no means all) of the religiously oriented seem to Nishitani to come nearest to Eastern Buddhism. Kierkegaard, for whom rationalized Christian doctrine was unable to provide the certainty needed for faith-induced decision and action, seems to be somewhat kindred in spirit to the Zen meditator facing the Great Death. St. Francis of Assisi commends himself to Nishitani—but as an atypical Christian—for his deep fellow-feeling toward all God's creatures, even the inanimate, by which he approaches the Buddhist sense of the organic oneness of the whole universe. But most markedly it is with Meister Eckhart that Nishitani feels existential and religious rapport. (No doubt he would agree with D. T. Suzuki's comment to me that "Eckhart is the leading Zen man in the West.") A godhead that is beyond all theologizing, that is interpenetrative of the deepest human essence and interpenetrated by the human essence in turn (and hence transcendently immanent in his "creation"), is very close to that Absolute Emptiness in which, as Nishitani maintains, all that is existent "lives, moves, and has its being," to use a Christian phrase.

III

From the way in which Nishitani has dealt with European thought and culture it is by now quite evident that the main encounter of his thought with Western philosophy and religion is in the existential realm rather than in that of formal theology or metaphysics, much less that of language analysis. Perhaps indeed for Buddhism in general, and for Nishitani's nonsectarian Zen and demythologized Buddhism particularly, the question of reality is an existential and religious one—religious in the sense of Tillich's ultimate concern, so that the proper role of philosophy is to advance existential interests, to make a fully existentialized human existence possible. As the translator notes in a perceptive phrasing:

> For the East the principle of salvation was made into a basic principle for all reality . . . the Kyoto school (of which Nishitani is a "member") simply transfers this process to an ontological level in accord with the Western scheme of things.

Hence the primary points at issue between East and West as set forth in this volume will be in the area of existential concern rather than in cosmological theory or reality-speculation. The "real" world for Zen Buddhism would seem to be the experienced, the lived-in, the existed-in context of human life; the philosophic and/or scientific names given to what surrounds us are considered of secondary importance to the religious, that is, fully existential life.

In passing it is of some interest to inquire why there has been little or no inclusion of any Anglo-American materials in Professor Nishitani's writings. Perhaps the reasons are not far afield. Since Japan's "opening to the West" her philosophers, for various incidental and cultural reasons, have been interested primarily in the Germanic tradition—and Nishitani was educated in this tradition. But doubtless the main reason is that the Anglo-American tradition has had little in it that has appealed to an Eastern and Buddhist-oriented culture. In the British tradition, for example, we have Reid's commonsense realism, practical, simplistic Utilitarianism, the empiricism and political philosophy of Locke, the God-centered idealism of Berkeley—none of which could have much appeal for a Buddhist-oriented thinker. As for American thought, almost the only American philosopher in whom Japan has taken any interest at all is John Dewey and his pragmatic "learning by doing" educational theories. Indeed for most of Japan, America is not a land of thinkers but of merchants, manufacturers, technical entrepreneurs, and practical-minded enterprise. What then can plausibly be projected about possible contact points, positive or negative, between Nishitani's thought and the American cultural scene?

In attempting to answer this question it must be insisted, in view of the nature of the thought pattern expressed in this volume, that feeling-tone is as important as formal thought-content for this encounter. The general cultural tradition, the contemporary mood and its interests, and like factors will be involved in the interaction and dictate the responses quite as much or more than the specific ideas involved.

On the face of it, and in keeping with what has just been said, the American scene would not look promising for a genuine encounter. American culture on the whole has been permeated by an optimistic and activist-progressive spirit, an onward-and-upward-forever hope-fulness stemming from both religious and secular sources. Characteristically, Americans have believed that determination, goodwill, and ingenious "know-how" could solve almost any problem in the universe, that success of our national efforts is guaranteed by Divine Will, evolution, and the historically active forces of "progress," in varying proportions! Hence traditionally, "Eastern pessimism"—of which Buddhism is judged to be the prime example—has been looked upon askance. Emerson, one of the few American thinkers to pay serious attention to Eastern philosophy and religion in the past, selected only a vaguely-conceived oriental Oversoul to place on the fringe of his self-reliance philosophy. So too, Americans tend to be scientifically-technologically oriented, perhaps no more confidently reliant upon technology to provide the "good life" than the Japanese, but without their tough resiliency in accepting misfortune and disappointment, product of a thousand years or so of the Buddhist teaching of karma. Will such a climate as this be at all receptive to Absolute Emptiness?

One must immediately add, of course, that the American optimism of the eighteenth and nineteenth centuries has lost much of its buoy-ancy and its naïve confidence in the future. The golden material prom-ises of limitless room and natural resources, and of a consequent "mani-fest destiny" to power and glory (a secular descendant of the Puritan sense of the Divine Purpose that was being fulfilled by their "holy experiment" in New England) have lost their credibility for most Americans, even though American affluence, relatively speaking, is still enormous. So, too, there are many who have become aware of the possibility of spiritual poverty in the midst of material plenty and are disillusioned with mere affluence.

One might add to this also a kind of eager grasping for other views of the universe than the traditional-popular perception of a Newtonian, material-causal clockwork structure. The seemingly greater flexibility offered by the newer doctrines of physics on particle indeterminacy and the relativity of time-space categories has seemed to some to represent a new breath of liberty within the ironclad rigidity of the cause-and-effect imposed by past scientific tradition, and to be somehow more encouraging to the "spiritual" values. Books such as Fritjof Capra's *The Tao of Physics*, setting forth extensive parallels between some Eastern religious-mythical views of the cosmos and the new world of physical theory, have been quite popular. There is also a considerable growth of natural environmental concern, a new awareness of the disastrous consequences of an exploiting and aggressive technological industrialism, that could find in the Buddhist sense of harmonic interaction between man and nature something more congenial than the biblical command given to Adam and his descendants to "subdue" the earth. Such then is the general atmosphere in which this presentation of Eastern values must make its way.

The American religious scene is also of interest and importance; for no matter how existentially and philosophically this book's ideas are presented, they come forth as a *Buddhist* view of life, and its existentialism is inherently and self-evidently religious in the deepest sense of that word. Though it is true that there is currently a revival of conservative-evangelical Christianity, and though both current values and antivalues in the United States embody or reflect Christian tradition, there is also a new openness to "foreign" religions, especially among the younger generation. Less than half of the country's population profess any of the varieties of Judaeo-Christian faith. For many the traditional churches and their teaching have become unconvincing and personally irrelevant—not so much as in Europe, yet substantially. Thus there has been a religious void, and a growing one in America, for the last few decades. Into this void has poured a plethora of importations, particularly from the Hindu-Buddhist East.

Of special interest here is the appearance of Zen on the American scene. It has been in America now for nearly fifty years in a religious-existential form. Some of the earlier interest in Zen, and the popularity of Suzuki-Zen in the sixties, was of a faddish sort, a wave of interest that then moved on to drug experiences for some, and to a renewed interest in traditional Christianity for others. But for still others, Zen meditation offered (and offers) a deeply personal and existential way of awareness and life more meaningful than the traditional ways of "salvation."

And as is well known, even in Christian circles, particularly the Catholic, there is considerable interest in and practice of a Christianized Zen-style meditation—to say nothing of the many Zen-fertilized personal-realization methods now current. Therefore it can be said that Zen, properly or improperly understood and practiced, is now a permanent part of the American religious scene.

For such groups this volume should be of considerable importance and interest. Here, for almost the first time, we have a serious attempt by a Buddhist philosopher to join issue *philosophically*, that is, not experientially but intellectually, with Western religion and philosophy. Up to the present, available Buddhist materials have largely been translations of Buddhist scriptures and related writings, expositions of these writings by Western linguists and historians of religion for university audiences (where this volume will also be quite welcome!), experimental psychological treatises on the "Zen experience," and manuals for the practice of *zazen*. But a continuing Zen movement in the West, mostly built on Zen *experience* so far, will sooner or later realize its need for a more intellectual presentation of a Zen world view than it possesses at present.

The relation of this volume to another important strand of American culture, with considerable inbuilt academic, religious, and personal interest, poses a problem. This is the psychological-psychiatric strand. Nishitani never mentions Freud, his successors, or opponents. Is it because Freudian-inspired techniques seem to be too much the mere manipulation of mental processes and emotional sets in order to better achieve traditional worldly goals, rather than the existential breakthrough Nishitani calls for? Yet this relationship, or lack of it, is of some consequence because part of the above-noted interest in Zen has been attributable to the strength of the psychological-psychiatric "tradition" in America. Indeed in the earlier days, and to some extent even yet, Zen has been viewed as a psychosomatic device to gain "inner peace" and to avoid or to finesse one's way past current social, ethical, and religious dilemmas.

Finally, and perhaps most important, it must be inquired whether the Buddhist philosophy of Absolute Emptiness can ever find a serious hearing among American philosophers. Here, as on the general cultural scene, prima facie prospects are not encouraging. There have, of course, been occasional contacts between Zen and American philosophy. D. T. Suzuki, for example, appeared some years ago at a Hawaiian East-West encounter, but it turned out to be more of a nonencounter; no *philosophical* answers were forthcoming from him, at least not Western-style "rational" ones. *Philosophy East and West* publishes occasional articles on Buddhist (and Zen) thought in comparison/ contrast with Western thought. So too an occasional philosopher, for example Paul Wienphal, has become deeply interested in the Zen mode of awareness. But by and large the American philosophical community has paid scant heed to Eastern philosophies in general, leaving them to departments of religious studies or Eastern linguistics. And Zen in particular has been given short philosophical shrift, being considered too Eastern-abstruse, non- or anti-intellectual, or semimystical and religious in nature.

Given the dominance of British empirical-realist schools of various types in the American philosophical heritage, this is not surprising. Of course there have been exceptions. Josiah Royce's absolute idealism attracted a few followers to an American idealist tradition, now mostly gone. The German idealists, so well known in Japan, have also had a few American followers. Naturalism comes to mind, described by its adherents a generation ago as a "temper" rather than a school of thought. There were also the realists who, along with the naturalists, were concerned to philosophize in the light of new scientific discoveries and the Darwinian theory of evolution. James's pragmatism, sometimes called the most characteristic American philosophy, viewed ideas not as essences or activity from some ontologically higher realm, but simply as plans of action whose truth or untruth was proven by their success in dealing with the situation to which they were addressed. Dewey, as observed, carried this philosophy on in the form of conceiving all thinking to be problem solving. Certainly the naturalist view which included man integrally in the natural order—strengthened here by Darwinism—and pragmatism's bringing ideation from its lofty Platonic heights into the push-and-pull world of concrete, living activity, might strike responsive chords in a Zen-oriented mind. Yet it is difficult to imagine any philosopher of these persuasions having a meaningful conversation with Buddhist philosophers, even though they might be sympathetic to the doctrines of codependent origination and the organic oneness of the universe. And from Nishitani's viewpoint, both philosophies would still be caught up in the Cartesian subject-object dualism, here crystallized in the "scientific method," and be philosophizing *in vacuo*, that is, nonexistentially and nonreligiously.

What then of the *present* philosophic scene? Here too the prevailing currents are not well adapted for a Buddhist dialogue because the dominant American philosophical mode of thought is embodied in the analytical and logical schools. The first, stimulated by Ludwig Wittgenstein, takes the structures and usages of ordinary language—Western-type language—for the proper field of philosophy. Metaphysical and ethical problems cannot be properly dealt with by philosophy because their truth or falsity cannot be determined. Their very presence in philosophy indicates a confusion about the structure, function, and "meaning" of language itself. Symbolic logic is, if possible, even further removed from metaphysical, religious, and ethical matters, being a semimathematical analysis of the formal structure of (Western?) language itself. It is concerned with the proper form of declarative, affirmative, and negative statement more than with the ontological "truth" or "reality" of any assertion or negation. In any event the only future for Eastern Buddhist philosophy here would be as a fleeting example for illustrating maximum philosophic aberration.

Even though they cannot claim large followings, there are other philosophical persuasions in America besides these two that would be less antagonistic or even friendly to Buddhist philosophical interchange. There is phenomenology, stemming from the German philosopher Edmund Husserl, a kind of meta-philosophy attempting to get behind (or above?) the ordinary modes of thinking to the structure of mentation itself, and not on a merely psychological level. "Bracketing" all normative terms and considerations, phenomenology tries to penetrate to the structure of the very possibility of having experience or ideas at all—Kant's trancendental unity of apperception under a new name? Yet the abstract superworldly nonexistential character of this kind of thinking would seem to be far removed from Buddhist existentialism.

There is also a group that consider themselves existentialist, influenced by Sartre and Heidegger, but, if one may judge, not so radically pessimistic as either—perhaps the influence of American optimism. The major emphasis among some of them is on "lived" values and life-reality apprehended in actual involved existence, rather than complete reliance upon purely logical, rationalistic, and "scientific" approaches to reality. Obviously the importance here of visceral and aesthetic values is considerable. In respect to Nishitani's presentation of the "nihility factory" in Nietzsche, Sartre, and to some extent in Heidegger, as *almost* providing the necessary degree of existential despair (a *zazen*-like "Why existence?" desperation) for a decisive breakthrough into the level of that genuine *śūnyatā*-awareness found in Buddhism, American existentialist despair may seem too mild to serve.

Nonetheless such a presentation of Buddhist philosophy as this may well find sympathetic hearers among American existentialists.

A more recent but very lively school of American thought—one for the moment more often to be found in departments of literature than in departments of philosophy or religion—is that derived from French structuralist and poststructuralist criticism, and in particular from the work of Jacques Derrida. A principal theme of this school has been the attack on the distinction between author and reader. At successive levels of generalization, this theme becomes an attack on the distinction between creator and interpreter, subject and object, and finally between self and nonself. When and if the methods of this critique begin to be employed on the traditional subject matter of theology, Nishitani's somewhat parallel critique of the Western crises of theism and selfhood may find a surprising kind of welcome.

One other possibility remains in the field of American philosophy, and one that has been slightly explored already. To this writer it seems to have the greatest potential for sustaining a full philosophical-religious contact between Buddhist East and Christian West of any thought pattern in America. This is the so-called process philosophy which had its roots in the thought of A. N. Whitehead, especially in his seminal *Process and Reality*. Again one must say that process philosophers are a small group, but the group is vigorous and has its religious counterpart in "process theology." This latter has grown especially from Whitehead's portrait of God as having a "primordial" and a "consequent" nature, that is, he is integral to the universe and vice versa, *he* develops, to some extent at least, in the development of the universe. He might be said to be transcendently immanent in it. One asks immediately whether there are possible likenesses here to the Buddhist *dharmakāya* or *śūnyatā*.

Without attempting to give even a cursory summary of Whitehead's thought, two or three possible points of contact with the Buddhist world view may be mentioned. First, there is clearly a biological-organic model underlying process philosophy's cosmology; indeed it has often been termed the philosophy of organism. In it each member of the universe, at whatever level, is intimately connected with every other by internal relations. Again process thought rejects any sharp division between "mind" and "matter" in the constitution of the cosmos; all existent entities, no matter how seemingly inorganic they may be, have a mental or feeling pole as well as a material pole. Its "ultimate reality"—though never quite so named—is creativity, superior even to God it seems. For process philosophy, flexibility and fluidity seem on the one hand to be in accord with Einsteinian relativity and Heisenbergian uncertainty principles; and on the other to be at least within speaking distance of the Buddhist view of the world as a fluxing tide of event-entities and characterized by the "circuminsessional interpenetration" of all its parts portrayed so often in this volume.

There are as well some evidences of actual rapprochement between process thought and Buddhist thought. Some Japanese graduate students in America have been struck by the "likeness" of Whitehead's thought to Buddhist thought. *Process and Reality* has recently been translated into Japanese. And there have been a few conferences between Japanese and American scholars devoted to an exploration of the similarities and differences of Whiteheadian and Buddhist viewpoints. Whether this will indeed grow into a full-scale and fruitful encounter between Eastern and Western philosophical and religious essences remains the secret of the future. But the potential for it is present, and the following pages may well contribute to its realization.

Emeritus Professor   Winston L. King
Vanderbilt University
Nashville, Tennessee

TRANSLATOR'S
INTRODUCTION

The fact that this staff is a staff is a fact in such a way as to involve at the same time the deliverance of the self. . . .

"Illuminating insight" does not stop at mere contemplation. It is integrated with the deliverance of all beings in time from the universal suffering of the world.[1]

In these few simple words we have, I believe, the deepest stirrings of a mind for whom the cognitive pursuit of reality is inseparably bound up with those ultimate concerns that have come to be known as religion. In them we have the very heart of the challenge that the thought of Keiji Nishitani poses to Western modes of philosophical reason and religious speculation.

It seems only fitting, therefore, that we look further into the meaning of this challenge, and the wider intellectual environment from which it stems, by way of introduction to the essays offered here in English translation.[2]

THE EASTERN BACKGROUND

It is a testimony to his integrity and seriousness as a philosopher that I must begin with the claim that Nishitani's thought can only be understood against the background of Japanese culture, both in its historical role as the final receptacle of the eastward drive of the cultures of India and China, and in its contemporary position as the one country in the world where East and West confront one another clearly and in full array. Indeed, one might say that the particular appeal of his thought for us lies precisely in the fact that its *universality* is mediated by this *regionality*.

In this regard, the following passage, appearing in the preface to the first substantial philosophical text of the Kyoto School (the tradition to which Nishitani belongs) to be presented to the English-speaking world over twenty years ago, is still very much to the point:

> While the history of Japanese metaphysical speculation, based on peculiarly Asian religious experiences, goes back to the eleventh century, Japanese philosophy as organized in accordance with Western concepts and assumptions is barely a century old. Ever since they came in contact with the culture and philosophy of the West, Japanese thinkers have considered it their task to search for a harmonious integration of two philosophical worlds; to reformulate, in the categories of an alien Western philosophy, the philosophical insights of their own past.[3]

In the case of the present book, the reader will no doubt soon observe that while Western philosophers are frequently brought into the discussion (and modern Japanese thinkers virtually passed over), Nishitani is particularly fond of calling to mind and "worrying to death" any number of old Japanese and Chinese texts, wrestling with them until he has secured the blessing he seeks. This material belongs almost entirely to the Buddhist tradition, which reached Japan by way of China and Korea in the sixth century of the Christian era, and has deeply impressed the mind of Japan and come to form the core of its intellectual life for these many centuries since.[4] The words of Dōgen, the thirteenth-century founder of the Sōtō Zen sect in Japan, will be found to loom especially large here. And indeed, Nishitani's works in general attest to a strong affinity with the thought of that extraordinary religious and intellectual giant whose works, in the pure pragmatism of their religious intent, can never be captured under the label of "spiritual reading" and leave us no choice but to speak of them as "metaphysical speculation."

In reading Nishitani, then, we must constantly keep in mind the way his thought follows along a path of Eastern speculation cut out of the same bedrock through which the Buddhist stream flows. Only when we are open to finding there a "rational" explication of an Eastern experience of life that is legitimately different from our own, and in many ways complementary to it, can we come to an appreciation of what Nishitani is trying to do. For at every turn Nishitani emphatically makes these Eastern insights his own while probing their relevance for contemporary life and their relationship to Western philosophical theories and religious tenets.

While there is no need even to attempt here a resumé of the rich variety of that speculative world, two ideas at least should be singled out as fundamental to the whole structure. Together they combine to render impossible, from the very start, the sort of dependency on and concentration of attention toward the subject-object relationship which characterizes Western thinking. In the first place, we have the notion of *pratītya-samutpāda* or "conditioned co-production," according to which reality is seen as a boundless web of interrelations whose momentary nodes make up the "things" of experience. It is pure relation without substance. It leaves covetous man with nothing to cling to, nothing to become attached to. But the grasping, clinging subject itself is no more substantial than things, because of a second notion, that of *anātman* or non-ego, according to which the basic self-affirmation through which man makes himself a permanent center of his world is undercut. In its stead, man is made to lose himself in an "All are One" or a "formless nothingness."

This may perhaps look less like an explanation of reality to us than like a pure and simple *reductio ad nihilum* of the facts of experience. To be sure, original Buddhism, where these ideas first found systematic expression, is world-negating in the extreme; and the reduction of all reality to a cosmic dream or "mind-only" is the ever-present and alluring Lorelei of Eastern speculation. Yet the main point for us to grasp here—and Nishitani goes to great lengths to make us see it—seems to be that this does not mean a mere doing away with the world, that it is not what we would call a simple negation of reality, but an alternative and ultimately positive view of reality that might even be termed a "radical empiricism."

In an effort to explain this, Japanese thinkers frequently refer us to Japanese and Chinese art:

> Eastern paintings do not aim at the expression of the real form of things; and even if they do portray the form of things, they do not portray the things themselves; by means of them they express the soul, but this soul is nothing other than the formless world. On the surface of the canvas the blank spaces dominate. These blank spaces are wholly different from the *backgrounds* of Western paintings. Instead the blank spaces are expressed by the form of the things portrayed.[5]

In this same regard we recall the famous words of Kitarō Nishida:

> In contradistinction to Western culture which considers form as existence and formation as good, the urge to see the form of the formless, and hear the sound of the soundless, lies at the foundation of Eastern culture.[6]

In brief, the Western mind cannot but think that all reality has been done away with when all "being" (form, substance) has been negated;

but the East has found that the removal of the immediate and over-powering face of reality is but a necessary condition for what is really real to appear.

Obviously this metaphysical position and everything it entails was not reached all at once. Indian art, for example, even in its overtly Buddhist representations, shows a marked difference from such a view. Its cluttered surfaces, tangled with figures that seem to undulate to-gether in a restless *pullulatio* of movement, seem to tell us: "form is fullness." In Hīnayāna Buddhism, on the other hand, we find the opposite extreme where all things are declared to be void: "form is emptiness." It is only in the Mahāyāna tradition, Nishitani would argue, that Buddhism reaches a synthesis of affirmation and negation. There things become an expression of the void, enabling the complete formulation that often serves it as a kind of motto: "form is emptiness, emptiness is form." Hīnayāna Buddhism finds its salvific negation or nirvāna (that is to say, its "sacred") in a world apart from and beyond the world of samsāra teeming with illusory appearances of individual reali-ties. Mahāyāna Buddhism, on the other hand, locates nirvāna squarely within this secular world of form and asserts that it is there that nirvāna finds its self-expression. The Kegon and Tendai philosophies that developed out of Chinese Buddhism surely represent important steps in the full elaboration of this view. Nishitani, however, seldom refers to them directly and, even then, reserves his allusions for the most part to those cases in which he finds their ideas reflected in Zen speculation. In contrast, the Indian originator of the complete viewpoint of emptiness, Nāgārjuna, seems to be granted a position of central importance.[7]

There can be no doubt, then, that we have in Nishitani a modern representative of an Eastern speculative tradition every bit as old and as variegated as the Western philosophical endeavor. But that tradition was also said to be "based on peculiarly Asian religious experiences." For the fact is that it is something that developed in unison with religious objectives and practices, without ever setting itself up as a system of "objective" knowledge, complete in itself and detached from the realm of the religious. In this sense, we might refer to it as "intrinsi-cally religious." Hence when we speak of "Buddhist philosophy," we need to understand thereby a mode of speculation that takes as its radical point of departure the Buddhist religious experience of reality as expressed in the Four Holy Truths, provides a systematic explanation of that religious doctrine and its attitude, and constructs for it an appropriate logic.

The Christian West does not possess anything comparable in the way of a "Christian philosophy." Even after the advent of Christianity, Western philosophy held fast to its Greek roots and did not make a fundamental shift in orientation to serve as an explanation of the Christian religious experience. The same could be said of either the Judaic or the Islamic religious experience vis-à-vis Western philosophy. As a result, we find religion and philosophy coexisting in conditions laden with tensions. The individual tends to assume one world view, for example, in moments of spiritual reading and another in moments of rational analysis. It is different with Buddhist philosophy, where the unity of the religious and the speculative has never been severed. The German theologian Hans Waldenfels puts it this way in speaking of Nāgārjuna: "Whatever he has to say philosophically all has to do with clearing the way for enlightenment and with the radical liberation of man from all false attachments that obstruct that way."[8] So, too, we find thinkers like Heinrich Dumoulin remarking similarly of Zen that it shows "the most intimate relationship between experience and doctrine. . . . Metaphysical speculation, religious practice, and mystical experience come very near each other and form a unity."[9]

The questions all this confronts us with seem to converge at three principal points. First: *What has this intrinsically religious logic to teach theology, especially Christian theology?* Second: *What has this speculation to teach us about the structure of reality in general?* A fair portion of the representatives of this speculation, and Nishitani is clearly among them, are carried along by the conviction that only on this level is truly *real* reality revealed to man: "When we speak of things 'as they truly are in themselves,' we are on the field of religion."[10] And third: *Can this speculation stand by itself, apart from religious practice, in logical autonomy and thus be considered philosophy in the Western sense?* On the one hand, we need to inquire into what D. T. Suzuki meant when he wrote that "Nishida's philosophy . . . is difficult to understand, I believe, unless one is passably acquainted with Zen experience."[11] On the other hand, if there is one thing that distinguishes Nishitani and his colleagues of the Kyoto School from their Buddhist predecessors, it is their confrontation with Western philosophy and their determination to see their speculation as expressly philosophical in some "scientific" sense or other of the term. It is to ask if the caesura the Kyoto School effects between religion and speculation is the same as that seen to obtain between religion and philosophy in the West. In its most precise form, the question asks after the logic adopted by the Kyoto School. Its representatives seem to agree that their logic is necessarily dialectical in the highest degree, indeed "more dialectical than Hegel's logic." But we want to know at what point this sort of logic not only stretches the confines of reason but springs free of those confines altogether.[12]

THE KYOTO SCHOOL

At this point something further needs to be said regarding the term "Kyoto School" that I have been using rather freely so far. Briefly put, the Kyoto School is a way of philosophizing—more of a philosophical ethos than a unified system of thought—which developed in the departments of philosophy and religion at the State University of Kyoto under the initial inspiration of Kitarō Nishida (1870–1945), widely acknowledged as the foremost philosopher of Japan since the time of the Meiji Restoration. In the words of Yoshinori Takeuchi, one of the principal contemporary representatives of the Kyoto School: "It is no exaggeration to say that in him Japan has had the first philosophical genius who knew how to build a system permeated with the spirit of Buddhist meditation by fully employing the Western method of thinking."[13]

The basic characteristics of the Kyoto School have already been hinted at: a thoroughgoing loyalty to its own traditions, a committed openness to Western traditions, and a deliberate attempt to bring about a synthesis of East and West. As Nishitani himself writes:

> We Japanese have fallen heir to two completely different cultures. . . . This is a great privilege that Westerners do not share in . . . but at the same time this puts a heavy responsibility on our shoulders: to lay the foundations of thought for a world in the making, for a new world united beyond differences of East and West.[14]

It is these characteristics, I would submit, together with the high level of competence with which the task they contain has been performed, that recommend the efforts of the Kyoto School to our attention, and make it altogether regrettable that this philosophical tradition has yet to be adequately introduced to the world at large.[15]

As noted above, the dream of a synthesis has been with Japanese intellectuals ever since the inclusion of philosophy as an integral part of the Western culture imported during the Meiji era. That such a dream should have been engendered is hardly to be wondered at, though we should not therefore overlook the overwhelming odds it faces to become a reality. In fact, during the first generations the appreciation of Western philosophy by Japanese scholars was somewhat superficial, which is understandable enough given their previous moorings in Confucian and Buddhist thought. At best their efforts led to a crude sort of syncretism. The past fifty years have brought pitfalls of their own. For one thing there is the conversion to a Westernized system of education, which may have contributed to a better appreciation of Western philosophy, but at the same time has left most Japanese intellectuals weakened in self-confidence toward their own traditions. Moreover, if we add to the higher levels of scholastic sophistication the peculiar Japanese tendency to compartmentalize, the inevitable result is that most Japanese scholars of Western philosophy get stuck within the narrow limits of their chosen field of specialization. While the degree of competence this enables is often remarkable indeed, there is every reason to deplore the fact that departments of Western philosophy (called *tetsugaku* 哲学 according to a neologism coined by its first advocates) and Indian philosophy (generally combined with Buddhist Studies and called *Indo tetsugaku*) carry on side by side in blissful ignorance of one another. Finally, we have to admit that departments of Western philosophy tend to mirror faithfully every movement taking place on the Western scene without showing much dynamism of their own or taking root in their native Japanese situation.

Against this backdrop the Kyoto School stands out as the single great exception, which the rest of Japanese academia does not very well know what to do with. To read through the works of its thinkers is to be struck by the resemblances to German idealism and its offshoots. And to be sure, that tradition has had considerable impact on Japan. As T. Shimomura notes, after the initial waves of French positivism and Anglo-Saxon utilitarianism, "in the 1890s, German philosophy became the mainstream." The reason for that special interest, he contends, "resides largely in the fact that that philosophy combines a deep moral and religious character with a strict logical and speculative character."[16] If we try to pin that affinity down more precisely, we come to two related traits: the recourse to dialectical logic and the resonances of mysticism.

The use of paradox is everywhere apparent in the writings of the Kyoto School, and contradiction is clearly considered not only to be logically meaningful but to be the sole means to drive the mind on to truly real reality. This trait is most pronounced in Nishida's definition of the real as a "self-identity of absolute contradictories" (or more freely and familiarly rendered, as a "coincidence of opposites"). Whatever other differences there may be between them, on this point Nishitani follows in the footsteps of Nishida, whose "dialectic is not so much the

process of thesis, antithesis, and synthesis, but a discovery of contradictions and the unity or identity in these contradictions."[17]

Now while style and terminology may remind us of German idealism, the real source of this dialectical language, let it be remembered, is
to be found in the Mahāyāna speculation alluded to earlier, and most
immediately in the paradoxical way of speaking peculiar to Zen. In this
connection, special attention needs to be given to the role of the con-
junctive *soku* [即] (translated here as *sive*) in Sino-Japanese Mahāyāna.
Put between two contradictory concepts (for instance in the formula,
"emptiness-*sive*-form, form-*sive*-emptiness"), it is meant to draw off the
total reality of the two poles into itself as their constitutive and ontologically prior unity. It indicates the only point or "place" at which the
opposites are *realized* and display their true reality. In order more
clearly to show the "inverse correspondence" or "identity through
negation" at work here, this has at times been referred to as the logic of
soku/hi (*sive/non*) [即非].

Before turning to the mystical element in the philosophy of the
Kyoto School—or rather, to establish its relationship with the element
of paradox more firmly—we may pause here for a brief look at Nishitani's peculiar use of spatial metaphor just referred to in the context of
the *soku*. At every turn we find him referring to the "place" or "point"
[ところ *tokoro*] at which events occur, to the "field" [場 *ba*] of being or
emptiness, to the "standpoint" [立場 *tachiba*] of the subject on its field,
and so forth. The use of such language, and the way of thinking behind
it, reverts back to Nishida who spoke of the absolute as the "locus of
absolute nothingness." While Nishitani himself does not often take the
word "locus" [場所 *basho*] into use as such in the present work, the
connection is unmistakable for those in the Kyoto School.

One's initial reaction might be to dismiss all of this as a mere vestige
of spatial imagination, along with the rest of the allusions to dimension,
horizon, plane, and so forth. There is, of course, no gainsaying the
danger of being led astray by metaphorical terminology. Yet the frequency and consistency with which such speech appears even in our
own descriptions of the absolute as a "transcendent"—whether "up
there" or "out there"—should give us pause to pay it greater attention.

The notion of "locus" was first suggested to Nishida, it would
appear, by the idea of *topos* in Plato's *Timaeus*, although he himself also
refers to Aristotle's notion of *hypokeimenon* and Lask's field theory to
explain its meaning. As Matao Noda has observed, "In this connection
the modern physical concept of field of force, taken by Einstein as a

cosmic field, seems to have suggested much to Nishida."[18] Perhaps the first thing to remember in trying to understand what Nishida, and with him Nishitani, has in mind is that our everyday idea of "place" is not a mere nonexistent "nothing" and yet neither is it an existent "something." It is more in the nature of what Jaspers calls an "encompassing" (*Umgreifendes*) that allows things to exist where they are: each on its own, and yet all together in a sort of oneness. The rest is a matter of degree. The place where things *are* can be envisaged at one end of the spectrum as determining things and binding them together in a purely external and superficial way; at the other, as defining their most intimate relationships and thus as constitutive of their very reality. The former is found in our commonsense notions of place; the latter is closer to the scientific idea of "field." In the transition from the one to the other, what was originally seen as a kind of detached background becomes more immediately immanent,[19] and the very idea of "background," usually understood as something secondary that sets the stage for things, comes to take on the richer sense of *das Hintergründliche*, the hidden, deeper reality of things normally hidden from view.

A technical analysis of the concept of locus in Nishida, as indicated, needs to probe further the special appeal that Aristotle's idea of matter has for him and to show how the notion of a *hypokeimenon*, as the non-being out of which all forms originate, was taken over by him. From there one would have to go into the dilemma in Aristotle's logic by virtue of which the individual is sought for but never reached through the specification of the universal; and the way in which this led Nishida to seek a *principium individuationis* in universality itself which, pushed to its limits, ends up ultimately in a transcendental indetermination. Finally, we should have to consider Kant's transcendental apperception as the unity of the subject, and the way in which this led Nishida to search for a unity wherein both subject and object would find their rightful place. Traces of all of these motifs are scattered throughout the essays presented here. It seems to me that this is not unconnected with the question about our sense of reality, about where we "locate" the truly real. In Christianity, all reality is said to be finally concentrated *in* the reality of God; for Plato, the really real is located in an intelligible world. For the Kyoto School, things are ultimately real on the field of emptiness, a place that is at once beyond our everyday encounter with things and yet where we do not encounter any reality—be it God or Idea—other than the reality of things themselves.

The critical importance of the concept of place is inseparable in turn from the concept of nothingness (more correctly, absolute nothingness) or emptiness, which, as Shimomura reminds us, is commonly considered the basis of existence in the East. An idea fraught with mysticism, it was Nishida's achievement to have succeeded in grounding the idea of nothingness conceptually and logically through his idea of locus.[20] Mention has already been made of the cardinal role that nothingness plays in the Buddhist tradition on the whole. It can now be seen more particularly to serve as the keystone that holds together the elements of the paradoxical and the mystical in the Kyoto School.

Takeuchi sets East and West against one another in sharp contrast here:

> The idea of "being" is the Archimedean point of Western thought. Not only philosophy and theology but the whole tradition of Western civilization have turned around this point. All is different in Eastern thought and Buddhism. The central notion from which Oriental religious intuition and belief as well as philosophical thought have been developed is the idea of "nothingness."[21]

Granted that this is basically the case, any attempt at a synthesis of East and West will have to reckon on bringing about a viable symbiosis. Provisionally, the way is left open either for assigning nothingness a fundamental role in Western modes of thought or for taking up being as a fundamental principle into Eastern modes of thought. As to which of these alternatives the Kyoto School follows in its pursuit of a synthesis, I would hazard the view that, at least on the surface, Nishida's writings seem rather to belong to the former, while the present work of Nishitani is clearly oriented to the latter.

In general, Oriental thinkers are fond of pointing out that, contrary to Western notions of nothingness, the Eastern notion is not a mere negative or *relative* nothingness, but an *absolute* nothingness that embraces both being and nothingness. In particular, Nishitani is said to have reached a "point" at which being coincides with nothingness.[22] The question then becomes whether the Western notion of being in its full length and breadth, with its enormous force of affirmation (*Bejahung*), and with all the aspirations to self-transcendence it embodies, is really subsumed under Eastern nothingness, or whether it is manipulated as a kind of "antithesis" or steppingstone to that nothingness. I only raise the issue here as one that the reader of these pages will hardly be able to avoid.

The dominant role of nothingness in Eastern culture is radically bound up with the world-negating aspect of its religion, especially Buddhism, and owes its basically positive connotations to the fact that this world-negation is seen from the outset as leading to, or containing in itself, salvation or true human realization. It is a "mystical idea" in the sense that life itself is seen not to have a direct value but rather to realize its value through death. Since the West possesses its own principles of world-negation or life-through-death, especially in Christianity, we are led to ask why the notion of nothingness never came to take a positive significance in the West and why it was never elevated to the status of a basic cultural principle. Perhaps an answer lies in the fact that for the East the principle of salvation was made into a basic principle for all reality—as for instance in Mahāyāna Buddhism's idea of samsāra-*sive*-nirvāna—and that the Kyoto School simply transfers this process to an ontological level in accord with the Western scheme of things. Would this not lead us to conclude that the West never made such a transference because the world-negation of its religion was not so radical, or because the whole content of its religion could not be represented in the aim of deliverance from this world?

As the words cited at the opening of this introduction testify, and as the book as a whole will confirm again and again, the philosophy of the Kyoto School is through and through religious. In the case of Nishida testimonies abound, all of them agreed that his philosophical inspiration belongs to Zen. To cite Shimomura once again: "Religious philosophy was the ultimate concern of his philosophical thinking from the very beginning until the very end. . . . Accordingly, he tried to include in philosophy also what in the West, perhaps as mysticism and as the limit of philosophical thought, philosophy stops short of."[24] Throughout the Kyoto School the conviction seems to hold sway that truly real reality is primarily to be found and its structure primarily revealed on the level of religion. "In religious Love or Compassion, the highest standpoint of all comes into view," writes Nishitani.[25] This would mean that the structure or logic of religious experience represents the prototype of every effort of the mind to grasp the truth of things. The question as to whether such a thing as "unsaved reality" can exist at all, and, if so, whether this might not have its own provisional structure and logic, is one that arises at once to the Western mind and appears to remain unanswered.

In a rather roundabout way, all of this may help to explain why a certain affinity with German idealism is to be found in the resonances of mysticism within the Kyoto School. More directly to the point perhaps is the passion for unity or *Alleinheit* that the two have in common. For Schinzinger, "Mahāyāna Buddhism is basically pantheistic; its prevailing idea is that Buddha is in all things, and that all things have Buddha-nature. To comprehend the Buddha-nature in all things, an approach is required which . . . experiences absolute oneness."[26] The label of pantheism, modeled as it is after Western patterns of *Alleinheit*, is not altogether appropriate, and it is with good reason that both Nishida and Nishitani explicitly reject it. Some kind of absolute standpoint, however, is needed to get a full view of that standpoint. The Kyoto School appears to share with German idealism the truly philosophical conviction of the possibility of such a standpoint.

KEIJI NISHITANI

Keiji Nishitani is universally recognized as the present "dean" of the Kyoto School and standard-bearer of the tradition that began with his teacher and master, Nishida. Nishitani was born on February 27, 1900, in the same rural district (Ishikawa Prefecture) of central Japan as Nishida. When he was seven years old, his family moved to Tokyo where he received the rest of his formal education. After graduating from Japan's most prestigious college at the time, the Daiichi Kōtōgak-kō, he moved to Kyoto where he has spent the rest of his adult life. In 1924 he graduated from the department of philosophy at the Kyoto Imperial University (since renamed Kyoto State University). In 1926 he took up a post lecturing in ethics and German at Kyoto's Imperial College and in 1928 assumed a lectureship at the Buddhist Ōtani University, both of which positions he held concurrently up until 1935, when he was called back to his alma mater and named professor in the department of religion. In 1955 he conceded his post in the department to Professor Yoshinori Takeuchi in order to assume the chair of modern philosophy until retiring in 1963. Since that time Kyoto has remained the center of his apparently unflagging activities as professor of philosophy and religion at Ōtani University, and as president of the Eastern Buddhist Society (founded by D. T. Suzuki), of the International Institute for Japan Studies (at the Christian Kanseigakuin University in Nishinomiya), and of the Conference on Religion in Modern Society (CORMOS).[27]

In his own account of his philosophical starting point, Nishitani has written:

Before I began my philosophical training as a disciple of Nishida, I was most attracted by Nietzsche and Dostoyevsky, Emerson and Carlyle, and also by the

Bible and St. Francis of Assisi. Among things Japanese, I liked best Sōseki
Natsume and books like the Buddhist talks of Hakuin and Takuan. Through all
these many interests, one fundamental concern was constantly at work, I
think. . . . In the center of that whirlpool lurked a doubt about the very existence
of the self, something like the Buddhist "Great Doubt." So it was that soon I
started paying attention to Zen.[28]

These words give us a good idea of the intellectual vectors coming
together in Nishitani's thought. To them we might add the influence of
Schelling, whose work on *The Essence of Human Freedom* he later translated into Japanese, of the existentalist philosophers, especially Heidegger with whom he studied in Freiburg from 1936 to 1939, and of a
lifelong interest in the German mystics, particularly Meister Eckhart.

In another biographical essay he speaks still more poignantly of the
birth of his philosophy:

My life as a young man can be described in a single phrase: it was a period
absolutely without hope. . . . My life at the time lay entirely in the grips of nihility
and despair. . . . My decision, then, to study philosophy was in fact—melodra-
matic as it might sound—a matter of life and death. . . . In the little history of my
soul, this decision meant a kind of conversion.[29]

The nihility that we see here will remain at the very core of Nishitani's
philosophical endeavors. This explains further why Marxism—or any
philosophy (or theology, for that matter) that stresses outer events to the
neglect of Existenz—was never able to tempt him:

It was inconceivable that this could ever solve my problem. That a materialistic
philosophy cannot answer the problems of the soul is clear to me from my own
experience. For me there is no way to doubt that the problems of the soul are the
fundamental ones for man.[30]

It was at that critical moment that Nishitani encountered Nishida
and Zen, the two forces he was to identify with most, though never to
the point of surrendering his own individuality. Indeed, they helped
him to get back in touch with himself and freed him to tackle the great
spiritual problems of his time. There are numerous references in his
works to the relationship between Zen and philosophy, especially as
regards his own life. I restrict myself here to two short but revealing
passages:

We consider it necessary for our philosophical inquiry to maintain a fundamental
religious attitude that accords with the spirit of free and critical thought of
philosophy. Since Zen has no dogmatics, and wishes to have none, it is easy to
understand why many of us keep rooted in the experience of Zen practice.[31]

And in the final essay of this book, after noting that it is the "original countenance of reality" that he is interested in pursuing, free of all religious and philosophical preconceptions, he goes on:

> If I have frequently had occasion to deal with the standpoints of Buddhism, and particularly Zen Buddhism, the fundamental reason is that this original countenance seems to me to appear there most plainly and unmistakably.[32]

Apropos of the same relationship in Nishida's work, Schinzinger notes suggestively: "Judging by all that has been said about Zen, everything depends on whether or not one can bring about a revelation of the essence of being in one's own existence."[33]

Waldenfels helps us here to put Nishitani's philosophy in the right perspective:

> For Nishitani it is a question of a fundamental religious option that he sees our historical situation grounded in a realm beyond space and time, a realm which is proclaimed in the mystical experiences of all times and in the basic Buddhist standpoint of emptiness. Nishitani's intention is to direct our modern dilemma to a solution through the basic notion of emptiness.[34]

We could go on lining up quotation after quotation from Nishitani in the same vein, but they all leave no doubt as to where Nishitani wants to locate the fundamental problem of our times: it is nihilism, and its alliance with scientism, that is undermining the very foundations of Western civilization, leaving man with no place to stand as man.

This constant preoccupation with nihilism also determines Nishitani's place within the Kyoto School. In one of his autobiographical passages, he remarks that the interest in Marxism and in the problems of scientific rationalism was already present in Nishida and Tanabe. His own inclinations led him elsewhere:

> It seemed to me that the problem of modern nihilism in Nietzsche and others was profoundly connected with all these matters. I am convinced that the problem of nihilism lies at the root of the mutual aversion of religion and science. And it was this that gave my philosophical engagement its starting point from which it grew larger and larger until it came to envelop nearly everything.[35]

In this way Nishitani came to see the conquest of nihilism as *the* task for himself as well as for contemporary philosophy and for future world culture in general. Once he had found his standpoint in Nishida's Eastern nothingness, his philosophy could take its basic orientation: nihility, or relative nothingness, can only be overcome by a radicalization of that nothingness, namely, by a "conversion" to absolute nothingness.

In all of this, we should not overlook the delicate balance of East and West, of Buddhism and Christianity which is present in Nishitani's vision. On the one hand, the true view of reality and the only hope for the global culture of the future is to be found (or at the very least strongly prefigured) in the Eastern heritage. While Nishida presents his idea of absolute nothingness as much as possible in continuity with Western ideas, Nishitani calls it by its Buddhist name, śūnyatā, and takes pains to show how in the East, too, the real idea of emptiness was born out of the conquest of the nihility at the ground of the human condition. On the other hand, the current dynamics of history seem to lean rather in the direction of the West. It is there that nihilism appears as the fundamental historical direction of an entire culture. Through the loss of God, its "absolute center," this affirmative-oriented culture of being has fallen into an abyss of nihility. From there it can never save itself through a simple return to affirmation, but "the negative direction must be pursued to its very end . . . where the negative converges, so to speak, with the positive."[36] Still, the West must do this, as it were, by its own dynamism, through a return to the ground of its own traditions. Put crudely and in its bare essentials, the question for Nishitani comes down to this: the West has nowhere to go but in the direction of the Eastern (Buddhist) ideal, but it cannot do so except from its own Western (Christian) premises.

Such is Nishitani's challenge to Western thought and to Western religion. The dilemmas of present-day culture are born out of Christianity and cannot be overcome without reference to Christianity. And yet in its present form Christianity is not suited to solving these problems. In order to rise to the task it has to break free of its Western provincialism, to reassess its appreciation of its own values and reorient itself according to a deeper appreciation of the fundamental values of Buddhism. Only in this way can Christianity become a standpoint of true affirmation, able to embrace and to overcome the negations it has engendered.

It bears repeating here that Nishitani sees his philosophy of emptiness, and Mahāyāna Buddhism in general, as radically positive. On this point he finds a convergence of his philosophy with the "original, pre-Buddhist, worldly nature" of Japanese culture. The question frequently arises from the outside whether Buddhism with its world-negating ways is not alien to the native Japanese religiosity as we find it expressed, for instance, in the Shinto celebration of life. If so, this would mean that the Buddhist inspiration of the Kyoto School is betraying the Japanese experience rather than honoring it. Nishitani is well aware of these questions, so much so that they can be said to flow through his writings like a steady undercurrent. Nowhere is the point stressed more forcefully than in the present book that the field of emptiness, while resulting from an absolute negation, forms the basis of an absolutely positive cultural attitude. Indeed the absoluteness of each immediately present individual thing cut off from all conditionings and relativizing elements, and the freedom and creativity of the self totally open to an infinite universality on the field of emptiness, are exalted here in almost lyrical terms.

We may round off this brief look at Nishitani's thought with two concluding remarks. First, let us return to the relationship between the thought of Nishitani and that of his master, Nishida. Nishida's works show him coming back again and again to the same struggle with finding, in concrete confrontation with Western philosophical systems, a logical expression for his initial Zen intuition of "pure experience," culminating in his talk of absolute nothingness. Nishitani takes up from there to concentrate on the fundamental problem of nihilism and on the two forces that can be looked to for its solution, Buddhism and Christianity. Most of the themes elaborated in the following pages—the search for truly real reality, the progression from being through relative nothingness to absolute nothingness (where the unity of nothingness and being is achieved), the relationship between world and individual, the identity of self and other, the motif of the *intimior intimo meo*, and so on—can be traced back to Nishida. But while the "volitional process" is central to many of Nishida's works and intuition is granted validity only in the context of praxis, Nishitani's thought seems to show a clearer orientation to contemplation within which the will appears as a disruptive and distorting element.

Second, a word about Nishitani's conception of history. From within the Kyoto School, the treatment of history in the final two essays has been received as the strongest and most original part of the book.[37] For the Western reader, on the other hand, these chapters may well be the hardest to digest. If it is in general the case that Nishitani offends our sensitivities with regard to reality and thereby sets us reflecting on our own presuppositions, this is particularly true here, where our view of history seems to be systematically dismantled before our very eyes, stone by stone. History, as a process that comes from somewhere (its beginning) and goes somewhere (its end); the unique position of cultural man as builder of history through the objectification of his actions; the irreversibility of time with its all-important distinction between the actual and the possible, past and future; the drama of events, decisions, and culpability—the whole construction is reduced to so much rubble.

Nishitani's outlook on natural, ontological reality, for all it differs from our commonsense "realistic" view of things, may find a ready ally in the contemporary view of science. For it has become commonplace to note that the solid, discrete objects that seem to make up our world belong to a buzzing confusion of fluid process where the presence of individuality and limitation seem more remarkable than their absence. But what of the reality of world-historical events?

Offhand, we might be tempted to remark that Nishitani is attempting the impossible in trying to bring an essentially ahistorical Eastern religiosity to bear on the philosophy of history. In fact, it would seem that Nishitani himself has occasionally had similar misgivings.[38] If anything has sustained him, it can only be the conviction expressed in the words with which he closes this book: "Unless the thought and deeds of men one and all be located on such a field [of emptiness], the sorts of problems that beset humanity have no chance of ever really being solved."

Meantime, it is certainly worth our while to follow him as he asks whether the standpoint of śūnyatā can contribute anything new to the view of history, and to take seriously his argument that the traditional Judaeo-Christian view of history does not really allow for selflessness. In so doing, we are obliged to reflect anew not only on the roots of the idea of history in Judaeo-Christian religion, but also on the possible effects of such a view on our concrete historical praxis. While it has become almost cliché to single out historicity as the dividing wall between Western and Eastern religions, and while Nishitani's attempts to break through that partition may not be totally successful, his work certainly illustrates for us a novel way of aligning Buddhism with ontology and the Judaeo-Christian tradition with history. The fact contained in the reality that "this staff is a staff" challenges here the reality contained in the fact that "Christ has died." The question that remains is whether it might also provoke in us new efforts to understand the import for all Western thought of the claim, that the man who died on the cross is the selfsame Word through whom all things were made.

I should like to conclude with a few words about this translation. Uprooting a tradition carefully bred and nurtured in its native Eastern soil and potting it in the alien and restricting categories of Western thought and language presents a constant danger at each step of the way in a translation such as this and leads to some unavoidable problems. Surely many factors argue in favor of the timeliness of such a venture at introducing the philosophy of emptiness into our familiar world of substantial being: the growing need for East and West to meet in the global village created by technology; the impact of process metaphysics on religious reflection; a certain preparedness in philosophical circles to reconsider the importance of nothingness, due to such figures as Heidegger; and so on. Yet the fact remains that the rhythms of life and thought in East and West are not yet simultaneous, let alone synchronized. The conditions for such a possibility are still in the making. At these initial stages, there is still a good deal of jostling and jarring whose echoes, I am only too well aware, resound throughout the pages of this translation.

Against this backdrop, every effort has been exerted to write English instead of trying to imitate the flavor of the Japanese by creating a prose that only those who straddle both languages could appreciate. At the same time, particular attention has been given to rendering every sentence, and practically every word, with as great a consistency as possible, in order not to make unnecessary interpretative decisions on behalf of the reader. I cannot flatter myself that the results make for easy reading. All too often the unfamiliar Oriental perspective that Nishitani slips into the discussion of familiar matters and the markedly different methods employed in philosophical argument inhibit the flow of the style.

In this respect we might first keep in mind the general Eastern antipathy to overly direct and assertive language in everyday intercourse. In place of an abrupt trumpeting of opinion in terms that the listener should not be able to disregard, Japanese prefers to circumnavigate an issue, tossing out subtle hints that permit only a careful listener to surmise where the unspoken core of the question lies. The same indirectness, or circularity, applies to philosophical argumentation. While the Western ideal of analysis prizes clarity and distinctness and progress in a straight line from one logical step to the next, Japanese philosophical style proceeds by way of concentric circles. The point has been noted often enough by both Eastern and Western thinkers:

> In general, it may be stated that Japanese thinking has the form of totality (*Ganzheit*): starting from the indistinct total aspect of a problem, Japanese thought

proceeds to a more distinct total grasp by which the relationship of all parts becomes intuitively clear.[39]

Like a musical theme, the basic theme is repeated and emphasized many times over, and while executing variations and performing spiral rotations continues to ascend.[40]

Nishitani certainly shows that "spiral repetitiveness" to the highest degree. His paragraphs not uncommonly run to several pages each and do not readily yield to being broken up. But whether this strikes one as magical incantation or simply gets on one's nerves, the loss is ours if we allow the foreignness of style to close us off altogether from the insights it orchestrates for us.

In addition, the reader may detect in Nishitani's prose a certain influence from Heidegger's philosophical style. Not only has this cracked the skull of a fair portion of his Japanese readership, it has also tempted me on more than one occasion to commit whole pages to the more supple demands of German grammar and vocabulary. In any event, like every creative philosophical thinker, Nishitani feels free to borrow philosophical jargon from others and give it a new twist better suited to his own aims. In such cases the reader will have to be the judge of nuances in meaning.

The notes in the text are the author's. In lieu of interposing clarifications of my own along the way, a glossary has been prepared to give some indication of the technical vocabulary employed, some of which may remain obscured by the English translation. It is meant to offer brief hints to certain of the Buddhist concepts adopted and some explanation of terms particularly difficult to translate. For those who are familiar with the writing system of Japanese, it may also serve to show how the translation was made and to highlight some of the subtle changes of meaning that have taken place in the transposition of Indian Buddhist terms into the framework of Chinese ideographic writing.

The history of the translation is an odyssey all its own. I recount it briefly only because it offers me an occasion to express my gratitude to those who helped it along its way from one stage to the next and whose names have every bit as much right as mine to appear under the title. An English translation of the first essay, signed by Janice D. Rowe, appeared back in 1960 in Vol. 2 of the journal *Philosophical Studies of Japan*. Five years later I prepared an initial draft of the remaining five essays over an eighteen-month period in collaboration with Seisaku Yamamoto, currently professor of philosophy in the department of general education at Kyoto State University. This was then passed on to Professor Nishitani who decided to have the translation published serially in *The Eastern Buddhist*, a journal that serves as an organ of the Eastern Buddhist Society of which he is the president. In preparation, the text was gone over painstakingly by the author himself, together with Norman Waddell, a member of the journal's editorial board and himself an accomplished translator of Japanese Buddhist texts. It appeared in this form over the years 1970–1980.

We should note here that in a concerted effort to make his line of argument more readily understandable to the Western reader, Nishitani took the liberty of adding occasional explanatory sentences and phrases at various points throughout the text. The reader who would compare this translation with the original Japanese should be informed that these English additions are authentic and not the woolgathering of the translator.

Finally, in preparation for publication in book form, the entire translation, including the first chapter, was gone over once more in comparison with the original Japanese for greater overall consistency and rather drastically revised for better readability by James Heisig, a co-member of the Nanzan Institute for Religion and Culture in Nagoya. At this stage the author was persuaded to allow his original title *What is Religion?* to be changed to what seemed to us a more suitable alternative.

It is my pleasant duty here to thank the editors of *Philosophical Studies of Japan* and *The Eastern Buddhist* for their generous willingness to waive their rights to the translation; and to express my deepest appreciation and sincerest gratitude to Seisaku Yamamoto, Norman Waddell, and James Heisig for their eminently capable and unselfish labors in behalf of this project. Finally, it is a special pleasure for me to be able to acknowledge in print the many efforts that Frederick Franck made in behalf of this project for several years prior to publication, and the constant help and good counsel that we received from John Russiano Miles and the University of California Press. Without them, we should never have brought the work to completion.

Nagoya, Japan   Jan Van Bragt
Christmas 1980

NOTES

1. See below, pp. 158, 183.

2. Obviously, this introduction itself can only be of an introductory nature. I refer the interested reader to Hans Waldenfels's book-length study of Nishitani's philosophy, *Absolute Nothingness* (New York: Paulist Press, 1980). Published as the opening volume of Nanzan Studies in Religion and Culture, it may be considered a companion to Nishitani's *opus major*, which we are proud to include as the second volume of that series. Pursuing the roots of Nishitani's thought all the way back to Sakyamuni, Professor Waldenfels not only outlines and analyzes, but takes significant steps to initiate a critical evaluation—or rather a dialogue—from a Christian standpoint. I have relied heavily on his pioneering work in the preparation of my remarks.

3. Kitarō Nishida, *Intelligibility and the Philosophy of Nothingness. Three philosophical essays*, trans. with an introduction by Robert Schinzinger (Tokyo: Maruzen, 1958). The passage cited here is taken from an unsigned preface.

4. The stress belongs here on "intellectual," which might as well have been written "speculative." Since the Japanese mind is often characterized as "antispeculative," I am inclined to agree fully with Professor Shimomura when he writes: "Japan had from very ancient times many outstanding Buddhist, Confucian, and later, Shinto thinkers. Their thought was philosophical in a high degree." Toratarō Shimomura, "Nishida Kitarō and Some Aspects of his Philosophical Thought," in Kitarō Nishida, *A Study of Good*, trans. V. H. Viglielmo (Tokyo: Japanese Government Printing Bureau, 1960), p. 191.

5. Ibid., pp.216–217. See also Yoshinori Takeuchi, "The Philosophy of Nishida," *Japanese Religions*, 3, no. 4 (1963): 11–17.

6. Shimomura, "Nishida," p. 211.

7. Waldenfels endeavors to show how Nāgārjuna's notion of śūnyatā ("emptiness") is pivotal for Buddhist thought and how it served as an inspiration for Nishitani's own efforts, concluding: "We may safely assert that in his own way Nishitani is seeking

the selfsame thing that Nāgārjuna had aimed at in the early years of our era." Waldenfels, *Nothingness*, p. 15; see also pp. 7, 15–23.

8. Ibid., p. 15.

9. H. Dumoulin, *Östliche Meditation und Christliche Mystik* (Freiburg-Munich: Karl Alber, 1966), p. 235.

10. Keiji Nishitani, "Nihon ni okeru shūkyō ishiki" [日本に於ける宗教意識 Religious Consciousness in Japan], in Kiyoko Takeda, ed., *Shisō no hōhō to taishō* (Tokyo: Sōbunsha, 1963), p. 254.

11. D. T. Suzuki, "How to Read Nishida," in K. Nishida, *A Study of Good*, p. iii.

12. In regard to these and related questions, readers of Japanese may find it worthwhile to consult the proceedings of a symposium that gathered the principal contemporary representatives of the Kyoto School together with Buddhist and Christian scholars to discuss the theme "Christianity and the Kyoto School of Philosophy." The symposium was held at the Nanzan Institute for Religion and Culture in the spring of 1980 and the results published in the following year by Shunjūsha of Tokyo under the title *Zettaimu to kami. Nishida-Tanabe tetsugaku no dentō tō kirisutokyō*— [絶対無と神－西田・田辺哲学の伝統とキリスト教 "Absolute Nothingness and God. The Nishida-Tanabe Philosophical Tradition and Christianity"].

13. Takeuchi, "The Philosophy of Nishida," pp. 3–4.

14. K. Nishitani, ed., *Gendai Nippon no tetsugaku* [現代日本の哲学 Philosophy in Contemporary Japan] (Kyoto: Yukonsha, 1967), pp. 2–4.

15. Comparatively speaking, the German philosophical scene is better informed on these matters than its counterpart in the English-speaking world. Of Nishida's translated works we have already referred to Schinzinger's translation of three essays (originally appearing in German under the title *Die intelligibele Welt*) and *A Study of Good*, Viglielmo's translation of Nishida's first and seminal work. In addition we may mention the following: *Fundamental Problems of Philosophy. The world of action and the dialectical world*, trans. D. A. Dilworth, (Tokyo: Sophia University, 1970); and *Art and Morality*, trans. D. A. Dilworth and V. H. Viglielmo (Honolulu; The University of Hawaii, 1973). Of the second philosopher of the Kyoto School, Hajime Tanabe (1885–1962), whose thought shows a stronger influence from the Pure Land Sect of Buddhism, we have no single book-length translation as of yet.

16. Shimomura, "Nishida," pp. 193, 195.

17. R. Schinzinger, *Three essays*, pp. 55–56.

18. Matao Noda "East-West Synthesis in Kitarō Nishida," *Philosophy East and West*, 4 (1955): 350.

19. A dialectic of "near side" and "far side" is frequently referred to in the present book. Nishitani uses it to combat possible misunderstandings that might arise concerning the "field of emptiness" as something that exists apart from things, lying beyond or behind things, and to combat every possible idea of a world beyond this everyday world, every "objective transcendence."

20. Shimomura, "Nishida," p. 212.

21. Y. Takeuchi, "Buddhism and Existentialism: The Dialogue Between Oriental and Occidental Thought," in W. Leibrecht, ed., *Religion and Culture: Essays in honor of Paul Tillich* (New York: Harper, 1959), p. 292.

22. See Masao Abe, "Nishitani Hakasecho 'Shūkyō to wa nanika' o yomite" [西谷博士著「宗教とは何か」を読みて On reading Professor Nishitani's *What is Religion?*], *Tetsugaku kenkyū* 42, no. 1 (1962): 83–104.

23. From a slightly different perspective I have touched on this question in my "Notulae on Emptiness and Dialogue: Reading Professor Nishitani's *What is Religion?*," *Japanese Religions*, 4, no. 4 (1966): 50–78.

24. Shimomura, "Nishida," pp. 205–206.

25. See below, p. 281.

26. Schinzinger, *Three essays*, p. 10.

27. As these titles should make sufficiently plain, Nishitani's concern with the dialogue between East and West, Buddhism and Christianity, has not confined itself to theoretical speculation but has also engaged him in practical activities.

28. "Watakushi no tetsugakuteki hossokuten" [私の哲学的発足点 My philosophical starting point], in Michitarō Tanaka, ed., *Kōza: Tetsugaku taikei* (Kyoto: Jimbunshoin, 1963), 1: 229. I have referred to this elsewhere in an essay entitled, "Nishitani on Japanese Religiosity," in Joseph Spae, *Japanese Religiosity* (Tokyo: Oriens Institute for Religious Research, 1971), pp. 271–272.

29. "Watakushi no seishun jidai" [私の青春時代 The Days of My Youth], in his *Kaze no kokoro* [風のこころ Heart in the Wind] (Tokyo: Shinchōsha, 1980), pp. 195, 198, 204.

30. Ibid., p. 198.

31. Foreword to Waldenfels, *Nothingness*, p. v.

32. See below, p. 261.

33. Schinzinger, *Three essays*, p. 16.

34. Waldenfels, *Nothingness*, p. 52.

35. Nishitani, "My Philosophical Starting Point," pp. 229–230.

36. Nishitani, "Science and Zen," *The Eastern Buddhist*, N.S. 1, 1 (1965): 102.

37. M. Abe, "Nishitani," pp. 93–94.

38. See below, p. 201.

39. Schinzinger, *Three essays*, p. 6.

40. Shimomura, "Nishida," p. 207.

PREFACE

Of the six essays that make up this book, the first four and part of the final essay have been published previously in the series *Lectures on Contemporary Religion* (現代宗教講座, vols. 1,2,4, and 6, Tokyo: Sō-bunsha, 1954–1955). I had originally been asked to write an article for the opening volume under the title "What is Religion?" but finding that what I wrote there did not adequately express what I wanted to say, I followed with a second article under a different title. Still feeling that justice had not been done to the subject, I kept on writing until I ended up with four essays. Even then I felt that something more had to be said on the subject and so added two more essays, which comprise the final two chapters of the present book. Such being the case, it is hardly to be wondered at that these pages do not possess the systematic unity of a work written from beginning to end with a definite plan in mind. Still, the work will, I hope, reveal a unity of thought throughout.

Some readers may, I fear, get the impression that the contents of what follows do not correspond to the title. On seeing the word *religion* on the front cover and glancing at the title of the initial chapter, one might expect a book by a specialist in the history of religions, a book that analyzes the range of phenomena that characterize the various historical religions and explains the universal traits of what we call religion. I believe that this is precisely what the editors of *Lectures on Contemporary Religion* had in mind when they approached me for a contribution. But the actual contents and line of thinking to be found in these pages are of another sort. They suggest that the phenomenon of religion and the question "What is religion?" can take on a meaning altogether different from such expectations: the attempt to come to one's own conclusions while asking questions of oneself. In the former approach, the author takes his lead from someone else's questions and treats his subject with scientific *objectivity*, offering conclusions based on the facts of history. In this latter approach, the quest is for the "home-ground" of religion, where religion emerges from man himself, as a *subject*, as a self living in the present.

Naturally, even in this second case we need to take into account the given facts as they have come down to us from the past. But at the same time there is the additional attitude of finding explanations that carry conviction for oneself as a contemporary individual, and in that sense of directing one's attention to what *ought to be* rather than simply what *has been*. The posture of turning one's gaze from the present to the past is complemented by the posture of turning one's gaze from the present toward the future. On this approach, the fundamental meaning of religion—what religion *is*—is not to be conceived of in terms of an understanding of what it *has been*. Our reflections take place at the borderline where understanding of what has been constantly turns into an investigation of what ought to be; and, conversely, where the conception of what ought to be never ceases to be a clarification of what has been. It is in this sense, and in accord with my own interests, that I interpret the question that marks the starting point of the first chapter. From the very outset, then, I have made it my concern to ask what it means to pose the question, "What is religion?"

The inquiry into religion attempted here proceeds by way of problems judged to lie hidden at the ground of the historical frontier we call "the modern world," with the aim of delving into the ground of human existence and, at the same time, searching anew for the wellsprings of reality itself. In so doing, I place myself squarely in a no-man's-land straddling the realms of the religious and the *anti*religious, or *a*religious (for to be unconcerned with religion will be taken here as already constituting a kind of relationship to religion), in a realm whose borders shift unevenly. Insofar as religion is being treated as a whole, I do not intend to base myself on the tenets or doctrines of any religion in particular, and any remarks made in that regard may be considered parenthetical to the main argument. For since it is religion in general, and not simply some particular brand of religion, that antireligious or areligious standpoints oppose or express their lack of concern with, it would follow as a matter of course that an investigation of matters religious on the general design described above must call into question religion itself as religion.

In modern times, as the universal concept "religion" came to take on a meaning of its own, it was inevitable that what we now call the philosophy of religion would come into being. In this sense, the essays gathered together here may be said to follow the lead of previous philosophies of religion. All philosophies of religion up until now, from the time of the classical systems of the nineteenth century, however, have based themselves on something "immanent" in man such as reason or intuition or feeling. In my view, it has since become impossible to institute such a standpoint, given the nature of the questions that have meantime given rise to the thought of the later Schelling, Schopenhauer, Kierkegaard, or even Feuerbach and Marx, and, above all, because of the appearance of positions like the nihilism of Nietzsche. Consequently, our considerations here take their stand at the point that traditional philosophies of religion have broken down or been broken through. In that sense, they may be said to go along with contemporary existential philosophies, all of which include a standpoint of "transcendence" of one sort or another.

Finally, this book deals directly with a few fundamental Buddhist concepts, such as *śūnyatā* and *karma*, and draws upon a number of terms connected with particular Buddhist sects, such as "becoming manifest," "circuminsession," "emergence into the nature of," and the like. But let me repeat: this does not mean that a position is being taken from the start on the doctrines of Buddhism as a particular religion or on the doctrines of one of its sects. I have borrowed these terms only insofar as they illuminate reality and the essence and actuality of man. Removed from the frame of their traditional conceptual determinations, therefore, they have been used rather freely and on occasion—although this is not pointed out in every case—introduced to suggest correlations with concepts of contemporary philosophy. From the viewpoint of traditional conceptual determinations, this way of using terminology may seem somewhat careless and, at times, ambiguous. As far as possible, it is best to avoid this sort of trouble; but it is not always possible when one is trying, as I am here, to take a stand at one and the same time within and without the confines of tradition. In this regard, I can do no other than rely on the reader's indulgence.

A great number of people have gone to considerable lengths to help this book along on its way to publication, among whom I would single out here the names of Ryōen Minamoto and Masakazu Ōhora. For all their kind help and hard work, I wish to express my heartfelt gratitude.

Kyoto, Japan   Keiji Nishitani

1

WHAT IS RELIGION?

I

"What is religion?" we ask ourselves, or, looking at it the other way around, "What is the purpose of religion for us? Why do we need it?" Though the question about the need for religion may be a familiar one, it already contains a problem. In one sense, for the person who poses the question, religion does not seem to be something he needs. The fact that he asks the question at all amounts to an admission that religion has not yet become a necessity for him. In another sense, however, it is surely in the nature of religion to be necessary for just such a person. Wherever questioning individuals like this are to be found, the need for religion is there as well. In short, the relationship we have to religion is a contradictory one: those for whom religion is *not* a necessity are, for that reason, the very ones for whom religion *is* a necessity. There is no other thing of which the same can be said.

When asked, "Why do we need learning and the arts?" we might try to explain in reply that such things are necessary for the advancement of mankind, for human happiness, for the cultivation of the individual, and so forth. Yet even if we can say why we need such things, this does not imply that we cannot get along without them. Somehow life would still go on. Learning and the arts may be indispensable to living well, but they are not indispensable to living. In that sense, they can be considered a kind of luxury.

Food, on the other hand, is essential to life. Nobody would turn to somebody else and ask him why he eats. Well, maybe an angel or some other celestial being who has no need to eat might ask such questions, but men do not. Religion, to judge from current conditions in which many people are in fact getting along without it, is clearly not the kind of necessity that food is. Yet this does not mean that it is merely something we need to live *well*. Religion has to do with life itself. Whether the life we are living will end up in extinction or in the attainment of eternal life is a matter of the utmost importance for life itself. In no sense is religion to be called a luxury. Indeed, this is why religion is an indispensable necessity for those very people who fail to see the need for it. Herein lies the distinctive feature of religion that sets it apart from the mere life of "nature" and from culture. Therefore, to say that we need religion for example, for the sake of social order, or human welfare, or public morals is a mistake, or at least a confusion of priorities. Religion must not be considered from the viewpoint of its *utility*, any more than life should. A religion concerned primarily with its own utility bears witness to its own degeneration. One can ask about the utility of things like eating for the natural life, or of things like learning and the arts for culture. In fact, in such matters the question of utility should be of constant concern. Our ordinary mode of being is restricted to these levels of natural or cultural life. But it is in breaking through that ordinary mode of being and overturning it from the ground up, in pressing us back to the elemental source of life where life itself is seen as useless, that religion becomes something we need—a *must* for human life.

Two points should be noted from what has just been said. First, religion is at all times the individual affair of each individual. This sets it apart from things like culture, which, while related to the individual, do not need to concern each individual. Accordingly, we cannot understand what religion is from the outside. The religious quest alone is the key to understanding it; there is no other way. This is the most important point to be made regarding the essence of religion.

Second, from the standpoint of the essence of religion, it is a mistake to ask "What is the purpose of religion for us?" and one that clearly betrays an attitude of trying to understand religion apart from the religious quest. It is a question that must be broken through by another question coming from within the person who asks it. There is no other road that can lead to an understanding of what religion is and what purpose it serves. The counterquestion that achieves this breakthrough is one that asks, "For what purpose do I myself exist?" Of everything else we can ask its purpose for us, but not of religion. With regard to everything else we can make a *telos* of ourselves as individuals, as man, or as mankind, and evaluate those things in relation to our life and existence. We put ourselves as individuals/man/mankind at the center and weigh the significance of everything as the *contents* of our lives as individuals/man/mankind. But religion upsets the posture from which we think of ourselves as *telos* and center for all things. Instead, religion poses as a starting point the question: "For what purpose do I exist?"

We become aware of religion as a need, as a must for life, only at the level of life at which everything else loses its necessity and its utility. Why do we exist at all? Is not our very existence and human life ultimately meaningless? Or, if there is a meaning or significance to it all, where do we find it? When we come to doubt the meaning of our existence in this way, when we have become a question to ourselves, the religious quest awakens within us. These questions and the quest they give rise to show up when the mode of looking at and thinking about everything in terms of how it relates to *us* is broken through, where the mode of living that puts us at the center of everything is overturned. This is why the question of religion in the form, "Why do we need religion?" obscures the way to its own answer from the very start. It blocks our becoming a question to ourselves.

The point at which the ordinarily necessary things of life, including learning and the arts, all lose their necessity and utility is found at those times when death, nihility, or sin—or any of those situations that entail a fundamental negation of our life, existence, and ideals, that undermine the roothold of our existence and bring the meaning of life into question—become pressing personal problems for us. This can occur through an illness that brings one face-to-face with death, or through some turn of events that robs one of what had made life worth living.

Take, for example, someone for whom life has become meaningless as a result of the loss of a loved one, or of the failure of an undertaking on which he had staked his all. All those things that had once been of use to him become good for nothing. This same process takes place when one comes face to face with death and the existence of the self—one's "self-existence"—stands out clearly in relief against the backdrop of nihility. Questions crowd in upon one: Why have I been alive? Where did I come from and where am I going? A void appears here that nothing in the world can fill; a gaping abyss opens up at the very ground on which one stands. In the face of this abyss, not one of all the things that had made up the stuff of life until then is of any use.

In fact, that abyss is always just underfoot. In the case of death, we do not face something that awaits us in some distant future, but something that we bring into the world with us at the moment we are born. Our life runs up against death at its every step; we keep one foot planted in the vale of death at all times. Our life stands poised at the brink of the abyss of nihility to which it may return at any moment. Our existence is an existence at one with nonexistence, swinging back and forth over nihility, ceaselessly passing away and ceaselessly regaining its existence. This is what is called the "incessant becoming" of existence.

Nihility refers to that which renders meaningless the meaning of life. When we become a question to ourselves and when the problem of why we exist arises, this means that nihility has emerged from the ground of our existence and that our very existence has turned into a question mark. The appearance of this nihility signals nothing less than that one's awareness of self-existence has penetrated to an extraordinary depth.

Normally we proceed through life, on and on, with our eye fixed on something or other, always caught up with something within or without ourselves. It is these engagements that prevent the deepening of awareness. They block off the way to an opening up of that horizon on which nihility appears and self-being becomes a question. This is even the case with learning and the arts and the whole range of other cultural engagements. But when this horizon does open up at the bottom of those engagements that keep life moving continually on and on, something seems to halt and linger before us. This something is the meaninglessness that lies in wait at the bottom of those very engagements that bring meaning to life. This is the point at which that sense of nihility, that sense that "everything is the same" we find in Nietzsche and Dostoevski, brings the restless, forward-advancing pace of life to a halt and makes it take a step back. In the Zen phrase, it "turns the light to what is directly underfoot."

In the forward progress of everyday life, the ground beneath our feet always falls behind as we move steadily ahead; we overlook it. Taking a step back to shed light on what is underfoot of the self—"stepping back to come to the self," as another ancient Zen phrase has it—marks a conversion in life itself. This fundamental conversion in life is occasioned by the opening up of the horizon of nihility at the ground of life. It is nothing less than a conversion from the self-centered (or man-centered) mode of being, which always asks what *use* things have for us (or for man), to an attitude that asks for what *purpose* we ourselves (or man) exist. Only when we stand at this turning point does the question "What is religion?" really become our own.

II

Being the multi-faceted reality that it is, religion can be approached from any number of different angles. It is commonly defined as the relationship of man to an absolute, like God. But as that definition may already be too narrow, there are those who prefer, for example, to speak in terms of the idea of the Holy. If this relationship is taken more concretely, however, still other possible angles of approach suggest themselves. For instance, the relationship of man to God may be spoken of as the abandonment of self-will in order to live according to the will of God; as the vision or knowledge of God; or, as the unveiling of God to the self, or in the self. Again, it may be thought of as the immediate perception of the absolute dependency of self-existence on divine existence, or as man's becoming one with God. One might as well pursue the view that it is only in religion that man becomes truly himself, that the self encounters its "original countenance." Furthermore, it is possible to regard the essence of religion, as Schleiermacher does in his *Reden über die Religion*, as the intuition of the infinite in the finite, as "feeling the Universe." On a variety of counts, of course, each of these views is open to criticism. Rather than enter any further into their discussion here, I should like instead to approach religion from a somewhat different angle, as the self-awareness of reality, or, more correctly, the *real* self-awareness of reality.

By the "self-awareness of reality" I mean both our becoming aware of reality and, at the same time, the reality realizing itself in our awareness. The English word "realize," with its twofold meaning of "actualize" and "understand," is particularly well suited to what I have in mind here, although I am told that its sense of "understand" does not necessarily connote the sense of reality coming to actualization in us. Be that as it may, I am using the word to indicate that our ability to perceive reality means that reality realizes (actualizes) itself in us; that this in turn is the only way that we can realize (appropriate through understanding) the fact that reality is so realizing itself in us; and that in so doing the self-realization of reality itself takes place.

It follows that realization in its sense of "appropriation" differs from philosophical cognition. What I am speaking of is not theoretical knowledge but a real appropriation (the *proprium* taken here to embrace the whole man, mind and body). This real appropriation provides our very mode of being with its essential determination. The real perception of reality is our real mode of being itself and constitutes the realness that is the true reality of our existence. This perception of reality can constitute the realness of our existence because it comes into being in unison with the self-realization of reality itself. In this sense, the realness of our existence, as the appropriation of reality, belongs to reality itself as the self-realization of reality itself. In other words, the self-realization of reality can only take place by causing our existence to become truly real.

The question will no doubt arise as to what this "reality" signifies. If the question is posed merely in the form of the usual request for knowledge, in expectation of a simple, conceptual response, then it is inappropriate to the reality I am speaking of here. In order for it to become a _real_ question, one that is asked with the whole self, body and mind, it must be returned to reality itself. The question that _asks about_ reality must itself become something that _belongs to_ reality. In that vein, I should like to try to interpret the religious quest as man's search for true reality in a _real_ way (that is, not theoretically and not in the form of concepts, as we do in ordinary knowledge and philosophical knowledge), and from that same angle to attempt an answer to the question of the essence of religion by tracing the process of the real pursuit of true reality.

When we think of "reality" from an everyday standpoint, we think first of all of the things and events _without_ us: the mountains and streams, the flowers and forests, and the entire visible universe all about us. We think, too, of other people, other societies and nations, and of the whole skein of human activities and historical events that envelop them. Next, we think of reality as the world _within_ us: our thoughts, our feelings, and our desires.

When we pass from the everyday standpoint to that of natural science, we find that it is the atoms, or the energy that makes them up, or the scientific laws that regulate that energy, rather than individual events and phenomena, that are now regarded as reality. In contrast, the social scientist, for his part, might posit that economic relations provide all human activity with its basis in reality. Or again, a metaphysician might argue that all those things are only the appearances of a phenomenal world, and that the true reality is to be found in the Ideas that lie behind them.

The problem with these various "realities" is that they lack unity among themselves and even seem to contradict one another. On the one hand, even if one assumes that things in the outer world are real, they cannot at bottom be separated from the laws of mathematics and natural science. The space the things of the outer world occupy and the movements they make conform to the laws of geometry and dynamics. Indeed, things cannot even exist apart from these laws. Moreover, our grasp of these laws obviously underlies the technology we have developed for controlling things and improving them. In a similar way, conscious phenomena such as feelings and desires cannot be separated from the laws of physiology and psychology; nor, as the stuff of concrete human existence, can they be considered apart from the kind of relationships that the social sciences take to be real.

On the other hand, no natural scientist would deny that the food he eats or the children seated at his table are all individual realities. No modern social scientist can help considering as very real the admiration he feels for a piece of Greek sculpture or the gloom he feels during the rainy season. On this point the scientist differs not in the least from men of ancient times. The same holds true for the metaphysician. Indeed, the relationship between ideas and sense objects, which has long been the most-debated problem in metaphysics, comes down to the question of deciding what is real.

In short, while the various standpoints of everyday life, science, philosophy, and the like all tell us what is real, there are grave discrepancies and contradictions among them. What the scientist takes to be real from the viewpoint of his science and what he takes to be real from the viewpoint of his everyday experience are completely at odds with each other, and yet he is unable to deny either of them. It is no simple matter to say what is truly real.

In addition to the things mentioned so far, death and nihility are also very real. Nihility is absolute negativity with regard to the very being of all those various things and phenomena just referred to; death is absolute negativity with regard to life itself. Thus, if life and things are said to be real, then death and nihility are equally real.[1] Wherever there are finite beings—and all things are finite—there must be nihility; wherever there is life, there must be death. In the face of death and nihility, all life and existence lose their certainty and their importance as reality, and come to look unreal instead. From time immemorial man has continually expressed this fleeting transience of life and existence, likening it to a dream, a shadow, or the shimmering haze of the summer's heat.

This brings us, then, to another sense of the real altogether different from the various meanings discussed so far. As an example of this sense of the real, I recall a passage from Dostoevski's *The House of the Dead*, recording how, one summer day during the author's term of imprisonment, while he was at work carrying bricks by the banks of a river, he was suddenly struck by the surrounding landscape and overcome with profound emotion. Reflecting on the wild and desolate steppes, the sun blazing overhead in the vast blue vault of heaven, and the distant chanting of the Khirgiz that floated his way from across the river, he writes:

> Sometimes I would fix my sight for a long while upon the poor smokey cabin of some *baïgouch*; I would study the bluish smoke as it curled in the air, the Kirghiz woman busy with her sheep. . . . The things I saw were wild, savage, poverty-stricken; but they were free. I would follow the flight of a bird threading its way in the pure transparent air; now it skims the water, now disappears in the azure sky, now suddenly comes to view again, a mere point in space. Even the poor wee floweret fading in a cleft of the bank, which would show itself when spring began, fixed my attention and would draw my tears.[2]

As Dostoevski himself tells us, this is the only spot at which he saw "God's world, a pure and bright horizon, the free desert steppes"; in casting his gaze across the immense desert space, he found he was able to forget his "wretched self."

The things that Dostoevski draws attention to—the curling smoke, the woman tending her sheep, the poor hut, the bird in flight—are all things we come in touch with in our everyday lives. We speak of them as real in the everyday sense of the word, and from there go on to our scientific and philosophical theories. But for such commonplace things to become the focus of so intense a concentration, to capture one's attention to that almost abnormal degree, is by no means an everyday occurrence. Nor does it spring from scientific or metaphysical reflection. Things that we are accustomed to speak of as real forced their reality upon him in a completely different dimension. He saw the same real things we all see, but the significance of their realness and the sense of the real in them that he experienced in perceiving them as real are something altogether qualitatively different. Thus was he able to forget his wretched self and to open his eyes to "God's world."

Later, in *A Raw Youth* and *The Brothers Karamazov*, Dostoevski tells us that God may be found in a single leaf at daybreak, in a beam of sunlight, or in the cry of an infant. This way of speaking suggests a great harmony among all things in the universe that brings them into being and sustains them in mutual dependence and cooperation, a mystical order that rules over all things so that God can be seen in the most trivial of things. This is, we might say, the backdrop against which the author's profound sense of the real in everyday things came into being. We know from *The House of the Dead* that his remarkable sensibility was connected with the prison life that had deprived him of his freedom; but the experience of such a sense of the real does not require such singular circumstances. On the contrary, it is an experience open to anyone and everyone. It is something to which poets and religious men and women have attested down through the ages.

Although we ordinarily think of things in the external world as real, we may not actually get in touch with the reality of those things. I would venture to say that in fact we do not. It is extremely rare for us so to "fix our attention" on things as to "lose ourselves" in them, in other words, to *become* the very things we are looking at. To see through them directly to "God's world," or to the universe in its infinitude, is even rarer. We are accustomed to seeing things from the standpoint of the self. One might say that we look out at things from within the citadel of the self, or that we sit like spectators in the cave of the self. Plato, it will be recalled, likened our ordinary relationship to things to being tied up inside a cave, watching the shadows passing to and fro across its walls, and calling those shadows "reality."

To look at things from the standpoint of the self is always to see things merely as objects, that is, to look at things *without* from a field *within* the self. It means assuming a position vis-à-vis things from which self and things remain fundamentally separated from one another. This standpoint of separation of subject and object, or opposition between within and without, is what we call the field of "consciousness." And it is from this field that we ordinarily relate to things by means of concepts and representations. Hence, for all our talk about the reality of things, things do not truly display their *real* reality to us. On the field of consciousness, it is not possible really to get in touch with things as they are, that is, to face them in their own mode of being and on their own home-ground. On the field of consciousness, self always occupies center stage.

We also think of our own selves, and of our "inner" thoughts, feelings, and desires as real. But here, too, it is doubtful whether we properly get in touch with ourselves, whether our feelings and desires and so forth are in the proper sense really present to us as they are, and whether those feelings should be said to be present on their own home-ground and in their own mode of being. Precisely because we face things on a field separated from things, and to the extent that we do so, we are forever separated from ourselves. Or, to put it in positive terms, we can get in touch with ourselves only through a mode of being that puts us in touch with things from the very midst of those things themselves. We are of course accustomed to set ourselves against what is *without* by looking at it from *within*, and then to think of ourselves as being in our own home-ground and in touch with ourselves when we do so. Such is the bias of consciousness. In fact, however, the self that is self-centered in its relation to the *without* is a self that is separated from things and closed up *within* itself alone. It is a self that continually faces itself in the same way. That is, the self is set ever against itself, as some *thing* called "self" and separated from other things. This is the self of self-consciousness, wherein a representation of the self in the shape of some "thing" or other is always intervening, keeping the self from being really and truly on its own home-ground. In self-consciousness, the self is not really and truly in touch with itself. The same can be said in the case of the internal "consciousness" of feelings, desires, and the like.

Things, the self, feelings, and so forth are all real, to be sure. On the field of consciousness where they are ordinarily taken for real, however, they are not present in their true reality but only in the form of representations. So long as the field of separation between *within* and *without* is not broken through, and so long as a conversion from that standpoint does not take place, the lack of unity and contradiction spoken of earlier cannot help but prevail among the things we take as real. This sort of contradiction shows up, for example, in the opposition between materialism and idealism; but even before it shows up on the level of thought, it is already there beneath the surface of our everyday modes of being and thought. The field that lies at the ground of our everyday lives is the field of an essential separation between self and things, the field of consciousness, within which a real self-presentation of reality cannot take place at all. Within it, reality appears only in the shape of shattered fragments, only in the shape of ineluctable self-contradictions.

This standpoint, which we may best call the self-contradiction of reality, has come to exercise a powerful control over us, never more so than since the emergence of the subjective autonomy of the ego in modern times. This latter appears most forcefully in the thought of Descartes, the father of modern philosophy. As is commonly known, Descartes set up a dualism between *res cogitans* (which has its essence in thought or consciousness) and *res extensa* (which has its essence in physical extension). On the one hand, he established the ego as a reality that is beyond all doubt and occupies the central position with regard to everything else that exists. His *cogito, ergo sum* expressed the mode of being of that ego as a self-centered assertion of its own realness. Along with this, on the other hand, the things in the natural world came to appear as bearing no living connection with the internal ego. They became, so to speak, the cold and lifeless world of death. Even animals and the body of man himself were thought of as mechanisms.

That such a mechanistic view of the world would come into being and that the world itself would turn into a world of death were, we might say, already implicit in Descartes' identification of matter with extension and his consideration of that extension as the essence of things. This did enable the image of the world we find in modern natural science to come about and did open the way for the control of nature by scientific technology. But it had other consequences. To the self-centered ego of man, the world came to look like so much raw material. By wielding his great power and authority in controlling the natural world, man came to surround himself with a cold, lifeless world. Inevitably, each individual ego became like a lonely but well-fortified island floating on a sea of dead matter. The life was snuffed out of nature and the things of nature; the living stream that flowed at the bottom of man and all things, and kept them bound together, dried up.

The idea of life as a living bond had been central to the prescientific, pre-Cartesian view of the world. Life was *alive* then not only in the sense of the individual lives of individual people, but, at the same time and in a very real way, as something uniting parents and children, brothers and sisters, and thence all men. It was as if each individual human being were born from the same life, like the individual leaves of a tree that sprout and grow and fall one by one and yet share in the same life of the tree. Not only human beings, but all living beings belonged to the larger tree of life. Even the soul (or psyche) was nothing more than life showing itself. Appearing as men, life took the form of a human soul; appearing as plants and animals, that of a plant or animal soul—for plants and animals, too, were thought to have their own souls.

Furthermore, on the basis of the life that linked individual things together at bottom, a sympathetic affinity was thought to obtain between one man's soul and another's. This "sympathy" was meant to bespeak a contact prior to and more immediate than consciousness. It was meant to point to the field of the most immediate encounter between man and man, at the ground of the instincts and drives that underlie all thought, feeling, and desire. More than that, this same sympathy was thought to exist not only among men, but among all living things. In other words, the vital connective that bound individual beings to one another was thought to appear as a field of "psychic sympathy" between souls. Of course, this view seems to have all but been wiped out completely by the modern mechanistic view of nature. But is that cause enough simply to dismiss it as antiquated?

On a summer's night, a mosquito flies into my room from the outside. It buzzes about merrily, as if cheering itself for having found its prey. With a single motion I catch it and squash it in the palm of my hand, and in that final moment it lets out a shrill sound of distress. This is the only word we can use to describe it. The sound it makes is different from the howling of a dog or the screams of a man, and yet in its "essence" it is the selfsame sound of distress. It may be that each of these sounds is but vibrations of air moving at different wavelengths, but they all possess the same quality or essence that makes us hear them as signals of distress. Does not our immediate intuition of the distress in the sound of the mosquito take place on a field of psychic sympathy? Might we not also see here the reason that the ancients believed animals to have souls? In this sense, whatever modern mechanistic physiologists or functionalist psychologists, who are busy trying to erase the notion of soul, might make of it, let it be said that there is something, even in animals, that we have no other name for than the one that has come down to us from the past: soul.

Just what this "something" ought to be said to consist of is, of course, another problem. It may no longer be necessary to think of the soul as some special substance. Perhaps it is not even possible to continue to think of it as something with an independent existence that takes up lodging "within" the body. This view requires us to look on the body, too, as something independent, a lifeless object with an existence all its own apart from the soul. It means considering body and soul as distinct substances, and then trying to determine how they come to be joined together.

It is also possible to approach the question from the opposite direction. For instance, Schopenhauer takes "the Will to Live" as the thing-in-itself and considers the body, as an organism, to be the objectification of that will, the form under which it appears to the eye of man. Bergson expresses a similar idea when he says that in its material aspect the body represents a point of relaxation for the tension inherent in life as it advances creatively. In both cases, individuals appear as individualizations of something else—be it "will" or "life"—that is at work within them. This is another possible way of viewing the soul. Along this same line, ancient peoples imagined that one soul could take on a variety of different animal bodies in succession, which belief then led to such notions as reincarnation and metempsychosis. We may wish to dismiss such ideas as extravagant fantasies, but we should still see behind them the view of soul just referred to.

Even granting that we cannot really get in touch with reality on the fields of consciousness and self-consciousness, neither can we stop short at the viewpoint of preconscious life and sympathy that we have described above. More than a few religions have in fact based themselves on a return to just such a preconscious level; but at that level, it is impossible to get deeply in touch with reality. Instead of regressing from the field of consciousness to a preconscious or subconscious one, we need rather to seek a new and more encompassing viewpoint that passes through, indeed *breaks through*, the field of consciousness to give us a new perspective.

III

The self of contemporary man is an ego of the Cartesian type, constituted self-consciously as something standing over against the world and all the things that are in it. Life, will, intellect, and so forth are attributed to that ego intrinsically as its faculties or activities. We are incapable of conceiving of the subjectivity of individual man without at the same time conceding to each individual his own ego, absolutely independent and irreplaceable. We designate as "subject" that entity which can in no way ever be made an object itself, or can never be derived from anything else, but is rather the point of departure from which everything else may be considered. The formula for expressing this is, of course, *cogito, ergo sum*. But that familiar phrase contains a fundamental problem. From the first, Descartes took the *cogito* as an immediately evident truth, the one thing that stood above all doubt and could therefore serve as a starting point for thinking about everything else. Because the *cogito, ergo sum* was self-evident, he did not see any further problem with it; which is to say, he was satisfied with thinking about the *cogito* from the standpoint of the *cogito* itself. But is there not in fact a difficulty here? For all its self-evidence, does the *cogito* really give us an adequate standpoint from which to think about the *cogito* itself? Does not that very self-evidence need to be brought out into the open at a more elemental level?

This is not to suggest that the origination of the *cogito* be explained on the basis of something like the "preconscious life of matter" spoken of earlier. Such an approach is altogether out of the question. It is absolutely inconceivable that the knower should be generated from or constituted by the known, since knowing always implies a transcendence over what is known. Neither do I suggest that the *cogito* be explained by means of something like "God." I do not have it in mind for the *cogito* to be *explained* through anything else at all, from "above" it or "below," and ultimately *reduced* to that something else. Rather, I want to turn to the ground of the subjectivity of the *cogito* and there to consider its origin from a point at which the orientation of the subject to its ground is more radical and thoroughgoing than it is with the *cogito*. The subject cannot emerge out of something objective. *Cogito, ergo sum* may be the most directly evident of truths, then, but that the field on which we think about the *cogito* ought to be the selfsame standpoint of the *cogito* is anything but evident. Far from being the one and only way of bringing out into the open the evident fact of the *cogito*, it is no more than one possible way of looking at that fact, one philosophical position among others. Specifically, it is the expression of one particular mode of being of the age, namely, the self-centered mode of being. Indeed, to think about the *cogito, ergo sum* by starting from the *cogito, ergo sum*—that is, to view self-consciousness and its self-evidence as mirrored on the field of that very self-consciousness itself—is only natural for the *ego* that is the subject of the *cogito*. We might even say that this ego arises in a field where self-consciousness mirrors itself at every turn. Hence, the self-evidence of self-consciousness—the very fact that the self is evident to itself—keeps us from feeling the need to look at that evident fact from a field beyond that fact itself.

As mentioned above, the self-evidence of the *cogito* can in no way be derived from the field of anything that is completely other than the ego, be it life, matter, or God. But because this ego is seen as self-consciousness mirroring self-consciousness at every turn and the *cogito* is seen from the standpoint of the *cogito* itself, ego becomes a mode of being of the self closed up within itself. In other words, ego means self in a state of self-attachment.

This also explains how problems that have their roots in the essence of the egoistic mode of being arise within the self. One thinks of the variety of ethical, philosophical, and religious doubts, anxieties, and demands tied up with the essence of the ego's mode of being. For example, questions of egoism, goodness and evil in human nature, radical evil and sin, loneliness and the loss of self in society, the possibility of knowledge, and the demand for salvation or deliverance, are all tied up with the mode of being of an ego that is a self centered on itself and clinging to itself. Eventually questions of this sort, and the mode of being of the ego itself, become questions for the ego. *Cogito, ergo sum* is the most immediately evident of truths, but as a result of being regarded from the field of the *cogito*, it becomes problematical instead, and, on a more fundamental level, turns into doubt. Its self-evidence becomes a kind of self-deception, or a fallacy unto itself, since the elemental ground of the ego itself has been closed off to the understanding of the ego. It is a process implicit from the very start in the origination of the ego itself.

The self-consciousness of the *cogito, ergo sum*, therefore, needs to be thought about by leaving its subjectivity as is and proceeding from a field more basic than self-consciousness, a field that I have been calling "elemental." Of course, when we say "thinking about," we do not mean the ordinary type of objective thinking. Thinking about the ego from an elemental field means that the ego itself opens up in subjective fashion an elemental field of existence within itself. In this sense, what we are saying is no different from saying that the elemental self-awareness of the ego itself comes to be an elemental self. This way of thinking about the *cogito* is "existential" thinking: more elemental thought must signal a more elemental mode of being of the self. On this view, the Cartesian *cogito, ergo sum* can secure its own truth only when the field of self-consciousness breaks open to the more elemental field of the elemental self. Where this does not take place, the self of that self-consciousness comes eventually to be a falsehood and a delusion unto itself.

This matter is something that comes to light in ancient philosophy and, in a special way, most acutely in religion. Looked at in this sense, the unique and characteristic mark of religion can be seen as the existential exposure of the problematic contained in the ordinary mode of self-being. It can be seen as the way of the great, elemental *ego cogito* elucidating the *ego sum*.

In order to explain this more concretely, I shall try to compare the method of doubt that Descartes adopted to arrive at his *cogito, ergo sum* with the doubt that appears in religion. Doubt and uncertainty show up in the vestibules of religion. We see them, for example, in the questions mentioned at the beginning of this chapter concerning the life and death of the self and the transience of all things coming to be and passing away in the world. Contained in the pain of losing a loved one forever is a fundamental uncertainty about the very existence of oneself and others. This doubt takes a variety of forms and is expressed in a variety of ways. For instance, Zen speaks of the "self-presentation of the Great Doubt." Its characterization as "Great" seems to hinge, for one thing, on the content of the doubt itself. The very condition of basic uncertainty regarding human existence in the world and the existence of self and others, as well as the suffering that this gives rise to, are surely matters of the utmost, elemental concern. As the Chinese adage has it, "Birth and death—the great matter." The word "Great," then, may also be said to refer to the consciousness of our mode of being and way of existing in response to this "great matter." This is a most important point.

As was noted earlier, we come to the realization of death and nihility when we see them within ourselves as constituting the basis of our life and existence. We awaken to their reality when we see them as extending beyond the subjective realm, lying concealed at the ground of all that exists, at the ground of the world itself. This awareness implies more than merely looking contemplatively at death and nihility. It means that the self realizes their presence at the foundations of its existence, that it sees them from the final frontier of its self-existence. To that extent the realization of nihility is nothing other than the realization of the self itself. It is not a question of observing nihility objectively or entertaining some representation of it. It is, rather, as if the self were itself to *become* that nihility, and in so doing become aware of itself from the limits of self-existence.

The realization we are speaking of here is not self-conscious, therefore, but consists rather in breaking through the field of consciousness and self-consciousness. Consciousness is the field of relationships between those entities characterized as self and things. That is, it is the field of *beings* at which the nihility that lies beneath the ground of being remains covered over. At this level, even the self in its very subjectivity is still only *represented* self-consciously as self. It is put through a kind of objectivization so as to be grasped as a being. Only when the self breaks through the field of consciousness, the field of *beings*, and stands on the ground of nihility is it able to achieve a subjectivity that can in no way be objectivized. This is the elemental realization that reaches deeper than self-consciousness. In standing subjectively on the field of nihility (I use the term "stand" and refer to nihility as a "field," but in fact there is literally *no place* to stand), the self becomes itself in a more elemental sense. When this takes place, the being of the self itself is *nullified* along with the being of everything else. "Nullification" does not mean that everything is simply "annihilated" out of existence. It means that nihility appears at the ground of everything that exists, that the field of consciousness with its separation of the *within* and the *without* is surpassed subjectively, and that nihility opens up at the ground of the *within* and the *without*.

This opening up of nihility is one of the elemental realizations of subjectivity. It is not "subjective" in the narrow sense of the field of consciousness that confronts the "objective" world as phenomena. Nor is it merely some form of psychological event. The self-presentation of nihility is rather a real presentation of what is actually concealed at the ground of the self and of everything in the world. On the field of consciousness this nihility is covered over and cannot make itself really present. When it does make itself present, however, everything that was taken for external and internal reality at the field of consciousness becomes unreal in its very reality: it is nullified but not annihilated. Self-being and the being of all things combine to make one question; all being becomes a single great question mark. This elementally subjective realization goes deeper than the self-evidence of self-consciousness clinging to itself like a *within* shut up inside itself. It is an awareness that can only emerge in the reality of an *Existenz* that oversteps the limits of being. It is an awareness that lies on the *far side* of everything that psychology can apprehend precisely by virtue of being all the more on the *near side* of the subject.

In this way, when we break through the field of self-consciousness and overstep the field of *beings* to come out on the field of nihility—in other words, when self-existence and the being of all things are transformed into a single question mark beyond the distinction between within and without (at the *far side* that is seen to be all the more at the *near side*)—that is when we may speak of the self as doubting. Here we come to something fundamentally different from the ordinary doubts we have about one thing or the other, that is, the doubts that have to do with objective matters. It is also fundamentally different from doubt understood as a state of consciousness. What I am talking about is the point at which the nihility that lies hidden as a reality at the ground of the self and all things makes itself present as a reality to the self in such a way that self-existence, together with the being of all things, turns into a single doubt. When the distinction between the doubter and the doubted drops away, when the field of that very distinction is over-stepped, the self becomes the Great Doubt.

I term it "Great" because it does not restrict its concern to the isolated self of self-consciousness but embraces at once the existence of the self and of all things. This Doubt cannot, therefore, be understood as a state of consciousness but only as a real doubt making itself present to the self out of the ground of the self and of all things. In appearing out of the depths of the one ground of self and world, this Doubt presents itself as *reality*. When this Doubt appears to the self, it does so with an inevitability quite beyond the control of the consciousness and arbitrary willfulness of the self. In its presence, the self *becomes* Doubt itself. The self *realizes* the doubt about *reality*. This is the "self-presentation of the Great Doubt." Through it the uncertainty that lies at the ground of the self and of all things is appropriated by the self.

This may also be called the doubt of the self, although it is not the "self" that does the doubting. In Buddhist terminology it is what is known as the doubt of *samādhi* ("concentration"). On some few occasions, of course, this kind of doubt may appear in pure and radical form, but in all cases the basic pattern remains the same: the doubt of the self about something or other is reflected back upon the self. Let us say, for example, that I am overcome with uneasiness and anxiety over the ideas or the way of life that I had all along assumed to be correct but am now beginning to have second thoughts about; or at a time when the sincerity of someone I love has suddenly been brought into question—so that the state of the self doubting about some particular matter passes over into the state of the real self-presentation of Doubt in the self, wherein the self and the object of its doubt at ground join together with one another. Whenever doubt becomes existentially serious and something real to the self, it contains the "self-presentation of the Great Doubt."

It is my view that the unique characteristic of the religious way of life, and the basic difference between religion and philosophy, comes to this: in religion one persistently pushes ahead in a direction where doubt becomes a reality for the self and makes itself really present to the self. This sort of real doubt may, of course, show up in philosophical skepsis, but philosophy tends to transfer it to the realm of theoretical reflection, and within those confines to seek an explanation and solution of the problem.

When Descartes entertained the possibility of doubting everything that presents itself to us by suspecting it all of being the illusion of a dream or the trick of a malicious demon, and so, considering that this doubt itself was the only thing beyond doubt, arrived at the conclusion *cogito, ergo sum*, he was engaged from the very start in a process of methodical doubt. This is something fundamentally different from the self-presentation of the Great Doubt. It cannot be the sort of doubt in which the self and all things are transformed into a single Doubt; it is not the Doubt that makes itself present in the self as the basic reality of the self and things; nor, again, is it that Doubt the very realization of which comes about within oneself, and in which the self realizes (appropriates) the fundamental uncertainty of the self and all things.

At the same time, the *cogito* of Descartes did not pass through the purgative fires in which the ego itself is transformed, along with all things, into a single Great Doubt. The *cogito* was conceived of simply on the field of the *cogito*. This is why the reality of the ego as such could not but become an unreality. Only after passing through those purgative fires and breaking through the nihility that makes itself present at the ground of the ego, can the reality of the *cogito* and the *sum*, together with the reality of all things, truly appear as real. Only then can this reality be actualized and appropriated. If we grant that Cartesian philosophy is the prime illustration of the mode of being of modern man, we may also say that it represents the fundamental problem lurking within that mode.

Along this same line, it would be an error to regard the self-presentation of the Great Doubt as a kind of psychological state that takes place in the course of religious practice, as even a great number of religious people seem to see it nowadays. In the state of Doubt, the self is concentrated single-mindedly on the doubt alone, to the exclusion of everything else, and *becomes* the pure doubt itself (samādhi). This much is certain, since it is no longer a question of a self that doubts something on the field of consciousness, but rather a point at which the field of consciousness has been erased. Of course, the fact remains that when doubt is concentrated on and brooded over, it produces its own psychological state. When we speak of a grief "deep enough to drown the world and oneself with it," or of a joy that "sets one's hands a-flutter and one's feet a-dancing," we have this same sense of single-mindedness or of *becoming* what one experiences. But it matters not whether we call it single-mindedness or samādhi—it is not to be interpreted as a mere psychological state. The "mind" of "single-mindedness" is not mind in any psychological sense. It is *reality* in the twofold sense that I have been using here. What is more, when I talk of overstepping the field of consciousness, I am not referring to the "unconscious," since the unconscious is not yet separated from the field of consciousness.

A monk named Ting Shan-tso (pronounced Jōjōza in Japanese) once inquired of the famous Zen master Lin-chi (in Japanese, Rinzai), "What is the heart of Buddhism?" Lin-chi gave him a slap and pushed him away. Ting Shan-tso, brought abruptly to a state of concentration, stood motionless and in such total self-oblivion that a monk nearby had to remind him to bow to his master. At the moment of bowing he is said to have attained the Great Enlightenment. That motionless self-oblivion does not indicate a mere psychological state. It is the momentous Great Reality I referred to earlier, making itself present and taking complete possession of the mind and body. Here we have the self-presentation of the Great Doubt. This sort of radical occurrence is probably the result of a great opportunity presenting itself after a good deal of religious discipline. But, to repeat what I said before, every doubt that is truly real, even if it is not so distinguished as the doubt of Ting Shan-tso, includes something of that same significance. There may be differences of depth and force, but qualitatively speaking—that is, in terms of its existential character—it comes to the same thing.

Of the many allusions in Zen literature to the encouragement of the Great Doubt, I should like to single out here a passage from the eighteenth-century *Sermons* of Takusui:

> The method to be practiced is as follows: you are to doubt regarding the subject in you that hears all sounds. All sounds are heard at a given moment because there is certainly a subject in you that hears. Although you may hear the sounds with your ears, the holes in your ears are not the subject that hears. If they were, dead men would also hear sounds. . . . You must doubt deeply, again and again, asking yourself what the subject of hearing could be. Pay no attention to the various illusory thoughts and ideas that may occur to you. Only doubt more and more deeply, gathering together in yourself all the strength that is in you, without aiming at anything or expecting anything in advance, without intending to be enlightened and without even intending not to intend to be enlightened; become like a child within your own breast . . . But however you go on doubting, you will find it impossible to locate the subject that hears. You must explore still further just there, where there is nothing to be found. Doubt deeply in a state of single-mindedness, looking neither ahead nor behind, neither right nor left, becoming completely like a dead man, unaware even of the presence of your own person. When this method is practiced more and more deeply, you will arrive at a state of being completely self-oblivious and empty. But even then you must bring up the Great Doubt, "What is the subject that hears?" and doubt still further, all the time

being like a dead man. And after that, when you are no longer aware of your being completely like a dead man, and are no more conscious of the procedure of the Great Doubt but become yourself, through and through, a great mass of doubt, there will come a moment, all of a sudden, at which you emerge into a transcendence called the Great Enlightenment, as if you had awoken from a great dream, or as if, having been completely dead, you had suddenly revived.

That the method of doubt described here is completely and qualitatively different from that of Descartes is clear. It belongs to the sort of doubt we have been considering here, in which death or nihility are *realized* in the self, both in the sense of becoming present to awareness as something real, and in the sense of becoming themselves something "spiritually" real. This method of doubt also helps us to understand why Zen Buddhism refers to radical doubt as the Great Death.

The Great Doubt comes to light from the ground of our existence only when we press our doubts (What am I? Why do I exist?) to their limits as conscious acts of the doubting self. The Great Doubt represents not only the apex of the doubting self but also the point of its "passing away" and ceasing to be "self." It is like the bean whose seed and shell break apart as it ripens: the shell is the tiny ego, and the seed the infinity of the Great Doubt that encompasses the whole world. It is the moment at which self is at the same time the nothingness of self, the moment that is the "locus" of nothingness where conversion beyond the Great Doubt takes place. For the Great Doubt always emerges as the opening up of the locus of nothingness as the field of conversion from the Great Doubt itself. This is why it is "Great."

This is also why it can be called the "Great Death." There are numerous Zen sayings referring to that conversion in such terms, for example: "In the Great Death heaven and earth become new," and "Beneath the Great Death, the Great Enlightenment." As in the case of doubt, this enlightenment must be an enlightenment of the self, but at the same time it must signal a "dropping off" of the mode of being in which "self" is seen as agent. It is something that presents itself as real from the one ground of the self and all things. It is the true reality of the self and all things, in which everything is present just as it is, in its *suchness*.

The reality that appears from the bottom of the Great Doubt and overturns it is none other than our "original countenance." To see "heaven and earth become new" is to look on the face of the original self. It is the full *realization* (actualization-*sive*-appropriation) of the reality of the self and all things. This is the Great <u>Wisdom</u> of which religion speaks, the wisdom that is, in fact, an aspect of the religious mode of being itself. We shall have to return to this matter later on.

IV

In line with this treatment of death and nihility, we must also see evil and sin as elemental issues for man and consider them as problems of reality. The usual thing is to pose questions about these things, too, simply from the field of consciousness. Particularly when it has to do with someone else, but even when it is only we ourselves involved, we speak of the self as committing evil. Actually we are making "self" and "evil" two separate realities, or at best imagining the self as if it were the trunk of a tree from which stem the leaves and branches of evil. This dichotomy comes about because we are thinking about self and evil by means of the representations that are proper to them on the field of consciousness.

Evil and sin become really and truly present as realities, however, only when they are constituted at a point beyond the field of the conscious self. It was on such a field that Kant conceived of "radical evil" as something having its roots in the ground of the subject itself—in the "ultimate subjective ground of all maxims"—and as an "intelligible act" (*intelligible That*)[3] of the subject itself, albeit as one preceding all temporal actions and experiences of the subject. In contrast, we are used to associating evil and sin with events in the world of temporal experience. But to stop there is to focus on the leaves and branches and miss the roots.

The radical awareness of evil comes about when the elemental source of particular evils within time is traced down to the ground of self-being itself. When Kant said that "radical evil" precedes all temporal experiences as something having its roots in the ground of the subject, he did not mean to imply a mere chronological precedence, as, for instance, we do when we speak of the "time before we were born." He meant that we become aware of evil as something residing directly beneath the present time, as something that breaks through time from within the very midst of time; that is, that we realize evil on the transtemporal ground of the subject. Or to put it another way, evil rises to awareness as a reality at the ground of self-existence out of that "moment" that Kierkegaard refers to as "the atom of eternity within time."

Inasmuch as evil makes itself present at the ground of the subject itself, we cannot remain content with speaking of evil as something that "the self commits." It is something substantial that becomes present in its own suchness at the ground of the *existence* of the self. It cannot be grasped from the standpoint of the self as agent. In this sense, it is "incomprehensible" to the ego precisely because it makes itself present as a reality, in its very suchness. Even so, radical evil is not something come to the self from somewhere outside the self. As a reality that makes its presence felt at the ground of the *subject*, it belongs only to the subject itself. Radical evil sinks its roots elementally into the ground of the subject. The subject itself through its realization (awareness) of radical evil, becomes, at its own ground, the realization (actualization) of the suchness of evil. This is why Kant found it necessary to conceive of radical evil as intelligible *act*.

Thus, evil rises to self-awareness in a truly subjective sense and in all its suchness, at a point beyond that field of consciousness where we can speak of the self having committed evil. Only then is the evil of the self truly and for the first time able to be "appropriated." An evil of the self itself, an evil whose elemental realization is the self, is not simply and exclusively a "self-ish" evil. It is not an evil immanent only in the self-consciously isolated "ego." As Kant had already seen to be the case with radical evil and as Kierkegaard had with original sin, this evil or sin is characteristic of humanity as a whole at the same time as it belongs to each individual. This evil lurking in the ground where the self is in unison with all things (or with all living things, or, at least, with all of mankind) presents itself as a Great Reality in the subjective ground of the self. It is precisely this that makes it a reality.

This also explains why Buddhism thinks of evil in terms of *karma* "from times past without beginning" and *avidyā* ("the darkness of ignorance"), and why Christianity turns to the notion of an "original sin" transmitted from one generation to the next. Each of these concepts contains a *real* perception of evil and sin. In Christianity, it is said that the sinful existence of man is the result of Adam's sin of disobedience against God, and this, in turn, is interpreted as we ourselves having committed sin in Adam. Put more subjectively and existentially, this simply means that both the sinfulness of the self and the sinfulness of all mankind make themselves present in an elemental sense as *one* reality, and are actualized and appropriated as such in the self. It is, so to speak, an appropriation of the evil of all men within the evil of the self, and, at the same time, of the evil of the self within the evil of all men. The

Buddhist notions of karma and avidyā should be taken as pointing to the same sense of the reality of evil.

It is only in religion that evil and sin can become present in their suchness, as the realities that they in fact are. Crime and evil are issues treated in such social sciences as law and economy, as well as in various branches of cultural studies, but for the most part they are handled there in an objective manner. They become problems in the subjective sense of the term primarily in the field of ethics, where, for the first time, crime and evil are related to the subject of each individual person and are made matters of individual responsibility. Only in ethics does the "personal" mode of being open up for each individual subject.

When morality and ethics are diluted and reduced to social and cultural questions, the so-called environmental conditioning theory of crime and evil appears. According to this theory, the evil and crimes wrought by men are entirely the responsibility of their environment. "Society is to blame," we are told. This one-sided way of looking at things blocks man from the way to personal awakening and, paradoxically, makes social life all the more evil. Hence the unique significance of ethics and the need for moral education.

However important ethics is, though, it still treats sin and evil only on the field of "ego," as something that "the self has committed." Although there are situations for which this treatment is adequate, its limitations prevent evil and sin from appearing in their true reality. In ethics, man does not yet attain an appropriation of the evil and sin of the self itself. This is possible only in religion. And this is why Kant, who had considered evil in his moral philosophy as simply the inclination toward "self love" immanent in man, could not avoid the concept of "radical evil" when he came to his philosophy of religion. This brings us back again to the basic difference between religion and ethics, paralleling the difference between religion and philosophy noted in the discussion of doubt.

We may recall here the famous controversy between Karl Barth and Emil Brunner over the problem of original sin. In contrast to Barth, for whom the "image of God" in man was completely corrupted by original sin, Brunner recognized this complete corruption but went on to argue that reason, as the "formal" aspect of the *imago Dei*, survives the corruption to provide an *Anknüpfungspunkt* ("point of contact") with divine grace. But if we take sin as a Great Reality, in the sense discussed above, that makes itself present at the very ground of self-being beyond the conscious self, it then becomes impossible to separate "form" from

"content" in the self-existence (and no less so in the "human" being) that
is the realization of that sin. Self-existence as a whole (and human being
in general) must be assumed to be corrupt.

Yet were complete corruption the last word on the actual condition
of the *imago Dei* in man, we should still be left with some unanswered
questions: How can man look for God, and how can he recognize when
he has found him? How can man become conscious of sin? How can
man hear when God calls out to him? It is not without reason, therefore,
that Brunner attempts to come up with some "point of contact." On the
other hand, though, if we set any limit at all to the completeness of the
corruption within man, we risk falling short of the full truth of human
sinfulness. Therefore, the place of "contact" must be present, in some
sense, *within* that complete corruption itself. It may be found, I think,
in the very awareness of the fact of complete corruption itself. Such
awareness would signal the realization (actualization-*sive*-appropria-
tion) of the utter powerlessness of the self to bring about its own
salvation, of the "spiritual" death of the self in sin, or of nihility itself.
When the self becomes the actualization of sin seen as a Great Reality,
when sin is appropriated, then the ensuing despair—that is, the loss of
all hope of the possibility of escape, and the awareness of the self that it
is nothingness and powerlessness—needs to be seen as a nothingness
become a field somehow capable of receiving redeeming love from God.
That all hope in the power of the self has revealed itself as hopeless, that
no horizon of possibility opens up before the self, amounts in fact to the
complete possession of the self by sin, to its identification with sin and
its becoming a member of sin. But then, in the twofold *realization* of sin,
we see the nothingness of the self rise up to serve as a locus (like the
χώρα that Plato speaks of in the *Timaeus*) for receiving redeeming love.

Since this locus is itself the point at which hope has run out for the
self, at which the self is pure nothingness, it can itself be said to have
been opened up from beyond by the love of God. But even so, it is
opened up as the locus to receive that very love, and so is not merely a
"point of contact." For Brunner, the *Anknüpfungspunkt* is posited in
human reason and, as such, is immanent in the self. The locus of
nothingness that I am speaking of here is the point at which the self is a
nothingness, at which the self has ceased to be a self any longer and has
become the *realization* of sin as a Great Reality. As it is itself nothingness, it is the locus wherein God's love can be accepted *really*, just as it
is.

Unlike reason, this nothingness is not an innate attribute of self-being. We cannot speak of it as either corrupted or uncorrupted. It is simply nothing at all, the nothingness that appears in the awareness that comes to man in limit-situations. If we are to speak of it as a kind of formal aspect of reality, then let it not be as a *form* distinct from *content*, but rather as the "form of non-form" for the whole content-and-form that is said to be corrupted as such. The love of God is also seen as the love of one who emptied himself (the *kenōsis* of God revealed in the *ekkenōsis* of Christ, who "emptied himself, taking the form of a servant") to save a sinful mankind. The "nothingness" that is constituted in the realization (appropriation) of sin may be thought of as correlative to this divine *kenōsis*.

The acceptance of divine love is called faith. Although this faith remains throughout a faith of the self, it is fundamentally different from the ordinary sense of faith which posits the self as its agent. In ordinary usage, faith is an *act* performed by the self, immanent in the self, and arising from *within* the self as an intentionality toward some object. It is the same even when we speak of believing in oneself. In all its forms, belief does not depart the field of consciousness and self-consciousness. In religion, however, faith comes about only on a horizon where this field has been overstepped and the framework of the "ego" has been broken through. Sin comes to be realized within the self as a reality emerging from the one ground of being of the self itself and of all men, or of all sentient beings (*sattva*). So, too, must the faith that signifies salvation as a conversion from that sin be a Great Reality.

We can find the concept of faith as a reality in this sense both in Christianity and in Buddhism. In Christianity, faith is considered to be a grace flowing from divine love. Buddhism distinguishes between "two types of profound faith." Faith is seen in its primordial sense as the turning of the "Power of the Original Vow" (that is, the saving will) of the *Tathāgata* (Buddha) in the direction of all sentient beings. This is known as the *dharma faith*. When this, in turn, meets with the real awareness of sin by man, it becomes *human faith*. In Christianity, faith in Christ means both man's witness to and appropriation of God's redeeming love, and also God's actualization of and witness to his own divine love in man. In both of these aspects, faith is the working of the Holy Spirit as the love of God which establishes a *real* bond between man and God, a bond that is both actualized and appropriated in faith. As it is written, "he who is united to the Lord becomes one spirit with him" (1 Cor. 6:17). In Buddhism, the name of Amida is taken to be the sign of the fulfillment of the Buddha's Vow of Compassion, and indeed is itself the name for the unity of the Buddha and all things. When that name is called to mind and pronounced on the lips of sentient beings, the actualization of the Buddha's Great Compassion and the witness of faith by sentient beings are seen to be really one, a single *realization*. In this regard we may draw attention to a passage from the *Shūjishō* of Kakunyo, a text from the tradition of Pure Land Buddhism:

> Without the practicing devotee who opens his heart to faith in the Name, Amida Buddha's Vow to save all and forsake none would not be fulfilled. Without the Buddha's Vow to save all and forsake none, how would the desire of the devotee for rebirth in the Pure land be fulfilled? Therefore it is said, "Is not the Vow the Name, and the Name the Vow? Is not the Vow the practicing devotee, and the devotee the Vow?"

In general, then, this sort of faith indicates the point at which the self truly becomes the self itself. The elemental realization of evil and sin, the field of nothingness opened up in that realization, and the acceptance in belief of the working of salvation all signify, each in its own way, the point at which the self becomes itself as something absolutely unique, the most "private" point in the self, the standpoint of the "solitary man" as Kierkegaard has it. Not only can no one else take the place of the self; but even the "self" of ordinary parlance, that is, the self as "ego," is equally incapable of replacing the true self. The ego represents the subjectivity of the individual, but as the standpoint of "ego" it can also be universalized into the standpoint of everyone else. This characteristic of the ego is already apparent, in the Cartesian *cogito, ergo sum*. Faith, in contrast, marks the point at which the self is really and truly a *solitary* self, and really and truly becomes the self itself. At the same time, however, this faith is not simply a thing of the self, but takes on the shape of a reality. We find this expressed in St. Paul as a faith in the one "who gave himself for me" (Gal. 2:20). Shinran notes, similarly: "When I carefully consider the Vow which Amida brought forth after five kalpas' contemplation, I find that it was solely for me, Shinran."[4]

This reality comes about at once as the absolute negation and the absolute affirmation of the solitary self. Salvation is referred to as the love of God, but it is a love that differs essentially from human love. For example, we hear Jesus proclaim: "Do not think that I have come to bring peace on earth; I have not come to bring peace, but a sword" (Matt. 10:34). In Zen this is known as the "sword that kills man" and the "sword that gives man life." It negates the ego-centered self of man, the self of elemental sin, from the very ground of its being. It cuts through the nihility and the "spiritual death" implied in sin and thereby makes it possible for man to inherit eternal life.

The love of which Jesus speaks is just such a sword: "For whoever would save his life will lose it, and whoever loses his life for my sake will find it" (Matt. 16:25). Faith, as a *realization* of the love of God (actualization-*sive*-appropriation) necessarily evolves into the "love of neighbor," and this love, too, comes to take on the significance of the sword. When St. Paul uses the word θεόπνευστος, "inspired by God" (2 Tim. 3:16), he does not mean that we have the Holy Spirit breathed *into us*, but rather that our very being becomes "God-breathed" through the breath (spiration) of God himself. This is the *reality* of faith and rebirth in faith. The ancients expressed a similar idea in the saying "The channel forms as the water flows." That is, water does not flow into a ready-made waterway called "man" but flows along freely its own way, and so makes its own waterway called "the new man." The reality of this rebirth, of this new creation, is the absolute affirmation born out of absolute negation. For the man who has been born anew, breathed through with the breath of God (the Holy Spirit), the love of neighbor must take on the character of love that is at the same time sword, and sword that is at the same time love. This is how faith and love must be in the world, if they are to bear witness to the love of the God who says of himself: "Those whom I love, I reprove and chasten" (Rev. 3:19).

In Buddhism it is said, "He who prays to be born into the Land of the Buddha will be reborn and reside there in a state of non-regression." The moment one pure act of faith springs up, this faith is constituted as a state of non-regression through which the believer enters a state of "right confirmation." This is so because this faith is not merely a conscious act of the self, but an actualization within the self of the reality we have been speaking of. It is called a state of non-regression because it is the moment at which the believer enters, instantly and irretrievably, into the certainty of rebirth. In that "atom of eternity in time," the *possibility* of rebirth is transformed into a *necessity* by the Power of the Original Vow of the Buddha. The word "direct" that appears in the phrase "the direct attainment of rebirth into the Pure Land" emphasizes the instantaneousness of the moment of conversion in which the delusory transitoriness of *karma* reaching back to times past without beginning is absolutely negated and birth into the Pure Land is secured and confirmed.

Earlier I used the expression "atom of time in eternity" in reference to the moment when radical evil makes itself present to self-awareness in the ground of the subject. At that time I also noted that the nothingness of the self makes itself present in that self-awareness of evil, and that this very nothingness becomes the locus of conversion. The direct attainment of birth into the Pure Land must represent the same sort of moment at which a change of heart takes place. It is the moment of conversion to birth through death, the moment wherein absolute negation and absolute affirmation are one, as stated in phrases like the following: "Receiving in faith the Original Vow is the first instant, the end to life; directly attaining birth into the Pure Land is the next instant, the immediate beginning of life." It is the moment of single-minded abandonment to Amida Buddha in a pure act of faith. Therefore, as Zendō (in Chinese, Shan-tao) writes in the *Hanshūsan*, "When we bow our heads in worship of the Buddha, we are still in this world; when we lift them up again, we have already entered into the realm of Amida."

Up to this point we have referred to various things as real: objects, events, and mental processes. But we also said that their reality can make itself present as the original reality of those things as they are in themselves only on a horizon where the field of consciousness has been overstepped. We have yet to touch on what this horizon ultimately consists of. We have merely stated that nihility becomes present when the field of consciousness is surpassed and that this nihility is also real, even though it means that objects and mental process become unreal.

Next came the problems of doubt and of sin and evil, which we treated as instances of nihility appearing in the form of a "spiritual" self-awareness at the ground of the self-conscious "ego" (that is, at the ground of what is usually thought of as subjectivity). We also touched on the question of faith as a conversion from doubt or from evil and sin. We noted that even though all these things belong to us as our very own, they are real primarily in themselves, and only *really* become our own when we ourselves become their realization. In other words, only when they make themselves present to us in their suchness are we able to be aware of the self in them. Taken in this sense, what we spoke of as conversion or change of heart, and as absolute negation and absolute affirmation, is a matter of reality itself and rises up within the Great Reality. To be sure, this reality is not something merely objective and separate from ourselves; if it were, we should still be on the field of consciousness. When we ourselves are thrown into the reality of evil or faith in such a way as to become ourselves the realization of their realness, a conversion takes place within reality itself with us as the hinge: we have a *real* change of heart.

Finally, in connection with the problem of belief we touched on God and Tathāgata (Buddha). Here the question of what is truly real takes on an added dimension, but before going any further into this question, I should like first to say something on the subject of modern atheism.

V

All along we have been making allusions to God, despite the fact that one of the questions of our times is whether or not there is a God at all. Not that atheism did not exist in former times; but there are special qualities of contemporary atheism that make it different from what it was before. We find ourselves at a point where atheism has been elevated to the position of serving as a substitute for theistic religions; where it seeks to serve as the ultimate basis for our human existence and to assign the ultimate *telos* of human life; and where it has come, accordingly, to offer itself as the only comprehensive, sufficient standpoint for modern man. These developments are visible in Marxism and in atheistic existentialism. As an example of the latter, we may look at the existentialism that Sartre presents as a humanism.

For Sartre, existentialism is nothing other than an attempt to draw out all the consequences of a coherent atheistic position: "God does not exist, and . . . it is necessary to draw the consequences of his absence right to the end."[5] As early as the last century, people were saying that God had become a useless, outdated hypothesis, and that it was possible to establish, simply from a standpoint of humanism, a set of *a priori* values that would yield norms for society, culture, morality, and so forth. This was an altogether optimistic brand of humanism, one of the most forceful expressions of which is to be found in the anthropological approach of Feuerbach. But the humanism of our time, says Sartre, is an existentialism that "finds it extremely embarrassing that God does not exist."[6] He cites the words of Dostoevski, "If God did not exist, everything would be permitted," to illustrate the starting point of existentialism.

For Sartre, the foundation of human existence is "nothingness" (*néant*). That man can find nothing to rely on, either within himself or without, constitutes the basis of existentialism. Moreover, the reason that existentialism is based on atheism is that we have awakened to the fact that the nothingness we encounter at the ground of our very being is itself one with that ground and is the basis of our very subjectivity. Accordingly, Sartre describes existentialism as a subjective standpoint. Atheism, or the assertion that man finds nothing to rely on either within himself or without, appears then as a deepening of human subjectivity.

Here Sartre connects to the Cartesian ego. On his view, it is from the standpoint of this ego that we possess the absolute truth of awakened consciousness. Aside from this, there is no other truth that can serve us as a starting point. Although Descartes took his starting point from a return to the *ego* of the *cogito, ergo sum*, his ego had no choice but to postulate a God beyond itself, a God whose veracity was above all doubt. For Sartre, the ego is constituted on a subjective nothingness. The existence of the self as a *res cogitans* is awakened to from the ground of this nothingness. While he is no less committed to the self-awareness of the ego than Descartes, Sartre has shifted the foundations of this awareness from God to nihility, from theism to atheism. In this shift we get a glimpse of the distance that modern man has gone since he began to pursue his own path to the awareness of subjectivity.

At the same time, the lack of anything to rely on either within the self or without signals for Sartre the freedom of man. As an existence grounded on a nothingness and thrown from this nothingness into its actual situatedness, human existence is free. Man is "condemned" to be free. With this freedom each individual, from within his actual situatedness, chooses his own mode of being. By his every action he casts himself ahead of himself, toward the future, as a series of undertakings and in so doing continually chooses himself as a self. Man is a "project." This is what Sartre means by the "existence" of man (what I have called Existenz). In its actual situatedness human existence goes out from its own being and is suspended in nothingness, therefore projecting the self ceaselessly outside of itself. In so doing, human existence is a mode of being that "acts." This constitutes its freedom.

Sartre tells us that he calls his existentialism a humanism because when a man chooses an existence for his "self," he chooses at the same time an image of what he believes man ought to be. In choosing himself, he is "thereby at the same time a legislator for the whole of mankind."[7] If a man decides, for example, that he ought to marry and have children, by that very action he not only chooses himself but also an attitude for how all of mankind ought to act. He establishes an image of man. The act of choice is always constituted to imply a responsibility to oneself and to the whole of mankind as well. This, Sartre claims, makes existentialism a humanism.

According to the Christian tradition, man is created in the image of God. The *imago Dei* is the essential being of man and precedes his actual being. But in the atheism of Sartre, which sees a nothingness at the ground of the self, the notion of the *imago Dei* as the essence of man is discarded; the standpoint of existentialism, in which the existence of man is said to precede his essence, naturally comes to take its place. In other words, when an actual individual takes himself as a project grounded on a nothingness and chooses a mode of being for himself, it is not God that is creating man by providing him with an "image of God" as his essence, but man who is creating an "image of man" for himself. This is the new humanism of existentialism.

This standpoint is a natural consequence, then, of the self-awareness of the Cartesian ego from which modern man set out. The problem that lay hidden from the start in modern man's standpoint of the ego can be said to have made itself immediately apparent in this development. As I have noted previously, even though the *cogito, ergo sum* is the most immediately real of facts, its evolution to modern man's standpoint of the ego is not the inevitable result it might seem to be at first glance. A subtle and easily overlooked problem lurks beneath the surface here. The standpoint of the ego is constituted by a duplication of the *cogito* in which the *cogito* is considered from the viewpoint of the *cogito* itself. This leads to subjectivity becoming a self shut up within itself: the self is bound up by itself in such a way that it cannot extricate itself from itself. The very existence of this self is marked by a "self-attachment," as if one had tied one's hands with one's own rope. Concealed within the depths of such a self is the demand for liberation from itself. This liberation, the real appearance of the realness of the *cogito* and its *sum*, is only possible within a horizon where the duplication of the *cogito* has first been broken down and the field of consciousness and self-consciousness has been overstepped. Subjectivity as well can only appear as primordial subjectivity when the standpoint of the Cartesian ego has been broken down.

Sartre claims that his theory "alone is compatible with the dignity of man, it is the only one which does not make man into an object."[8] We may well appreciate his intentions, but, as we noted before, so long as we maintain the standpoint of self-consciousness, the tendency to take ourselves as objects remains, no matter how much we stress subjectivity. Moreover, even though Sartre's theory appears to preserve the dignity of man in his subjective autonomy and freedom, the real dignity of man seems to me to belong only to one who has been "reborn," only in the "new man" that emerges in us when we are born by dying, when we break through nihility.

Sartre also describes the existence of man as a "project" of continually going beyond the self and going outside of the self, or as a mode of being continually overstepping itself. He recognizes a transcendence here that is a form of *ek-stasis*: a standing-outside-of-oneself. But for Sartre this transcendence is not transcendent in the sense that God is. This transcendence means that nothingness is constituted at the ground of self-existence. Man uses that nothingness as a springboard from which to keep going beyond himself. But insofar as Sartre locates subjectivity at the standpoint of the Cartesian ego, his nothingness is not even the "death" of which Heidegger speaks. The mode of being of this ego is not a "being unto death." Nor is it anything like the Great Death that we referred to above as the place of nihility that opens up through the Great Doubt, since the Great Doubt signals nothing less than the bankruptcy of the Cartesian ego.

Even less so are we dealing here with the Buddhist notion of *śūnyatā* ("nothingness," "emptiness"). Nothingness in Buddhism is "non-ego," while the nothingness in Sartre is immanent to the ego. Whatever transcendence this may allow for remains glued to the ego. Sartre considers his nothingness to be the ground of the subject, and yet he presents it like a wall at the bottom of the ego or like a springboard underfoot of the ego. This turns his nothingness into a basic principle that shuts the ego up within itself. By virtue of this partition that nothingness sets up at the ground of the self, the ego becomes like a vast and desolate cave. It reminds us of what ancient Zen tradition calls "life inside the Black Mountain" or "living in the Demon's Cavern." One is holed up inside the cave of the self-conscious ego that has nothingness at its ground. And as long as this nothingness is still set up as something called nothingness-at-the-bottom-of-the-self, it remains what Buddhism repudiates as "the emptiness perversely clung to." The subjectivity of man may be fundamentally deepened, but it still hangs on with devilish tenacity. The self that sets up this nothingness is thereby bound by it and attached to it. Nothingness may seem here to be a denial of self-attachment, but in fact that attachment is rather exponentialized and concealed. Nothingness may seem here to be a negation of being, but as long as it makes itself present as an *object* of consciousness in representative form—in other words, as long as the self is still attached to it—it remains a kind of being, a kind of object.

In fact, this is what is usually meant by nihility. It cannot be a true negation of the self and all things because it exempts the subject to which it is attached through the negation, and thereby becomes itself a sort of "being." Nor can it be a true and effective affirmation of the self and all things that makes them present as reality, because it is no more than mere negation, a mere "nay-saying" that turns everything into unreality.

Buddhism goes further to speak of "the emptiness of the nihilizing view," by which it means to stress that "absolute emptiness" in which nihilizing emptiness would itself be emptied. In this absolute emptiness, the field of consciousness that looks upon the self and things as merely internal or external realities, and the nihility set up at the ground of this field, can for the first time be overstepped. Here both the "nihilizing view," that merely negative attitude found in every sort of nihilism, as well as the "view of constancy," the merely positive attitude found in all kinds of positivism and naive realism, are both overcome. All attachment is negated: both the subject and the way in which "things" appear as objects of attachment are emptied. Everything is now truly empty, and this means that all things make themselves present here and now, just as they are, in their original reality. They present themselves in their suchness, their *tathatā*. This is non-attachment.

To see nothingness at the ground of the existence of the self, in the way that Sartre does, is to see the self as having no ground to stand on. But the nothingness that means "there is *no* ground" positions itself like a wall to block one's path and turns itself into a kind of ground, so we can still say that "there *is* a ground." Only absolute emptiness is the true no-ground (*Ungrund*). Here all things—from a flower or a stone to stellar nebulae and galactic systems, and even life and death themselves—become present as bottomless realities. They disclose their bottomless suchness. True freedom lies in this no-ground. Sartre's freedom is still a bondage, a kind of hole that has the ego projected into it like a stake driven into the ground for the self to be tied to. This is the standpoint of "attachment." To a certain extent it might be called freedom, but in a more elemental sense, it is rather the deepest bondage.

For Sartre, "there is no reality except in action," and "every man realizes himself in realizing a type of humanity."[9] The sense of these words should be clear from what we have already said. The question is, however: from what horizon is the "action" referred to here to be performed, from what horizon are we to realize the self in realizing a "type of humanity"? In order for action to be true action, it cannot stem from the kind of nothingness that Sartre is speaking of. He writes, for example: "Every one of us makes the absolute by breathing, by eating, by sleeping, or by behaving in any fashion whatsoever. There is no difference between free being . . . and absolute being."[10] These words make him sound like a Zen master; but the fact that such activities as eating, drinking, and sleeping are absolute in themselves as activities does not emerge from such a standpoint. Neither is the realization of a "type of humanity" possible at the standpoint of humanism as Sartre understands it. It must rather be something that points to the realization of a "new man," that originates from the absolute negation of the "human." Our individual actions get to be truly "absolute" activities only when they originate from the horizon that opens up when man breaks out of the hermit's cave of the ego and breaks through the nothingness at the base of the ego; only when they become *manifest* from a point at which the field of consciousness, where actions are said to be "of the self," is broken through, while all the time remaining actions of the self.

It is only natural that an existentialism of this sort, resting as it does on the Cartesian subjective ego, should provoke criticism from the opposite pole of materialism. In the essay just cited, Sartre includes a discussion with a certain Marxist who stresses the materialistic standpoint: "The primary reality is that of nature, of which human reality is only one function. . . . The primary condition is a natural condition and not a human condition."[11] Looking at things this way, however, renders it impossible to explain the subjectivity of the ego. Nor can a critique based on such a standpoint demonstrate sufficient understanding of the human existence that Sartre had been stressing. The critique does, however, have its validity. For as long as we do not step beyond the field of a fundamental separation of subject and object, a conflict between considering the object from the standpoint of the subject and considering the subject from the standpoint of the object will arise. In either case, as explained earlier, we do not really and truly get in touch with the realness of either the self or things.

VI

Sartre's position of atheistic existentialism is not yet the ultimate standpoint. On the contrary, the world of religion comes into being precisely at the point that such a position is broken through. Still, it is not without reason that a position like Sartre's has made its appearance: it is the very reason why the mode of human existence of modern man itself had to appear. And this brings us fundamentally back to a problem contained in Christianity.

Christianity has long considered the egoistic mode of being that is basic to the reality of man as a form of disobedience against God, as an original sin. The alternative it offers is the way to a new man who, rather than following his own will, forsakes it to follow the will of God, who dies to self in order to live in God. This is where Christianity locates the true freedom of man. This freedom can only come about at one with obedience to the will of God. The autonomy of man can only come about in unison with the recognition of and submission to the absolute authority of God above.

In modern times, however, man began to awaken to his own independence as something that cannot be restricted by any authority whatsoever, even the very authority of God. Principles in the realms of academics, arts, politics, ethics, and so forth have all been loosened from their religious moorings and set adrift in the widespread "secularization" of human life. It is this estrangement of the actualities of human life from religion that presents the fundamental problem in the story of modern man. As a result, atheism has appeared in a variety of persuasions, finally serving as the foundation for the subjective mode of being of man itself. In this way the standpoint of atheism has itself come to be subjectivized.

This position may be called a natural outgrowth of modern *Geistesgeschichte*. It maintains that only a standpoint of subjectivized atheism— the atheism of the man who sees nothing at all either within or without himself on which to rely, and who is aware of a nothingness at the ground of his self-being—can truly bring about human Existenz and freedom. As noted above, however, at this standpoint man runs up against a wall inside the self, and his freedom becomes a freedom of the deepest bondage. We cannot stop here. We must seek the point at which this barrier is broken through and there seek out the world of religion.

The traditional standpoint of Christianity implies an estrangement from the awakened subjectivity of modern man. Might it not be that these two mutually exclusive positions—the freedom of man carried all the way through to a subjective nothingness and a subjectivized atheism, and the religious freedom appearing in traditional Christianity— require some sort of higher synthesis in our times? Christianity cannot, and must not, look on modern atheism merely as something to be eliminated. It must instead accept atheism as a mediation to a new development of Christianity itself. Be that as it may, the question needs to be asked: At what point has Christianity become so problematic for modern man as to make him advance in the direction of an estrangement from Christianity? I should like to consider this question briefly with regard to the Christian view of God and, in particular, the transcendence and personal character of the Christian God.

Christianity speaks of a *creatio ex nihilo*: God created everything from a point at which there was nothing at all. And since all things have this *nihilum* at the ground of their being, they are absolutely distinct from their Creator. This idea is a plain expression of the absolute transcendence of God. Compared to the Greek notion of a demiurge who fashioned things by giving shape to already existing material, the notion of a God creating everything from nothing at all represents a more advanced idea of God in that it enables us to conceive of the absoluteness of God.

At the same time, though, this development made it inevitable that the ontological relationship between God and creatures would become a perennial problem within Christianity. Insofar as God is the one and only absolute *being*, all other things consist fundamentally of *nothingness*. But as there is no way around the admission that things do in fact exist, the question arises of how we are to consider the relationship between their being and the absolute being of God. The problem was a difficult one, and things like the Platonic idea of "participation" and the idea of an *analogia entis* were advanced to solve it. Even up to our own day, the issue has not been resolved at a conceptual level.

The most important thing in this regard, however, is that the problem needs to become an existential question, in the Existenz of religious man. Take, for example, the question of the omnipresence of God. Augustine notes in his *Confessions*: "Lo, heaven and earth exist: they cry out that they have been created."[12] Taken merely at the conceptual level, these words stop short of expressing a view on divine omnipresence. But if all things were *really* crying something out to us, and if we were *really* to listen to what they have to say, these words would turn into a question for our very own Existenz. And in that case, what would they mean? If things are telling us that they were created by God, then they also are telling us that they are not themselves God. To that extent, we do not encounter God anywhere in the world. Instead, we find everywhere, at the ground of everything that is, the nihility of the *creatio ex nihilo*. This nihility stands like a great iron wall that absolutely separates all things from God. Accordingly, to encounter this nihility means necessarily to encounter God as an iron wall, to meet with the absolute negativity of God: God is not his creatures; creatures cannot be God.

At the same time, to say that things exist as they actually are in spite of this nihility means, from the standpoint of the believer, that one encounters in them the grace and power of God breaking through nihility, bestowing being on things and sustaining them in existence. The words of Augustine just cited carry this double sense of the encounter with God: in our very inability to encounter God wherever we turn in the world, we encounter God no matter where we turn.

If the omnipresence of God can be considered in such a paradoxical way, what becomes of the Existenz of the self as a being in such a world? In the final analysis it comes to this: one is pressed from all sides for a decision, whether one faces a single atom, a grain of sand, or an earthworm. Each and every one of us is brought directly up against the iron wall of God. One who has been able to come to faith may face it and pass through it. But even one who has not found his way to God cannot fail to encounter that iron wall wherever he looks, wherever he turns, even should he turn into himself; he cannot flee God and the absolute negativity he represents. The omnipresence of God must be something like this. People of old used to say that if God so desired, the whole world would vanish from existence in an instant and return to nothingness. God is omnipresent as one who graciously bestows being and one who absolutely takes it away; it is his to pronounce the absolute Yes as well as the absolute No over all created existence.

Hence for anyone, whoever he happens to be, encountering the omnipresence of God existentially must begin with a sense of having been cast out into the middle of a desert of death. When the omnipresent God is accepted at the existential standpoint, it becomes a paradox for the existence of the self that finds God at every turn and at every moment, like being in a desert from which one cannot escape, but within which one cannot survive either. The omnipresence of God, then, must make itself present as something that deprives us of a locus to stand in self-existence, a locus where we can live and breathe.

Our existence is said to be a sinful one, an existence of rebellion against God. In existential terms, however, the "ontological" relationship between our being and the being of God can be considered in the sense just described. The omnipresence of an absolutely transcendent God presses as close as possible to our existence, our Existenz. It allows neither for advance nor for retreat, but presses us for a decision and fixes itself resolutely to the comings and goings, the ins and outs of our daily lives.

It seems to me that we get a glimpse of this sort of existential condition in Moses and the prophets, and in such figures as St. Paul, St. Francis of Assisi, and Luther. To the ordinary Christian way of thinking, however, the transcendence of God is linked with representations and images that set God "up in heaven" or "upon the clouds," standing aloof from creatures and from the world as a whole. Is it not somewhat rare for Christians to accept the transcendence of God as a problem relevant to their own Existenz? Is it not rather more frequently the case that the omnipresence of the absolutely transcendent God is *not* accepted as a presence directly confronting the self? And yet, as we have been saying all along here, all created beings cry out that they have been created by God. This means that no matter where we turn, God is not there; at the same time, wherever we turn, we come face to face with God. That is, the God before whom all of creation is as nothing makes himself present through all of creation. The Christian must be able to pick up a single pebble or blade of grass and see the same consuming fire of God and the same pillar of fire, hear the same thunderous roar, and feel the same "fear and trembling" that Moses experienced.

The ordinary view is that the encounter with the absolute transcendent God in "fear and trembling" takes place in a personal relationship with God through the awareness of sin. That it is to be encountered in the created *world* seldom seems to come into consideration. The idea of perceiving God in all the things of the world is usually rejected as "pantheism," and the correct view is taken to be a "theism" based on a personal relationship with God. But to say that God is omnipresent implies the possibility of meeting God everywhere in the world. This is not pantheism in the usual sense of the word, since it does not mean that the world is God or that God is the immanent life of the world itself. It means that an absolutely transcendent God is absolutely immanent.

That a thing is created *ex nihilo* means that this *nihil* is more immanent in that thing than the very being of that thing is "immanent" in the thing itself. This is why we speak of "absolute immanence." It is an immanence of absolute negation, for the being of the created is grounded upon a *nothingness* and seen fundamentally to be a nothingness. At the same time, it is an immanence of absolute affirmation, for the nothingness of the created is the ground of its *being*. This is the omnipresence of God in all things that have their being as a *creatio ex nihilo*. It follows that this omnipresence can be said to represent for man the dynamic *motif* of the transposition of absolute negation and absolute affirmation. To entrust the self to this *motif*, to let onself be driven by it so as to die to the self and live in God, is what constitutes faith.

The advent of Christ can then be seen as the corporeal apparition to man of this *motif* of conversion as it occurs within God himself. The gospel proclamation that the Kingdom of God is at hand presses man to the decision to die and be born anew. The fact that the gospel of the Kingdom of God has an eschatological dimension signifies, from the existential standpoint, that the *motif* of conversion for man implied in divine omnipresence confronts man with an urgency that presses him to a decision on the spot: either eternal life or eternal death. This is the meaning of what was said earlier about the love of Christ being at one and the same time a sword that kills man and a sword that gives man life. It means that there is an undercurrent running through the gospel to the effect that no matter where a man is or what he is doing, he comes into touch with the cutting sword of *de-cision*. Only in this way might eschatology be said to be a problem of human Existenz. He who dies and regains life by this sword of *agapē* can become God-breathed, an expiration of the Holy Spirit.

Now taken in such an existential way, the transcendence and transcendent omnipresence of God can also be termed a personal relationship between God and man, though only in a sense very different from what is usually meant by "personal." Compared to the usual meaning we find in the case of relationships like that between God and the soul, or some other "spiritual" relationship that is called "personal," what we are speaking of here would be considered as *impersonal*. But we are not using the term "impersonal" in its ordinary sense, as the antonym of "personal." The pantheistic notions of the life or creative power of the universe are instances of the impersonal in its usual sense. But when the omnipresence of God is encountered existentially as the absolute negation of the being of all creatures, and presents itself as an iron wall that blocks all movement forward or backward, it is not impersonal in that usual sense.

We have here the possibility of a totally different way of viewing the personal, and, therefore, the impersonal. It is what we should call an "impersonally personal relationship" or a "personally impersonal relationship." The original meaning of *persona* probably comes close to what we are speaking of. In Christianity, the Holy Spirit has this characteristic. While being thought of as one *persona* of the Trinity, it is at the same time the very love of God itself, the breath of God; it is a sort of impersonal person or personal nonperson, as it were. But once such a point of view is introduced, not only the character of the Holy Spirit, but also that of God himself who contains this spirit, and of man in his "spiritual" relationship with God (as well as the character of that relationship itself), have to be seen on a new horizon. And in the eyes of those who are breathed by this kind of Holy Spirit and are reborn with this breath as their eternal life, that is, in the eyes of those who have been given faith (the living bond with God, or *religio*), all creatures are seen as God-breathed.

It should, therefore, also be possible for Christianity to proclaim: "In the Great Death heaven and earth become new." St. Paul writes: "I know and am persuaded in the Lord Jesus that nothing is unclean in itself; but it is unclean for anyone who thinks it unclean" (Rom. 14:14). Implied in Paul's faith in Christ is what Buddhism calls a "faith-knowledge" that all things are pure in themselves. In a word, in all these cases there is no stopping at a notion of God as personal in the traditional sense of the word, or at a notion of the relationship between God and man as simply a personal relationship. Rather, God must be encountered as a reality omnipresent in all the things of the world in such a way as to be absolutely immanent as absolutely transcendent. It must be an impersonally personal (or personally impersonal) encounter, in which God's reality is realized as impersonally personal (or personally impersonal). God's reality must be conceived of on a horizon where there is neither *within* nor *without*. The existence of a man who meets with that reality must not be thought of simply as "internally" personal existence.

VII

In the foregoing we discussed the transcendence of God and the ontological relationship between God and created things by looking at the notion of divine omnipresence and its acceptance at the existential level. We might equally well have begun with another notion, that of divine omnipotence. In this concluding section I should like to touch briefly on that subject, although what I shall have to say does not differ fundamentally from what has been said above.

Someone, as the story goes, once asked a Christian in jest, "If God is omnipotent, could he deign to sneeze?" The Christian stood and thought awhile, and then replied that probably God could not, since he has no autonomic nervous system. Whimsical though it be, this exchange contains a' fundamental question. If there were something, anything whatsoever, that God could not do, then God would not be all-powerful and thus would not be an absolute being. Conversely, if God were to sneeze like creatures, he could not be considered absolutely transcendent. What shall we do with the dilemma this presents?

In essence, the story points to nothing other than the same serious problem of the relationship between divine order and evil that people have been cudgelling their brains over since time immemorial. If God is all-powerful, all-knowing, and all-good; and if every being, every act, and every event in the world is constituted by divine decree and maintained within a divine order proceeding from that decree; then how can there be evil in the world of God's creation? If the all-knowing God must have known that evil would come about in the world, how is it that he did not create a world that was only good? How is it that the all-powerful God does not wipe out evil altogether instead of allowing it to go on existing? These questions belong to what is known as "theodicy," where they have been given various answers by various thinkers through the years.

Man sneezes, God does not. When a man without faith sneezes, he encounters the nihility of the self because the existence of a creature that sneezes is constituted from the very first on a nihility. When a man of faith sneezes, he, too, encounters the nihility of the self because he believes himself to have been created by God *ex nihilo*. But if the believer stops short at that insight, he does not get beyond the standpoint of entertaining that sort of idea about God, of thinking about his impressions of God. This then brings him to the dilemma of transcendence and omnipotence in God: man sneezes and God cannot; therefore, man is capable of something that God is not.

The situation is different when viewed from an existential standpoint. Man was made by God in such a way that he *can* sneeze, and that is a display of divine omnipotence. Even when he sneezes, man does so within the omnipotence of God. There is no sneezing without it. Thus, from the existential standpoint, even in something so trivial as a sneeze man encounters the nihility of the self and at the same time the omnipotence of God. Here divine omnipotence means that man encounters the separation of absolute negation and absolute affirmation of the self in the comings and goings, the ins and outs of daily life. It means that the self in its entirety, body and mind, is brought to the crossroads of life and death. In the words of Jesus:

> Do not fear those who kill the body, and after have no more that they can do. But I will warn you whom to fear: fear him who, after he has killed, has power to cast into hell; yes, I tell you, fear him! Are not five sparrows sold for two pennies? And not one of them is forgotten before God. Why, even the hairs of your head are all numbered. [Luke 12:4–7]

Thus the omnipotence of God must be something that one can encounter at any time, listening to the radio, reading the paper, or chatting with a friend. Moreover, it must be something encountered as capable of destroying both body and soul, something that makes man fear and tremble and presses him to a decision. Without this sense of urgency, for all our talk about them, divine omnipotence and God himself, remain mere concepts. The omnipotence of God must be accepted as altogether near at hand, that is to say, present in the comings and goings, the ins and outs of daily life, bringing us to fear and trembling. Only then is it really accepted as a reality.

When divine omnipotence is thus really accepted, the faith that drives out fear is also constituted as a reality:

> Why, even the hairs of your head are all numbered. Fear not; you are of more value than many sparrows. And I tell you, every one who acknowledges me before men, the Son of man also will acknowledge before the angels of God; but he who denies me before men will be denied before the angels of God. [Luke 12:7–9]

We remarked earlier that faith as dying to self and living in God means letting oneself be driven by the *motif* of conversion contained within God himself (in his relationship to man) from absolute negation to absolute affirmation. There may be no need to repeat the point here, but, briefly put, it means that the *motif* of that conversion is actualized in the self which thereby appropriates it.

No doubt, a lot of people will claim that they do not encounter the omnipotence of God when listening to the radio. At those times, then, such a man should encounter the nihility of the self instead. But if he insists that he does not encounter nihility either, or that he is too busy and has no time for nihility, that he is not a man of leisure or that his intellect does not recognize such things as nihility, then he encounters nihility in his way of not encountering it. Nihility makes its presence felt in the very fact that he does not encounter nihility. Whatever sort of fellow he be, however busy or intellectual, or rather the more busy and more intellectual he is, the more he is unable to retreat so much as a single step from nihility. Even if his consciousness and intellect do not encounter nihility, his *being* does. Nihility is apparent in his busy or intellectual mode of being itself. On the contrary, if he were to encounter nihility directly, that would enable him to take his first step away from it. But the fact that he does not, only entrenches him all the more deeply within it. Such is the nature of nihility.

As stated above, the incongruence between a world order dependent on divine omnipotence and the evil in human existence has long been a perplexing problem. Basically, though, it is no different from the problem contained in sneezing or listening to the radio. God does not sneeze, but he made some of his creatures so that they do. The omnipotence of God makes itself present in the sneezing of those creatures, and that primarily as an absolute negativity: as the grounding of all things in *nihilum* through creation. Similarly, God created man with the freedom to do evil. Even the evil acts of man, therefore, fall within the compass of that divine omnipotence that makes itself present in man's power to do evil and use that power. Here, too, it shows up primarily as an absolute negativity: divine wrath. But even this stems from the fact that man's ability to commit evil arises out of the nihility that lies at the ground of his existence by virtue of his having been created *ex nihilo*. And when man himself becomes the locus of nihility in his awareness of radical evil, as discussed above, when the conversion of faith becomes a reality, then salvation is realized even though man remains a sinner unable to rid himself of evil. Here divine omnipotence is realized as the absolute affirmation that permits evil even while persisting in its absolute negation. This absolute affirmation as negation directed at the evildoer is nothing other than the pardoning of evil in the man of faith. It is divine love. There is absolutely no evil in God, and yet evil falls absolutely within the compass of divine omnipotence.

In the problems of evil and sin, the relationship of God and man becomes *personal* in the original sense of the word. Christianity speaks of the punishment of man in the "first Adam" and his redemption through the "second Adam." Modern theologians, with their modern notions of personality, even assert a radical distinction between evil and sin, the latter only being possible in a "personal" relationship with God. But in a relationship grounded on absolute affirmation as absolute negation, an evil act and an involuntary reflex action like sneezing are the same. They both depend on the createdness of man, that is, on the nihility at the ground of his very being. And seen on that basis, even a personal relationship can be called impersonally personal (or personally impersonal) in the sense outlined above.

It seems to me that once we look at the notion of person as applied to both God and to man in terms of the approach given here—which provides a broader base than was formerly the case by locating a point beyond the opposition of personal and impersonal—the problem of religion and science can then really be taken on. Indeed one of the reasons that I have ventured this line of thought is precisely that I am seeking a horizon within which we can really get in touch with the problem of religion and science. In the following chapter, I should like to take up that question in greater detail, as well as to expound more fully the notions of the personal and the impersonal in religion.

2

THE PERSONAL AND THE IMPERSONAL IN RELIGION

I

The problem of religion and science is the most fundamental problem facing contemporary man. In former times an idea gained prevalence that religion was fated to be overrun by the advance of science and left to its eventual demise. There are those who still think this way. But it takes only a passing glance at the fabric of intellectual history over the past hundred years to realize that such a simplistic view of the problem has been left behind. What is most important, though, is that ideas like this inhibit our ability to understand what man is.

Science is not something separate from the people who engage in it, and that engagement, in turn, represents only one aspect of human knowledge. Even the scientist, as an individual human being, may come face to face with nihility. He may feel well up within him doubts about the meaning of the very existence of the self, and the very existence of all things. The horizon on which such doubt occurs—and on which a response to it is made possible—extends far beyond the reaches of the scientific enterprise. It is a horizon opening up to the ground of human existence itself.

One may reply that all the efforts of man ultimately come to naught, and that things cannot be otherwise, so that everything, including science, becomes fundamentally meaningless. And yet even here, in the reply of so-called pessimistic nihilism along with its accompanying doubt, we find ourselves outside the horizon of science and in the realm of philosophy and religion, where nihilism is but one possible response. Indeed, the overcoming of this pessimistic nihilism represents the single greatest issue facing philosophy and religion in our times. As we remarked earlier, even those who claim that things like nihility are not a problem for them will sooner or later be swallowed up by nihility itself. It is already very much there, right under their feet, and by refusing to make it a problem for themselves they only slip deeper into its clutches.

The contemporary problematic, therefore, has to do with inverting the view that religion will pass away with scientific progress. For in its very efforts to deny religion and to block off the horizons of the religious quest, the advance of science has had the effect of bringing the question of the ultimate meaning of human existence or life into even sharper relief. And herein looms large the problem of nihilism.

Given these broad horizons, then, science itself becomes part of the problem. Modern science has completely transformed the old view of nature, resulting in the birth of various forms of atheism and the fomenting of an indifference to religion in general. The atheistic existentialism of Sartre is one example of this. This turn of events can hardly be without relevance to the question of God as it affects all religions, but in particular as it affects the kind of clearly defined theism we find in Christianity. Until the problem of religion and science reaches a level that is fundamental enough to render the approach to the question of God itself problematical, we cannot say that the issue has really been faced. It is as serious as that.

The laws of the natural world used to be regarded as part of the divine order, a visible expression of the providence of God. The order of the natural world and the order of the human world were united in a single great cosmic order. This meant that everything in the universe existed by virtue of being assigned a specific place in the whole. As an *order*, it was conceived teleologically; and as a *cosmic* order, it was seen to witness to the existence of God. In this sense, the problem of order has traditionally been, and continues to be, of major importance for religion as much as for philosophy. Augustine, for example, notes in *De ordine*, VII, 19: "If, as we have been taught and as the necessity of order itself persuades us to feel, God is just, then he is just because he renders to each thing what is its just due." Augustine here sees a "great order," and beyond that, a "divine providence."

The idea of a cosmic order may be traced back to Pythagoras and Plato, before them to the Upanishads, and still further back to several peoples of the ancient world. Even in modern times, such natural scientists as Kepler and Newton regarded their own research and pursuit of the laws of nature as a quest for the secrets of a divine cosmic economy. Then, as is well known, once natural science and its image of the world had been established, the teleological conception of the natural world gave way to a mechanistic one, bringing a fundamental change in the relation between man and nature. It was a process of disengaging the approach to nature from the religious world view that had been its matrix.

The great Lisbon earthquake of 1755 affords an appropriate symbol of what was taking place. On the one side, we see the English clergy, for instance, attributing the earthquake to the Catholicism of the city's inhabitants. On the other, we see the people of Lisbon thinking that they had brought the disaster upon themselves by permitting heretics (Protestants) to reside in their city. But behind these controversies was the profound and extensive shock that the earthquake inflicted on the mind of Europe. The chronicles of the history of philosophy tell us of the ill will the disaster engendered between Voltaire and Rousseau. We know, too, that Kant wrote a treatise on the disaster in the following year, in which he attacked as blasphemous the "misguided human teleology" that would label such a natural phenomenon as divine punishment or presume to detect in it "the aims of divine solicitude."

As this intellectual process continued, the natural world assumed more and more the features of a world cold and dead, governed by laws of mechanical necessity, completely indifferent to the fact of man. While it continues to be the world in which we live and is inseparably bound up with our existence, it is a world in which we find ourselves unable to live as *man*, in which our *human* mode of being is edged out of the picture or even obliterated. We can neither take this world as it is nor leave it. This is the paradoxical position from which the world makes itself present to us, a position much like what Dostoevski describes in *Notes from the Underground*: unable to affirm, unable to deny, and no recourse left but to bang one's head against it. It is a world that leads man to despair. But for Dostoevski the matter did not end there, for from within that very despair there came to birth an awareness of nihility penetrating deep beneath the world of natural laws and in-human rationality with which science is preoccupied. At this depth the awareness of nihility opens up a horizon that enables a freedom beyond necessity and a life beyond rationality. This is life in the "underground." For Dostoevski it meant reinstating the question of religion together with and over against the question of nihilism.

The discovery of this complex of problems at the depths of human existence was not, of course, a matter for Dostoevski alone. Indeed, within the world of nature and its scientific laws, all of which has become both indifferent to and paradoxical for human existence, we can see unfolding in our times a problem fundamental for all religions. A religion based merely on the old teleological view of nature is, to say the least, inadequate for our day and age. But is it possible for us to regard a natural order so indifferent to our *human* mode of being as to rub it out, as belonging to a greater divine order? Or is such an indifferent natural order altogether incompatible with the concept of God? Whichever be the case, it cannot help but seriously bring into question former notions of God and of man. Still, religion has yet to confront science at this fundamental level.

In the past most religions tended to be motivated solely by human interests, by the question of man. Their basis was, to borrow a phrase from Nietzsche, "human, all too human." This comes as no surprise— religion has to do with the salvation of man. But being concerned with the salvation of man is different from concluding that the enabling ground of salvation lies within the realm of human interests. What is more, at present the very ground of religion has been shaken by a world grown indifferent to human interests. In short, the problem comes down to this: when the relationship between man and an insensitive world on the one hand, and between this same world and God on the other, are made the ground of religion, what becomes of the relationship between God and man which is religion?

So long as the world could be seen from a teleological standpoint, there was no real difficulty. A fundamental harmony was seen between the world and the existence of man in that world. Man was taken to be the supreme representative of all things in the world. He stood at its center. The meaning and *telos* of human existence formed the criteria for the meaning and *telos* of the world. As a consequence, the relationship between God and man became like its own axis with the world pushed out on to the periphery. Whether the world was thought of positively as the creation of God or negatively as something to be cast aside made no difference. For once this axis had been set up, it was possible to establish a relationship between God and man based exclusively on human interests, and beyond that made into something exclusively "personal."

A world that has become indifferent to the fact of man, however, and that engages man in that paradoxical situation mentioned earlier, in which man can neither abide in it nor abandon it, can no longer remain at the periphery of the relationship between God and man. The world cuts across the vertical God-man axis, so to speak, and sets up an independent horizontal axis all its own. With regard to the human mode of existence, the former model of teleological harmony gives way to that of a paradoxical contradiction. And with regard to God, it is then no longer possible to see the world as simply ordered according to divine providence or divine will. Thus, the total impersonality of the world came to appear as something qualitatively different from either human or divine "personality." In effect, the world cut through the personal relationship between God and man.

This means that man is no longer merely *personally* in the world. As a being who is both completely material and completely biological, he is ruled by the indifferent laws of nature. Those laws embrace everything in the world—non-living, living, and human—and govern without regard for such distinctions. Human interests make no difference, either. For example, when somebody tosses a crust of bread and a dog jumps up and catches it in midair, the movement of the person's arm, the flight of the bread, and the response of the dog are all subject to the laws of nature. Or again, whether atomic power is employed to kill off vast numbers of people or applied to peaceful objectives matters not to the natural laws at work. These laws display in both cases the same cold inhumanity, the same indifference to human interests. Those laws still rule over everything that exists, including man.

Up until now, religions have tended to put the emphasis exclusively on the aspect of life. "Soul" has been viewed only from the side of life. Notions of "personality" and "spirit," too, have been based on this aspect of life. And yet from the very outset life is at one with death. This means that all living things, just as they are, can be seen under the Form of death.

In Buddhism there is a method of meditation known as the "death's-head contemplation." (In its early stages, Christianity may have had something similar.) Japanese artists have often painted this theme by portraying a skull lying in pampas grass. The great poet Bashō introduces one of his haiku with the remark:

> In the house of Honma Shume, on the wall of his Noh stage, there hangs a painting: a tableau of skeletons with flutes and hand-drums. Truth to tell, can the face of life be anything other than just this? And that ancient tale about the man who used a skull for a pillow and ended up unable to distinguish dream from reality—that, too, tells us something about life.

His haiku follows:

> Lightning flashes—
> Close by my face,
> The pampas grass!

During the course of his wanderings Bashō was obliged on one occasion to pass the night in the wilds. A sudden flash of lightning in the dark showed him that he had taken to bed in a meadow, with the pampas grass alongside his face. The tradition of Buddhist death's-head contemplation and the frequency of the theme in art form must have led him to his poem. But there is also something new here. A living man experiences himself, as living, in the image of the skull on the pampas grass. There is more to be seen here than simply a meadow. It is what is being pointed to in the Zen saying, "Death's heads all over the field." Let the field stand for the Ginza or Broadway: sooner or later the time will come when they will turn to grassy meadows.

> And as he came out of the temple, one of his disciples said to him, "Look, Teacher, what wonderful stones and what wonderful buildings!" And Jesus said to him, "Do you see these great buildings? There will not be left here one stone upon another, that will not be thrown down." [Mark 13:1–2]

There is no need for the buildings actually to crumble and go to seed. One can see the Ginza, for instance, just as it is, in all its magnificence, as a field of pampas grass. One can look at it as if it were a double exposure—which is, after all, its real portrait. For in truth, reality itself is two-layered. A hundred years hence, not one of the people now walking the Ginza will be alive, neither the young nor the old, the men nor the women. As the old saying goes, "With a single thought, ten thousand years. And with ten thousand years, a single thought." In a flash of lightning before the mind's eye, what is to be actual a hundred years hence is already an actuality today. We can look at the living as they walk full of health down the Ginza and see, in double exposure, a picture of the dead. Bashō's lines are also about the Ginza.

This kind of double vision is to be found among modern Western poets, as well. T. S. Eliot writes in *The Wasteland*:

> Unreal City,
> Under the brown fog of a winter dawn,
> A crowd flowed over London Bridge, so many,
> I had not thought death had undone so many.

The last line is taken from the procession of the dead in Dante's *Inferno*,[1] which in Eliot's vision becomes streams of people flowing over London

Bridge. The real London before his eyes discloses itself as unreal, as dead. (In the concluding section of *The Wasteland*, Eliot turns his double lens on history as well. Jerusalem, Athens, Alexandria, and Vienna— centers of the development of Western culture—are all seen as "Unreal.")

This kind of double exposure is true vision of reality. Reality itself requires it. In it, spirit, personality, life, and matter all come together and lose their separateness. They appear like the various tomographic plates of a single subject. Each plate belongs to reality, but the basic reality is the superimposition of all the plates into a single whole that admits to being represented layer by layer. It is not as if only one of the representations were true, so that all the others can be reduced to it. Reality eludes all such attempts at reduction. In the same sense, the aspect of life and the aspect of death are equally real, and reality is that which appears now as life and now as death. It is *both* life and death, and at the same time is *neither* life nor death. It is what we have to call the nonduality of life and death. This question may be put aside for later consideration. Suffice it to note here that the crosscut of reality which discloses the aspect of death has heretofore been called the *material*, and that which discloses the aspect of life, the *vital*. Soul, personality, spirit, and the like have been viewed exclusively from this latter aspect of life; so has been God.

Since ancient times calamities both natural and man-made have often been spoken of as the punishment of heaven, the wrath of God, or the like. For the prophets, the fall of Israel was like a lash from the whip of an angry God whose people had turned against him. Both Christians and those of other faiths regarded the sack of Rome by Alaric and his troops as a divine punishment, each blaming the other. Such examples as these show that the order of nature and history had come to be viewed teleologically, as dependent on a divine personality, and that the relationship between God and man had come to be viewed mainly as a matter of *human* interests. But the laws of the natural world that rule over life and matter alike, that govern life as well as death, are in themselves indifferent to questions of our life and death, of the fortune and misfortune that comes our way, of the good and evil we do. Nature greets with indifference distinctions like these which belong to the concerns of man. Nature's insensitivity is felt in the circle of man as distant and unfeeling, at times even as coldhearted and cruel.

If these same laws of nature are attributed to God as part of the order created by him, then perhaps there is a side to God other than the personal for containing this cold indifference. Or perhaps we should conclude that the laws of nature do not belong to God at all, in which case God would lose his absoluteness and thus cease to be God. What should we do with this problem? Basically, it calls for a reexamination of the notion of "personality" as used up until now to refer to God and man.

In addition to the conflict between the modern scientific view of nature and that of traditional religion (in particular, Christianity), the problem of religion and science also brings us up against the question of modern man's awareness of his own subjectivity. Since these two issues are in fact interrelated, it is necessary to touch, however briefly, on the latter.

II

Since the advent of modern times, the world view of natural science has been tied up with the question of atheism. The rejection of the existence of a personal God arose as a consequence of the rejection of a teleological view of the world. Generally speaking this atheism has taken the standpoint of scientific rationalism. Its contents boil down to a form of materialism. And its spirit is "progress."

The element of materialism in modern atheism relates to the fact that it has taken the essence of the things of the world to be matter. The element of scientific rationalism stems from an assertion of the power and right of human reason to control such a world. In contrast to the standpoint of an earlier metaphysical rationality that considered itself constituted by and made subject to the divine order of creation, the new rationalism has represented human reason as coming forth to dismantle the framework of divine order. The world has been seen as materialistic and mechanistic because its order lost the sense of dependence on the *personal* will of God it once had under the teleological scheme. The character of the world came to be divorced from the personal character of God. This meant, in turn, that the world was considered to be completely accessible to human reason, inasmuch as the materialistic world view implied that the stuff of the world is absolutely passive to the control of man. Conversely put, in conformity with the notion that all things in the world are essentially reducible to matter, and from the perspective of the one who controls the world, man arrived at an awareness of his own reason as something absolutely active and absolutely free. Human reason was thus transferred to a field on which it seemed to enjoy absolute authority, where it no longer had the need, nor even the opportunity, to see itself as belonging to a divine order or as subordinate to the will of God.

In this way, out of the union of the passive, raw material of the world and the absolute formative agent of human reason, the idea of "progress" emerged. In a totally passive world, reason finds itself able to advance in self-awareness and in the imposition of rational form on the world. Indeed, this is the way reason *must* function, giving rise to a future that opens up like a path to unlimited progress. Such was the optimism of the atheism that grew out of the Enlightenment.

Three elements, then, compose modern atheism: materialism, scientific rationalism, and the idea of progress. Taken together, they show the awakening of man to free and independent subjectivity. In other words, what may be called "progress atheism" resulted from the coalition of the awakening of subjectivity in reason and the materialistic view of the world, both of which entail a denial of the existence of God.

In our times, however, atheism has gone a step further. For one thing, there is a sense of the meaninglessness of a purely materialistic and mechanistic world and an accompanying awareness of the nihility that lies concealed just beneath the surface of the world. For another, it seems possible to speak of subjectivity today only as an awakening to a nihility within human nature that lies beyond the reach of reason and yet constitutes the very ground on which we stand. To feel this nihility underfoot is to break through the "existence" of things all at once, to pass beyond that dimension in which each and every thing in the world is thought to have an objective existence, and to uncover for man a standpoint of subjectivity that can never be reduced to mere objective existence. As I mentioned earlier, this is the form of subjectivization in modern atheism.

Translating this into a comparison with Christianity, the consciousness of a nihility underlying all things in the world and the world itself that we find in atheism has its counterpart in the *nihilum* that appears in the Christian conception of divine creation as a *creatio ex nihilo*. Again, the posture in which the subject takes its stand on nihility—the subjectification of nihility—by deciding to depend on nothing outside of itself is analogous to the absolute subjectivity of God who says of himself: "I am who I am." For the awareness of nihility within contemporary atheism, the *nihilum* in *creatio ex nihilo* turns into an abyss in which the existence of God is denied and replaced by nihility. In this abyss of nihility both self and world find their ground. Here we see manifest the awakening to subjectivity that modern atheism has invited from the start.

This is clear in the case of Nietzsche. Sartre, too, as we touched on earlier, shows similar tendencies. In each of them atheism is bound up with existentialism. That is, atheism has been subjectivized, nihility has become the field of the so-called *ekstasis* of self-existence, and the horizon of transcendence opens up not in an orientation to God but in an orientation to nihility. As a matter of course, such an atheism no longer subscribes to the idea of progress found in earlier atheism, nor can it allow itself to be so naively optimistic. On the contrary, the characteristic features of current atheism are as follows: an awareness of a most fundamental human crisis; a suffering that is one with existence itself; and an impassioned decision to uphold resolutely the independence of human selfhood, relying on nothing outside of the self, striving to be completely oneself, and thereby to break out of the fundamental crisis of human existence.

Of the two, Nietzsche's position on atheism and existentialism is far more comprehensive and penetrating than Sartre's. The existentialism of Sartre is confined to a humanistic frame that displaces the absolute affirmation of God onto man. But the question of atheism is not originally tied up with human existence alone. It has to do with the existence of all things, that is to say, of the world as such. Atheism must also signal a fundamental conversion in one's way of looking at the world.

To borrow an analogy from Nietzsche, what we are dealing with here is a catastrophic change similar to what took place in natural history when dry lands rose up out of the sea and the many animals that had once lived in the sea were forced to become inhabitants of the land. This meant radically altering their way of living, their way of looking at things, and their habits—in short, a fundamental reorientation in their way of being and valuing. The shift to atheism is like the entire land sinking back again into the sea, forcing all the land animals to revert back into sea animals. It represents a change so fundamental that not only the human mode of existence but even the very visible form of the world itself must undergo a radical transformation. Individual things, for example, lose their substantiality when they are grounded on nihility and come to look instead like the waves of the sea. This is how the world looks from the viewpoint of the "eternal return." It requires, moreover, a fundamental conversion in the human way of being in the world which shows up in Nietzsche as the impulse to a new religiosity—basically different from former religions but nonetheless a new religiosity—that he refers to symbolically as the Dionysian.

Although we speak here of "atheism" or of a "godless man" (as Nietzsche does in *Thus Spoke Zarathustra*), we do so in a sense fundamentally different from the sense in which they are used to refer to previous forms of atheism or to ordinary atheists. Similarly, although Nietzsche emphasized an "un-human" way of being, he was not advocating something to replace, on the same plane, what is normally spoken of as the "human." His is rather an attempt to posit a new way of being human beyond the frame of the "human," to forge a new form of the human from the "far side," beyond the limits of man-centered existence, from "beyond good and evil." This is the sense of his image of the "Overman," who embodies the doctrine that "Man is something that shall be overcome."[2] This seemingly fanciful idea of Nietzsche's results from the attempt to follow through radically on the fundamental conversion that atheism implies in one's way of being human and viewing the world.

For his part, Sartre would also claim that existentialism attempts to pursue the consequences of atheism. The difference is that he restricts his grasp of man to the field of consciousness. What is more, although he does allow Existenz to come into being out of nothingness, as far as the world and the things in it are concerned, he does not abandon his way of looking at them from the field of consciousness. The fact that he has not followed through the consequences of atheism radically seems clear from his presentation of existentialism as a humanism. It is primarily in Nietzsche that atheism comes to its truly radical subjectivization, that nihility comes to possess a transcendent quality by becoming the field of the ecstasy of self-being, and that the freedom and self-reliance of man are brought to an out-and-out confrontation with the question of dependence on God.

Kierkegaard, as we know, sought to resolve this same confrontation in the direction of faith. In his case, existentialism—or the emphasis on subjectivity—consists in locating man at the point of decision, where he must choose between these two options: either to see his existence as grounded on and upheld by divine salvation; or to suffer the despair of the "sickness unto death" that admits of no salvation, and so to fall into an inauthentic existence. In this latter case, one is deluded into assuming that the existence of the self that desires to be itself without grounding itself on God is the real existence, and hence calls forth the nihility at the ground of self-existence which, in due time, leads one to eternal damnation.

For Nietzsche and Kierkegaard, then, existentialism takes on a fundamentally religious significance as a confrontation between human subjectivity and God, and thereafter splits into its atheistic and theistic tendencies. But whereas Nietzsche's thought came to maturity after passing through the purgative fires of the mechanistic world view and so was able to enter into confrontation with the new way of being human concealed in the emergence of modern natural science,[3] there is no such radical confrontation to be found in Kierkegaard's thought. Consequently nihility does not take on for him the sense of the abyss where the self-being of man comes to its ecstatic transcendence. The germ of this idea can be seen in *The Concept of Dread*, but it did not develop within his general thought to an adequate encounter with the problem of religion and science.

III

In the opening section we noted that the laws of nature in the modern scientific view have become completely indifferent to man and his interests. The world these laws control has come to appear as something cutting across the personal relationship between God and man that was once present in religious experience. This world, we saw, has taken on the characteristics of being essentially unrelated to God and man insofar as they are personal entities, or, rather, has shown itself essentially incompatible with the idea of "personality." We suggested that the idea of personality entertained in the past with regard to both God and man stands now in need of reexamination.

In the preceding section we spoke of the awakening of subjectivity in modern man as it is interwoven with the problem of the modern scientific view of nature. We noted that in our day this awareness has reached its culmination in the subjectivization of atheism. In other words, the nihility that spells the death of God emerges from deep beneath the material, mechanical world and is perceived by modern man as an abyss in which he experiences the ecstatic transcendence of his self-being. Only when a man has felt such an abyss open at the ground of his existence does his subjectivity become subjectivity in the true sense of the word: only then does he awaken to himself as truly free and independent.

Historically speaking, these questions are intimately related to Christianity, which has functioned at once as the matrix and the antagonist of modern science since its beginnings in the Renaissance or even before. It is the same with modern atheism, whose variety of forms is unthinkable apart from Christianity. If we trace the genealogy of the ideas that make up the ingredients of modern atheism—for example, the idea of a natural law of unyielding necessity, the idea of progress, and the idea of social justice that has motivated so many social revolutions—we come back eventually to Christianity. In shaping his radical attack against Christianity, Nietzsche was giving utterance to an attitude that had been nurtured within Christianity itself, namely, the constant and uncompromising pursuit of the truth. Let us therefore first look at our problem with an eye to its Christian origins.

I should like to preface this consideration with a famous passage from the gospel according to Matthew:

> You have heard that it was said, "You shall love your neighbor and hate your enemy." But I say to you, Love your enemies and pray for those who persecute you, so that you may be sons of your Father who is in heaven; for he makes his sun rise on the evil and on the good, and sends rain on the just and on the unjust. For if you love those who love you, what reward have you? Do not even the tax collectors do the same? And if you salute only your brethren, what more are you doing than others? Do not even the Gentiles do the same? You, therefore, must be perfect, as your heavenly Father is perfect. [Matt. 5:43–48]

There are two points to be noted in this passage. First is the command to love one's enemies as one's friends, which is presented as the way to becoming perfect as God is perfect. In Buddhism this is what is known as "non-differentiating love beyond enmity and friendship." Second, God's causing the sun ro rise on the evil as well as the good, and the rain to fall on the unjust and just alike, is cited as an example of this perfection. The phenomenon this speaks to is similar to what I referred to before as the indifference of nature, except that here it is not a cold and insensitive indifference, but the indifference of love. It is a non-differentiating love that transcends the distinctions men make between good and evil, justice and injustice.

The indifference of nature reduces everything to the level of a highest abstract common denominator, be it matter or some particular physical element. In contrast, the indifference of love embraces all things in their most concrete Form—for example, good men and evil men—and accepts the differences for what they are.

What is it like, this non-differentiating love, this *agape*, that loves even enemies? In a word, it is "making oneself empty." In the case of Christ, it meant taking the form of man and becoming a servant, in accordance with the will of God, who is the origin of the *ekkenōsis* or "making himself empty" of Christ. God's love is such that it shows itself willing to forgive even the sinner who has turned against him, and this forgiving love is an expression of the "perfection" of God who embraces without distinction the evil as well as the good. Accordingly, the meaning of self-emptying may be said to be contained within God himself. In Christ, *ekkenōsis* is realized in the fact that one who was in the shape of God took on the shape of a servant; with God, it is implied already in his original perfection. That is to say, the very fact itself of God's being God essentially entails the characteristic of "having made himself empty." With Christ we speak of a deed that has been accomplished; with God, of an original nature. What is *ekkenōsis* for the Son is *kenōsis* for the Father. In the East, this would be called *anātman,* or non-ego.[4]

Hating one's enemies and loving one's friends are sentiments typical of human love. They belong to the field of the ego. Indifferent love belongs rather to the realm of non-ego. And it is this characteristic of non-ego that is contained by nature in the perfection of God. For man to actualize this perfection of God, to be perfect as the Father in heaven is perfect and so to "become a son of God," man must engage himself in loving his enemies. This requires a transition from differentiating human love to non-differentiating divine love. It means denying *eros* and turning to *agapē*, denying ego and turning to non-ego. Christ embodies this perfection of God through the love by which he "emptied himself" of his equality with God to take on the shape of a servant among men. The Christian is said to practice or imitate that self-emptying perfection when he converts from a human differentiating love to a divine non-differentiating love.

Although self-emptying, ego-negating love may be taken as characteristic of divine perfection, we point more expressly to that perfection when we speak of a perfect mode of *being* rather than of the *activity* of self-emptying or of *loving* that is typified in Christ and commanded of man. In other words, as alluded to in the first chapter, the sort of quality we refer to as self-emptied can be seen as essentially entailed from the beginning in the notion of the perfection of God, and the activity of love as consisting in the embodiment or practice of that perfection. Considered in its relation to love as deed or activity, the perfection of God can also be called love. But if the activity of love has a personal character to it—as I think it does—then there is no way around the conclusion that the perfection of God and love in the sense of that perfection point to something elemental, more basic than the "personal," and that it is as the embodiment or imitation of this perfection that the "personal" first comes into being. A quality is implied here of *transpersonality*, or *impersonality*.

As observed, the term "impersonal" is not to be taken as the opposite of the "personal," but as the "personally impersonal." We get an idea of this personal impersonality from the nondifferentiating love that makes the sun rise on the evil as well as the good, and the rain fall on the just and the unjust alike. In an earlier passage from the gospel of Matthew, heaven is called God's throne, and the earth his footstool. The same sense of the personally impersonal adopted in our discussion of the omnipresence and omnipotence of God might well be applied here as well to the impersonality with which God preempts and stands above the positions of the simply personal, and from which personality derives.

The non-differentiating love that makes the sun rise on the evil as well as the good, on the enemy as well as the ally, contains, as we said, the quality of non-ego. Non-ego (*anātman*) represents the fundamental standpoint of Buddhism, where it is called the Great Wisdom (*mahā-prajñā*) and the Great Compassion (*mahā-karuna*). I have already had occasion to touch briefly on the former in the first chapter; suffice it here to add a word about *mahā-karuna*, the Great Compassionate Heart, the essential equivalent of the biblical analogy that tells us there is no such thing as selfish or selective sunshine. The sun in the sky makes no choices about where to shine its rays and shows no preferences as to likes or dislikes. There is no selfishness in its shining. This lack of selfishness is what is meant by non-ego, or "emptiness" (*śūnyatā*). The perfection of God has this point in common with the Great Compassionate Heart of Buddhism. And that same divine perfection is then demanded of man.

From what has been said, it should be clear that this *perfectness* of God is something qualitatively very different, for instance, from the *personal* absoluteness of the God who singled out the people of Israel as his elect, who commands with absolute will and authority, who loves the righteous and punishes the sinful. If perfection is taken to mean a non-selective non-ego, then personality that engages in making choices can in no sense be taken as a form of perfection. We have here two different ways of looking at God from the Bible. In the past, Christianity has tended to focus only on the aspect of the personal in God. Instances in which attention has been given to the impersonal aspect are few.

My purpose in taking up this problem here, however, is to relate it to the problem of religion and science. On the one hand, we want to know whether nature as understood by modern natural science, in spite of its insensitivity and indifference to the good and evil, the fortunes and misfortunes of men, can still be thought of as belonging to God; and on the other, whether this modern view of nature as insensitive is connected to the question of the free independence of man and the awakening of his subjectivity. It is because this manifold problem has proved so difficult to dispose of in our times that we must question the notion of the personal in God and inquire into the realm of the transpersonal.

The history of Christian dogmatics does not, I think, provide us with a ready-made theological apparatus for coping with this manifold problem. Indeed the view of nature which modern science has given us has only recently become the acute problem for religion that it is; I cannot see that during this time Christianity has produced any thought capable of making deep enough contact with the issue or confronting it authentically. Only with regard to questions of the free independence of man, and his awakening to subjectivity, have attempts to uncover the aspect of the transpersonal in God been not wholly lacking. These attempts belong to the tradition known as negative theology. If we start from the problem of religion and science, questions of freedom and autonomy seem to be only indirectly relevant. But since all along we have taken them as indicating another facet of the same question, I should like first to address myself to this issue before going any further.

IV

Let us begin by having a look at the thought of Meister Eckhart who offers us the most radical example of negative theology. Eckhart is well known for his distinction between God and godhead (*Gottheit*), the latter of which he calls the "essence" of God. In spite of his terminology, he did not, of course, think in terms of two Gods. Godhead means what God is in himself—what Eckhart speaks of as *absolute nothingness*.[5]

Absolute nothingness signals, for Eckhart, the point at which all modes of being are transcended, at which not only the various modes of created being but even the modes of divine being—such as Creator or Divine Love—are transcended. Creator, he says, is the Form of God that is bared to creatures and seen from the standpoint of creatures, and as such is not to be taken as what God is in himself, as the essence of God. It is the same when God is said to be Love or to be Good. The essence of God that renders ineffable each and every mode of being (and each and every Form) can only be expressed as absolute nothingness. (Strictly speaking, even to speak of "essence" is already inadequate.)

Now, when we say that man has been made in the image of God, this includes the godhead of absolute nothingness. When the image of that God becomes active in the soul of man, through the working of the Holy Spirit, man is said to become a "son of God." Eckhart calls this the "birth of God" in the soul.

As an event of history, the incarnation of God in Christ represents the "birth of God" in the world of man. What Eckhart does is to draw that event into the interior of the soul of man. When a human being thus becomes the living image of God, there opens up within his soul a path leading all the way to the essence of God. This is so by virtue of the fact that the God who comes to birth within him—the Christ alive within his soul—includes not only the entire *God* of the Trinity but also the *godhead*. For the soul, ascent of the path that has opened up means to enter, step by step, deep within God and finally to attain union with him. The union spoken of here is not the simple approach of two objects from opposite directions that meet and then join together. The whole process, rather, means that from ever deeper within the soul itself, the element of self is broken through again and again.

The birth of God in the soul already represents a breakdown of egoity or self-will or the ego-centered mode of being of the soul; but this is only the first step. The soul proceeds further, penetrating into the God that has been born within it, into the revelation of the depths of God breaking its way up from the soul's innermost recesses. Even in so doing, the soul returns more and more deeply to itself and becomes more and more truly itself. Eckhart conceived of this as the soul "breaking through" God, with its final consummation at the break-through to the essence of God: absolute nothingness, a point at which not a single thing remains. He calls this the "desert" of the godhead.

Here the soul is completely deprived of its egoity. This is the final ground of the soul, its *bottomless ground*. Although it marks the point at which the soul can for the first time return to be itself, it is at the same time the point at which God is in himself. It is the ground of God: "As God breaks through me, so I, in turn, break through him. God leads my spirit into the desert and into his self-identity, where he is a pure One, springing up within himself."[6]

One cannot really speak here any longer of "union." Indeed, Eckhart himself stresses that it is not a matter of being united with God (*Deo unitum esse*) but of being one with God (*unum esse cum Deo*). It is, if you will, the self-identity of the soul that is self-identical with the self-identity of God. It brings the soul to a desert of absolute death, and at the same time discloses a fountainhead "springing up within itself" of absolute life. It is at once the source of the eternal life of God and of the eternal life of the soul. In this one fountainhead, God and soul are as a single living "pure One." Elsewhere Eckhart expresses it in these terms: "The ground of God is the ground of my soul; the ground of my soul is the ground of God. . . . Here I live out of my own authentic nature [*Eigen*] even as God lives from his. . . . The eye with which I see God is the eye with which God sees me."[7]

The originality of Eckhart's thinking strikes us on a number of counts. First, he locates the "essence" of God at a point beyond the personal God who stands over against created beings. Second, this essence of God, or godhead, is seen as an absolute nothingness, and moreover becomes the field of our absolute death-*sive*-life.[8] Third, only in the godhead can man truly be himself, and only in the openness of absolute nothingness can the consummation of the freedom and independence of man in subjectivity be effected.

Of course, in speaking of subjectivity here I do not mean the subjectivity of the ego. Quite to the contrary, it is the subjectivity that comes about from the absolute death of ego (what Eckhart calls *Abgeschiedenheit*) and from pure oneness with God. In this connection "pure" points to the sheer nonobjective character of this oneness. For Eckhart even the *unio mystica*, which had traditionally been regarded as the final stage of perfection in mystical experience and was assumed to represent union with God (*Deo unitum esse*), still considered the being of God as an object to be united with. Lurking behind these presuppositions was a dualism of subject and object. The perfect achievement of mystical union is not yet wholly free of the shell it has broken open; it does not yet signal a return to the self and an awakening to its true nature. This can only take place in losing oneself in God, in an absolute oneness.

In Eckhart, then, the pursuit of subjectivity necessitates the distinction between God and godhead. For the ground of subjectivity is to be found only at the point that one reaches beyond God for the absolute nothingness of godhead. This is the field of the "uncreated *I am*," where, Eckhart tells us, the self has been positioned eternally from before the creation of the world, standing in the godhead already before God spoke his Word. He further considers that it is on this ground that God bares himself most essentially through the soul, and that the soul bears witness to God as present in the Dasein of the soul itself.

Having said all of this, we must not suppose that Eckhart looked on absolute nothingness and the "uncreated *I am*" as a never-never land far removed from actuality, or as a self-intoxicated isolation from reality. In fact he strongly warns against such tendencies and has high praise for the practical activities of everyday life.[9] Even though the field of godhead is called an absolute nothingness, Eckhart insists that it needs to be lived right in the midst of everyday life in the immediacy of which it discloses itself. Or again, even though he refers to that ground as the "uncreated *I am*" and as the source of eternal life, this does not mean that it is to be sought apart from the created self and the temporal life. In the *I am*, createdness and uncreatedness are subjectively one; in life, eternality and temporality are a living one. Nor can "standing in the godhead" be interpreted as the contemplation of God, since it is already beyond all intellectual understanding, including even the intuitive intellection that is proper to the contemplation of God. It is rather the *realization* (in the twofold sense spoken of earlier as actualization and appropriation) within everyday life of the nothingness of the godhead.

To repeat: the very distinction between God and godhead is necessitated by the opening up of the path to subjectivity. "I flee from God for the sake of God," writes Eckhart. "I beg of God that he make me rid of God." Fleeing God for God's sake seems to mean that the here-and-now Dasein of man can bear witness *essentially* to God only through man's truly finding himself in the nothingness of the godhead. He adds further on:

> When I break through and stand emptied [*ledig steben*] of my own will, of the will of God, of all the works of God, and of God himself, I am beyond all creatures, and I am neither God nor creature but am what I was and what I should remain now and forever more.[10]

With this sort of thought Eckhart brings into extremely sharp relief the very confrontation between the free autonomy of man, or subjectivity, and God that is the basic concern of present-day existentialism. But it is not the atheism of Nietzsche or the theism of Kierkegaard we find in Eckhart. He sees the *nothingness* of godhead at the ground of the personal *God* from the far side, beyond theism and atheism, at a point where the autonomy of the *soul* is rooted firmly in essential oneness with the essence of God. It would seem worth our while to take a closer look at the difference between this standpoint and that of modern atheistic existentialism.

As we noted earlier, Christianity thinks in terms of a *creatio ex nihilo* by a God who transcends the nihility that forms the ground of the entities he creates. Atheistic existentialism, in addition to denying the existence of this God, replaces him with nihility which, as the field of the *ekstasis* of self-being, is then perceived as the ground of the subject itself. Thus the nihility of *creatio ex nihilo* penetrates as such the place once held by God, deepens into an abyss, and then comes to appear as the ground of subjectivity.

The "nothingness" of godhead that Eckhart sees at the very ground of God himself must be said to be still more profound than the nihility that contemporary existentialism has put in the place of God. What is more, we seem to find in Eckhart a more penetrating view of the awareness of subjectivity in man. This can be seen in his reasoning that the awareness of subjectivity arises out of an absolute negation passing over into an absolute affirmation. The subjectivity of the uncreated *I am* appears in Eckhart only after passing through the complete negation of—or detachment (*Abgeschiedenheit*) from—the subjectivity of egoity. Furthermore, the subjectivity of the uncreated *I am* is not viewed as something cut off from the *I am* of the creature living in the here and now. *I am* is only possible as a single, unique *I am*, and as such is it absolutely affirmed.

The authentic awareness of subjectivity that Eckhart sets up as an absolute negation-*sive*-affirmation, as absolute death-*sive*-life, figures in contemporary existentialism without passing through absolute negation. Nihility appears at the ground of self-being and renders it ecstatic, but this ecstasy is not yet the absolute negation of being, and thus does not open up to absolute nothingness.

Sartre, for example, considers existence an ecstatic "project" constituted on nihility but continues to view that existence as consciousness. For him, nihility is not given as the field where the conscious ego is negated or negates itself. The self-affirmation of the subject appears at the point that the existence of the self can be said to be an existence freely chosen and posited by the self itself in the face of nihility. But this is not yet a self-affirmation that has plumbed nihility to its depths.

In contrast Nietzsche, as early as in *The Birth of Tragedy*, took up a position well beyond the standpoint of the ego. In his later thought the standpoint of an absolute negation-*sive*-affirmation is fairly clear. But this absolute affirmation, or *Ja-sagen*, comes about in things like "life" and the "Will to Power," so that it is not sufficiently clear in his case precisely to what extent the recovery of such a standpoint includes the sense of a subjective awakening wherein the self truly becomes the self.

At any rate, Nietzsche does not seem to have attained Eckhart's standpoint of an absolute nothingness that takes its stand on the immediacy of everyday life. And here we can see reflected the difference between a nihility proclaiming that "God is dead" and an absolute nothingness reaching a point beyond even "God"; or between life forcing its way through nihility to gush forth and life as absolute death-*sive*-life. In short, if the *nihilum* of *creatio ex nihilo* (as a negative referring to the relative existence of created being) may be called relative nothingness, and if the nothingness of godhead in Eckhart (as the point at which all of existence, including subjective existence, stands out in its true-to-life reality) may be called absolute nothingness, then perhaps we might say that the nihility of Nietzsche's nihilism should be called a standpoint of *relative absolute nothingness*.

Be that as it may, these hastily drawn comparisons should give some glimpse into the significance of Eckhart's thought. No doubt what he has to say is markedly distant from orthodox Christian faith, and it is not without reason that he was regarded as heretical in his own times, despite his considerable influence. In our times, when human subjectivity and the confrontation between that subjectivity and God have become the great problems that they are, the thought of Meister Eckhart seems to me to merit serious reconsideration.

The point becomes all the more clear when we turn to a comparison with the thought of contemporary Christian theology. Emil Brunner, for example, argues that God is always treated in the Bible as God-toward-man (*Gott-zum-Menschen-hin*) and man as man-from-God (*Mensch-von-Gott-her*). For Brunner, the Bible contains no doctrinal statement whatsoever concerning what God and man are in themselves. The relationship between God and man is altogether personal, and in this personal relationship man stands over against God as a freely independent reality (*ein reales Gegenüber*).

> God wills his own real counterpoint, he creates it as such and sets it up as something that is not himself but nevertheless is because God so wills it. . . . The world, and above all man, stands truly really over against God. God himself wills it so, has arranged it that way, and will remain by that arrangement through all eternity. He gives the creature a being in counterpoint to his own, not independent but yet self-sustaining in its dependence on him. He supplies the creature with the ability to be something that stands over against him, indeed to be itself precisely in its standing over against him.[11]

On the whole this reflects accepted Christian thought, but it seems to me to leave a problem unanswered. When it is said that God wills the existence in reality of free and independent creatures standing over against himself, what field are we to posit for this independent existence? Brunner himself speaks of creation as God's calling man forth out of nothingness or of imprinting his *imago Dei* onto nothingness. And it is precisely for this reason, he argues, that man can be thought of as absolutely dependent on God. But does this mean that the nihility of *creatio ex nihilo* is to be the field appointed for free and independent existence? If so, then since such existence can be made to return to nihility at any moment by a single act of divine will, its freedom and independence are really grounded on nihility.

We have already noted how contemporary existentialism subjectifies nihility by making it the field of the ecstasy of self-existence. As a result, nihility is shifted to the side of the subject itself, and the freedom or autonomy of the subject is said to be a function of existence (Existenz) stepping over itself into the midst of nihility. In contemporary theology, however, nihility belongs on the side of divine will, so that creature existence is seen merely as existence, without any ecstasy into nihility. As a result, even though one may speak of a "freedom" or "independence" in such an existence, these things do not have their roothold within the subject itself. They end up, in the final analysis, as no more than an apparent freedom and the illusory appearance of an independence. To the extent that a nihility belonging to divine will is their ground, neither freedom nor independence are actually real. On this view, accordingly, man cannot truly be said to be a "reality standing over against God" that is "not God himself" but "*itself*, over against God." In such an approach, it seems to me, the questions of human subjectivization and confrontation with God have not really been thought through radically enough.

When something that is not God but stands by itself over against God is posited, the field to which it is appointed—that is, the ground of its existence—must be a point within God where God is not God himself. In other words, it must be a point that is not the nihility of *creatio ex nihilo* but rather something like the absolute nothingness of godhead that we saw in Eckhart. Godhead is the place within God where God is not God himself.

When it is said that God wills a free existence that stands over against himself, the field in which that will unfolds itself must be understood as an absolute nothingness. In this way it becomes possible for the first time to think of creatures that are free beings, who are not God but stand by themselves over against God, as nonetheless posited within God.

We observed, further, that godhead is the point within God where God is not God himself. This may seem to contradict what I said earlier abut godhead being what God is in himself, but in fact these two statements come to the same thing. To say that God is what God is in himself precisely in that absolute nothingness in which God is not God himself means nothing other than to consider ecstasy as applying to the existence of God as well as of man. In the same way that human existence can be thought of as subjective only when it is ecstatic, so too it is possible to think of divine being as achieving subjectivity for the first time—albeit as an absolute subjectivity in absolute nothingness— in *ekstasis*. If we take in its strictly ontological sense this notion that for both man and God existence is subjective, and if we grant that this existence is only possible in *ekstasis*, then it seems natural to conclude with Eckhart that the point at which human subjectivity reaches its consummation is in a subjective "oneness" with divine subjectivity. The subjective coincidence of subject with subject can no longer be called a "union."

In short, since the nihility of *creatio ex nihilo* may be spoken of as a simple relative nothingness, the existence that comes about on the ground of that nothingness can never be truly independent. Truly free existence can only be posited on and rooted in absolute nothingness. This, it seems to me, is the kind of nothingness Eckhart has in mind when he says, "The ground of God is the ground of my soul; the ground of my soul is the ground of God."

As we have just been saying, subjective existence is realized in ecstasy, that is, in a mode of being wherein the self *is* in itself at the point that it has stepped over itself. If we take this a stage further, however, this sense of ecstasy turns out to be inadequate. It leaves out the more profound and comprehensive standpoint of absolute negation-*sive*-affirmation spoken of earlier. Ecstasy represents an orientation from self to the *ground* of self, from God to the *ground* of God—from being to nothingness. Negation-*sive*-affirmation represents an orientation from nothingness to being. The difference in orientation points to a reversal of standpoints. (It is not without good reason that Heidegger made an about-face from his earlier course to rethink his stance on *ekstasis* in an orientation proceeding from the *ground*.) Up to now I have, for the most part, followed the course of ecstasy in pursuing the questions of subjectivity and of the personal and the impersonal. If these issues are to be delved into more deeply, the kind of reversal we have just referred to will be necessary.

V

The idea of man as person is without doubt the highest conception of man yet to appear. The same may be said of the idea of God as person. Once the awareness of subjectivity had been established in modern times, the notion of man as a personal being became practically self-evident. But is the way of thinking about person that has so far prevailed really the only possible way of thinking about person?

Put simply, until now the person has been viewed from the standpoint of the person itself. It has been a person-centered view of person. In the modern period—as we see, for instance, with Descartes—even the ontologically more basic ego was viewed from the ego-centered perspective of the ego itself and grasped from the standpoint of the *ego cogito*. It has been the same with person. Inasmuch as ego and person from the very outset entail inward self-reflection, without which they cannot come into being as ego and person, it is only natural that this kind of self-immanent self-prehension should come about. So long as the need for a more elemental mode of reflection does not arise, people automatically stay within this mode of grasping ego and person.

The person-centered prehension of person, however, is by no means self-evident. Indeed, it stems from a bias rooted deep within the self-consciousness of man. More fundamentally, the ego-centered grasp and interpretation of ego which we find in modern man is no less of a bias and hardly as self-evident as it is assumed to be. These biases signal a confinement of self-being to the perspective of self-immanence from which man prehends his own egoity and personality, a confinement that inevitably ushers in the narcissistic mode of grasping the self wherein the self gets caught up in itself.

Person is rather a phenomenon that appears out of what cannot itself be called personal and does not entail any confinement of self-being. In referring to person as a "phenomenon," I do not mean to contrast it with the thing-in-itself, as Kant might. It would be a mistake here to think that there is some thing-in-itself subsisting apart from the phenomenon, or that this thing-in-itself makes its appearance in some Form other than its own Form, like an actor putting on a mask. The interpretation of person as phenomenon does not make it a temporary exterior that can be donned and doffed at will. To think of person in that way is to lose sight of the subjective element in the personal which engages the self in a process of unlimited self-determination.

The ancient concept of *persona* originally carried the meaning of such a mask. When I say that person is a phenomenon, however, I do not wish to imply that there is some other "thing" behind personal being, like an actor behind a mask. Person is an appearance with nothing at all behind it to make an appearance. That is to say, "nothing at all" is what is behind person; complete nothingness, not one single thing, occupies the position behind person.

While this complete nothingness is wholly other than person and means the absolute negation of person, it is not some "thing" or some entity different from person. It brings into being the thing called person and becomes one with it. Accordingly, it is inaccurate to say that complete nothingness "is" behind person. Nothingness is not a "thing" that *is* nothingness. Or again, to speak of nothingness as standing "behind" person does not imply a duality between nothingness and person. In describing this nothingness as "something" wholly other, we do not mean that there is actually some "thing" that is wholly other. Rather, true nothingness means that there is no thing that is nothingness, and this is *absolute nothingness*.

"Nothingness" is generally forced into a relationship with "being" and made to serve as its negation, leading to its conception as something that "is" nothingness because it "is not" being. This seems to be especially evident in Western thought, even in the "nihility" of nihilism. But insofar as one stops here, nothingness remains a mere concept, a nothingness only in thought. Absolute nothingness, wherein even that "is" is negated, is not possible as a nothingness that is thought but only as a nothingness that is lived. It was remarked above that behind person there is nothing at all, that is, that "nothing at all" is what stands behind person. But this assertion does not come about as a conceptual conversion, but only as an existential conversion away from the mode of being of person-centered person. Granted what we have said about the person-centered self-prehension of person as being intertwined with the very essence and realization of the personal, the negation of person-centeredness must amount to an existential self-negation of man as person. The shift of man as person from person-centered self-prehension to self-revelation as the manifestation of absolute nothingness—of which I shall speak next—requires an existential conversion, a change of heart within man himself.

Existential conversion consists in extricating oneself from a person-centered mode of being to come out on the *near side*, in a mode of personal being in the immediacy of the actual self. The "nothing at all" behind the person comes out into the open on the side of the self, the original self. If person be regarded as the sheer mode of self-being itself, "behind" which there is nothing, this is so because the matter is being looked at from the side of the person. In this case, nothingness only goes as far as being looked at or thought about. When the "nothing at all" opens up on the near side of the personal self, however, and is seen as the sheer self itself, then nothingness really becomes actualized in the self as the true self. Then it is appropriated in the self. Self-existence, in the sense spoken of earlier, becomes the realization of nothingness. "Appropriating" is not "looking at." Pressed to give it a name, we might call it a "seeing of not-seeing," a seeing that sees without seeing. True nothingness is a living nothingness, and a living nothingness can only be self-attested.

In this kind of existential conversion, the self does not cease being a personal being. What is left behind is only the person-centered mode of grasping *person*, that is, the mode of being wherein the person is caught up in itself. In that very conversion the personal mode of being becomes more real, draws closer to the self, and appears in its true suchness. When person-centered self-prehension is broken down and nothingness is really actualized in the self, personal existence also comes really and truly to actualization in the self. This is what is meant by absolute negation-*sive*-affirmation, and it is here that some "thing" called personality is constituted in unison with absolute nothingness. Without a nothingness that is living and a conversion that is existential, this would make no sense.

This is what I had in mind in speaking of person as an appearance with nothing at all behind it to make an appearance. Person is constituted at one with absolute nothingness as that in which absolute nothingness becomes manifest. It is actualized as a "Form of non-Form."

In this sense we can understand person as *persona*—the "face" that an actor puts on to indicate the role he is to play on stage—but only as the *persona* of absolute nothingness. We can even call it a "mask" in the ordinary sense of a face that has been taken on temporarily, provided that we do not imply that there is some other "true" or "real" thing that it cloaks, or that it is something artificial devised to deceive, or that it is a mere "illusory appearance." Person is through and through real. It is the most real of realities. It comes into being only as a real form of human being that contains not the slightest bit of deception or artificiality. But at the same time it is in the most elemental sense an "illusion" precisely because it is the highest mode of being, constituted in unison with absolute nothingness and becoming manifest as such. Man thus comes into being as an absolute nothingness-*sive*-being rooted elementally in the personal mode of being. In the terms of the Tendai school of Buddhism, man comes into being as the "middle" between "illusion" and "emptiness."

Dostoevski often speaks of the "face" to point to the sense of a mystical side of man that lies hidden in the depths of personality. Nietzsche draws frequently on the image of the "mask," as, for example, when he writes in *Beyond Good and Evil*: "Whatever is profound loves masks. . . . Every profound spirit needs a mask: even more, around every profound spirit a mask is growing continually."[12] This is typical Nietzsche, deep in insight and full of subtlety. In both cases, what is being referred to has something in common with the sense of "mask" or "face" we have related to the standpoint of absolute nothingness-*sive*-being, being-*sive*-nothingness. And yet they are not the same.

Personality is something altogether alive. Even if we consider it to be "spirit," it is a mask of absolute nothingness precisely as *living* spirit. Were nothingness to be thought of apart from its mask, it would become an idea. Were we to deal with the mask apart from nothingness, person could not avoid becoming self-centered. The living activity of person, in its very aliveness, is a manifestation of absolute nothingness. And spirit, as a lived spirituality, is one with the transspiritual and the aspiritual that it manifests. Only in this way does person truly come into being as a *reality*.

What we have here is no longer that subjectivity usually attributed to personality, but rather the very negation of that subjectivity that person ascribes to itself in its person-centered self-prehension. This negation means a conversion within the self-enclosed personality, an outburst of altogether fresh vitality. It is like a key to that innermost depth of personality that has been closed off since the very beginning— the "beginning without beginning"—of personal being. Through this negation the person is broken through from within and the personal self discloses itself as subjectivity in its elemental sense, as truly absolute selfhood.

We find an example of this in the words that Gasan Jōseki (1275– 1365), a Sōtō Zen master of Japan five generations removed from Dōgen, inscribed over a self-portrait he had made:

> The heart and mind of this shadowy man
> At all occasions is to me most familiar—
> From long ago mysteriously wondrous,
> It is neither I nor other.

The self as human existence, the self as a real being in the actual world, the whole self ranging from personality to the bodily flesh is called here "this´shadowy man." The various activities of personality and consciousness that make up the "heart and mind"—from thinking, feeling, and will to sensations and actions—are no less shadowy. "Shadow" here means the same as what I called "illusion" above. It is the completely unreal, because all the activities of man become manifest as themselves only in unison with absolute nothingness. And yet precisely at this point they are seen to be the most real of realities because they are nothing other than the manifestation of absolute selfhood.

Absolute selfhood opens up as nonobjectifiable nothingness in the conversion that takes place within personality. Through that conversion every bodily, mental, and spiritual activity that belongs to person displays itself as a play of shadows moving across the stage of nothingness. This stage represents the near side of the personal self. It is the field commonly seen as "outermost" by the personal self and referred to as the external world actually present in the here and now, ever changing. At the same time, it is the field of nothingness bursting forth from within the innermost depths of personal self. It is the ultimate realization and expression of nonobjectifiable—and, in that sense, elementally subjective—nothingness. It is the point beyond the innermost depth at which the subject transcends itself and converts into the outermost. It is the point of de-internalization, so to speak. Here the *without* is more *within* than the innermost. The "outer world" emerges here as a self-realization of nonobjectifiable nothingness, or, rather, makes itself present such as it is, in oneness with nothingness.

The field of true human existence opens up beyond the outer and the inner, at a point where the "shadowy man" is in oneness with absolute selfhood. We have here an absolute self-identity. Thinking, feeling, and action are, on every occasion, entirely illusory appearances with nothing behind them, the shadowy heart and mind of the shadowy man. And yet, on every occasion they are one with the selfhood that is aware of itself as the absolute, nonobjectifiable nothingness beyond all time and occasion. This oneness is a self-identity. For the self that stands in absolute selfhood, those activities of consciousness are "most familiar."

Still, the field that self occupies at that time is not the standpoint of mere personality or consciousness but the field of nothingness. It is not the mere standpoint of personal self-immanence within personality itself or of conscious self-immanence within consciousness itself.

Insofar as the field of nothingness is completely one with personality and consciousness, the whole of this oneness is present within personality and consciousness. Conversely, insofar as personality and consciousness can be what they are only in oneness with absolute nothingness, the same complete oneness stands ecstatically outside of personality and consciousness. The absolute *within* and absolute *without* are here one and the same. What renders this possible is that we are arrived at the standpoint of absolute nothingness, that is of absolute nothingness-*sive*-being, being-*sive*-nothingness. Insofar as personal being with its heart and mind is completely one with absolute selfhood, it is utterly real; insofar as personal being is completely apart from absolute selfhood, it is utterly illusory and shadowlike. For this reason the supremely unreal heart and mind of the shadowy man, although they originate from moment to moment as things completely temporary and completely in the world of time, at the same time and on every occasion, in their very temporality they stand ecstatically outside of time. They are altogether "eternal" in their temporality. Coming into being and passing away at each fleeting moment as they do, the heart and mind of the shadowy man are on every occasion "from long ago mysteriously wondrous."

The self in this absolute selfhood is not what is ordinarily termed the personal or conscious "self" or "ego," and yet again does not *exist* as something other than that personal or conscious self. It is not another man: it is neither *another* man nor another *man*. For although self and other are completely apart from each other as men, "man" (that is, conscious personality), such as he is in all his living activities and modes of being, is a phenomenon that presents itself as "man" in unison with that which is not "man"—namely, with absolute nothingness. Seen from that aspect, every man, such as he is in the real Form of his suchness, is *not* man. He is impersonal. In other words, he is "man" as an appearance with nothing at all behind it to make an appearance.

We ordinarily find ourselves on the standpoint of personal, conscious being. Because of this, self and other, as human realities, tend to be grasped as absolutely two. But looked at from a point closer to the near side, self and other, while remaining absolutely two as *persons*, are at the same time and in their very duality absolutely nondual in their nonhumanity, in their *impersonality*. It is only from such a standpoint that we can say of the heart and mind of the shadowy man that they are "neither I nor other." This is the standpoint of absolute selfhood, of the true self that is personal-*sive*-impersonal, impersonal-*sive*-personal.

At his death Gasan Jōseki left behind him these lines:

> It is ninety-one years
> Since my skin and bones were put together;
> This midnight, as always,
> I lay myself down in the Yellow Springs.[13]

The absolute selfhood that is described in terms of "neither I nor other" is the self of man into which "skin and bones were put together," his actual conscious and personal existence with its living activities. But at the same time, in the very midst of those activities, it is ever ecstatic, ever "laying itself down in the Yellow Springs." From one moment to the next of human activity, it is absolutely death-*sive*-life, life-*sive*-death; absolutely being-*sive*-nothingness, nothingness-*sive*-being. Similarly, Eckhart says that the soul finds its spring of eternal life incessantly gushing up out of itself in the desert of godhead: in the nothingness that lies beyond even the being of God, the nothingness that is the field of the absolute death of the soul.[14]

From the standpoint of absolute selfhood, life and death of themselves both belong to the self, each at its own time and each in its own Form. At each of their moments, life and death are constituted completely within "time." Inside and out, through and through, they are temporal. But at the same time, from one moment to the next and in their very temporal mode of being, life and death are ecstatic. They *are* ecstatically. Viewed from the standpoint of absolute selfhood, there is no change in life at death. That is the sense of the words in the death verse just quoted: "This midnight, as always."

We are reminded here of Nietzsche's image of midnight and noon becoming one. Absolute life-*sive*-death, death-*sive*-life becomes manifest from moment to moment in "human" life, as if midnight were falling at noon, in brilliant sunlight. When the eighth-century Chinese Zen master, Ma-tsu, was paid a visit as he lay abed seriously ill and was asked about his condition, he replied, "Sun-faced Buddha, moon-faced Buddha." Groaning with pain and breathing one's last are, as such, "sun-faced Buddha, moon-faced Buddha."

In the *Vimalakirti Sutra*, Vimalakirti states that he suffers illness because all sentient beings suffer illness. His illness is indeed a real illness, albeit an occasion for showing Great Compassion for all living things. There is not the slightest hint here of a feigned illness, nor should his remark be understood in a metaphorical or symbolic sense. So long as the illness that all living things suffer is real, the suffering that

Vimalakirti undergoes from the field of an absolute non-duality of self and other is no less real. The illness he suffers is through and through, inside and out, real. That his suffering is said to be "empty" does not mean, however, that somewhere "behind" it or "at the interior" there is health to be found. It means that his absolutely real illness, as such, is one with "emptiness." As the saying goes, water does not wet water, nor fire burn fire. This points to the central meaning of emptiness. To the extent that water cannot wet, it is not water; and to the extent that fire cannot burn, it is not fire. But to say that water does not wet itself does not mean that water is not in fact water. Quite the contrary, it means that the fact that water is really water is the real Form of water itself. "Emptiness" is the real form of reality. Real Form as such is a "non-Form." Only in its non-Form does a fact become manifest as a fact. This is what Vimalakirti has in mind when he says, "My illness has no form and is invisible."

It was remarked earlier that the real Form of all things, including man, comes to be a "double exposure" of life and death. All living things can be seen under the Form of death without thereby being separated from their proper Form of life. The real appearance of these things must be seen at ground to rest on the basis of absolute being-*sive*-nothingness, nothingness-*sive*-being, or of the absolute non-duality of life and death as we have just described it. This seems to me the only possible starting point for pursuing reflection on the problem of science and religion.

3

NIHILITY AND ŚŪNYATĀ

I

As we have gone to some lengths to point out in the previous chapter, one of the greatest, most fundmental problems all religions face in our times is their relationship to science. The world view prevalent in science and the scientific way of thinking in general appear to be fundamentally incompatible with the world view and ontology which traditional religions have by and large made their basis. Now the objection might be raised that these latter world views and ontologies, while they may be referred to as metaphysics or philosophy, are not to be called religion and bear no relationship to the essential life of religion. There is an element of truth to this, but it is not the whole truth. Every religion, when it takes concrete shape—as an actual historical reality— invariably bases itself on some world view or ontology. For a religion this basic "philosophy" is not something that can be changed at will, like a suit of clothes. It is to religion what water is to a fish: an essential condition for life. Water is neither the life of the fish as such nor its body, and yet it is essentially linked to both of them. A change of world view or ontology is a matter no less fatal to a religion than a change from salt water to fresh is to a fish.

One often hears that religion and science each has its proper domain and task, and that the two need never come into conflict with one another as long as they remain confined to those original boundaries. This is inadequate. A boundary separates one area from another and yet at the same time belongs to both of them. The foundations of the conflict between religion and science lie surely concealed in just such a boundary. In fact, since ancient times metaphysics and philosophy have consisted in the exploration of the borderlines between science and religion.

In our own times, the problem of the boundary has come to focus on whether there even is such a borderline or not. Present-day science does not feel the need to concern itself with the limits of its own standpoint. The scientific point of view displays a tendency—probably an essential tendency—to overlook not only religion but philosophy as well (that is, if we exempt the kind of "scientific" philosophy that takes the scientific standpoint as such to be a philosophical one). Science thus seems to regard its own scientific standpoint as a position of unquestionable truth from which it can assert itself in all directions. Hence the air of absoluteness that always accompanies scientific knowledge. In short, we can no longer content ourselves with merely fixing limits and drawing borderlines between science and religion as we have become accustomed to doing. The problem is even more critical than the so-called theology of crisis had first thought it to be.

The basic reason that science is able to regard its own standpoint as absolute truth rests in the complete objectivity of the laws of nature that afford scientific knowledge both its premises and its content. One cannot "get a word in" regarding the explanations science gives to the laws of nature from any point of view other than the scientific one. Criticisms and corrections may only be brought to bear from the scientific standpoint itself. Thus, even inherently hypothetical scientific explanations are always presented as objective fact. This may account for the unique power that science enjoys, for the authority with which the "scientific" has come to be invested.

Such being the case, does this mean that, in virtue of the character of absoluteness affixed to scientific knowledge, things like religion, philosophy, and the arts come to no more than subjective opinion? Is the scientific truth with its absoluteness the whole of truth? Is it really impossible that absolute truths originate from other realms as well? At first glance, a plurality of absolute truths does not seem feasible. Common sense tells us that the idea of two absolute truths is a *contradictio in terminis*, that only one or the other can be truth. But is this really so self-evident? Does it not stem from one specific and fixed idea of the absolute and the relative? Is a new way of looking at the absolute and the relative, according to which two absolutes could come into being conjointly, utterly unthinkable? Have we no other way to conceive of the relative than in terms of setting limits—as we do, for instance, when we divide a sheet of paper into two by drawing a line across it? Might we not conceive of a way of looking at the absolute and the relative whereby two things, in spite of, or rather *because* of, their both being absolute, can turn out to be relative to one another—like a single sheet of paper seen at one moment from the front and at another from the reverse? In order to look into these questions I would like to approach the problem of the relationship between science and philosophy from a new angle.

The first question we face, if we accept the objectivity of the laws of nature as beyond doubt, is this: on what horizon are these laws encountered and on what dimension are they received? To repeat an example from the previous chapter, when someone tosses a crust of bread and a dog leaps up in the air to catch it, every "thing" involved (the man, the dog, the bread), as well as all of their movements, are subject to certain physico-chemical laws. Seen from this point of view, the concrete particularities of each of these things and their movements are dismissed, or rather dissolved into a homogeneous and uniform set of relations among atoms and particles. One might then conclude that the real Form of these concrete things and their movements is to be found precisely within those relationships and the laws that control them. Of course, in addition to the physico-chemical realm there is assumed to be a biological one as well, and beyond that a psychological one, which in its turn leads to the realms of "spirit" and "personality." But on each of these levels, all phenomena would still be regarded as reducible, one way or another, to physico-chemical relations and laws, and as able to be explained in terms of them.

From another point of view, however, there is no denying that such things as a crust of bread, a dog, and a man exist in their own proper mode of being and their own proper form (*eidos*), and that as such they maintain a special relationship among themselves. In the case of the dog, for instance, the piece of bread and the man belong to the dog's "environment," and the same can be said of the man in his relationship to the bread and the dog. The respective properties, manner of movement, and physical shape characteristic of the human being and the dog are inconceivable apart from the special characteristics of their respective environments.

Moreover, in this relationship of things to environment, the laws of nature may be said to be "received" on a variety of different dimensions. In the example just given, the dog and the man *live* the laws of nature, as it were, through their respective actions. The laws of nature are here lived laws: they show up in all living things as the laws lived in the lives of those things. What is more, in the case of a dog and a human being within whose lives the laws are lived—for instance, in the act of the man tossing the crust of bread and the dog jumping up at it—their activities in some sense also imply an *appropriation* of the laws of nature. It is a kind of *apprehension* prior to apprehension proper, an apprehension to which the ambiguous term "instinct" is usually applied.

I cannot here consider the notion of instinct in the same detail and to the same depth that Bergson and others have. In any event, we might say that it is consistently based, on the one hand, on the mutual relationship of an individual organism to its environment, which determines that organism's properties, activities, physical structure, and the like; and on the other, on the "specific" mode of being that is inherited as individual eidetic form by the individual offspring from the individual parent. What is called instinct can be said to come into play at the dynamic intersection of these two processes. Such generalizations do not, of course, even begin to take into account the basic distinction between plants and animals, but for the time being we shall have to leave the matter rest there.

It is in the nature of the standpoint of natural science that the laws of nature are said to be "at work" controlling the activities of living organisms. My point here is rather that these controlling laws become manifest in living organisms as something lived and acted out in a sort of "instinctive appropriation." The laws of nature only appear when these organisms live and act, and thereby embody and appropriate those laws. In the world of concrete things, the hegemony of the laws of nature comes to light only when the laws are actualized by those things. This means that in the case of living organisms, the rule of law is encountered on the dimension of instinct. In other words, the very way in which these laws are encountered as manifest in living organisms (namely, as laws that are lived and acted out), is the very thing we have in mind when we speak of "instinct." Instinctive behavior is the law of nature become manifest.

That the activities of living organisms only occur in accordance with these laws means that the laws are "at work" *in* those activities and *as* those activities. At the dimension of living things, the rational order of existence becomes manifest as an embodied and appropriated rational order. Generally speaking, in becoming manifest this way, rational order displays a purposive or teleological character. The rational order of existence comes to assume a teleological character on the field wherein living organisms come into being and instinct becomes active. Physico-chemical laws are here synthesized in a teleological structure and become, so to speak, its raw material.

The unique contribution of man in all of this is technology. His apprehension of the relation between a specific goal aimed at and the specific means required for realizing that goal involves a knowledge of the laws of nature. Unlike simple instinct, technology implies an intellectual apprehension of these laws of one sort or another. When pre-civilized man learned to make tools and to use them—for instance, in making fire—this skill contained in embryo an understanding of the laws of nature *qua* laws. The use of tools and skills for work originates only through such knowledge.

Conversely, knowledge advances and develops through the technological labors of man; and the advance of knowledge in turn advances technology. As a law comes to be understood, this law is lived and acted out through instrumental skill. Yet even here, in the work that man performs through his technological activity in accordance with the laws of nature, these laws remain "at work" and indeed *are* that very work itself. They become manifest as laws through the technology of man. In this case, however, unlike the case of instinct, the laws become manifest in activity by being refracted through knowledge. It is precisely this manifestation that we name technology. Here the laws become manifest on a field where knowledge and action work together and develop together. It is on such a field that the rule of law is encountered and "received."

The same can be said in the case of knowledge and technology becoming scientific. In the natural sciences, laws become known purely as laws in their abstractness and universality; the technology that contains that knowledge becomes a mechanized technology. In this case, too, the development of technology through the improvement of equipment for observation and experiment promotes the advance of scientific knowledge. And the progress of knowledge, in turn, promotes the development of technique. The tempo of this reciprocal advancement of knowledge and technology has been accelerating rapidly since the mechanization of technology. The significance of man operating in accord with the laws of nature, as well as of the laws of nature becoming manifest through and as the work of man, is more thoroughly visible in a technology dependent on machinery. It is precisely on this field of mechanical technology, where knowledge and purposive activity make the greatest advances and work in closest unity, that the fog lifts from the laws of nature to lay bare their character as laws most clearly. This field represents our closest encounter with the laws of nature. Machines and mechanical technology are man's ultimate embodiment and appropriation of the laws of nature.

The laws of nature thus become manifest on various dimensions and various fields, and we encounter them on all of these dimensions. We encounter them as much on the field of instinct, where man finds himself on a par with a dog, and on the field of physical inertia, where man finds himself on a par with a crust of bread, as we do on the field of our technological activities, where we use tools and machines. Moreover, we have come to look on the history of human "progress" as wrapped up with this distinction of levels. In a word, a blessing has been pronounced on the tendency of man to rationalize his understanding of nature through science, which includes the rationalizing of his intellect itself and of his entire actual daily life.

Now within the process I have just described, two elements are fused into one. First, the laws of nature govern all things, ranging from inanimate objects to human beings, according to the mode of being proper to each dimension. Here we see the control, that law exercises over things, permeating them on various dimensions. While inanimate things exist merely as matter, animate things are possessed of life as well; and in addition to existing as matter and life, human beings are further endowed with intellect. The control of the laws of nature that pervades these various dimensions as they unfold one after another within the domain of existence reveals a gradual deepening of the control of natural law over those things. The rational order of existence exhibits a manifold perspective whose *teleological* character becomes increasingly more marked as it ascends the levels of being until it eventually comes to complete actualization in the machine, where the purposive activity of man functions in a purely *mechanical* manner. Here the rule of the laws of nature may be said to attain its final and deepest point.

The second element is the appearance of a gradual deepening in the power of things to make use of the laws of nature parallel to the relative strength of those laws. This second aspect means that the release of things from the laws of nature, from bondage through the use of those very same laws of nature, and the freedom that this leads to becomes manifest ever more deeply in those things.

These two elements, to repeat, are linked to one another. The higher we proceed up the chain of being, the deeper the reach of the rule of law; but, at the same time, the more fully actualized the freedom of things that use those laws. Inanimate things are completely passive to the rule of law. To that extent the rule of law may be referred to as direct, albeit to that same extent shallow and external. When we come to the instinctive behavior of living things, law appears as something lived and acted out. This means that the rule of law makes its appearance in a deeper and more internalized form than it had with inanimate things. Even if the behavior and life of living things cannot take a single step away from the laws of nature, at the same time the living of these laws already represents a step in the direction of freedom from their control. In short, already in their mode of being as living things, the implication is at least faintly present that subordination to law directly entails emancipation from its bondage. The manifestation of the laws of nature and their utilization can be considered to come together immediately in "instinctive" life and behavior. Yet insofar as that unity is merely *immediate*, the world of living things remains bound by those laws.

When man uses tools and acts technically, however, the rule of the laws of nature appears in more internalized fashion. At the same time, the use of laws is also seen with greater clarity. This is so because the laws become manifest in human work through the *mediation* of intellect. It is only in human work that it is clearly seen that obedience to the laws directly implies freedom from their bondage. Nowhere is this more radically apparent than at the level where technology becomes mechanized.

Seen from one side, the emergence of the machine in or through the work of man means that the laws of nature become manifest in their most profound and obvious mode. In the machine, human work can be said to have passed beyond the character of human work itself, to have objectified itself and assumed the character of an immediate working of the laws of nature themselves.

Machines are pure products of human intellect, constructed for man's own purposes. They are nowhere to be found in the world of nature (as products of nature); yet the workings of the laws of nature find their purest expression in machines, purer than in any of the products of nature itself. The laws of nature work directly in machines, with an immediacy not to be found in the products of nature. In the machine, nature is brought back to itself in a manner more purified (abstracted) than is possible in nature itself. As such, the operations of the machine have become an expression of the work of man. With an abstractness more pure than anything in the products of nature, that is to say, with a kind of abstractness impossible for natural events, the expression of the laws of nature has become an expression of the work of man. This shows the *depth* of the control of the laws of nature. These laws disclose their domination most deeply in their permeation of the life and work of man, so deeply as to pass beyond the pale of the "human" and return once again to nature itself (in its abstracted mode). This is the very deepest mode in which the rule of the laws of nature appears to things in general.

Seen from the other side, however, the emergence of the machine marks the supreme emancipation from the rule of the laws of nature, the supreme apparition of freedom in using those laws. In the machine the work of man is completely objectified; purposive human agency is incorporated, as it were, within nature as part of the things of nature, and thereby the control over nature is radicalized. It is a rule over nature more far-reaching than the self-rule of nature itself. Hence, we see here in greatest clarity a relationship according to which subordination to the control of law directly implies liberation from it. It is the field of a relationship that first comes to light in the machine and expresses itself through the machine.

II

Of utmost importance for us here, however, is a serious problem that has come about since the relationship between the laws of nature and things entered its final stage with the emergence of the machine. Simply put, that relationship is now in a process of inversion. We are in a situation in which we must speak of the controller becoming the controlled.

As noted in the previous section, the rule of the laws of nature intensifies as we ascend to higher levels of being, and this means at the same time that things gradually free themselves from the control of those laws and come instead to make use of them for a *telos* of their own. In this sense, a relationship of control obtains on both sides: laws rule over things and things rule over laws. With the emergence of the machine, the relationship reached an extreme which in turn has given rise to a new situation.

On the one hand, on the field where the machine emerges into being, that is, where the rule of the laws of nature has become fully present deep in the work of man and the very things of his life, human life and work as a whole have become progressively mechanized and impersonalized. The field on which man located himself when he produced the machine and which has ever since been growing more extensive, is a field of mutual alliance between two factors: on the side of man, an abstract intellect seeking scientific rationality; and on the side of nature, what we might call a "denaturalized" nature that I described above as "purer than nature itself." This field is gradually coming to look like something that deprives man of his very humanity. When this relationship of reciprocal control between the laws of nature and the things of nature reaches its extreme in the machine, it does so on a field that goes beyond the original, natural ties between man and the world of nature. It is a relationship that breaks down the barrier between the humanness of man and the naturalness of nature, and in so doing is fully radicalized. But at the same time a profound perversion takes place at this very extreme: an inversion of the more elemental relationship in which man took control of the laws of nature by means of the control that those laws wrought over the life and work of man; here the laws of nature come to reassume control over man who controls the laws of nature. This situation is usually referred to as the tendency toward the *mechanization* of man, toward the loss of the human. Needless to say, it points to one of the basic features constituting the contemporary "crisis of culture."

On the other hand, this inverted relationship points up another situation tied in to that of the mechanization of man. Just as the mechanization of man is an inversion of his rule over the laws of nature, so too an inversion occurs in the rule of the laws of nature over man. Here the rule of the laws of nature, arrived at the extreme of a profound, internal control of man, opens up a mode of being in which man behaves as if he stood entirely outside of the laws of nature. Simply put, it is a mode of being at whose ground nihility opens up. Eventually the field on which the machine comes into being—referred to above as a field of mutual alliance between abstract intellect in quest of scientific rationality and denaturalized nature—discloses nihility both at the ground of man who relies on that intellect and at the ground of the world of nature.

Only by taking a stance on this nihility is man able to find complete freedom from the laws of nature and to disengage himself from their radical control. It is, we might say, a standpoint from which man looks at the laws of nature as if they were entirely external to him. From time immemorial man has spoken of a life in keeping with the law or order of nature. Here that mode of being is completely broken through. In its place there appears a mode of being wherein a man situates himself on the freedom of nihility and behaves as if he were using the laws of nature entirely from without. It is the mode of being of the subject that has adapted itself to a life of raw and impetuous desire, of naked vitality. In this sense it takes on a form close to "instinct"; but as the mode of being of a subject situated on nihility, it is, in fact, diametrically opposed to "instinct."

Now, this mode of being of the subject, which adapts itself to the naked vitality of life while standing its ground on nihility, exhibits a variety of forms, depending on the depth or shallowness of its adaptation. For instance, nihility lurks beneath the contemporary tendencies of great masses of people to devote themselves passionately to the races, to sports, and to other amusements. Though it merely float about in the atmosphere of life without clearly coming to awareness, yet it is there—as a "crypto-nihilism."[1] Or again, there is the type of nihilism that shows up in the solitary Existenz that turns away from the trends of the masses to opt for nihility as the ground of being with clear consciousness and decisiveness. Between these two fall a whole spectrum of nihilisms. But all of them have this in common: they belong to a mode of being that both stands steadfast on nihility and points to a subject given over to the naked vitality of life. It is a mode of being in which man uses the laws of nature as if he stood entirely outside of them. This mode of being human represents the inversion of the rule of the laws of nature pushed to its extreme.

The laws of nature rule over man in the very process of becoming manifest through the work of man. This is the "rationalization" of human life that has been assumed from the Age of Enlightenment in the eighteenth century right up to the present to represent the progress of man. In fact, however, from the ground of this rationalized human life, life itself—in the sense of something altogether preceding rationalization—has gradually come to appear as resting on a nihility that looks to be altogether inaccessible to rationalization. Keeping pace with the advance of the rationalization of life, yet standing behind it, another standpoint continues to gather strength: the growing affirmation of a prereflective human mode of being that is totally non-rational and non-spiritual, the stance of the subject that locates itself on nihility as it pursues its own desires unreservedly. This, too, constitutes one of the basic elements of the contemporary crisis of culture.

No matter which side one looks at things from, therefore, the inversion of controller and controlled keeps rearing its head. At the extreme of the freedom of the self in controlling the laws of nature, man shows the countertendency to forfeit his human nature and to mechanize it. At the extreme of the wholesale controls that the laws of nature exercise through human work, these laws come under the control of man as a subject in pursuit of desires, of one who behaves as if he stood outside of all law and control. The emergence of the mechanization of human life and the transformation of man into a completely non-rational subject in pursuit of its desires are fundamentally bound up with one another.

Accordingly, it is within mechanical technology—that is, within the disclosure at the interior of human life of the field where the machine emerges into being—that the sort of situation referred to earlier in which the subordination to law directly implies an emancipation from law unveils its most radical Form. But at the same time, the truly real Form of the situation is perverted and kept hidden from view. What ought to be the original Form of the relationship between man and nature seems instead to have been perverted into its opposite. This is what is meant by the frequently heard claim that man is being dragged along by the machines he himself has built. This also underlies the problem of the imbalance between the progress of science and the progress of human morality. The crux of the matter is not so much an imbalance as a movement in opposite directions.

Obviously, these things show up in more intensified form in the problem of nuclear weaponry. And even should we go on to extend our argument from the mechanization of man and his transformation into a subject in pursuit of its own desires to include historical and social issues, such as the various forms of political institutions in the contemporary world, we end up in the same problematic. In communist countries, the political institution exhibits a tendency toward totalitarianism that implies an orientation to the mechanization of institutions as well as of man. In liberalist countries, the freedom of individuals under democracy is apt to be oriented to the mere freedom of the subject in pursuit of its desires. These two differing orientations, however, derive from the same source and are bound up with one another. Here again, viewed as a whole, the problem of a mechanized civilization and political institutions can be traced back finally to one and the same source: the point from which contemporary nihilism is being generated, whether in overt or cryptic fashion.

As we noted earlier on, in our own day and age nihilism takes its start from an awakening to a meaninglessness at the ground of the world and man himself. It is an awareness that has accompanied the appearance of the mechanistic image of the world of modern science and the tendency toward the mechanization of man that has increasingly permeated not only the social structures of the modern world but the inner life of man as well. There is a tendency for human life to be mechanized socially as well as psychologically, to be perceived itself as a kind of mechanism; only as a subject in pursuit of its desires and situating itself (aware or not) on the nihility that has opened up at the bottom of that mechanism, has man succeeded in helping his self-existence escape from being dissolved into a mechanism.

To repeat, the perversion that occurred in the original relationship of man to the laws of nature has taken the shape of a fundamental intertwining of the mechanization of man and his transformation into a subject in pursuit of its desires, at the ground of which nihility has opened up as a sense of the meaninglessness of the whole business. This nihility itself has come to look like a fitting accompaniment to the basic situation in which man finds himself in the contemporary world. Accordingly, it is not something that can escape our notice. If we look at our own existence as it is, without deluding ourselves, there is no way to avoid becoming aware of it. It is for this reason that many contemporary existentialists, out of a sense of honesty to their own self-being, have decisively and of their own accord set their feet firmly on nihility. This sort of positive nihilism in existentialism represents a clear intent to step away from the mechanization of man and from the degradation of man to the level of a subject in pursuit of its desires inherent in a nihilism that has yet to reach self-awareness. In other words, it exhibits the effort to climb up out of the pit into which man is slipping in our times through the perversion of his original relationship to nature.

At the same time, man cannot escape that perversion so long as he takes a stand on nihility, because it was precisely through that perversion that nihility came to light: the pit that lies open at the bottom of that perversion is nothing other than nihility itself. Nihility cannot shake free of nihility by itself. Therefore, nihilism is thwarted in its positive intentions by the very nihility on which it stands so steadfastly. This, we may say, is the standpoint of the dilemma that nihilism and the realization of nihility entail. Moreover, if this nihilism can be said to have come about from the rule of the laws of nature and the regulative role played by science and technology as they affect how man relates to the world and to himself, we can also say that in this nihilism, and the dilemma it involves, the problem of science and religion takes shape in its most condensed and fundamental form.

III

In the preceding section we spoke of the control of science and scientific technology, or, more fundamentally, of the field on which they are constituted: the mutual alliance of abstract, impersonal intellect and the mechanistic image of the world. We also had something to say regarding the consequent emergence of a twofold tendency toward the mechanization of the inner life and social relationships of man on the one hand, and the transformation of man into a subject in pursuit of its desires on the other. In a word, we have dealt with the tendency toward the loss of the human.

The traditional religions conceive of God and man and the relationship between them in personal terms. Faced with contemporary problems, these religions have struck on a singularly fundamental and difficult question. To elevate the standpoint of the personality or spirit of man is, of course, to oppose the tendency toward the loss of the human. That much is indispensable to the mode of being proper to man. It is also why ethics, art, and philosophy are of such great significance. In a certain sense, it is even possible to draw a basic line of opposition that puts these things on one side and the control of science on the other. In addition, at the root of the personal-spiritual realm a relationship to God as absolute personality or absolute spirit was seen to obtain, and this religious relationship alone was considered capable of providing the personality and spirit of man with an unshakable foundation.

The orientation opposed to the sovereignty of science has drawn its impulse, for the most part, from this realm of religion. Consequently, resistance against the tendency toward the loss of the human has up until now assumed the form of setting limits to the standpoint of science from a position based in the realm of things religious. Traces of such efforts are to be found everywhere in the history of philosophy since Descartes. This is so because personality or spirit constitutes the core of what is genuinely human.

As noted earlier, however, the image of the natural world has undergone a complete change since the Renaissance as a result of the development of the natural sciences. The world has come to appear completely unfeeling and altogether indifferent to human interests.

The world has cut across the personal relationship between God and man. As a result, talk of a world order dependent on God, of a providence in history, and even of the very existence of God has become alien to the mind of man. Man grows increasingly indifferent to such notions as these and eventually to his own humanness as well. Man continues to be dehumanized and mechanized.

Faced with such a situation, and looking at it merely from the standpoint of personality or spirit, or from that of the personal relationship between God and man, we cannot help but think we are up against something beyond all solution. At this point the demand arises for a transpersonal field to open up—beyond the standpoint of personality or spirit, and yet the only sort of field on which personality and spirit can become manifest. Furthermore, because we detected an element of transpersonality in the Christian notion of God, it was possible to see in the omnipresence of God in the world, or in the non-differentiating love or "perfection" of God that makes the sun to rise on good and evil alike, a personal-impersonal quality. Eckhart pointed to such a standpoint in explaining the "essence" of the personal God as absolute nothingness. He conceived of it as the kind of field of absolute negativity that even breaks through subjectivity (in the sense of the personality) as something lying directly underfoot of our subjectivity, and at the same time as the kind of field of absolute affirmation on which our personality also becomes manifest. In a word, he took it as a field of absolute death-*sive*-life.

Such a field cannot lie on a far side, beyond *this* world and *this* earthly life of ours, as something merely transcendent. It must lie on the near side, even more so than we ourselves and our own lives in the here and now are ordinarily supposed to be. The "detachment" that Eckhart spoke of as a radical departure not only from self and world but even from "God"—the flight from God for the sake of God—must rest, as it were, in an absolutely transcendent near side. He himself claimed that the ground of God lies within the self, nearer to the self than the self is to itself.

In the Buddhist standpoint of *śūnyatā* ("emptiness"), this point comes to light still more clearly. Śūnyatā is the point at which we become manifest in our own suchness as concrete human beings, as individuals with both body and personality. And at the same time, it is the point at which everything around us becomes manifest in its own suchness. As noted before, it can also be spoken of as the point at which the words "In the Great Death heaven and earth become new" can simultaneously signify a rebirth of the self. Even though this be spoken of as a "rebirth," what is meant here is the appearance of the self in its original countenance. It is the return of the self to itself in its original mode of being.

Might it not be, then, that we need to revert to such a standpoint in order for the sort of relationship referred to earlier—in which subordination to the rule of law is at once an emancipation from it—to come about properly? And is it not further the case that the possibility of human existence also properly emerges only in connection with the enabling of this relationship in its proper sense? In other words, is this not the only place that a standpoint is to be found that is properly capable of overcoming a situation in which, as a result of the sovereignty of science, that relationship has become perverted and given impulse to the loss of the human? Is it not here that we find a standpoint properly able to conquer the nihilism generated by the perversion of that relationship?

IV

The claim has just been made that śūnyatā represents an absolutely transcendent field, and, at the same time, a field that is not situated on the far side of where we find ourselves, but on our near side, more so than we are with respect to ourselves; and further, that its disclosure represents a conversion properly described as absolute death-*sive*-life. It is in the nature of this death-*sive*-life that it be dealt with seriously and honestly, and in as radical a fashion as possible.

Talk of birth through death has long been and continues to be a part of many religions. We hear of things like dying to finite life to be reborn into eternal life, and dying to self to live in God. In these cases, as observed earlier, the main stress falls on the side of life. What is called "soul" or "spirit" or "personality" has long been seen from the side of life, as well. (This holds true even in the case of the dead, whose souls or spirits are spoken of as "ghosts.") Given such an orientation, the life of animate things was located a rank above the inanimate level of things. Along this same line, the notion of a gradual *ascent* to soul, spirit, and personality came about, an ascent that culminates in one final leap to the standpoint of religion as a personal relationship between God and man.

In contrast, the orientation that puts the stress on death is spoken of in terms of a *reduction* that proceeds backward through personality, spirit, soul, and life to arrive at inanimate things, where everything is considered to be based upon and reducible to materiality. The scientific way of looking at things is fundamentally constituted on such an orientation. As noted above, it culminates in a leap to the nihility and meaninglessness that opens up at the ground of all things, including life itself, and the awareness of these things, in turn, gives rise to nihilism.

So brief a sketch as this is obviously inadequate to the complexities involved. For instance, insofar as all things are considered to have been created *ex nihilo*, as in Christian teaching, the personal relationship of God and man comes into being as a kind of salvation by means of an eternal life that is bestowed from beyond by breaking through that *nihilum*. Since such a notion of salvation implies birth through a death, it therefore contains something that cannot simply be classified as part of the orientation of life.

Or again, when a man commits himself to be himself uncompromisingly, without God and simply as the finite being that he is, the nihility or death experienced as an absolute separation from God shows up in his self-awareness as a sin that leads him in revolt against God. Sin is, as it were, death or nihility in sublimated form, come to light in an existence aware of itself. The roots of this "original sin" spread out beyond the spirit and personality of "natural" man and reach deep into his soul and animal life as well. Hence salvation as the forgiveness of sin implies the conquest of nihility and death in that basic sublimated and comprehensive form. Birth through death can also be spoken of in this more fundamental sense. The orientation to life we spoke of, therefore, can only arrive at the realm of religion by profoundly overcoming death—in a sort of leap.

In contrast, while the opposing orientation to death permits us to speak of meaninglessness and nihility opening up at the ground of all things, including life itself, this does not simply mean that God is lost sight of with only the *nihilum* of the *creatio ex nihilo* left behind. Nor does it mean that a nihility is felt simply behind the "being" of finite beings. Were this the case, we should still find ourselves in one of the typical forms of traditional nihilism. In contemporary nihilism, this nihility extends, as we said before, into the field of the very existence of God whence it deepens into an abyss. On that abyssal, godless nihility, all life whatsoever, be it animal life and the soul, or even spiritual-personal life, takes on the features of a fundamental meaninglessness.

But at the same time, on such a view man enables himself to attain to true subjectivity and to become truly free and independent only when he commits himself decisively to take a stand on that abyss of nihility. Nihility is seen, then, as the field of the ecstatic transcendence of human existence, that is, the field on which human Existenz comes into being. It is on this field that Existenz assumes responsibility for creating new meanings for the meaninglessness and nihility of life and existence. It is here that Existenz seeks to draw forth the strength to affirm life in all its absurdity from the impassioned commitment to stand its ground unswervingly amidst the absurdity of life. In place of the image of God, the image of the "Overman" or the image of the fully human "man" is generally held up here as the object of man's intrinsic intentions.

In any case, something within nihilism shows up when viewed in terms of Existenz that we cannot deal with merely in terms of the orientation to death: the point at which nihility becomes the ground-work for a new (existential) mode of being, at which dying becomes the groundwork for a new and different way of living. This is why we stated that nihilism comes to light through a leap beyond the orientation to death out of which the scientific point of view was generated.

In brief, matters are never very pure and simple when we have to do with standpoints oriented to life or to death. Still, in spite of everything, it seems to me that traditional religions spin on a life-oriented axis, while the line running from the scientific viewpoint to nihilism represents a death-oriented axis. Perhaps this will seem clearer if we contrast them both with the standpoint of śūnyatā alluded to earlier.

To repeat what was said there, the emergence of any given thing in the Form of its true suchness can be considered as the point at which the orientation to life and the orientation to death intersect. Everything can be seen as a kind of "double exposure" of life and death, of being and nihility. In saying this, I do not have in mind the sort of thing Plato did in speaking of things in the sensible world as impermanent entities in constant flux because of a "mixture" of being and non-being. Neither do I mean that being and non-being mingle together in each thing as if they were quantitative elements; and certainly not that death comes about when life wears down to its end, or that nihility appears when being disappears. I mean instead that while life remains life to the very end, and death remains death, they both become manifest in any given thing, and therefore that the aspect of life and the aspect of death in a given thing can be superimposed in such a way that both become simultaneously visible. In this sense, such a mode of being might be termed life-*sive*-death, death-*sive*-life. It should then seem natural to continue to look at something directly and see life-*sive*-death or death-*sive*-life as its proper Form without ever having to turn away from the actual Form of the thing itself.

In the two orientations contrasted above, the one tries to grasp the real form of things such as they are on a life-oriented axis, the other on a death-oriented axis. The former brings about an upward developing viewpoint, ascending from life and soul to spirit or personality. Ultimately, the "death" implied throughout spirit or personality, soul, and life rises to awareness as sin (or "original sin," as it is called in Christian teaching) in the sense of a disobedience or a rebellion against God who is absolute life. Meantime, the standpoint of a personal communion with God, in which death is overcome by passing through the bottom of death, appears as the result of a final leap.

The death orientation seeks to reduce everything to material relationships. Ultimately, the "life" implied throughout all of life and soul and spirit or personality, emerges into self-awareness as meaninglessness. In this case, it is the standpoint of Existenz in the midst of nihilism—where meaninglessness is overcome by passing through the bottom of nihilism—that appears in a final leap.

But now, what would happen if we were to stick to looking at things directly, as they are in their proper Form of life-*sive*-death, death-*sive*-life? It might be that a leap would take place here, too, though it would not be a leap upward along a line of development ascending toward personality, nor a leap downward along a line of reduction descending toward materiality. Rather, it would have to take place directly underfoot of the proper Form of things as life-*sive*-death, death-*sive*-life. This would give rise to a viewpoint completely different from those that distinguish various stages or levels in between material and personality, and which lead to talk of "ascent" to higher stages or "reduction" to lower ones. We would then be able to come up with a standpoint in which personality and materiality, usually considered as altogether mutually exclusive, could be seen in a sort of "double exposure," free of the fixed idea normally attached to them. This could also be called a standpoint of absolute "equality," in which personality, while continuing to be personality, would nonetheless be seen as equal to material things; and material things, while retaining their materiality, would nonetheless be seen as equal to personality.

It is the very standpoint of śūnyatā itself that enables such a viewpoint to come about. But what does all of this mean? How does it come to be a standpoint of śūnyatā? To answer these questions it is necessary to turn our attention first of all to the difference between the standpoint of nihility on which nihilism positions itself, and the standpoint of śūnyatā.

V

As we have already had occasion to observe, the traditional view of personality has looked at personality from the point of view of personality itself: as a personality grasping itself from itself. This means that up until now, our view of personality has been constituted with a self-centered prehension of personality as its nucleus. This way of understanding personality, as personality's self-centered prehension of itself, can already be said to represent a form of captivity or self-attachment. Accordingly, in the preceding chapter I came to speak of a standpoint of absolute nothingness or emptiness that would break through this self-attachment and deny the self-centered prehension of personality. I went on further to speak of personality as becoming manifest in its Form of true suchness only in unison with absolute nothingness, which is its original mode of being. Yet this standpoint of absolute nothingness, we saw, does not lie on the far side of what we are accustomed to call our own personality or ego; it opens up instead on the near side, as the absolute near side, so to speak. This emptiness, or śūnyatā, is another thing altogether from the nihility of nihilism.

In the preceding section we saw how in modern nihilism, nihility has deepened into an abyss: the nihility that one becomes aware of at the ground of the self and the world extends all the way to the locus of the divine. Nihilism here makes the claim that only by taking a stance on nihility can man truly attain to subjectivity and freedom. With this subjectivization of the abyss of nihility, a realm opened up at the ground of the self-existence of man beyond the pale of the divine order hitherto considered to be essentially in control of the self, a realm that allows nothing to preside over it, not even God. Here the autonomy of man truly came into being for the first time. The anxiety of having nothing to rely on, the sense of instability at being deprived of all basis for settling down firmly and peacefully, was directly transformed as such into the standpoint of a creative freedom that did not affix itself to anything existing up to that time. For the self-existence of man, nihility became a field of ecstatic self-detachment. Nihilism had become existential.

In spite of this, however, the representation of nothingness in nihilism still shows traces of the bias of objectification, of taking nothingness as some "thing" called nothingness. To be sure, this does not mean that nothingness was reified in such a way as to question the existential standpoint of nihilism, the subjectivized standpoint of nihility, or even the seemingly subjective existence of nihility. The notion of nothingness or the representation of nothingness are simply not problems in such a context. The nihilism we are speaking of takes a firm stance on the awareness of the real experience of nihility at the foundation of ourselves and of all things. It is a standpoint in which we ourselves *become* nihility, a standpoint which, to revert to earlier remarks, can itself be called the "realization" of nihility.

Nevertheless, nihility is still being viewed here from the bias of self-existence as the groundlessness (*Grundlosigkeit*) of existence lying at the ground of self-existence. This means that it is seen lying outside of the "existence" of the self, and therefore also as something more than that "existence," or distinct from it. We find this, for example, even in Heidegger's talk of self-existence as "held suspended in nothingness," despite the fundamental difference of his standpoint from other brands of contemporary existentialism or nihilism. The very fact that he speaks of the "abyss" of nihility already tells us as much. In Heidegger's case, traces of the representation of nothingness as some "thing" that is nothingness still remain.

Here again, though, the representation of nothingness is not the issue. What is at issue is rather the nihility we find opening up before us at the ground of self-existence when we take a stand there, a nihility that really stretches out like an abyss over which the existence of the self is held in suspense. The point here is simply that nihility is always a nihility *for self-existence*, that is to say, a nihility that we contact when we posit ourselves on the side of the "existence" of our self-existence. From this it follows that nihility comes to be represented as something outside of the existence of the self and all things, as some "thing" absolutely other than existence, some "thing" called nothingness. The problem is that traces of the common view that simply sets nothingness over against existence as a mere conceptual negation persist. The longstanding Western view of nothingness has yet to divest itself of this way of thinking. The śūnyatā we speak of points to a fundamentally different viewpoint.

Emptiness in the sense of śūnyatā is emptiness only when it empties itself even of the standpoint that represents it as some "thing" that is emptiness. It is, in its original Form, self-emptying. In this meaning, true emptiness is not to be posited as something outside of and other than "being." Rather, it is to be realized as something united to and self-identical with being.

When we say "being-*sive*-nothingness," or "form is emptiness; emptiness is form," we do not mean that what are initially conceived of as *being* on one side and *nothingness* on the other have later been joined together. In the context of Mahāyāna thought, the primary principle of which is to transcend all duality emerging from logical analysis, the phrase "being-*sive*-nothingness" requires that one take up the stance of the "*sive*" and from there view being as being and nothingness as nothingness. Ordinarily, of course, we occupy a standpoint shackled to being, from which being is viewed solely as being. Should such a standpoint be broken through and denied, nihility appears. But this standpoint of nihility in turn becomes a standpoint shackled to nothingness, from which nothingness is viewed solely as nothingness, so that it, too, needs to be negated. It is here that emptiness, as a standpoint of absolute non-attachment liberated from this double confinement, comes to the fore.

Viewed in terms of this process, śūnyatā represents the endpoint of an orientation to negation. It can be termed an *absolute negativity*, inasmuch as it is a standpoint that has negated and thereby transcended nihility, which was itself the transcendence-through-negation of all being. It can also be termed an *absolute transcendence of being*, as it absolutely denies and distances itself from any standpoint shackled in any way whatsoever to being. In this sense, emptiness can well be described as "outside" of and absolutely "other" than the standpoint shackled to being, provided we avoid the misconception that emptiness is some "thing" distinct from being and subsisting "outside" of it.

In spite of its transcendence of the standpoint shackled to being, or rather because of it, emptiness can only appear as a self-identity with being, in a relationship of *sive* by which both being and emptiness are seen as co-present from the start and structurally inseparable from one another. Hence, talk of transcendence does not entail withdrawing off to some transcendent "thing" called emptiness or nothingness. Emptiness lies absolutely on the near side, more so than what we normally regard as our own self. Emptiness, or nothingness, is not something we can turn to. It is not something "out there" in front of us. It defies objective representation; no sooner do we assume such an attitude toward it than emptiness withdraws into hiding.

It has often been pointed out that the subjectivity of the ego resolutely refuses to be viewed objectively. And yet, the self shows a constant tendency to comprehend itself representationally as some "thing" that is called "I." This tendency is inherent in the very essence of the ego as self-consciousness. Therefore it marks a great step forward when the standpoint of Existenz-in-ecstasy, held suspended in nothingness, appears as a standpoint of truly subjective self-existence. Nonetheless, traces of the representation of nothingness as the positing of some "thing" that is nothingness are still to be seen here. The standpoint of śūnyatā, however, is absolutely nonobjectifiable, since it transcends this subjectivistic nihility to a point more on the near side than the subjectivity of existential nihilism.

For these reasons, what we have called the abyss of nihility can only be constituted in emptiness. Even for nihility to be so *represented* is possible only in emptiness. In this sense, just as nihility is an abyss for anything that exists, emptiness may be said to be an abyss even for that abyss of nihility. As a valley unfathomably deep may be imagined set within an endless expanse of sky, so it is with nihility and emptiness. But the sky we have in mind here is more than the vault above that spreads out far and wide over the valley below. It is a cosmic sky enveloping the earth and man and the countless legions of stars that move and have their being within it. It lies beneath the ground we tread, its bottom reaching beneath the valley's bottom. If the place where the omnipresent God resides be called heaven, then heaven would also have to reach beneath the bottomless pit of hell: heaven would be an abyss for hell. This is the sense in which emptiness is an abyss for the abyss of nihility.

Furthermore, the abyss of emptiness opens up more to the near side, more immediately here and now than what we call ego, or subjectivity. Just as we overlook the cosmic sky that envelops us while we move and have our being within it, and stare only at the patch of sky overhead, so too we fail to realize that we stand more to the near side of ourselves in emptiness than we do in self-consciousness.

From what has been said so far regarding the basic differences between the standpoint of śūnyatā and contemporary nihilism, it should be clear that the former is not atheistic in the same sense as the latter. Still less is it akin to the atheisms of positivism or materialism, which are of an altogether different orientation from that of nihilism. In virtue of what it denies, the standpoint of emptiness expressed in such phrases as "being-*sive*-emptiness," or "form is emptiness, emptiness is form," transcends nihilism on the one hand, and materialism and positivism on the other. And yet to be sure, it seems to imply the possibility of bringing into higher synthesis the basic orientations and motives contained in the two opposing standpoints. This problem will be touched upon later.

If the standpoint of śūnyatā is not an atheism in the usual sense of the word, even less should it be classed as a form of what is normally called theism. In the preceding chapter, Eckhart exemplified a standpoint that does not set up an either/or alternative between theism and atheism. While taking the personal relationship of God and man as a living relationship between the "image of God" in the soul and its "original image," he refers to the "essence" of God that is free of all form—the completely "image-free" (bildlos) godhead—as "nothingness," and considers the soul to return to itself and acquire absolute freedom only when it becomes totally one with the "nothingness" of godhead. This is not mere theism, but neither, of course, is it mere atheism. (For this reason, it was even mistakenly called pantheism.) As the "ground" of the personal God, this "nothingness" lay on the far side, in the background of God, and yet was immediately realized as being "my ground," lying directly on the near side, at the foreground of the self. We find here in Eckhart a turn to the sort of standpoint I spoke of as the absolute near side. The standpoint of śūnyatā appears when such a turn has been achieved clearly and distinctly.

To be sure, even in Buddhism, where we find the standpoint of emptiness expounded, a transcendence to the far side, or the "yonder shore," is spoken of. But this yonder shore may be called an absolute near side in the sense that it has gone beyond the usual opposition of the near and the far. Indeed, the distinguishing feature of Buddhism consists in its being the religion of the absolute near side.

In the case of Eckhart, the "nothingness" in which God's ground is my own, and my ground is God's own, is the field that brings about a personal relationship between God and man. It is on this field of "nothingness" that the actual Form—the visible Form or Bild—of everything that exists, including God, comes to light. Only in this "nothingness" is everything that is represented as God or soul, and the relationships between them, made possible.

It is the same with the standpoint of emptiness. As I said before, only in emptiness does the abyss of nihility appear, and only in emptiness can it be represented as an abyss. Moreover, it is only on the field of this same emptiness that God and man, and the relationships between them, are constituted in a personal Form, and that their respective representations are made possible. And still this field of emptiness opens up on the absolute near side of what is spoken of as our ego or subjectivity.

VI

It may sound like a curious, almost fantastic, bit of folly to claim that emptiness is the only field upon which such things as what modern nihilism calls the abyss of nothingness and what older religions have called the personal relationship of God and man, come into view and then to describe this emptiness as an absolute near side. Perhaps it is, to our everyday point of view or to philosophical and theological ways of thinking. But is this really the case? Might it not be instead that the stuff of "fantasy"—in its original meaning as representation or image-making—still survives in talk of an abyss and a personal relationship between God and man?

Of course, to say that image-making and representative features remain does not imply that we are dealing here merely with mental images, mere products of the imagination, as Feuerbach and other critics of religion would have it. Nihility is not a subjectivistic feeling or fantasy or idea, but a reality every bit as real as our actual existence. Nor is nihility something removed from the ordinary level on which we live. It is something in which we find ourselves every day. Simply because our every day is all too "everyday," because we are so stuck in our everydayness, we fail to pay attention to the reality of nihility.

We like to feel that we are close to our family and friends and know them well. But do we really, after all, essentially know those whom we are most familiar with? The failure to know a person "essentially" does not refer to what happens when one man fails to understand the inmost heart of another, even though the two be close to one another; nor to the fact that even between the most intimate of companions misunderstandings inevitably occur. If that were our meaning, we could not even claim to adequately understand our own inmost hearts and our own personalities.

I use the word "essentially" rather in a sense related to the "home-ground" of a familiar individual as he becomes manifest directly before us. We no more know whence our closest friend comes and whither he is going than we know where we ourselves come from and where we are headed. At his home-ground, a friend remains originally and essentially a stranger, an "unknown." Of course, my friend is not a stranger in the sense of a person I chance to meet along the roadside in the course of my journeys. I know him well and am close to him. Nevertheless, this familiarity of ours is essentially a familiarity breached by an absolute abyss, compared to which even a stranger along the roadside is the most intimate of friends. Essentially speaking, then, all men, be they the most intimate of friends or the most distant of acquaintances, are exactly to the same degree "unknown."

This is not only true of men. Take the tiny flower blooming away out in my garden. It grew from a single seed and will one day return to the earth, never again to return so long as this world exists. Yet we do not know where its pretty little face appeared from nor where it will disappear to. Behind it lies absolute nihility: the same nihility that lies behind us, the same nihility that lies in the space between flowers and men. Separated from me by the abyss of that nihility, the flower in my garden is an unknown entity.

People give names to persons and things, and then suppose that if they know the names, they know that which the names refer to. So, too, people presume that just because they "have seen" something before, they know what it is. The deeper our "association" with certain persons and things, the more we converse with them and mix with them, so much the better do we get to know them and to become more intimate with them. They become *our* acquaintances, *our* family members, *our* primroses.

Seen essentially, that is, as existing in nihility and as manifest in nihility, everything and everyone is nameless, unnameable, and un- knowable. Now the reality of this nihility is covered over in an every- day world which is in its proper element when it traffics in names. The home-ground of existence passes into oblivion. The world about us comes to consist only of what already is, or else can become, known and familiar. It becomes an all too "everyday" world. We get stuck in our familiarity with it. We forget the essence of persons and things even as we mingle with them.

But what is it like, this abyss of nihility that distances us from even what is closest to us? It lies behind everything in the world. Even the galaxies and nebulae cannot divest themselves of it. And this cosmic nihility is the very same nihility that distances us from one another. Even as we sit chatting with one another, the stars and planets of the Milky Way whirl about us in the bottomless breach that separates us from one another. There is a sense in which we who sit together in the same room each stand apart from the entire universe. One sits in front of another with body and mind manifest in nihility such that one cannot say whence the other comes nor whither he is going. This is the abyss of nihility.

If emptiness is seen as an abyss even to that abyss of nihility, then what has just been said of the abyss of nihility also applies to emptiness in a truly absolute sense. In the mode of being where form is emptiness and emptiness form, "forms" (that is, all things) are absolutely nameless, absolutely unknown and unknowable, distanced from one another by an absolute breach. In contrast to the field of nihility on which the desolate and bottomless abyss distances even the most intimate of persons or things from one another, on the field of emptiness that absolute breach points directly to a most intimate encounter with everything that exists. Emptiness is the field on which an essential encounter can take place between entities normally taken to be most distantly related, even at enmity with each other, no less than between those that are most closely related.

This encounter is called "essential" because it takes place at the source of existence common to the one and the other and yet at a point where each is truly itself. It is here that all things can encounter one another on a level of equality beyond distinctions of gratitude and revenge, free of differences between ill will and good. Indeed, it is even inadequate to speak any longer of an "encounter." Just as a single beam of white light breaks up into rays of various colors when it passes through a prism, so we have here an absolute self-identity in which the one and the other are yet truly themselves, at once abolutely broken apart and absolutely joined together. They are an absolute *two* and at the same time an absolute *one*. In the words of the Zen Master Daitō Kokushi: "Separated from one another by a hundred million kalpas, yet not apart a single moment; sitting face-to-face all day long, yet not opposed for an instant." Later on I should like to return to a more detailed discussion of such a mode of being in the field of emptiness.

VII

The absolute near side referred to above is entirely united to and self-identical with what we ourselves are as body and mind. It is like the poem of Gasan Jōseki cited in an earlier chapter:

> The heart and mind of this shadowy man
> At all occasions is to me most familiar—
> From long ago mysteriously wondrous,
> It is neither I nor other.

This has often been explained with the help of the ancient metaphor of waves and water. The waves that roll on one after another in endless succession all return to the one great water, which in turn swells up again into its waves. No "waves" exist apart from their water, nor does "water" exist apart from its waves. Rather, at the point that water and waves are self-identical (as water-waves), this flowing wetness emerges into reality for what it is, water there being water and waves there being waves. And this is precisely the point that we are calling the field of the absolute near side.

Insofar as we do not transfer to this near side, however, stopping short at being as entities possessed of body and mind, or even as rational or personal entities, the absolute near side remains forever a far side absolutely beyond us. Yet this is none other than the mode of being that we ordinarily find ourselves in.

In this ordinary mode of being—that is, insofar as we stop short at being entities possessed of body and mind, or at being rational or personal entities—our body-mind (fundamentally, our self-consciousness) grasps itself from itself; our reason grasps itself from the posture of reason; and our personality grasps itself from within the personality itself. In each case we can speak of a self-immanent self-prehension or a self-centeredness, at the core of what is taking place. In each case the body-and-mind, reason, or personality constitutes a self-enclosed confinement and self-entangled unity. What is more, that core of self-prehension remains forever shackled, as we observed before, to its own narcissism. It is a grasping *of* the self *by* the self, a confinement of the self by the self that spells attachment *to* the self. Even reason and personality do not emerge without being accompanied by self-attachment in this essential (or ontological) sense.

The prehension of the self by the self is forever an act that we ourselves perform. As beings possessed of body and psyche we grasp ourselves and thereby get caught by ourselves in our own bodies and minds. As rational or personal beings, we grasp ourselves and thereby get caught by our own reason or personality. While this is our own act, it is not something we are free to do as we please. It is not a mere act of will that we can arbitrarily cease any time we so desire. The force of destiny is at work here, impelling us to be and to act in this manner. The whole variety of possible beings possessed of body and mind, and all possible rational or personal beings appearing in this world, demonstrate this mode of being and perform in this manner. Universal life, consciousness, reason, and personality emerge from the depths of the world to become immanent and individualized in every being, each of whom falls into narcissistic self-attachment. This force of destiny is not a destiny in the ordinary sense of something that simply rules over us and controls us from without. Nor is it merely something like blind will. It is a destiny that appears only in the shape of the acts we ourselves perform, only as one with our own actions.

At any rate, so long as we stop short at being entities possessed of body and mind, or at being rational or personal entities, we remain within our own grasp. To that extent we are essentially self-attached. In other words, we shut ourselves off from the standpoint of emptiness which is our absolute near side. Again, to that same extent the absolute near side remains forever an absolute far side for us. The basic determinant of our ordinary mode of being consists precisely of this self-attachment and self-confinement.

In my view, it is in this sort of situation that the far side truly carries its absoluteness for us. In other circumstances, by comparison, the far side is not yet absolute. For instance, when Plato conceives of a world of Ideas as the far side of this sensible world, the *beyond* he has in mind is only beyond to the extent that it is something like a celestial world "on high" beyond this terrestial world. It is a far side viewed perpendicularly from the earth upward. It consists only of a 90° turn from the preoccupations of ordinary, everyday life. For those who take their stand on earth, and for those who position themselves within a ptolemaic world view, this represents the far side. But for those who take a stand on a field analogous to the field of cosmic space where heaven and earth are posited on the same level, that is to say, for those who position themselves on the field of emptiness, such a far side ceases to be a far side.

Similarly, a personal God who is thought to reveal himself vertically from heaven down to earth, as commonly represented in Christianity, is considered to be seated beyond, on the far side. Since in this case we speak of a revelation from beyond, the far side is more to the far side than it was with Plato. It is a far side revealed vertically from heaven to earth. Yet even here the situation remains fundamentally unchanged. It is still the farsidedness of a heaven situated above an earth below. The only difference is that in Plato we have an orientation from earth to heaven (*eros*), while in Christianity the orientation is from heaven to earth (*agape*). In both cases the far side comes about through a 90° turn.

Although Christian teaching posits an absolute breach between God and man, it still allows room for God, man, and the breach between them to be represented within the same field. Indeed, the continued efforts of metaphysics to institute standpoints of reason or *logos* to serve as such a field has been a part of philosophy within Western intellectual history since ancient times. Reason develops a plane of "thought" on which far side and near side, God and man, usually considered not to belong to the same plane, can be represented alongside each other. And when an absolute breach or unrelatedness is held to obtain between them, philosophical reason develops a plane of "dialectical" thought on which even such an unrelatedness can be represented as a sort of relationship of "unrelatedness," that is, as a "dialectical" relationship.

Returning to the abyss of nihility, we see that it is not a far side in the original sense of the two cases just mentioned. It belongs to the near side. Still, to the extent that it is represented as the sort of thing that we can look down and see open up at the ground beneath us, something of the far side remains present in it. It is as if we were looking down from a position *on* the earth to what lies *under* the earth, turning 90° in the opposite direction of the Platonic or the Christian sense. Nonetheless, we have come to rest at a point where what is on the earth and what is under the earth can be represented on the same field. In other words, the "nothingness" of nihilism can be represented philosophically on the same level as "being."

The standpoint of emptiness is altogether different: it is an absolute openness. It presents us with the sort of field on which the "far side" of the orientation toward heaven as well as the "opposite direction" of the orientation toward what is under the earth can both be constituted and represented; yet it is not a field that can itself be represented, that is, a field on an absolute near side. Thus, both the abyss of nihility and the personal relationship of God and man can come about in and be represented in emptiness.

The standpoint of emptiness makes its appearance in a kind of 180° turn, as a field that simultaneously comprises both the 90° turns of the formally opposing orientations upward to heaven and downward to under the earth. We might compare it to taking a canvas painted on one side with images of heaven and on the other by images of earth, and turning it over from front to back. In contrast, the other instances of the far side, namely, those relative to the breach between Ideas and sense objects, God and man, existence and nihility—however absolutely that breach be conceived—can be compared to something painted on one and the same front surface of the canvas.

Furthermore, when the standpoint of emptiness is radicalized—

and the corresponding orientation is one in which emptiness itself is also emptied—this is like a 360° turn. Front and back appear as one. The point at which emptiness is emptied to become true emptiness is the very point at which each and every thing becomes manifest in possession of its own suchness. It is the point at which 0° means 360°. And thus, in spite of its being originally an absolute near side, or rather for that very reason, it can also be an absolute far side. For only 0° can at the same time be 360°.

This means that the absolute near side is the field of the essential death of beings viewed as possessing body and mind, or as rational or personal entities. It is the field of essential disentanglement from the self-attachment spoken of earlier. In a word, it is the field of what Buddhist teaching calls *emancipation*, or what Eckhart refers to as *Abgeschiedenheit* ("detachment"). It is also and at the same time the field of the essential life of those same beings, the field where what is absolutely unnameable has a name and lives in the everyday world of names. It signifies the field of absolute death-*sive*-life, life-*sive*-death for the whole man in his every mode of being, as body and mind, as rational, and as personal.

As the absolute near side, emptiness cannot, of course, exist some "where" as some "thing." Whatever is represented as emptiness, or posited as emptiness, is not true emptiness. True emptiness is nothing less than what reaches awareness in all of us as our own absolute *self-nature*. In addition, this emptiness is the point at which each and every entity that is said to exist becomes manifest: as what it is in itself, in the Form of its true suchness. It is the field on which the awareness of our true self-nature—or, what is the same thing, self-nature as true self-awareness—and the selfness of each and every thing in the form of its suchness come about simultaneously, or rather in unison, or perhaps better still, self-identically.

The terms "awareness" and "self-awareness" do not refer here to self-consciousness, any more than "self-nature" should be taken to refer to the egoity or subjectivity of the ego. Nor does our talk of the "real Form of suchness" carry the sense it ordinarily would in realism or materialism. In those perspectives, things are already objectified and represented in opposition to and outside of the ego. No matter how emphatically things are said to be "outside" of consciousness, there is no avoiding the implication that insofar as they are conceived as being "outside," they are still viewed from the field of consciousness. On the other hand, the real Form of suchness means a cutting off from all representation or thought and does not admit of prehension by the ego. It is what is known in Buddhism as the "unattainable" mode of being, wherein something is what it is on its own home-ground.

For this reason, even though we speak of the thing itself, what we have in mind is altogether different from the Kantian notion of the *Ding-an-sich*, "thing-in-itself"). Again, even though we speak of the self-identical constitution of self-nature and the Form of the suchness of things, this does not refer to a "unity" of subject and object such as we find it variously explained in the history of philosophic thought East and West. That is to say, we do not presuppose a separation of subject and object and then work toward their unification. The unity of the absolute near side is not the result of a process but rather the original identity of absolute openness and absolute emptiness. Its standpoint is neither a monism nor a dualism of any sort. It is the absolute one, the absolute self-identity of the absolutely two: the home-ground on which *we* are what we are in our self-nature and the home-ground on which *things* are what they are in themselves.

The question will no doubt arise as to whether this is possible, and if so, how. What sort of mode of being do we have in mind when we say that a thing is only on its home-ground when it is in emptiness? Or, to put it the other way around, what do we mean by "in emptiness" when we say that things are a reality only in emptiness? When we say, "form is emptiness, emptiness is form," what is the mode of being of "form" (existing things)? And what is the significance of "emptiness"? Furthermore, if we say that things are "really" and "in their suchness" on their own home-ground and cut off from all representation and conceptualization—in short, that things are themselves—this cannot but imply directly that our self-nature opens up *on* the absolute near side and *as* an absolute near side, that there is an awareness of self-nature. But how is this possible?

This problem appears, for example, in the famous passage from the opening of the "Genjōkōan" chapter of Dōgen's *Shōbōgenzō*:

> To practice and confirm all things by conveying one's self to them, is illusion: for all things [dharmas] to advance forward and practice and confirm the self, is enlightenment.

And elsewhere in the same work:

> To learn the Buddha Way is to learn one's self. To learn one's self is to forget one's self. To forget one's self is to be confirmed by all things [dharmas]. To be confirmed

by all dharmas is to effect the dropping off of one's own body-and-mind and the mind-and-body of others as well.[2]

What mode of being renders it possible for all things to come forth and practice and confirm the self, or for the self to be confirmed by all things? Why should this be at once a dropping off of the body and mind of one's own self and a dropping off of the body and mind of other selves?

Two passages from the *Muchū mondō* ("Questions and Answers in a Dream") of Musō Kokushi offer a further example:

> Hills and rivers, the earth, plants and trees, tiles and stones, all of these are the self's own original part.

> It is not that the field of that original part lies in body-and-mind, or that it lies outside body-and-mind, or that body-and-mind are precisely the place of the original part, or that the original part is sentient or non-sentient, or that it is the wisdom of Buddhas and saints. Out of the realm of the original part have arisen all things: from the wisdom of Buddhas and saints to the body-and-mind of every sentient being, and all lands and worlds.

To what does this "original part of the self" point? What does it mean that hills and rivers, the earth, plants and trees, tiles and stones, all constitute the original part of the self, that they have all arisen out of the realm of that original part?

VIII

On the field of consciousness things are all "received" as objective entities by the self-conscious ego posited as a subjective entity. Things are set in opposition to consciousness as "external" actualities. This is so, as noted earlier, because the very possibility of things being viewed externally already implies the field of consciousness. Even to say of something merely that it lies outside of subjectivity is still an act of subjectivity. An *object* is nothing other than something that has been *represented as an object*, and even the very idea of something independent of representation can only come about as a representation. This is the paradox essential to representation (and hence to the "object" as well), an *aporia* inherent in the field of consciousness itself.

When the field of consciousness is broken through, allowing nihility to open forth at its ground, and when things are "nullified" and become unreal or deactualized, subjective existence takes this nihility as a field of *ek-stasis* and reverts nearer to an original subjectivity. So, too, when we say that things are deactualized or made unreal, we do not mean that they are transformed into mere illusory appearances. We mean that, deprived of the character of external actuality, things also escape the subjectivism, the representationalism that lurks behind so-called external actualities. And with that we move a step further away from the paradox of representation.

On the field of nihility, things cease to be "objects" and, as a result, appear as realities cut off from representation. As we understand it here, being cut off from representation is diametrically opposed to subsisting as an objective being apart from representation. On the field of consciousness, the very idea of an external actuality independent of representation only arises as a representation. Conversely, on the field of nihility, when things cease to be external actualities or objects, they escape representation and appear in their own reality. When the field of nihility opens up simultaneously at the ground of both subject and object, when it appears behind the relationship of subject and object, it always presents itself as a field that has been there from the first at the ground of that relationship. What seems to make things and ourselves unreal in fact makes them emerge more really. In Heidegger's terms, the being of beings discloses itself in the nullifying of nothingness (*das Nicht nichtet*). The field of nihility is thus the very field where the subject becomes more originally subjective and, at the same time, where everything appears more in accord with its suchness.

Moving further along, then, and converting from the field of nihility to that of emptiness (turning from 90° to 180°, or even to 360°), we are led to ask: in what mode of being do things appear? This was the question I posed earlier.

On the field of emptiness, of course, things are not simply the subjective representations that idealism takes them for, nor are they merely the objective entities or external actualities independent of consciousness posited by realism and materialism. However independent things may be of consciousness—although this, as pointed out before, is not so simple as one might suppose—they cannot be independent of nihility. No thing, whatever it be, can be divested of nihility. Sooner or later all things return to nihility. Things cannot be actual without being deactualized; things cannot really exist except as unreal. Indeed it is in their very unreality that things are originally real. Moreover, in nihility the existence of existing things is able to be revealed, questioned, and perceived. The existence of things is seen to be at one with the existence of the subject itself by the subject that has become its original subjectivity. This is why we say that nothing whatsoever can exist independently of nihility. The field of nihility goes far beyond the field of consciousness on which the opposition between materialism and idealism is constituted.

This is all the more true of the field of emptiness where the abyss of nihility first becomes possible. Neither the field of consciousness nor the field of nihility can come about apart from the field of emptiness. Prior to the appearance that things take on the field of consciousness, where they are objectivized as external realities, and prior to the more original appearance things assume on the field of nihility, where they are nullified, all things are on the field of emptiness in their truly elemental and original appearances. In emptiness things come to rest on their own home-ground. At the same time, prior to the consciousness of objects which has representation as its cornerstone, and prior to coming to know of existence in nihility, an elemental and truly original intellection comes about within the absolute near side of emptiness. It is an intellection that arises at the very point at which "all things advance forward and confirm the self," or that "hills, rivers, the earth, plants and trees, tiles and stones, all of these are the self's original part." Pressed to give it a name, we might call it a "knowing of non-knowing." It is the point at which the self is truly on its own home-ground. Here plants and trees have penetrated to the bottom to be themselves; here tiles and stones are through and through tiles and stones; and here, too, in self-identity with everything, the self is radically itself. This is the knowing of non-knowing, the field of emptiness itself. Let us consider this in somewhat greater detail.

Throughout the history of Western thought, from the days of ancient Greece right up to the present, being or existence has, by and large, been thought of in terms of either the category of "substance" or that of "the subject." Whether animate or inanimate, man or even God, insofar as an entity is considered to exist in itself, to be on its own ground, it has been conceived of as substance. The concept of substance points to that which makes a thing to be what it is and makes it preserve its self-identity in spite of the incessant changes that occur in its various "accidental" properties. Now *being* is looked upon as substance because, from the very outset, *beings* are looked upon as objects; and thus also, conversely, because beings set before the subject representationally are viewed from the subject's point of view. The paradox of representation mentioned above comes into play here. It is the same with "life" or "soul" when these are conceived of in terms of substance.

Once the circumstances lying behind the formation of the concept of substance are brought to light, it is natural to propose, as Kant did, the basic position that all objects are representations, and therefore "appearances"; and to interpret substance as one of the *a priori* concepts of pure reason, as something that thought "thinks into" (*hineindenkt*) objects. (In spite of this, the paradox of representation remains unsolved. Kant tried to avoid it by means of the distinction between "appearances" and "things-in-themselves," between *phenomena* and *noumena*.)

The circumstances underlying the formation of the concept of substance cry out for the standpoint of a "subject" resistant to all objective comprehension. No doubt Kant marks a milestone in the awareness of such a subject. Since his time, the process of awakening to subjectivity has progressed rapidly, arriving at the notion of ecstatic existence within nihility, that is, at the notion of subjectivity in Existenz. The same subject now comes to exist within nihility "essentially," that is, in such a way as to disclose its very "existence" in nihility.

Generally speaking, that nihility opens up at the ground of a being means that the field of that being's "existence," of its essential mode of being, opens up. In nihility both things and the subject return to their respective essential modes of being, to their very own home-ground where they are what they originally are. But at the same time, their "existence" itself then turns into a single great question mark. It becomes something of which we know neither whence it comes nor whither it goes, something essentially incomprehensible and unnameable. Each and every thing, no matter how well acquainted the self may be with it, remains at bottom, in its essential mode of being, an unknown. Even should the self itself, as subject, seek to return to its home-ground, to its very existence as such, it becomes something nameless and hard to pin down. This is what I meant when, speaking of the Great Doubt, I said that the self becomes a realization of doubt. With the disclosure of the very existence of things in nihility, existence itself is disclosed as a real "doubt," and the subject itself appears in its original Form: both return to their essential modes of being.

The ontology we have received from the ancients has not pursued the problem of being to that point. Within its confines, the field is yet to be opened, even up to our own day, on which the existence of the very one inquiring into existence is transformed into a question. Traditional ontology was unable to move beyond a simply "theoretical" standpoint of merely inquiring into existence, a standpoint at which the questioned and the questioner were set apart from each other. Traditional ontology was incapable of descending to the kind of field where questioner and questioned are both transformed into a single great question mark so that nothing is present save one great question, to the kind of field that may be referred to as the "self-presentation of the Great Doubt." Ontology needs to pass through nihility and shift to an entirely new field, different from what it has known hitherto.

But if existence is transformed into a question, then its disclosure in nihility cannot provide the standpoint for resolving that question. The standpoint of nihility merely advises of the ineluctable demand for a conversion. If in nihility everything that exists reveals its original Form as a question mark at one with the subject itself, then the standpoint of nihility itself needs in turn to be transcended. It is at this point, as I have repeatedly pointed out above, that the standpoint of emptiness opens up.

It should be clear, therefore, that on the standpoint of emptiness what exists can no longer be said to exist as substance or subject, since these have both already been brought into question at the level of nihility. Dare we conceive of a mode of being that is neither subjective nor substantial? However difficult it may be to think in such terms, we must. If the idea of substance, as something tied to objective existence, constitutionally presupposes the subject as its counterpart, in the same way that the idea of the subject presupposes an object as its counterpart; and if, when the field of this relation is broken through in nihility, subject and substance together are transformed into a single question; then the necessary consequence of the further conversion from nihility to emptiness is that the modes of being of things and of the self can no longer be described as object and subject. The mode of being of things when they are what they are in themselves, on their own home-ground, cut off from the sort of mode of being reflected in the subject-object relation, cannot be substantial, much less subjective. So, too, the mode of being of the self under those same circumstances can be neither subjective nor substantial. That being the case, what is the mode of being of something that is "in itself" and yet neither substance nor subject?

IX

In the first place, the concepts of substance and subject determine a mode of being according to which an entity preserves itself self-identically; that is, this mode signals a point within constantly changing conditions at which an entity continues to be, or to be seen, as what it is. To that extent, substance and subject are able, each in its own way, to indicate the mode of being of a thing in itself. But do they speak to the true suchness of that mode of being?

Let us say a child is making a fire in the yard. There *is* a fire out there. Its "substance" comprises *what* the fire is, what keeps it from being something else. What distinguishes the fire from the ground, the grill, the brazier, the tongs, the firewood stacked nearby, and so forth, what brings about the unique properties of fire—namely, the power and activity of combustion—may be said to form the substance of fire. It points to the mode of being of fire in itself.

In this case, however, the mode of being of the thing itself is clearly grasped in the Form under which it displays itself to us, and thus also to the extent that we recognize it as such. The substance of fire is the "form" (*eidos*) of fire. Fire here displays *itself*, and displays itself *to us*. This is its *eidos*. Only on such an eidetic field can we distinguish fire from anything else and recognize its unique properties of combustion. Furthermore, this field enables us to classify intellectually and to analyze scientifically the process involved in combustion and thereby to demonstrate what fire is, that is, what its substance is. If we grant this as the "definition" of fire, then combustion may be said to represent a constitutive element in the core content of the definition (the so-called specific difference) of fire. In any case, substance is presented here in terms of *logos*, as something that can be explained in terms of "logical" structures or interpreted "theoretically." It is given as something that can be viewed from the standpoint of reason. In other words, "substance" indicates the mode of being of a thing in itself, though only in the eidetic form it turns to us for the seeing, only as it is rationally recognizable.

To sum up, the field where the mode of things as they are in themselves is grasped eidetically and where the concept of substance comes into being, has a twofold character: on the one hand, it is the field on which *things* come to display what they are in themselves; and on the other, the field on which *we* grasp what things are in themselves. Such are the distinguishing features of the field of *logos* or reason. On this field things are still grasped as objects and thus, conversely, still seen from the standpoint of the subject. However much we speak of "substance" as representing things seen from the inside out, what they are in themselves, we are still on a field that discloses itself in such a way as to lead us to speak of the imposition of reason into the interior of things.

From ancient times, reason has been referred to as the standpoint of the identification of the subjective and the objective. The field of reason is the point at which the seer and the seen are discovered, at ground, to be one. That is to say it is the field where things disclose what they themselves are, where rational cognition possesses an objectivity that differentiates it from thought colored by affect. Despite the fact that this identification of seer and seen is constitutive of reason, time and again through the course of history traces of the duality of seer and seen have survived in contemplation or intellectual intuition. In other words, while talk of the objectivity of rational cognition implies that things are grasped from within as what they are in themselves, these things still maintain vestiges of an objective existence being viewed from without. This is the sort of standpoint that reason is: on its field, what things are in themselves is prehended as "substance."

This is why the field of reason is not the field where a thing is on its home-ground as the thing it is in itself. Reason is not the proper field to give rise to the true mode of being of things as they are in themselves. In order to approach the fact *that* fire is, reason invariably goes the route of asking *what* fire is. It approaches actual being by way of essential being.

On my view, there is no better example of this line of thought than Aristotle. That fire actually burns is due to the burning of something that is burnable—for instance, firewood. The actual existence of fire is upheld by the firewood. That firewood is burnable, his argument goes on, is due to the nature or *physis* of fire being latent in the firewood. In Aristotle's own terminology, combustion is something that develops from latent possibility, or *dynamis*, to real actuality, or *energeia*.

Firewood, however, cannot catch fire by itself; it needs actual fire to be kindled. In the same way, a child's learning the alphabet and learning to read is the actualization of an ability (or possibility) that lies within him but is in need of a teacher, one who already knows how to read, in order to be brought out. A pine tree is an outgrowth of the nature (*physis*) latent in its seed, but this seed in turn has been generated by a parent tree possessed of the same nature. Everything partakes of this cyclical process of actuality and potentiality. And this cyclical process of development is governed by the essential being—the *physis* of the fire or the pine tree—that permeates it.

Having accepted essential being as the natural essence or *physis* of a thing, Aristotle then forged ahead from essential being to actual being, where he conceived of the structure of being as consisting of "form" (*eidos*) and "matter." In the actuality of fire, that is to say, in its combustive activity, the very mode of being of fire becomes manifest as *eidos*, and that manifestation occurs as an emergence into being from a potentiality latent in the combustible "matter." To think of a process of development from potentiality to actuality is an attempt to join *eidos* to matter, and to look in the direction of the latter for the substrate of the former. Clearly, from the standpoint of rationality the being of things is grasped as objective being.

Seen from the opposite side, the being of things is still grasped from the viewpoint of the subject. This is what we pointed to earlier as characteristic of the position that thinks in terms of the *logos*-structure of being. In fact, the dynamic, developmental view of the relationship of potentiality to actuality as well as the static, structural view of the relationship of matter to *eidos* are both conceived in the light of the logical relationship of the notion of *genus* to that of *species* (specific difference) as we find it in "logical" definitions.

In short, when the ontological, structural connections within things as they are in themselves are perceived as a set of necessary relations obtaining within the thought content of the subject concerned with those things, we find ourselves firmly set on the standpoint of reason. It is from that standpoint that we attempt to pursue the fact *that* something is (its actual being) through the medium of *what* it is (its essential being). Thus, this standpoint does not enter directly and immediately to the point at which something *is*. It does not put one directly in touch with the home-ground of a thing, with the thing itself. But then again, is it even possible to assume such a standpoint at all? And if so, what might the mode of being of things be like there? And what would our own mode of being be like were we to stand there?

X

Substance, as we have indicated, represents the point at which a thing preserves its self-identity: Substance indicates what a thing is in itself only to the extent of the eidetic form in which the thing discloses itself to us. But if this is so, what is the thing's mode of being completely apart from this disclosure to us? As noted earlier, Eckhart speaks of the godhead, or the "essence" of God, in terms of an altogether formless, absolute "nothingness" wherein God is on his own home-ground beyond any of the forms in which he discloses himself to his creatures, and in particular beyond the "personal" forms through which he reveals himself to man. "Essence" here is taken in a similar sense, covering all that exists, even "plants and trees, tiles and stones." We are concerned with a mode of being in which a thing truly exists on its home-ground as the thing it is, in which it preserves its own self-identity.

In my view, the key to this question is contained in something that has been present in the Eastern mind since ancient times. We find it expressed in such phrases as: "Fire does not burn fire," "Water does not wash water," "The eye does not see the eye." The saying that fire does not burn fire refers, of course, to the self-identity of fire. But this is not the self-identity of fire as a "substance" viewed from a standpoint at which we view fire as an object. It is rather the self-identity of fire as fire in itself, on its own home-ground: the self-identity of fire to fire itself.

It is the same when we say that water does not get water wet, or that the eye does not look at itself. In the sense that fire is something incapable of burning fire, the words, "Fire does not burn fire," speak of the *essential* being of fire. They also mean that fire does *actually* burn and that there is actually a fire burning. That a fire has been kindled and is burning brightly means that the fire does not burn itself, that it insists on being itself and existing as what it is. In this fact of fire's not burning itself, therefore, the essential being and actual being of fire are one. These words express the self-identity of fire, the self-identity of fire in itself on its own home-ground. They point directly to the "selfness" of fire.

This is fundamentally different from the case in which "substance" is considered to denote the selfness of fire. Here the term "self-identi-cal" could never mean substance. Substance denotes the self-identity of fire that is recognized in its *energeia* (its state of being at the work of combustion), that is, in the mode of being in which fire is actually burning and actually fire. On the contrary, the assertion that fire does not burn fire indicates the fact of the fire's "not burning," an action of non-action.

Distinguish, for the time being, between fire as that which burns firewood and fire as that which does not burn itself. The burning that takes place when the fire burns firewood points to the selfness of fire, but so does the fact that fire does not burn itself. The two are here one and the same. As something that burns firewood, fire does not burn itself; as something that does not burn itself, it burns firewood. This is the mode of being of fire as fire, the self-identity of fire. Only where it does not burn itself is fire truly on its own home-ground. In other words, we speak not only of the selfness of fire for us, but also of the selfness of fire for fire itself. This is something altogether different from a "substance" that recognizes the self-identity of fire only in its *energeia* of burning. If the "substance" of fire is recognized in the *energeia* of combustion, then the fact that fire continues to combust only as something that does not at the same time burn itself can truly be said to point directly to the selfness of fire. That fire does not burn itself shows that at the ground of its mode of being, where it is what it is, fire is not simply substance, that the selfness of fire differs from what is expressed by the notion of substance.

As I have repeatedly stated, it has generally been held that the fact that a thing is itself, that it is self-identical, comes to be by virtue of its "substance." This way of looking at things begins from the standpoint of reason; it takes place on the field of *logos*. Here the self-identity of a thing is grasped logically as a "category" in the logic of being. Or perhaps better, it is grasped in a shape that renders it susceptible to being grasped logically. This is the shape in terms of which we usually conceive of self-identity (that is, of the fact that a thing is itself) and as such represents a constitutive element in the metaphysics of traditional ontology.

The true mode of being of a thing as it is in itself, its selfness for itself, cannot, however, be a self-identity in the sense of such a substance. Indeed, this true mode must include a complete negation of such self-identity and with it a conversion of the standpoint of reason and all its logical thinking. To return to our example, faced with the sort of viewpoint that recognizes the self-identity of fire only through fixing attention on the work of combustion going on (the *energeia* of fire), wherein fire actually *is* and actually is *fire*, the selfness of fire expressed in the fact that fire does not burn itself implies the complete negation of that self-identity. If we suppose that the natural, essential quality (*physis*)—or, in Buddhist terms, "self-nature"—resides in the power and work of combustion, then the selfness of fire resides at the point of its so-called *non*-self-nature. In contrast to the notion of substance which comprehends the selfness of fire in its fire-nature (and thus as *being*), the true selfness of fire is its non-fire-nature. The selfness of fire lies in non-combustion. Of course, this non-combustion is not something apart from combustion: fire is non-combustive in its very act of combustion. It does not burn itself. To withdraw the non-combustion of fire from the discussion is to make combustion in truth unthinkable. That a fire sustains itself while it is in the act of burning means precisely that it does not burn itself. Combustion has its ground in non-combustion. Because of non-combustion, combustion is combustion. The non-self-nature of fire is its home-ground of being. The same could be said of water: it washes because it does not wash itself.

For this reason, we have to admit that even the self-identity of a fire as the fire it is, is unthinkable without its non-combustion. Self-nature is such as it is only as the self-nature of *non*-self-nature. The true self-identity of fire does not emerge from the self-identity it enjoys in combustion as a "substance" or a "self-nature," but only from the absolute negation of that self-identity, from its non-combustion.

Put in more concrete terms, genuine self-identity consists in the self-identity of the self-identity of self-nature (as being) on the one hand, and its absolute negation on the other. What we usually say (from a standpoint that recognizes the self-nature of fire in combustion), that "this is fire," is not yet true. Rather, we speak the truth when we negate that standpoint and say that "this is not fire," instead. Only on a field where this sort of utterance is possible does it become truthful to claim that "this is fire." "This is not fire, therefore it is fire"—to adopt a formula from the *Diamond Sutra*—is the truth of "this is fire." It is the authentic way of pointing directly to the selfness of fire and of expressing the reality of fire in its suchness.

If all this sounds strange, it is only because we are used to positioning ourselves on the standpoint of reason. We may look upon things and make judgments about things one way in daily life, another way in science, and still another way in philosophy. And yet in each case, we position ourselves, in the broad sense of the term, on a standpoint of reason where we cannot come in touch with the reality of things. We are able to touch that reality only at a point cut off from the judgment and contemplation proper to reason, only on a field absolutely different from and absolutely *surpassing* such judgment and contemplation. We speak here of the field of the selfness of things, the self-identity of things where they appear *pro seipsis* and not *pro nobis*. And since this field is absolutely other than the standpoint of everyday life, of science, or of philosophical thinking, the self-identity of a thing on this field—for instance, the fact that this is fire—can be truly expressed in the paradox: "This is not fire, therefore it is fire."

This absolutely surpassing field is none other than the field of śūnyatā spoken of earlier as the absolute near side. An adequate explanation of the standpoint of śūnyatā is only possible if we take into consideration not only the concept of substance but also that of the subject. This would then allow us to pursue in depth the issues introduced above: the problem of personality and materiality, as well as the problem of the modes of being of things and the self implied in the claim that all things come forth and "confirm the self," or that "hills and rivers, the earth, plants and trees, tiles and stones, all are the self's own original part."

4

THE STANDPOINT OF ŚŪNYATĀ

I

In the preceding chapter, I discussed the notion of "substance." Ordinarily, it is thought that substance makes a thing exist as itself. Substance is used to point out the essence of a thing, the self-identity in which a thing is what it is in itself. In other words, it is the *being* of a being. All beings possess a variety of qualities or attributes, their so-called accidents, such as size, shape, and so forth; but what unites these accidents and provides them with a basis is "substance." To speak a bit more concretely, substance expresses what a thing is, what *kind* of thing it has its being as. Suppose, for example, that this "thing" were a human being. Then substance would denote the "beingness" of such a reality in its mode of "being as a man." It is generally held that substance is imperceptible to the senses, that as the selfness of a thing lying behind various sensory appearances, it can only be grasped through thinking. This is the notion of substance that has up until now represented a constitutive element in ontological reflection.

The question remains, however, as to whether that which makes a thing to be something, whether the point at which a thing can be said to "be" what it itself is, in a word, whether the *selfness* of a thing can really be grasped and really given expression by means of the notion of substance. To be sure, the concept of substance brings to the surface the mode of being of the thing as it is in itself. Yet this invariably restricts the selfness of a thing to the way that thing is disclosed to us on the field of reason. That is to say, on the field of reason the selfness of things merely represents the sort of Form in which they appear to us who happen to be thinking about them. The function of thinking, as an activity of reason in us, is to journey beyond the field of sense perception to a field on which things can be made to disclose their selfness. Therein lies the particular significance of thinking. But for that very reason, the "substance" grasped on the field of reason cannot but be the mode of being of a thing in its selfness insofar as it appears *to us* and insofar as it is seen *by us*. We would be hard put to show that this points straight to the thing itself in its mode of being where it could be said to be on its own home-ground. Such *original* selfness must lie beyond the reach of reason and be impervious to thought.

Neither, of course, does the reality of an "object," in the sense that traditional brands of realism or materialism think of it (for instance, a reality seen in terms of its materiality), express the original selfness of a thing. Such reality is represented as the point within things appearing on the field of sensation as objects of sense perception which goes beyond immediate perception and beyond perceiving subjectivity. But this manner of representation stems from a field on which the subjective and the objective are set in opposition to one another, from the field of objects and their representations. What pretends to go beyond the opposition of subject and object is, in fact, still being viewed from within the perspective of one of the two opposing orientations—namely, that of the object. To that extent, we have yet to rid ourselves of thinking in terms of the opposition of subject and object. In general, no matter how much we think of an objectivity within things and events lying beyond our consciousness and its representations, so long as they are envisaged as things and events in the ordinary sense of those words—that is, so long as they are looked upon objectively as objects—their objective reality has yet to elude the contradiction of being represented as something lying beyond representation.

Looked at from another angle, the mode of being which is said to have rid itself of its relationship to the subjective has simply been constituted through a covert inclusion of a relationship to the subjective, and so cannot, after all, escape the charge of constituting a mode of being defined through its appearance *to us*. This is precisely what I referred to earlier as the "paradox of representation."

Again, it might be thought that we can only get in touch with the reality of things through our action or praxis where the standpoint of representation has already been passed beyond. But here, too, the problem remains: on what field does this ability to get directly in touch with the reality of things through our action (be it individual or social) obtain? On what kind of field is such praxis initially possible?

The story is told of Dr. Johnson that, upon hearing of Berkeley's theory that for a thing "to be" means for it "to be perceived," he promptly pretended to trip his foot against a stone in refutation. However much truth we may find concealed in this refutation-by-action, it does not of itself really offer proof to the contrary. The question still remains as to what sort of field Dr. Johnson's action originated from. Did it, for instance, merely take place on a field of sense perception similar to what we find in animals? Or did it occur on a field proper to the mode of being of man with his clarity of consciousness and intellect? Or again, did it take place on a field beyond consciousness and intellect?

Let us suppose for a moment that Dr. Johnson's refutation falls in the first category. In that case, his action cannot be said to touch the "being" or reality of things. In contrast, Berkeley's assertion with regard to the stone, the foot, or the act of kicking itself, that the "being" of these things consists in their "being perceived," really takes a step deeper into the inner reality of things. But then this assertion itself, of course, falls into the second category, being nothing more than a contraction of the field of the opposition of subject and object in favor of the *subject*. If, on the contrary, the field where the activity of Dr. Johnson takes place is the domain of the reality (that is, materiality) of things as objects in the sense discussed above, then this would amount to a contraction of the field of the opposition of subject and object in favor of the *object*. In that case, the covert inclusion of a relationship to the subject is unavoidable.

This means that materialism, no less than idealism, does not even begin to open up a field on which immediate contact with the very reality of things through praxis would be possible. Both materialism and idealism lose sight of the basic field where the reality of things and praxis initially come about; they lose sight of the sort of field where things become manifest in their suchness, where every action, no matter how slight, emerges into being from its point of origin.

This is what I take to be the third possibility mentioned above, namely a field that goes beyond consciousness and intellect. It would have to be a field of śūnyatā or emptiness. It would appear as the field of a wisdom that we might call a "knowing of non-knowing." From this field we could even take a second look at conscious or intellectual knowing and see it reduced finally to nothing other than a "knowing of non-knowing." Similarly, it would be a field of a praxis that might be called an "action of non-action," whence we could even take a second look at all of our activity and see it as nothing other than an "action of non-action." And lastly, it would be a standpoint where knowledge and praxis are one, a field where things would become manifest in their suchness.

We shall have more to say of this later on. For the time being, I only wish it to be understood that merely to talk about action or praxis does not of itself resolve the question of what sort of field this praxis emerges from in the first place. This is so even when this practice is spoken of as a social praxis.

Passage beyond the whole field of the opposition of subject and object—either the field of sense perception or the field of rational thinking—comes about as nihility appears at the ground of those fields and as subject and object alike are "nullified" from the ground up. In that both subject and object are affected, the field of nihility differs from the field of "materiality" and the field of "Ideas." *Materiality* is represented as going beyond the opposition of subject and object through an orientation to the "matter" of things appearing on the field of sensation; that is, a passageway to the "matter of things" is made available on the field of sensation. On the other hand, *Ideas* are represented as going beyond the opposition of subject and object through an orientation favoring the "form" (*eidos*) or "substance" of things appearing on the field of reason.

The two are identical in that both are conceived of in terms of things that appear as "objects" on the field of the opposition of subject and object. Put the other way around, both are conceived of on the basis of the form of things under which things show themselves to us, the "subjects." The field of nihility, on the other hand, appears at the point of breaking loose of all this entanglement in the subjective and the objective. On the field of nihility, all that is ordinarily said to exist or to be real on the fields of sensation and reason is unmasked as having nihility at its ground, as lacking roots from the very beginning.

The act of *con-centration* by which every being gathers itself within itself—in other words, the "beingness" of a "being"—is stretched out as it were over an abyss and seems to fade away into bottomlessness. From somewhere deep beneath the ground of all things, the Form of "things falling apart and scattering" floats up to the surface. It matters not how gigantic the mountain, how robust the man, nor how sturdy the personality. Nihility is a question that touches the essential quality of all existing things. And "nullification," then, is nothing more than a display of the form of "illusory appearance" essential to all beings. When all things return to nihility, they leave not a trace behind. From ancient times people have spoken of the *impermanence* of things. The nihility that permits not a trace to be left behind lies at the base of all things from the very start: that is the meaning of impermanence.

As remarked in an earlier context, however, the nihility seen to lie at the ground of existence is still looked upon as something outside of existence; it is still being viewed from the side of existence. It is a nothingness represented from the side of being, a nothingness set in opposition to being, a *relative nothingness*. And this brings us to the necessity of having nihility go a step further and convert to śūnyatā.

The emptiness of śūnyatā is not an emptiness represented as some "thing" outside of being and other than being. It is not simply an "empty nothing," but rather an *absolute emptiness*, emptied even of these representations of emptiness. And for that reason, it is at bottom one with being, even as being is at bottom one with emptiness. At the elemental source where being appears as one with emptiness, at the home-ground of being, emptiness appears as one with being. We speak of an elemental source, but this does not mean some point recessed behind the things that we see with our eyes and think of with our minds. The source is as close as can be, "within hand," of the things themselves. And the things as they are in themselves, where they are on their own home-ground, just what they are and in their *suchness*, are one with emptiness. For the field of emptiness stands opened at the very point that things emerge into being.

We are used to representing things, however, as objects on the field of sensation or the field of reason, thus keeping them at a distance from ourselves. This distance means that we are drawn to things, and that we in turn draw things to ourselves. (In this sense, "will," or desire and attachment, can also be posited at the ground of "representation.") As long as we stand in such a relationship to things, we can go on thinking of ourselves as incapable of coming within hand of things, and of things in themselves as forever unknowable and out of our reach.

To say that being makes its appearance as something in unison with emptiness at bottom—or that on the field of emptiness each thing that is becomes manifest according to its own mode of being—means that everything that showed its Form of dispersion and dissolution in nihility is once more restored to being. Each and every thing that is recovers once again its power of concentration for gathering itself into itself. All are returned to the possibility of existence. Each thing is restored anew to its own *virtus*—that individual capacity that each thing possesses as a display of its own possibility of existence. The pine tree is returned to the *virtus* of the pine, the bamboo to the *virtus* of the bamboo, man to the *virtus* of his humanity. In that sense, emptiness might be called the field of "be-ification" (*Ichtung*) in contrast to nihility which is the field of "nullification" (*Nichtung*). To speak in Nietzschean terms, this field of be-ification is the field of the Great Affirmation, where we can say Yes to all things. (I shall come back to this later.)

That everything that is gets restored to its being, means that everything appears once again as possessed of substance. The substance of things laid bare on the field of reason scatters and fades away like fog over a bottomless abyss when laid out on the field of nihility. The essential *eidos* of things falls apart in nihility, which permits nothing to leave a trace of itself behind. That is to say, it is no longer clear what things are any more. Nay, it is not even clear what I myself am. Man ordinarily grasps himself on the field of reason as a rational being. But once on the field of nihility, he is no longer able to express *what* his self itself is. Self and things alike, at the ground of their existence, turn into a single great question mark.

On the field of emptiness all things appear again as substances, each possessed of its own individual self-nature, though of course not in the same sense that each possessed on the field of reason. An essential difference shows up in the passage through nihility: the difference between what is grasped as the selfness of the thing on the field of reason, and the selfness of the thing as it is on its own home-ground.

On the field of reason, the selfness of a thing is expressed by speaking of it as "being one thing or another" or as "existing as one thing or another." We say things, for instance, like "this is a man" or "he exists as a human being." And here, again, the concept of substance comes into play (some philosophers locating it in the universal eidetic form, "human being," others in "this" specific individual man).

On the field of emptiness, however, the selfness of a thing cannot be expressed simply in terms of its "being one thing or another." It is rather disclosed precisely as something that cannot be so expressed. Selfness is laid bare as something that cannot on the whole be expressed in the ordinary language of reason, nor for that matter in any language containing logical form. Should we be forced to put it into words all the same, we can only express it in terms of a paradox, such as: "It is *not* this thing or that, therefore it *is* this thing or that."

Being is only being if it is one with emptiness. Everything that is stands on its own home-ground only on the field of emptiness, where it is itself in its own suchness. Even when we speak of things reappearing in their substance, we mean only a substantiality that emerges from a unity with emptiness. On the field of emptiness, substantiality is an absolutely non-substantial substantiality. So long as we propose to adopt the rational idiom and intellectual concepts to which talk about substance belongs, we have no choice but to speak of the selfness of things in such terms. For we are faced with something that cannot be expressed originally with words.

The "what" of a thing is a real "what" only when it is absolutely no "what" at all. The eidetic form of a thing is truly form only when it is one with absolute non-form. For example, the form "human being" of "this is a human being" emerges at the point that the form has cut itself off from all such form. Within every human being a field of absolute non-form opens up as a point indeterminable as "human being" or some other "what." To say that man becomes manifest as man from such a point is nothing other than the original meaning of the claim that he exists as a man.

II

The assertion that being is only being in unison with emptiness belongs in its fullest and most proper sense to the point of view that speaks of the "substance" of things. This was what I had in mind in saying that the mode of being of things as they are in themselves is not substance but something that might be called non-substantial substance.

As observed in the concluding section of the previous chapter, the ancients pointed to the selfness of things in terms such as these: "Fire does not burn fire," "The sword does not cut the sword," "The eye does not see the eye." Fire does not burn itself in the act of combustion. Non-combustion consists of the fact that fire preserves itself while it is burning. Combustion is non-combustion, and non-combustion is combustion. The paradox bespeaks the selfness by virtue of which the fire is on its own home-ground in the act of combustion.

This applies, however, not only to the substance of things but to their various "attributes," as well. For instance, when we say that fire is hot, we can also say that the heat itself is not hot. Of course, this does not mean that apart from the fact "it is hot," there would be some other distinct fact, "it is not hot." Nor when we say "it is not hot" do we point to some such fact as a sub-zero temperature. When something is hot, no matter what its temperature, the fact that "there is not heat" conforms to the fact that "there is heat." The "is not" of "there is not heat" is not a nothingness relative to the "is" of "there is heat." It is a nothingness altogether beyond the field of the relativity of being and nothingness. It is a non-heat spoken of on a completely different field, one that passes completely beyond the field where arise the separation of hot and cold and the correlative opposition of heat and cold. It is a field signifying the absolute negation of that field.

When we maintain that "it is cold," this field of non-heat is the field of non-cold. The separation of hot and cold occurs on the field of sense perception, the cornerstone on which rest our everyday judgments of perception and conceptualization, as well as our scientific and philosophical considerations. The field of non-heat/non-cold is a completely different field, the absolute negation of all those standpoints. It is the field of an absolute "nothingness."

This non-heat, then, is nothing other than the primary fact of heat itself. Heat and non-heat are self-identically a single fact. Were there no self-identity here, neither the fact of heat nor the field of that fact could come into being. This non-heat is simply an indication that the fact of heat becomes manifest on a field of absolute "nothingness" which surpasses both the realm of the senses and the realm of reason. It indicates the point at which the fact of heat emerges into being, as it were, in *ek-stasis* from itself.

That fire is hot is a sense datum belonging ontologically to the category "quality." As a quantity measurable on a thermometer, it can be said to belong to the category of "quantity." But the fact of heat, at the point of its facticity, is a primary fact that cannot be grasped by the categories of quality and quantity. To say that the hotness of fire "is not hot" does not signify its nature of being hot or cold; this non-heat cannot be measured on a thermometer. The fact of heat manifests itself ecstatically as a primary fact on the yonder side (actually the hither side) of the categories of quality and quantity.

Of course, when we say that hotness as such is not hot, we do not mean that the concept "hotness" is not hot. We are calling into question, on a field that transcends even the realm of reason where concepts are constituted, a fact that has become manifest in its suchness. If we look only at the aspect of transcendence, a realm of Ideas such as Plato had in mind might come near to what I am thinking of here. If we can conceive of something like the Idea of "hotness," it would be something that surpasses sense-perceptual hotness and is itself not hot. However, if one considers the transcendent non-heat as some "thing" that is the Idea of heat, if one conceives of a world of Ideas as true realities existing somewhere apart from the sensory world, one remains stuck in the standpoint of contemplative reason. That is, transcendent non-heat must remain self-identical with the fact of heat.

The field of non-heat is not a world apart, an "intelligible world" of Ideas. As the field of absolute nothingness, it has to be at one with the world of primary fact. On the other hand, the world of primary fact is not simply a "sensory world." The primary fact as the self-identity of non-heat and heat is neither sensible hotness nor hotness as an Idea. It is a fact that pervades both the realm of the senses and the realm of reason, as it were, without belonging to either of them as such. On a standpoint that gives expression to heat exclusively by cutting it off from every-thing else, hotness would indeed be a sense datum. If we think of non-heat exclusively by cutting it off from everything else, we would probably have something like the Idea of heat. But the sheer fact of hotness is neither.

The "world" of this primary fact is one. There are not two worlds, a sensory one and a supersensory one (in Kantian terms, a world of *phenomena* and a world of *noumena*). We usually take the world as an extended environment that envelops us and serves as our field of be-havior. And from there, as it happens, we go on to think up another, invisible world behind that first one. But neither of them is the world in its suchness. Neither of them is the world we actually live in. The very fact that we can consider our extended environment to be a world, and then think up a supersensory world behind it, happens in the first place only because we are actually living in a world of primary fact.

To sum up, a hot thing emerges into being as what it is in itself at a point beyond all categories of substance, quality, quantity and the like—namely, on the field of śūnyatā, or absolute nothingness. There a thing becomes master of itself. It is, we might say, the autonomous mode of being of that thing. By autonomous we do not mean a mode of being of things in which they are revealed *to us*, in which the face they turn in our direction is merely, as it were, the front side or "surface" of things. It is rather a mode of being that has nothing at all to do with our representations or judgments; yet it is not the back side, or hidden aspect of things. Such expressions already imply a view of things from where *we* stand. On its own home-ground, a thing has no front and no back. It is purely and simply itself, as it is in its selfness and nothing more.

At the same time, of course, when we speak of this mode of being as autonomous, we do not have in mind a "subjectivity" as a self-conscious ego. We are not thinking of things anthropomorphically. Insofar as we can speak of a thing in itself, we imply a quality that draws it into the compass of the concept of substantiality; and insofar as we are able to speak of a thing as autonomous, we imply a quality that fastens it to the concept of subjectivity. But of itself it is neither substance nor subject.

We have here a completely different concept of existence, one that has not up to now become a question for people in their daily lives, one that even philosophers have yet to give consideration. The haiku poet Bashō seems to hint at it when he writes:

> From the pine tree
> learn of the pine tree,
> And from the bamboo
> of the bamboo.

He does not simply mean that we should "observe the pine tree carefully." Still less does he mean for us to "study the pine tree scientifically." He means for us to enter into the mode of being where the pine tree is the pine tree itself, and the bamboo is the bamboo itself, and from there to look at the pine tree and the bamboo. He calls on us to betake ourselves to the dimension where things become manifest in their suchness, to attune ourselves to the selfness of the pine tree and the selfness of the bamboo. The Japanese word for "learn" (*narau*) carries the sense of "taking after" something, of making an effort to stand essentially in the same mode of being as the thing one wishes to learn about. It is on the field of śūnyatā that this becomes possible.

The mode of being of things in their selfness consists of the fact that things take up a position grounded in themselves and settle themselves on that position. They center in on themselves and do not get scattered. From ancient times the word *samādhi* ("settling") has been used to designate the state of mind in which a man gathers his own mind together and focuses it on a central point, thereby taking a step beyond the sphere of ordinary conscious and self-conscious mind and, in that sense, forgetting his ego. While the word refers in the first place to a mental state, it also applies to the mode of being of a thing in itself when it has settled into its own position. In that sense, we might call such a mode of being "samādhi-being." The form of things as they are on their own home-ground is similar to the appearance of things in samādhi. (To speak of the fact that fire is burning, we could say that the fire is in its fire-samādhi.)

Of course, this is no different from designating something as a "definite" thing, settled into being this specific thing and none other.

Ordinarily, though, a thing is defined from a point outside of the thing itself. On the standpoint of reason, for instance, this is expressed by means of a "definition" as the "form" of that thing. Or again, one may consider a specific individual to originate as an amalgam of eidetic form and matter, with matter functioning as the so-called principle of individuation. In either case, things are being viewed from the outside.

In contrast, the sheer definition of the selfness of a thing may be expressed as its samādhi-being (its mode of being "settled"). In such a mode of being, that a certain thing *is* is constituted as an absolute fact. Even the fact "it is hot" that comes to be one moment and disappears the next is absolute as a fact—as absolute as if it were the only fact throughout all of heaven and earth. As the saying goes for a period of particularly sultry weather, heat "fills the heavens and girds the earth." It is a "bottomless" hotness (though not, of course, in any thermometric sense). Or to take another example, "A single falling leaf—fall is everywhere" is more than a figure of speech. It belongs to a field where the fall of a single leaf is taken as an absolute fact, where the samādhi-form of the falling leaf is an immediate experience. One might even say that poetic truth and true poetry come into being when facts find expression on such a field.

III

That being is only being in unison with emptiness means that being possesses at its ground the character of an "illusion," that everything that is, is in essence fleeting, illusory appearance. It also means that the being of things in emptiness is more truly real than what the reality or real being of things is usually taken to be (for instance, their substance). It signifies, namely, the *elemental* mode of being of things on their own home-ground and tells us that this is the thing itself as it is.

Therefore, the elemental mode of being, as such, is illusory appearance. And things themselves, as such, are phenomena. Consequently, when we speak of illusory appearance, we do not mean that there are real beings in addition that merely happen to adopt illusory guises to appear in. Precisely because it is *appearance*, and not some*thing* that appears, this appearance is illusory at the elemental level in its very reality, and real in its very illusoriness. In my view, we can use the term the ancients used, "the middle," to denote this, since it is a term that seems to bring out the distinctive feature of the mode of being of things in themselves.

As noted above, the various "shapes" that things assume on the field of sensation (the various sense-determined modalities of things) as well as the various "shapes" that they display on the field of reason (whether as eidetic forms of things or as categories in the sense of "forms" of discursive thought) are all the Form that things take insofar as they appear *to us*. They all show the way things are *for us*. They are merely the "front" that things put up before us, the shapes in which things appear to us as reflections of their relationship to us. Rather than show the manner of being of things as they are on their own home-ground, shapes are the Form of things removed from their own home-ground and transferred into our "consciousness," into our senses and our intellect. These shapes are, so to speak, radiations from the things themselves, like rays of light issuing from a common source.

To change metaphors, the shapes that things assume for us on the fields of sensation and reason are the *Forms* that appear on the perimeter. We are used to viewing the selfness of things from their circumference: we skirt around the outside of things; so things do not reveal their own selfness to us. The things themselves reveal themselves to us only when we leap from the circumference to the center, into their very selfness. The *leap* represents the opening up within ourselves of the field of śūnyatā as the absolute near side which, as we pointed out earlier, is more to the near side than we ourselves are. The *center* represents the point at which the being of things is constituted in unison with empti-ness, the point at which things establish themselves, affirm themselves, and assume a "position." And there, settled in their position, things are in their samādhi-being.

In contrast, the shapes of things that appear on the fields of sensa-tion and reason, are nothing more than the simple negative of the things themselves. This is the case even with substance. These shapes are a negation of the "position" (or self-positing) of things; they transform things into mere reflections and transfer them from their position to some other location. This is what the later Schelling had in mind in characterizing all the philosophy of reason up to Hegel as negative philosophy, and designating his own as a positive philosophy (al-though, of course, in terms of content, what we are saying here is altogether different from Schelling's philosophy). In any case, at the center, things posit themselves as they are and in such a way as not to permit contact from the outside.

Above I suggested we call such a mode of being "the middle." It has been said, "If you try to explain something by comparing it with something else, you fail to hit the middle."[1] We can say something similar with regard to the thing as it is in itself. If, for example, from the standpoint of reason, one conceives of the being of a thing in itself as a substance and explains *what* it is substantially, one does not thereby find the thing itself but only an eidetic form "comparable" to the thing itself. In even trying to ordain it as one thing or another by means of thought, one has already missed the thing itself. The thing itself goes on positing itself as it is; it goes on being in its own "middle," a shape without shape, a form of non-form.

Looked at from the circumference, then, the various shapes of a thing do not fit the thing itself. But looking back from the selfness of the thing—that is, from its center—its "middle" mode of being pervades all shapes. In a word, all sensory modes and all supersensory eidetic forms of a thing are not to be seen apart from the "position" (the self-positing mode of being) of the thing. They are all appearances of the thing itself, which remains through it all in the mode of being of a shape without shape, a form of non-form, in its "middle" mode of being.

The words of the ancient philosopher, "All things have a hold on themselves,"[2] may be said to point to such a mode of being. This would apply to the visible appearances of things as well, which is the guise under which things keep a hold on themselves and affirm themselves. And the field where all things have a hold on themselves is none other than the field of śūnyatā that, having passed beyond the standpoints of sensation and reason, and having passed through nihility, opens up as an absolute near side. On that field of śūnyatā each thing becomes manifest in its suchness in its very act of affirming itself, according to its own particular potential and *virtus* and in its own particular shape. For us as human beings, to revert to that field entails at one and the same time an elemental affirmation of the existence of all things (the world) and an elemental affirmation of our own existence. The field of śūnyatā is nothing other than the field of the Great Affirmation.

IV

Parallel to talk of substance with regard to *things* goes talk of the subject, which is the particular regard of *human existence*. The notion of substance expresses something that subsists as the ground of the various attributes of a thing. It expresses the mode of being in which a thing comes into being as itself. Similarly, the notion of the subject expresses something that subsists in a given human being at the basis of his various faculties as a unifying factor. It indicates the mode of being whereby man comes to view himself as he himself is. But, we may ask, does this concept of subject, when all is said and done, truly express man in himself, as he is on his own home-ground? Is it not rather the case that this concept, like its parallel concept of substance, merely points to man in himself insofar as he is laid bare *to* himself *within* himself, on the field of his own consciousness?

That the notion of the subject expresses the essence of human existence has become almost too self-evident to bear mention. This is particularly the case in modern times, where the essence of human existence has come to be identified with self-consciousness. This sort of self-interpretation found in modern man can already be seen at work in the *cogito* that Descartes made the fundamental principle of his philosophy, and appears in sharpest relief in Kant, who took up the same orientation and followed it all the way through to the end. In both his theoretical and his practical philosophy, Kant presents a standpoint of the subject radically and thoroughly sounded to its depths.

In the theoretical philosophy of Kant, the standpoint of the subject appears as what he himself calls a "Copernican Revolution." Our cognition or experience of an object does not result from the intuitions and concepts we have concerning the object being in accord with that object; but on the contrary, says Kant, it results from the object being in accord with the a priori characteristics of our faculty of sense intuition and the a priori concepts of understanding. By thus giving the foundations of cognition an orientation exactly opposite to that of the entire tradition before him, Kant opened up a critical philosophical standpoint halfway between the standpoint of traditional metaphysics (which had tried to grasp the thing-in-itself dogmatically by pure rational thinking) and that of Humean skepticism (which had shaken that metaphysics to its foundations). As is well known, Kant went on to argue that the range of epistemic possibilities is limited for us to the phenomenal world, while the thing-in-itself is behind the phenomenal: actual reality, alone and of itself, but as such unknowable by us.

Be that as it may, at least the totality of all objects of experience that make up nature or the world of phenomena is clearly something constructed by the a priori formalities of sensation and understanding. And the awareness of man as the bearer of this power has, with modern man, come to show itself as a self-awareness of the subject. One might say that the subject that lies at the ground of the various faculties of consciousness has come at the same time, by means of the a priori forms of these various faculties, to lie at the ground of the visible world and all things therein. This shows up especially in Kant's idea of the "transcendental apperception of self-consciousness," in which we can glimpse links to the Cartesian *cogito*. In Kant's case, however, this self-awareness means two things. On the one hand, the investigation of the a priori nature of the various faculties of consciousness involves a deep penetration into the existence of the object and a clarification of its foundations. In so doing, the awareness of the competence proper to the subject reaches its highest point. But, on the other hand, this awareness of the competence of man, by virtue of its completeness, signals the arrival of an awareness of the limits of that competence, as we see in the sharp distinction between the phenomenal world and the world of things-in-themselves.

As is well known, the concept of the thing-in-itself that occasioned the distinction between these two worlds contains serious theoretical problems. Beginning with Fichte, German idealism sought to step beyond those limitations to a standpoint of metaphysical reason, culminating in Hegel's standpoint of absolute reason. From there we find a turnabout to such positions as the radical subjectivity and existentialism of Kierkegaard, the aggressive nihilism and Will to Power of Nietzsche, the historical materialism of Marx, and so forth on up to the present day.

If we follow the history of these changing ideas back, if we approach the issue more fundamentally by considering how these problems are rooted ultimately in Kantian philosophy, our attention is immediately drawn to one point: Kant looks on things from the very outset as *objects*; or, to put it the other way around, his standpoint is that of *representation*. In his theoretical philosophy, an objective, representational point of view is presupposed as a constant base.

The problem of the thing-in-itself developed, in fact, from the presupposition of such a base. To view things as objects is, after all, to grasp things on the field of consciousness, under the Form they display insofar as they unveil themselves to us. In that case, as a matter of course, all objects are received as representations. A concept of substance similar to that explained above also arises out of the orientation given to the pursuit of this mode of being of things. A substance accessible to reason, such as that found in the old metaphysics, might be thought to signify the objective "being" of things as they are in themselves, but by the time a thing is received as an object and seen as "outside" of the subject, the reverse has become the case: it has already been represented by the subject as such an "outside" thing. On the contrary, then, it is the standpoint of representation that lends support from the back side for the concept of substance that is advanced as the "being" of the thing-in-itself.

The old metaphysics had not delved deeply into that contradiction. Believing uncritically in the power of reason, it thought that the "being" of the thing-in-itself could be grasped by rational thought. It considered knowledge to consist in the complete "correspondence" (*adequatio*) of concepts to things. When a thing as it is in itself is set up objectively "outside" of the subject, it is in fact represented as such *by* the subject. This paradox, along with the dialectic it implies, is covered over by that one-dimensional relationship of "correspondence" between thing and concept. However, when the hidden basis of that metaphysics was laid bare by Hume and the naive trust in reason had crumbled under the weight of his critique, it was only natural for this paradoxical situation to rise to the level of reflection. So it was that Kant's so-called standpoint of self-critical reason opened up.

Arguing on the grounds that all objects are representations, Kant reached the conclusion that "substance" does not designate the "being" of things as they are in themselves; but rather, as one a priori concept or category of pure reason (in this case, of pure understanding), it designates something that the subject "thinks into" (*hineindenkt*) things. In other words, substance was changed into one of the elements that go into the makeup of things insofar as they appear as phenomena. Thus at the same time, there came into being a sharp distinction between the phenomenal world and the world of things-in-themselves.

In brief, for the old metaphysics, ontology centered on a concept of substance that designated the "being" of things as they are in themselves. But with the disclosure of the real situation underlying the origination of this concept, substance was transformed into a "form" of pure understanding, one of the "norms" of its cognitive activity. And with that, the standpoint of the subject with its self-awareness came forth as the center of a system of the critique of knowledge replacing the former ontology.

Now what I have tried to say in this all too crude outline is that the old metaphysics and the critical philosophy of Kant do not differ on the fundamental point of taking the standpoint of the object and its representation as basic and presupposed. The only change is that the relationship between the object and its representation which operated as a *covert* basis in the former was made *overt* in the latter and there given approval. The old metaphysics took its orientation from the stance that our representations fashion themselves after their objects, and accordingly held that the speculative concept formulating "what a thing is"—namely, "substance"—can adequately correspond to the object as the thing it is in itself. Kant, however, took his stand on an opposite orientation: that objects fashion themselves after our representations of them. For him, accordingly, the object of our knowledge cannot be the thing-in-itself, and substance becomes but one of the formalities of understanding that go into the composition of the object insofar as it appears phenomenally.

Of course, the difference in orientation of these two standpoints is not simply a matter of opposing orientations on the same plane. As I noted before, Kant's standpoint that the object is modeled after our representation of it lay concealed within the standpoint of the old metaphysics, according to which representations were modeled after their objects. It was only for Kant to bring this to light. (To interpret this as an opposing orientation on the same plane would be to identify the transcendental critique of Kant with the sort of idealism we find in Berkeley.) In spite of all this, or rather because of it, we are able to assert that the objective-representational point of view is basic to both conceptions and a presupposition common to both. The revolution of thought that Kant occasioned, turning the standpoint of the old metaphysics on its head, is, at a more fundamental level, still grounded in the same presupposition. It is, properly speaking, the inverse of the old metaphysics. The concept of substance, central to the old metaphysics, and the standpoint of subject, central to Kantian philosophy, stand on the same base. From that footing, Kant's Copernican Revolution brought about an awareness of the competence of the subject vis-à-vis the world as the totality of objects of experience. In that sense, both his theoretical philosophy and his practical philosophy, which we shall touch on later, gave profound expression to the essential mode of being of modern man.

As also observed, however, after Kant, modern man's subject-oriented standpoint ran its course precipitously until it could go no further. Eventually it reached the standpoint of reason, of absolute reason; and then, breaking through still further, it laid bare the nihility at its own ground. We may say that the standpoint of the *subject* laid bare its ground only when it advanced to an ecstatic self-transcendence on the field of nihility.

But this meant that at the same time nihility was opened up at the ground of the existence of *things*. For Kant, the rational knowledge of nature is possible only if reason itself conforms to what reason *a priori* "thinks into" (*hineindenkt*) nature. In the same way, the nihility that opens up at the ground of the subject by breaking through that field of reason is simultaneously "inserted into" (*hineingelegt*) the ground of the totality of things. But when the concept of substance, which was supposed to express the selfness of things, and the concept of subject, which was supposed to express the selfness of the self, strike against nihility at their very ground and are there negated, they make a leap forward onto a field where the things and the self they were out to prehend manifest their selfness. This means that, on the field of nihility, neither things nor the self are objects of cognition and, hence, can no longer be prehended or expressed conceptually (as *logos*). They are no longer determined either as substance or as subject. We seem no longer to be able to say "what" they are.

Hence, to say that the nihility opening up at the ground of the subject is inserted into the ground of things, should not be thought of in the same sense in which reason is said to "insert" or "think in" its own principles into nature (in the case of the knowledge of objects). On the contrary, the insertion of nihility at the ground of things means, in fact, that nihility looms up from the ground of all existing things, assaults us, and inserts itself into the ground of our existence. With that, the existence of things and of the self are both transformed into something utterly incomprehensible, of which we can no longer say "what" it is. In the sense spoken of earlier, the existence of things and the self appear as the Doubt that is characteristic of the Great Reality.

On this point, the standpoint of nihility differs fundamentally from traditional brands of skepticism, as for instance that which Hume represents. In skepticism, we doubt a certain matter; on the standpoint of nihility, all things without exception, as well as we ourselves, join together to become a real doubt. And this, in turn, means drawing a step nearer to the true manifestation of the selfness of things and the self. Or perhaps better, it means drawing nigh to the field on which their selfness has at bottom been manifest from the very beginning—to the field of śūnyatā as the absolute near side.

On the field of nihility, where the field of reason has been broken through, cognition is no longer the issue. Things and the self are no longer objects of cognition. The field of nihility is rather the appearance of the self-awareness that the selfness of things and the self are utterly beyond the grasp of cognition. Once on the field of nihility, objects (things and the self as objects) and their cognition cease to be problems; the problem is the *reality* of things and the self. Moreover, this reality and our apprehension of it are made possible not by returning from the field of nihility to the field of reason, but only by advancing from the field of nihility to arrive at a field where things and the self become manifest in their real nature, where they are *realized*. The field of nihility appears at the point that one breaks a step away from the field of consciousness and reason; and this is at the same time a step further in the direction of the field of śūnyatā, or emptiness.

As I have already touched from time to time on the conversion from the standpoint of nihility to the standpoint of emptiness, we shall not enter into it further here.

To put it simply, the standpoint of nihility is not a far side in the sense that we usually think of God or the world of Ideas as lying in the "beyond." And yet, all the same, it does go *beyond* the standpoint of everyday understanding straddling sensation and reason to prehend the existence of things and the self. In that sense, it is not simply a standpoint of the near side; it is a transcendence of the near side, albeit a transcendence more oriented to the near side than is our ordinary near side.

At the same time, however, nihility still stands over against existence; it is situated alone, by itself, "outside" of existence. That is, it is still taken as some "thing" called nihility. It is not an object of consciousness, and yet there remains a sense in which nihility is still viewed objectively. It is not the standpoint of consciousness, and yet there remains a sense in which nihility is still viewed representationally as nihility. In a word, nihility is still, to a certain degree, seen as a far side, and hence at the same time still clings to the standpoint of a near side looking beyond to a far side. Its character is essentially a transitional one.

Nihility is an absolute negation aimed at all "existence," and thus is related to existence. The essence of nihility consists in a purely negative (antipodal) negativity. Its standpoint contains the self-contradiction that it can neither abide in existence nor abide being away from it. It is a standpoint torn in two from within. Therein lies its transitional character. We call it the *standpoint* of nihility, but in fact it is not a field one can stand on in the proper sense of the term. It is no more than a spot we have to "run quickly across."[3] As essentially transitional and a negative negativity, it is radically real; but the standpoint itself is essentially hollow and void, a nihility. The very standpoint of nihility is itself essentially a nihility, and only as such can it be the standpoint of nihility.

The standpoint of śūnyatā is another thing altogether. It is not a standpoint of simply negative negativity, nor is it an essentially transitional standpoint. It is the standpoint at which absolute negation is at the same time, in the sense explained above, a Great Affirmation. It is not a standpoint that only states that the self and things are empty. If this were so, it would be no different from the way that nihility opens up at the ground of things and the self. The foundations of the standpoint of śūnyatā lie elsewhere: not that the self is empty, but that emptiness is the self; not that things are empty, but that emptiness is things. Once this conversion has taken place, we are able to pass beyond the standpoint on which nihility is seen as the far side of existence. Only then does the standpoint appear at which we can maintain not merely a far side that is *beyond* us, but a far side that we have *arrived* at. Only on this standpoint do we really transcend the standpoint still hidden behind the field of nihility, namely of a near side looking out at a far side. This "arrival at the far side"[4] is the realization of the far side. As a standpoint assumed at the far side itself, it is, of course, an absolute conversion from the mere near side. But it is also an absolute conversion from a near side looking out at a far side beyond. The arrival at the far side is nothing less than an absolute near side.

On the field of śūnyatā, the Dasein of things is not "phenomenal" in the Kantian sense, namely, the mode of being of things insofar as they appear to us. It is the mode of being of things as they are in themselves, in which things are on their own home-ground. But neither is it the *Ding-an-sich* that Kant spoke of, namely, that mode of being of things sharply distinguished from phenomena and unknowable by us. It is the *original* mode of being of things as they are in themselves and as they in fact actually exist. There is no distinction here between the phenomenon and the thing-in-itself. The original thing is the thing that appears to us as what it is, without front side or back.

This is not, however, to speak of things in the sense of objective realities, as all sorts of realism have come to conceive of them on the fields of sensation or reason. It says rather that all things are illusory in their true selfness as such. I have explained above how a "dogmatic" standpoint that simply takes the so-called outer objective reality for the thing itself shelters a self-contradiction, and how the Kantian critique with its split between two completely irreconcilable modes of being, phenomenon and noumenon, came to be advocated. On the standpoint of śūnyatā, where these two irreconcilable modes of being are pushed to their limits, they are both seen to come about as one and the same mode of being of the thing.

On the one hand, the thing itself is truly itself on this field, for in contrast with what is called objective reality, it has shaken off its ties with the subject. This does not mean, however, that it is utterly unknowable. For reason, it is indeed unknowable; but when we turn and enter into the field of emptiness, where the thing itself is always and ever manifest as such, its *realization* is able to come about. On the other hand, on this field the being of a thing is at one with emptiness, and thus radically illusory. It is not, however, an illusory appearance in the sense that dogmatism uses the word to denote what is not objectively real. Neither is it a "phenomenon" in the sense, say, that critical philosophy uses the word to distinguish it from the thing-in-itself. A thing is truly an illusory appearance at the precise point that it is truly a thing in itself.

As the saying goes, "A bird flies and it is like a bird. A fish swims and it looks like a fish." The selfness of the flying bird in flight consists of its being *like* a bird; the selfness of the fish as it swims consists of looking *like* a fish. Or put the other way around, the "likeness" of the flying bird and the swimming fish is nothing other than their true "suchness." We spoke earlier of this mode of being in which a thing is on its own home-ground as a mode of being in the "middle" or in its own "position." We also referred to it as "samādhi-being."

On this field of emptiness, modern man's standpoint of subjective self-consciousness, which had been opened up by Kant's Copernican Revolution, has to be revolutionized once again. We appear to have come to the point that the relationship in knowledge whereby the object is said to fashion itself after our a priori patterns of intuition and thought has to be inverted yet again so the self may fashion itself after things and correspond to them. The field of emptiness goes beyond both the field of sense intuition and rational thinking; but that does not mean that the subject turns to the object and complies with it, as is the case with sensual realism or dogmatic metaphysics. It pertains to the realization (manifestation-*sive*-apprehension) of the thing itself, which cannot be prehended by sensation or reason. This is not cognition of an object, but a non-cognitive knowing of the non-objective thing in itself; it is what we might call a knowing of non-knowing, a sort of *docta ignorantia*.

This is a field where by denying the subject we pass beyond the subject in its usual sense (the self set up in opposition to an object) to its absolute near side; so we cannot speak of a "knowing self." We cannot say "self" and so neither can we say "know." Strictly speaking, it is no longer proper to speak in the terms we did earlier, borrowing on Kant, of a self adjusting to things or fashioning itself (*sich richten*) after them. In other words, we cannot say that the self takes things as its standard, orients itself in their direction, and straightens itself out accordingly. Talk of such an orientation, along with the implied something that orients and something that is oriented, belongs to the standpoint of knowing. We are able to speak of a knowing of non-knowing only when we have gotten beyond all of that. By virtue of the very fact that we seek to orient ourselves to the thing itself, it has already become an object, and our knowing (the knowing of non-knowing) has already turned to cognition.

The thing in itself becomes manifest at bottom in its own "middle," which can in no way ever be objectified. Non-objective knowledge of it, the knowing of non-knowing, means that we revert to the "middle" of the thing itself. It means that we straighten ourselves out by turning to what does not respond to our turning, orientating ourselves to what negates our every orientation. Even a single stone or blade of grass demands as much from us. The pine demands that we learn of the pine, the bamboo that we learn of bamboo. By pulling away from our ordinary self-centered mode of being (where, in our attempts to grasp the self, we get caught in its grasp), and by taking hold of things where things have a hold on themselves, so do we revert to the "middle" of things themselves. (Of course, this "middle" does not denote an "inside" as opposed to an "outside," as I pointed out earlier on.)

Since olden times, the cognitive power of reason has been called a "natural light." But the real "natural light" is not the light of reason. It is rather, if I may so designate it, the light of each and every thing. What we call the knowing of non-knowing is, as it were, the gathering together and concentration on a single point of the light of all things. Or better still, it is a reverting to the point where things themselves are all gathered into one. All of this goes contrary to our ordinary way of thinking, and, as such, must sound strange. To make its meaning more clear, it is necessary that we enter further into the questions posed by the statements, "Being is only being in unison with emptiness," and "Emptiness is self." In what follows, with the aid of an analogy, I hope to shed some light on the meaning of these expressions.

V

In explaining the selfness of things, it was stated that the mode of being of things that appear to us as objects on the fields of sensation and reason is the Form of things visible *from their circumference*, while the things themselves constitute the mode of being in which they are rather, as it were, *at their own center*. This latter, non-objective mode of being was also termed the "middle" mode of being of things.

It was further noted that the shapes of things as objects of sense intuition and rational thinking are reflected within ourselves as things that have left their own home-ground in order to move into a relationship with us, a relationship that may be likened to a beam of light radiating from its source. Therefore, the Form of things seen on the fields of sensation and reason is not the selfness of things. On the other hand, when looked at from the center, all such Forms of things are seen to be appearances of the things themselves and to be permeated by the non-objective mode of being of things in their "middle."

To simplify things for a moment, let us represent the fields of sensation and reason as the circumferences of two concentric circles. Then let a single radius cross the two circumferences at two points, designated as a^1 and a^2, to represent the objective forms under which a certain thing, A, appears on the fields of sensation and reason respectively. This means, in effect, that a^1 and a^2 are actually $a^1(A)$ and $a^2(A)$. Meantime, the thing itself, A, is situated in the center of the circle. This mode of being of a thing as it is in itself, as a nonobjective way of

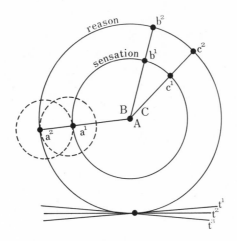

being-in-the-middle, permeates a^1 and a^2 such that they can be seen as apparitions of A itself: A is $A(a^1, a^2)$.

All other things, B, C, D . . . , can be represented in the same way. The infinity of possible points on the circumferences, a^1, b^1, c^1 . . . or a^2, b^2, c^2 . . . (up to a^n, b^n, c^n, . . .) are each conceived as a distinct point, while in the center the infinite number of points, A, B, C . . . , are situated in the same center, concentrated into one. On the fields of sensation and reason, things are each seen as a sensible thing with independent individuality, or as the "substantial form" thereof. In the non-objective mode of being, which they share as things in themselves, they are all concentrated into one simultaneously.

Of course, such a concentration is unthinkable from the standpoint of the conscious self in its everyday experience, which always establishes itself within the bounds of sensation and reason; as it is also from the idea of "being" which gets its start from a foothold in those experiences (and here I mean to include traditional Western ontology as a whole, with its focus on "being" to the neglect of "nothingness"). We have, for example, standpoints like those of medieval nominalism and modern empiricism, which take sensation as their basis and put sensible things at the core of their considerations of "being." Conversely, medieval realism and modern rationalistic ontology take reason as their basis and put substantial form at the core of their considerations of "being." To return to the analogy of the two concentric circles, such standpoints amount to taking a^1 or a^2 as the center, with the result that the other (a^2 or a^1) is made into a point on the circumference of a new and smaller circle that marks off the confines of the consideration of "being" (indicated in the diagram by the broken lines). They think of the "being" of A only as a^1 (a^2) or as a^2 (a^1), and so on with B, C, D. . . .

From such a standpoint, all kinds of complicated systems have been devised, but on the whole and fundamentally, they all start from the standpoint of the ordinary conscious self that conceives of all things as distinct and separate individual entities. It is another thing altogether with the thing in itself, which cannot be grasped on the fields of sensation and reason, and which cannot be seen from the circumference. Here the "thing" is unable to be conceived of if we center our thinking in the mode of being that appears on the fields of sensation and reason. We are unable to consider the mode of being of things as they are in themselves by drawing distinct, individual, small circles, each of which takes a point on the circumference (of which an infinite number are possible) as its center.

As noted earlier, such a way of viewing being is broken down when the field of nihility appears at the ground of the fields of sensation and reason. The further conversion that takes place by then passing through the field of nihility to the field of śūnyatā means that all things in their selfness are gathered into one, as the different points on a circumference are drawn into a single center. It seems to follow, therefore, as a matter of course that this mode of being of the thing itself could not really have arisen in traditional Western ontology, where considerations of being have left nothingness essentially out of the picture.

Naturally, viewpoints that speak of a concentration into the One have shown up in the West from time to time. Examples are numerous, beginning in ancient Greece with Xenophanes' notion of "One and All" ("What we call all things, that is One") and Parmenides' idea of "Being" ("To think and to be are one and the same"), and including such thinkers as Plotinus, Spinoza, and Schelling. The absolute One they had in mind, however, was either conceived of as absolute reason or, when it went beyond the standpoint of reason, at least as an extension of that standpoint in unbroken continuity with it. At the same time, that absolute One was conceived of in terms of a negation of the multiplicity and differentiation of existing things as deceptive and illusory appearances. At each point, the One means something completely different from the situation we spoke of as the concentration of all things in their selfness into one. This is so, primarily, because such an absolute One does not pass through the field of nihility before making its appearance.

Nihility is something that can appear from behind any experience on the fields of sensation and reason, and from out of the ground of "being" experienced there, as that which nullifies that experience and that ground of being. This is shown on our diagram by the fact that tangents (t^1, t^2, t^3 . . .) can be drawn at will from any given point on either of the two circumferences. This shows how any point whatsoever on the circumference contains within itself an orientation to infinite dispersion in all directions and thus hangs permanently suspended over a bottomless abyss.

The field of nihility is the field of such an infinite dispersion. The fields of sensation and reason, on the contrary, are systems of "existence" set up as the negation of such an orientation toward infinite dispersion. They are a "world" in which everything that exists is gathered together and united. And this is made possible, we might say, by the concentration of all things into a single center, a center that makes the world what it is.

Now the absolute One of traditional philosophy just referred to assumed such a system of "existence" or such a "world"—whether the sensible world or the intelligible world, or again a composite of the two—to the exclusion of the nihility opening up at its ground. As a result, the center where all beings revert to one is only thought of within a system of being, only within the world. And this center, in turn, is taken as some sort of "being" itself. It is as if the circle were only being thought of from within the circle itself, and as if the center were always and only to be thought of as the center of a circle. This is also the reason why, as was pointed out before, the absolute One is converted into the standpoint of absolute reason or, at least, considered as a continuation of absolute reason. On this view, the center is always seen from the circumference. In other words, the One is seen as the point at which all beings may be reduced to one. This also explains why it is that the absolute One is inevitably conceived of as something abstracted from the multiplicity and differentiations of all beings. In a system of being that excludes nothingness, the idea that "all beings are One" leads to the positing of a One seen as mere non-differentiation. It is precisely from this sort of standpoint that absolute unity is symbolized as a circle or sphere.

For multiplicity and differentiation to become really meaningful, then, the system of being must be seen as something that opens up *nihility* at its ground, and not merely as a system of *being*. The circle must not be looked at only from within the circle itself, but as something that includes tangents at all points on the circumference. In so doing, it becomes apparent that all those points imply an absolute negation of the orientation to revert to oneness at the center (the orientation given to them as properties of a circle), such that each point implies an orientation toward infinite dispersion. They then cease to be merely the defined loci of points situated equidistant from a common center. Of themselves, these points are not merely uniform and un-differentiated. They do not sink into a One that has had all multiplicity and differentiation extracted from it. Instead, each of them displays an orientation toward pluriformity that absolutely denies such a reduction to oneness, an orientation toward infinite tangential dispersion. And these orientations, showing up as they do in a unique manner at each particular point, as belonging only to that point, bring about an infinite differentiation.

Multiplicity and differentiation, that is, the fact that it is impossible to substitute any one given thing for any other, the fact that each thing has its being as something absolutely unique, become really apparent only when the field of nihility opens up at the ground of the system of being. One might say that only when a thing has lost any point to be reduced to, only when it has nothing more to rely on, can it be thrown back upon itself. This is the mode of being that we referred to earlier as the Great Doubt.

Furthermore, when the unique existence of all things and multiplicity and differentiation in the world appear on the field of nihility, all things appear isolated from one another by an abyss. Each thing has its being as a one-and-only, a solitariness absolutely shut up within itself. We call such a state of absolute self-enclosure "nihilistic." In human awareness, this solitariness is expressed as being suspended, all alone, over a limitless void. Raskolnikov in *Crime and Punishment* and Stavrogin in *The Possessed* inspired unspeakable terror even in their own mothers, such was the abyss of their solitariness. An existence isolated abyssally from everything else, deprived of even its ties to its own mother and estranged from all order (in the sense of a "world"), is an existence aware of an abyssal nihility at its own ground. Out of the depth of all things, as we remarked earlier, nihility rises into view and insinuates itself into the ground of such an existence. This is the "nullification" in which nihility appears as a "negative negativity."

In our diagram, we drew the small circles a^1 (a^2) and a^2 (a^1) to represent the modes of being that have their centers respectively in sensation and reason. Even in these modes of being, things are individual, multiple, and self-enclosed. But insofar as things are considered only within a system of being, they are thought of always as having some connection with one another, as belonging within an order and a unity. Ultimately they are thought of as returning to the unity of an absolute One that is, in turn, itself a being. Basically, this is the approach of our ordinary consciousness of things, as well as the approach of every standpoint of thought that takes this consciousness as its *point de départ*.

On the field of nihility, though, all nexus and unity is broken down and the self-enclosure of things is absolute. All things that are scatter apart from one another endlessly. And even the "being" of each thing that is shatters in every direction, riding atop its tangents, as it were, of which we know not whence they come nor whither they go. This existence seems to evaporate into a bottomless nihility; its possibility of existence seems to continually sink away into an impossibility of existence.

On the field of śūnyatā, however, things are brought back again to the possibility of existence. Or rather, things are made to appear in the possibility of existence that they possess at bottom. They appear from the home-ground (elemental source) of their existence, from the selfness lying at their home-ground. This means that the sensible and rational forms of a thing recuperate original meaning as apparitions of the non-objective mode of being of the thing in itself, as the *positions* of that thing. This is what was referred to earlier as the process of "beification." To return to our analogy, the field of śūnyatā is a void of infinite space, without limit or orientation, a void in which the circles and all the tangents that intersect them come into being. Here the mode of being of things as they are in themselves, even though it arise from the sort of center where "All are One," is not reduced to a One that has had all multiplicity and differentiation extracted from it.

Since there is no circumference on the field of śūnyatā, "All are One" cannot be symbolized by a circle (or sphere). Even though we say that the mode of being of things in their selfness appears in the return from the circumference (namely, from the fields of sensation and reason) to the center (the home-ground of things themselves), this center is no longer the center of a circle; it is no longer a center with a circumference. It is, as it were, a circumference-less center, a center that is only center and nothing else, a center on a field of emptiness. That is to say, on the field of śūnyatā, *the center is everywhere*. Each thing in its own selfness shows the mode of being of the center of all things. Each and every thing becomes the center of all things and, in that sense, becomes an absolute center. This is the absolute uniqueness of things, their reality.

Still, to treat each thing as an absolute center is not to imply an absolute dispersion. Quite to the contrary, as a totality of absolute centers, the All is One. The analogy of the circle used up to this point is incapable of illustrating such a state of affairs in which the center of all things is everywhere, and yet all things are One. What we are speaking of here cannot be thought of as a system of "being." "All are One" can only really be conceived in terms of a gathering of things together, each of which is by itself the All, each of which is an absolute center. And the only field in which this is possible is the field of śūnyatā, which can have its circumference nowhere and its center everywhere. Only on the field of śūnyatā can the totality of things, each of which is absolutely unique and an absolute center of all things, at the same time be gathered into one.

"All are One" signifies the "world" as the unifying order or system of all that is. The shape of that world may be said to be such as I have just explained it. Earlier on, we referred to the non-objective mode of being of things as they are in themselves, whereby each is on its own home-ground, as a "middle." In its mode of being as a "middle," even the tiniest thing, to the extent that it "is," is an absolute center, situated at the center of all things. This is its "being," its reality. The "world," then, is nothing but the gathering together of that "being." It is the "All are One" of all that is in that mode of being—that is, the real world we actually live in and actually see. The possibility of all things gathering together and constituting one world, and the possibility of existence where each thing can "be" itself by gathering itself into itself, can only be constituted on the field of śūnyatā. (As noted above, the possibility of existence for "things" cannot be conceived of apart from the possibility of a "world.")

To summarize, a system of being becomes genuinely possible, not on a field where the system of being is seen only as a system of being, but on a field of emptiness where being is seen as being-*sive*-nothingness, nothingness-*sive*-being, where the *reality* of beings at the same time bears the stamp of *illusion*. On this field, a mode of being is constituted wherein things, just as they are in their real suchness, are illusory appearances, wherein as things-in-themselves they are phenomena.

VI

That a thing actually *is* means that it is absolutely unique. No two things in the world can be completely the same. The absolute uniqueness of a thing means, in other words, that it is situated in the absolute center of all other things. It is situated, as it were, in the position of *master*, with all other things positioned relative to it as *servants*.

To our ordinary way of thinking, though, it is simply a contradiction to claim that this is how it is with everything that "is," and yet that the "world" is constituted through all such things being gathered into one. How is it possible that something in the position of master to other things can at the same time stand in the position of servant to all other things? If we grant that each and every thing, in its mode of being as what it is in itself, enjoys an absolute autonomy and occupies the rank of master seated at the center of everything, how are we to avoid thinking of such a situation as complete anarchy and utter chaos? Is this not diametrically opposed to conceiving of the world as an order of being?

This sort of objection arises because one is only thinking on the field of ordinary consciousness, which covers the expanse between sensation and reason and leaves the field of śūnyatā out of the picture. That beings one and all are gathered into one, while each one remains absolutely unique in its "being," points to a relationship in which, as we said above, all things are master and servant to one another. We may call this relationship, which is only possible on the field of śūnyatā, "circuminsessional."

To say that a certain thing is situated in a position of servant to every other thing means that it lies at the ground of all other things, that it is a constitutive element in the being of every other thing, making it to be what it is and thus to be situated in a position of autonomy as master of itself. It assumes a position at the home-ground of every other thing as that of a retainer upholding his lord. The fact that A is so related to B, C, D . . . amounts, then, to an absolute negation of the standpoint of A as master, along with its uniqueness and so, too, its "being." In other words, it means that A possesses no substantiality in the ordinary sense, that it is a *non*-self-nature. Its being is a being in unison with emptiness, a being possessed of the character of an illusion.

Seen from the other side, however, the same could be said respectively of B, C, D . . . and every other thing that is. That is to say, from that perspective, they all stand in a position of servant to A, supporting its position as master and functioning as a constitutive element of A, making it what it is. Thus, that a thing *is*—its absolute autonomy—comes about only in unison with a subordination *of* all other things. It comes about only on the field of śūnyatā, where the being of all other things, while remaining to the very end the being that it is, is emptied out. Moreover, this means that the autonomy of this one thing is only constituted through a subordination *to* all other things. Its autonomy comes about only on a standpoint from which it makes all other things to be what they are, and in so doing is emptied of its own being.

In short, it is only on a field where the being of all things is a being at one with emptiness that it is possible for all things to gather into one, even while each retains its reality as an absolutely unique being. Here the being of all things, as well as the world as a system of being, become possible. If we exclude the field of śūnyatā and try to conceive at the same time of the *reality* of things (the fact that things *are*), and the fact that all things gather into one, we find that the more deeply we think it over, the more we swing toward anarchy and chaos.

All things that are in the world are linked together, one way or the other. Not a single thing comes into being without some relationship to every other thing. Scientific intellect thinks here in terms of natural laws of necessary causality; mythico-poetic imagination perceives an organic, living connection; philosophic reason contemplates an absolute One. But on a more essential level, a system of circuminsession has to be seen here, according to which, on the field of śūnyatā, all things are in a process of becoming master and servant to one another. In this system, each thing is itself in not being itself, and is not itself in being itself. Its being is illusion in its truth and truth in its illusion. This may sound strange the first time one hears it, but in fact it enables us for the first time to conceive of a *force* by virtue of which all things are gathered together and brought into relationship with one another, a force which, since ancient times, has gone by the name of "nature" (*physis*).

To say *that a thing is not itself* means that, while continuing to be itself, it is in the home-ground of everything else. Figuratively speaking, its roots reach across into the ground of all other things and helps to hold them up and keep them standing. It serves as a constitutive element of their being so that they can be what they are, and thus provides an ingredient of their being. *That a thing is itself* means that all other things, while continuing to be themselves, are in the home-ground of that thing; that precisely when a thing is on its own home-ground, everything else is there too; that the roots of every other thing spread across into its home-ground. This way that everything has of being on the home-ground of everything else, without ceasing to be on its own home-ground, means that the being of each thing is held up, kept standing, and made to be what it is by means of the being of all other things; or, put the other way around, that each thing holds up the being of every other thing, keeps it standing, and makes it what it is. In a word, it means that all things "are" in the "world."

To imply that when a thing is on its own home-ground, it must at the same time be on the home-ground of all other things sounds absurd; but in fact it constitutes the "essence" of the existence of things. The being of things in themselves is essentially circuminsessional. This is what we mean by speaking of beings as "being that is in unison with emptiness," and "being on the field of emptiness." For this circuminsessional system is only possible on the field of emptiness of or śūnyatā.

As I have already noted, if the field of śūnyatā be excluded, for a thing to be on its own home-ground and to be "itself" would be for it not to be in the home-ground of all other things; and, conversely, for it to be on the home-ground of other things would be for it not to be itself. In that case, there would in truth be no way for us to explain the fact that all things "are" in the "world." Only on the field of śūnyatā, where being is seen as being-*sive*-nothingness, nothingness-*sive*-being, is it possible for each *to be itself* with every other, and so, too, for each *not to be itself* with every other.

The interpenetration of all things that comes about here is the most essential of all relationships, one that is closer to the ground of things than any relationship ever conceived on the fields of sensation and reason by science, myth, or philosophy.

Even the likes of Leibniz's system of monads reflecting one another like living mirrors of the universe, for example, can in the final analysis, be returned to this point.

Now the circuminsessional system itself, whereby each thing in its being enters into the home-ground of every other thing, is not itself and yet precisely as such (namely, as located on the field of śūnyatā) never ceases to be itself, is nothing other than the *force* that links all things together into one. It is the very force that makes the world and lets it be a world. The field of śūnyatā is a *field of force*. The force of the world makes itself manifest in the force of each and every thing in the world.

To return to a terminology adopted earlier on, the force of the world, or "nature," becomes manifest in the pine tree as the *virtus* of the pine, and in the bamboo as the *virtus* of the bamboo. Even the very tiniest thing, to the extent that it "is," displays in its act of being the whole web of circuminsessional interpenetration that links all things together. In its being, we might say, the world "worlds." Such a mode of being is the mode of being of things as they are in themselves, their non-objective, "middle" mode of being as the selfness that they are.

VII

In the circuminsessional relationship as we have just described it, each thing is on the home-ground of every other thing even as it remains on its own home-ground. This means that in the being of things, the world *worlds*, and that things *are* in the world. All this is possible only on the field of śūnyatā. As the field of circuminsessional relationship, the field of śūnyatā is the field of a force by virtue of which all things as they are in themselves gather themselves together into one: the field of the possibility of the world. At the same time (and in an elemental sense, this comes to the same thing), it is the field of the force by virtue of which a given thing gathers itself together: the field of the possibility of the existence of things.

For us, this field of emptiness is something we are aware of as an absolute near side. It opens up more to the near side than we, in our ordinary consciousness, take our own self to be. It opens up, so to speak, still closer to us than what we ordinarily think of as ourselves. In other words, by turning from what we ordinarily call "self" to the field of śūnyatā, we become truly ourselves. The meaning of this turn to the field of śūnyatā has already been explained. Namely, when nihility opens up at the ground of the self itself, it is not only perceived simply as a nihility that seems to be outside of the self. It is drawn into the self itself by the subject that views the self as empty. It becomes the field of ecstatic transcendence of the subject, and from there turns once more to the standpoint of śūnyatā as the absolute near side where emptiness is self.

This means that the field of the so-called self, the field of self-consciousness and consciousness, is broken down. In a more elemental sense, it means that we take leave of the essential self-attachment that lurks in the essence of self-consciousness and by virtue of which we get caught in our own grasp in trying to grasp ourselves. It means also that we take leave of the essential attachment to things that lurks in the essence of consciousness and by virtue of which we get caught in the grasp of things in trying to grasp them in an objective, representational manner.

What does it mean, though, to say that "emptiness is self"? We said that emptiness is the field of the possibility of the world and also the field of the possibility of the existence of things. "Emptiness is self" means that, at bottom and in its own home-ground, the self has its being as such a field. The self is not merely what the self is conscious of as self. The field of śūnyatā within which the world and things become possible opens up at the home-ground of the self as a self that is truly on the home-ground of the self itself, that is, the *original self in itself*.

As a field of "possibility," the home-ground of the self in the self precedes the world and things. Of course, I speak here not of temporal precedence, since time, too, becomes possible on the field where the world becomes possible. For this reason, it is perfectly all right to claim that nothing can be conceived of as temporally prior to the world, and to regard the world as continuing infinitely in time. Still, the home-ground of the self and the self itself that is truly on its home-ground are still essentially *before* the world and things. The self has its home-ground at a point disengaged from the world and things and, at bottom, that is where it comes to rest. One might call this a "transcendence" in a sense similar to that found in contemporary existential philosophy (although there are differences as to how this is conceived.)

In sum, when we are on our own home-ground and are truly ourselves, we are on a field—and have our being *as* that field—where the "world," in the sense of a circuminsessional system of being referred to in the preceding section, becomes possible and where "things" at the same time possess their possibility of existence. It may be said that all of us, as individual human beings, are also "things" in the world and that our existence is an illusory appearance precisely as the truly real beings that we are. And we may then go on to say that where this being of ours "is" at an elemental level at one with emptiness, the world and the totality of things become manifest from our own home-ground.

To be on such a home-ground of our own is, for us, true *self-awareness*. Of course, that self-awareness is not a self-consciousness or a self-knowledge, nor is it anything akin to intellectual intuition. We are used to seeing the self as something that knows itself. We think of the self as becoming conscious of itself, understanding itself, or intellectually intuiting itself. But what is called here "self-awareness" is in no sense the self's knowing of itself. Quite to the contrary, it is the point at which such a "self" and such "knowledge" are emptied. In what sense might this, then, be said to be our true self-awareness?

In speaking of things, it was observed that expressions such as "Fire does not burn fire" and "The eye does not see the eye itself" point to the non-objective mode of being of things as they are in themselves. An eye is an eye because it sees things, but when the eye is on the home-ground of the eye itself, there is an essential *not-seeing*. Could the eye see the eye itself, it would not be able to see anything else. The eye would cease to be an eye. The eye is an eye through that essential not-seeing; and because of that essential not-seeing, seeing is possible. Not being an eye (not-seeing) constitutes the possibility of being an eye (seeing). For that reason, the being of the eye, as mentioned earlier, can only be formulated in such terms as these: the eye is an eye because it is not an eye.

This means that the possibility of the existence of being rests in emptiness. Of course, what we here call "being" is the non-objective being of things as they are in themselves. In our example, the eye's not-seeing only comes to be a not-seeing in unison with the eye's activity of actually seeing something. Likewise, that activity of seeing only comes to be a seeing in unison with not-seeing. This contradictory state of affairs, in which seeing and not-seeing only come to be as a unity, constitutes the self-identity of the eye in its nonobjective mode of being as what it is in itself.

Quite literally, then, we may speak of an essential "blindness" simultaneously present in seeing. The point of blindness comes at the very point that seeing is seeing as such: it is right at hand and manifest in the act of seeing. It is, of course, not a visual defect we speak of. It is not the objective phenomenon of sightlessness. What we have in mind is a not-seeing squarely positioned *within* the activity where seeing becomes manifest as seeing, a not-seeing that is there for the sake of the possibility of seeing to be seeing. It is not that sight in an objective, phenomenal sense is not present, but that in the non-objective way that it is what it is in itself, it is empty. Emptiness here means that the eye does not see the eye, that seeing is seeing because it is not-seeing. It means that the very sensation or perception called seeing (and consciousness as a whole) is, at bottom, empty. All consciousness as such is empty at its very roots: it can only become manifest on the field of emptiness. Consciousness is *originally* emptiness. Yet this original emptiness is not distinct from the fact, for instance, that seeing is seeing itself. That seeing is a groundless activity (empty already from its own-ground) means that seeing, strictly speaking, is seeing bottomlessly. Even the ordinary activity of sight is, as it were, an "action of non-action."

Put in more general terms, there is a *non-consciousness* at the base of all consciousness, though not in the sense of what is called the "unconscious." The realm of the unconscious, no matter how deeply it reaches into the strata underlying consciousness, remains after all continuous with the realm of consciousness and on a dimension where, together with consciousness, it can become the subject matter of psychology. We speak of a non-consciousness here to indicate that the unconscious as such is also empty from its very roots up.

In that sense, as something that transcends the conscious and the unconscious, we might call the *non*-conscious a *trans*consciousness. But that would not mean, of course, that there is some "thing" that is a transconsciousness. We speak of emptiness but do not imply that there is some "thing" that is emptiness. Transconsciousness, as the original emptiness of consciousness, is one with consciousness itself. (Seeing is at one with seeing as the absolute negativity of seeing.) It is in that sense that we call it a *non*-consciousness. In the words of a haiku that comes to us from an unknown poet on his deathbed:

> Now that I am deaf
> it is clear for me to hear
> the sound of the dew

It is the same with the self-awareness we were speaking of before. The self is the self as something that knows the self; but in the self in itself, as it is on the home-ground of the self, there is an essential *not-knowing* that is one with the *knowing* of the self. Were the self in itself something that knew the self in itself, the self would be completely unable to attain to the knowledge of knowing anything at all (just as if the field of emptiness were a sort of being and we would be left with only one Spinozistic "substance," while the world and all things would melt away). In this case no *knowing* in the sense of knowing oneself through intellectual intuition or through conscious or cognitive knowledge, and no *self*, in the sense of a "subject" that comes to know itself in such ways, could come about. The result would be that not even the knowing whereby that self knows other things (as subject knowing its objects) could come about.

At the ground of all knowing from the standpoint of the "subject," there lies an essential not-knowing. The standpoints of conscious and discursive (discerning) intellect and intuitive intellect are broken. The standpoint of the subject that knows things objectively, and likewise knows itself objectively as a thing called the self, is broken down. This not-knowing is the self as an absolutely non-objective selfness, and the self-awareness that comes about at the point of that not-knowing comes down to a "knowing of non-knowing." This self-awareness, in contrast with what is usually taken as the self's knowing of itself, is not a "knowing" that consists in the self's turning to itself and refracting into itself. It is not a "reflective" knowing. What is more, the intuitive knowledge or intellectual intuition that are ordinarily set up in opposition to reflective knowledge leave in their wake a duality of seer and seen, and to that extent still show traces of "reflection."

I call this self-awareness a knowing of non-knowing because it is a knowing that comes about not as a *refraction* of the self bent into the self but only on a position that is, as it were, absolutely straightforward or *protensive*. This is so because it is a knowing that originates in the "middle." It is an absolutely non-objective knowing of the absolutely non-objective self in itself; it is a completely non-reflective knowing. This self-awareness is constituted only on the field of śūnyatā, on a standpoint where emptiness is self. The absolutely protensive position referred to is the point at which the self is truly the self in itself, and where the being of the self essentially posits itself. The knowing of non-knowing comes about only as the *realization* (manifestation-*sive*-apprehension) of such being as it is in itself on the field of śūnyatā. On all other fields the self is at all times reflective and, as we said before, caught in its own grasp in the act of grasping itself, and caught in the grasp of things in its attempt to grasp them. It can never be absolutely protensive; it can never be the "straight heart" of which the ancients speak.

When Emperor Wu of the Liang Dynasty asked Bodhidharma, "What is the first principle of the holy teachings?" the Patriarch replied, "Emptiness, no holiness." The Emperor, confused by this answer, inquired further, "Who is this standing before me?" "No knowing," answered Bodhidharma.[5] The story as such is well enough known, but what I should like to suggest here is that this "No knowing" that strikes out from beneath the very bottom of the universe like a bolt of lightning is quite the same thing we have been speaking of as the not-knowing in which the self is on its own home-ground as what it is in itself.

It is only through making this non-objective self in itself (and its non-objective self-awareness) a home-ground that the self as subject becomes possible. To begin with, the standpoint of the subject always comes about as the unity of two orientations: on the one hand, its orientation toward a subjectivity that persists in being a non-objective existence and refuses to be an object; and on the other hand, its orientation to know objects and relate to them as the subjectivity that it is. At the point where these two orientations intersect, the subject comes into being with the structure of self-consciousness as something that persists in being non-objective and yet is set up in a kind of permanent opposition to objects. In other words, its being comes about in the reflective knowing whereby the self knows itself.

Now the first of these two orientations, the persistent non-objectivity of subjectivity in the subject, is only possible by virtue of the absolute non-objectivity of the selfness of the self. Subjectivity is nothing else than the selfness of the self reflected onto the field of consciousness. The "subject" is made possible by the self itself. (Therefore, conversely, the selfness of the self can be called the elemental subject.)

The second orientation, the reflective knowledge whereby the self knows itself and objects, is also made possible by the fact that the self in itself is a not-knowing. If the knowing of the self in itself (which is, in fact, a knowing of non-knowing) were reflective knowing, then the standpoint of a subject that is related to the self itself (knows the self) while still persisting in its relationship with the object (knowing the object), would be impossible, as would all reflective knowledge on that standpoint. Just as the essential function of the eye, to see things, is possible by virtue of the selfness of the eye, whereby the eye does not see the eye itself; and just as the fact that fire burns things is possible by virtue of the selfness of fire, whereby the fire does not burn itself; so, too, the knowing of the subject is rendered possible by the not-knowing of the self in itself. Thus we can say in general that the self in itself makes the existence of the self as a subject possible, and that this not-knowing constitutes the essential possibility of knowing.

Furthermore, just as the seeing and not-seeing of the eye—"to be an eye" and "not to be an eye"—only come about in a unity that also spells the self-identity of the eye in itself; and just as the combustion and non combustion of fire—"to be fire" and "not to be fire"—only come about in a unity that also spells the self-identity of fire in itself; so, too, the knowing and not-knowing of the self—"to be a self" and "not to be a self"—only come about as a unison that constitutes the *concrete* self-identity of the self in itself.

If we look at things in terms of the self as subject, projected on the fields of sensation and reason (on the field of consciousness as a whole), oriented toward the home-ground of the self, then the pure selfness of the self, or its pure self-identity, appears at the point that the being of the self as it is in itself is a being on the field of śūnyatā, a being at one with emptiness. This pure selfness appears at the point that the self is an absolutely protensive position (in the sense that the being of the self is the self's positing of itself). But when we turn this around to look at the other side, not only the so-called subject but even the body is an apparition of selfness. It is—in unity with pure selfness—the position of the being of selfness. In other words, the self in itself consists, concretely speaking, in the self-identity of the selfness itself, subject and body. This is the same sense in which I spoke above of the various sensible and rational forms as all pervaded by the mode of being of the "middle" and becoming its disclosure.

On the field of śūnyatā, our selfness goes beyond the so-called subject. Our selfness is the point at which all modes of being of the self—personal, conscious, corporeal, and so forth—have all been cast off. There "being" is a mode of being that can no longer be called self. There the self is what is *not* the self. This mode of being, however, pervades the various modes of being of the self—personal, conscious, corporeal, and so on—and constitutes, together with them, one "being," one "position." From that point of view, our self remains through to the end the very self we are conscious of and know about, the everyday self with its bodily behavior, its joys and its wrath, its sorrows and its pleasures, busy employing its discernment and keeping active in social life. It is the self that *is* the self. Hence finally, concretely speaking, the point of self-identity, at which "to be a self" and "not to be a self" are one, is nothing other than the self in itself. We have no choice but to express our self in itself as "that which is not self in being self" and as "that which is self in not being self."

VIII

"Being self in not being self" means that the being of the self as a personal, conscious, corporeal human and the existence of the self as subject are essentially illusory appearances. It means, moreover, that the various phenomena of human body and human mind, and all of reflective knowledge wherein the self knows the self and objects, are essentially illusory appearances: what the ancients called "vain discernment" (*vikalpa*). No matter how objectively true these phenomena are in themselves (for instance, as scientific cognition), in this very truth they are essentially illusory appearances. Or, put the other way around, it is precisely on the field of śūnyatā that these phenomena, at one with emptiness, are nothing less than actual reality at an essential level. It is what we spoke of earlier as "true suchness" (*tāthatā*). Or again, if you will, it is the "likeness" contained in the assertion "the bird flies and it is like a bird."

In another context, I have spoken of this same thing as "primal fact," remarking there:

> Goethe says that things that will pass are metaphors of the Eternal . . . yet so long as there is nothing like an eternal thing to serve as its archetype, the metaphor as such is the primal reality or fact. It is metaphor even as primal fact, and primal fact even as metaphor. A Zen master extends his staff and says: "If you call this a staff you cling to it; if you do not call it a staff you depart from the facts. So what should you call it then?" The staff he has in mind is not the sensible wooden object, but neither is it not the sensible object. The staff is always the staff, but at the same time it is not the staff. Even though we say of it "form is emptiness, emptiness is

form," our words are not spoken from a contemplative standpoint. . . . The fact
that this staff is this staff is a fact in such a way as to involve at the same time a
deliverance of the self. In this the fact appears as a primal factuality. The point at
which this fact can be comprehended in a primal manner is the point of deliverance
where one becomes a Son of God, a Son of Buddha.

It is not that it is *not* the world of sense perception, matter, and life, but only
that it is the *primal* world of these things. It is the world of these things brought
back to what is primal, stripped of the discerning intellect that infiltrates our
ordinary talk of sense perception, matter, and life without our realizing it.[6]

When a fact is on its own home-ground, it is a fact without bottom.
There it rises above anything that might provide a roothold of support.
On whatever dimension one seeks to make a ground of its "cause," or
"reason," or "purpose"—not only in matter, sensibility, life, and so on,
but also in discursive understanding with its categories, speculative
reason with its Ideas, or even the Will to Power as a metaphysical
principle—one is unable to reach the facts themselves on their own
home-ground.

On the field of śūnyatā, fact as primal fact, that is fact as the very
fact it is in its own true reality, is groundlessly itself. It is simultaneously the far side and the near side of every roothold and every
ground, on every dimension. It is simply itself, cut off from every How
and Why and Wherefore. And this being, a being bottomlessly on the
field of śūnyatā, is precisely what we have been calling illusory appearance. Our subjective existence and all its facts can also be called a
"likeness" of that sort.

"Not being self in being self," on the other hand, means that on the
field of śūnyatā the selfness of the self has its being in the home-ground
of all other things. On the field of śūnyatā, the center is everywhere.
Each and every thing in its nonobjective and "middle" selfness is an
absolute center. To that extent, it is impossible for the self on the field of
śūnyatā to be self-centered like the "self" seen as ego or subject. Rather,
the absolute negation of that very self-centeredness enables the field of
śūnyatā to open up in the first place.

To the extent that the being of the self is present in the home-
ground of all other things, the self is not the self. The self is not a small,
self-centered circle. Together with emptiness it is free of all outer
limits. It is, so to speak, something with no circumference whatsoever.
This is elemental self-awareness.

As a being in unison with emptiness, then, the self is one absolute
center, and, to that extent, all things are in the home-ground of the self.
And so far as our self is at the home-ground of all things, that is, on the

field of śūnyatā, all things are also at the home-ground of the self. Such a circuminsessional interpenetration, as we said before, can only come about when all things, including ourselves, are in a nonobjective, "middle" mode of being. As we also noted there, through this circuminsessional interpenetration, all things are gathered together, and as such render possible an order of being, a "world," and consequently enable the existence of things as well.

The "force" by virtue of which each and every thing is able to exist, or perhaps better, the force by virtue of which all things make one another exist—the primal force by virtue of which things that exist appear as existing things— emanates from this circuminsessional relationship. All things "are" in the home-ground of any given thing and make it to "be" what it is. With that thing as the absolute center, all things assemble at its home-ground. This assembly is the force that makes the thing in question be, the force of the thing's own ability to be. In that sense, we also said that when a thing *is*, the world *worlds*, and that as the field of circuminsessional interpenetration, the field of śūnyatā is a field of force.

Now this field can also open up in the self when the self is truly in the self's home-ground. It lies at the home-ground of the self. It is, as it were, directly underfoot, directly at hand for the self. The roothold of the possibility of the world and of the existence of things, namely, the place where the world and the existence of things "take hold of their ground," can be said to lie in the home-ground of each man, underfoot and right at hand.

In this way, the selfness of the self—insofar as the self is said to "be a self"—lies radically in *time*, or, rather, is bottomlessly in time. At the same time, on the field of śūnyatā—insofar as the being of the self is at bottom only being in unison with emptiness, insofar as the self is said "not to be a self"—the self is, at every moment of time, ecstatically outside of time. It was in this sense that we spoke above of the self of each man as at bottom preceding the world and things.

We are born in time and we die in time. "To be in time" means to be constantly within the cycle of birth-and-death. But we are not merely within time and within the cycle of birth-and-death. On our own home-ground, we are not simply drifting about in birth-and-death: we live and die birth-and-death. We do not simply live in time: we live time. From one moment in time to the next we are making time to be time, we are bringing time to the "fullness of time." That is the sense of what we referred to earlier as "being bottomlessly in time."

But now, thus to be bottomlessly within time and within the cycle of birth-and-death means to stand ecstatically outside of time and outside of that cycle. It means to precede the world and things, to be their master. This, at bottom, is the sort of thing we "are" in our home-ground, in our selfness. And when we become aware of that fact, namely, when we truly *are* in our own home-ground, we stand from one moment of time to the next *outside* of time, even as we rest from one moment to the next bottomlessly *inside* of time. Even as we stand radically, or rather bottomlessly (groundlessly and with nothing to rely on), inside the world, we stand at the same time outside of it. In this case, having nothing to rely on means absolute freedom.

Passing out of time and onto the field of śūnyatā is no different from radicalizing the mode of being in time, that is, from living *positively* in the vicissitudes of time. This means that our existence goes beyond all possible things to rely on. This "reliance on nothing" is absolute freedom.

Precisely as the absolute freedom that bottomlessly makes being and time to be being and time, emptiness is also a knowledge. It is the standpoint of an insight that knows everything in its true suchness. But similar to what we have noted often enough before, this suchness can be spoken of as phantom-like. This knowledge is a "phantom-like Wisdom."

In the words of the *Avatamsaka Sutra*:

> The phantom-like Wisdom of the Buddha, without hindrance, completely penetrates with its light all dharmas of the three worlds, and enters into the mental activities of all sentient beings. Here it is the domain of the Good Heavenly Being of the North. Its all-inclusiveness knows no limits at all. . . . Here, it is the deliverance of the Great Light.[7]

A little further on, the sutra compares the dwelling of the Tathāgata in "phantom-like Wisdom" to a magician's magic (literally, the phantom acts of the phantom master):

> It is as with the magician accomplished in his art who dwells at the crossroads, producing all kinds of magical effects. On one day, a fleeting instant, he conjures up a full day or a full night, even seven days or seven nights, a fortnight, a month, a year, a hundred years. And always everything is there: cities and hamlets, wells, rivulets, rivers and seas, sun and moon, clouds and rain, palaces and houses. The original day or hour is not done away with simply because a great stretch of years has been shown in that time; and the days, months, and years of the phantasmagoria are not destroyed simply because the original time was so very short.

What this passage says is that in a fleeting instant, in the twinkling of an eye, the temporal span of a whole day or a hundred years appears phantasmally, and this phantasm is the day or the hundred years in actuality. At the same time, since the phantasmal span is revealed here in its suchness, this actual instant does not cease to be this actual instant. "With a single thought, ten thousand years. And with ten thousand years, a single thought."

On the field of emptiness, all time enters into each moment of time passing from one moment to the next. In this circuminsessional interpenetration of time, or in time itself that only comes about as such an interpenetration, namely, in the *absolute relativity* of time on the field of śūnyatā, the whole of time is phantom-like, and the whole of the being of things in time is no less phantom-like.

But in spite of this, on the field of śūnyatā, each time, in its very actuality, is the suchness of this time or that time. We might say, in other words, that because in the field of śūnyatā each time is bottomlessly in time, all times enter into each time. And only as something bottomless that all times can enter into does each time actually emerge in its manifestation as this or that time, such as it is. This suchness and phantom-likeness must needs be one. Therein, to be sure, lies the essence of time.

Should one be inclined to dismiss this view of time as a mere fantasy, one might recall, for example, that Kierkegaard speaks of a "transcendence" in the "moment," and along with that of a "simultaneity" coming to be in the "moment." In fact, past and present can be simultaneous without "destroying" the temporal sequence of before and after. Without such a field of simultaneity not even culture, let alone religion, could come into being. We can encounter Sakyamuni and Jesus, Bashō and Beethoven in the present. That religion and culture can arise within and be handed down historically through time points to the very essence of time.

The *Avatamsaka Sūtra* speaks of the same idea not only in connection with time but also with place:

> The magician, staying in one place, produces all kinds of magical effects of magical places; but he does not thereby destroy his original place. . . . He does not destroy this one world by the fact that those worlds are many, nor are those many worlds destroyed by the fact that this world is one.

That time and place consist of a circuminsessional interpenetration in which all enter into each, in other words, the absolute relativity of time and space, means that all things have their being temporally and spatially; "earth, water, fire, air, oceans and mountains, towns and hamlets," and the very "halls of heaven"—in short, the "world"—arise in the interpenetration in the being of each and every thing, in the elemental relativity of existence.

In addition, that the world comes into being as a single totality, as a single "world," means that it originates in a circuminsessional inter-penetration with many "worlds." This world of ours is one relative world. Any number of other possible or actual (in Leibniz's idiom, *possible* or *compossible*) worlds are conceivable. On the field of śūnyatā, where they can be conceived, each such world is able to reflect all the others without ceasing to be the real world that it is of itself. The one world itself comes into being on the field of śūnyatā as a field of absolute relativity.

(On the field of śūnyatā, we can also find a point from which to conceive of the workings of reason in fixing its "ideas" and "ideals" representationally from within itself; or to conceive of the workings of the creative power of the artist—what the seventeenth-century haiku poet Kikaku, in speaking of one of the poems of his master, Bashō, calls the "phantom technique." The poem reads:

> The first wintry shower—
> Even the monkeys seem to long
> For a small straw coat.

Indeed, these words seem to conjure up the image of the poet himself in his straw raincoat, winding his way along along a solitary mountain pass. Here, however, we restrict our concerns to the field of śūnyatā as a "knowing.")

In brief, the totality of things in the world, and also the world itself, have their being bottomlessly on the field of śūnyatā and, therefore, *are* in their phantomness-*sive*-suchness by virtue of the circuminsessional interpenetration whereby all are in each. Here the suchness of the bird consists in the fact that "The bird flies and it is like a bird." And the mode of being of we who stand on that field, namely, our selfness returned to its own home-ground, comes about at the point where "to dwell in the world is to dwell in the void." As it is written, "One does not enter the world outside of the void, nor enter the void outside of the world. And why? Because there is no difference between void and world." This is what it is "to dwell, with a boundless heart, in the phantom-like Wisdom of the Tathāgata," "to know everything such as it is," and "to know that all dharmas are without ego."

To know things such as they are is to restore things to their own home-ground. And if the fact that the bird looks like a bird when it is flying points to the fact that the bird is flying, and is thus precisely what we called above its primal factuality, then knowing its suchness is no different from knowing that "this fact is this fact" and "this fact has its being as this fact." The identity of "being" and "knowing" is more primal than traditional metaphysics has taken it to be.

As we said above, on the field of śūnyatā, our self is at bottom prior to the world and things, and therein lies the roothold of the possibility of the world and the existence of things. This does not mean, as in Kant's philosophy, that the cognition of objects (and, consequently, of phenomena insofar as they are objects of cognition) would be a construction from a priori formalities of sensation and understanding. I speak here of the nonobjective "selfness" of things prior to any separation between materiality and formality or between matter and eidetic form, and prior to any consideration of the distinction between the phenomenon and the thing-in-itself. The point where the manifestation of things as they are in themselves "takes hold" rests in our own home-ground: on the field of śūnyatā.

Such knowledge of things in themselves (the knowing of non-knowing) means precisely that in truly returning to our own home-ground, we return to the home-ground of things that become manifest in the world. This knowledge is a realization (apprehension) in the sense of a reentry to the home-ground where things are manifest in their suchness. This reentry to the point where things in themselves realize themselves nonobjectively and posit themselves (on their *position* or samādhi-being), means for the self a direct reentry to the home-ground of the self itself. This is a knowing of non-knowing.

In a word, it is the nonobjective knowing of the nonobjective thing as it is in itself that we speak of. It is not a knowledge, therefore, that depends on rational capacity. As remarked earlier, reason has traditionally been called the "natural light," but the true "natural light" is not reason. If we call nature a *force* that gathers all things into one and arranges them into an order to bring about a "world," then this force belongs to the field of śūnyatā, which renders possible a circuminsessional interpenetration among all things. Returning to take a stand there means returning to the home-ground of the world and of things; and this, in turn, means a return of the self to the home-ground of the self. Therefore, once we grant that this is where the knowing of non-knowing originates, *this* knowledge has to be the true "natural light."

As opposed to reason, this light is not something apart from the very "being" of all things themselves. On the field of śūnyatā, the very being of all things, each of which becomes manifest as itself even as it is being gathered into unison with every other thing, is the being of the light of our knowledge (a knowing of non-knowing) returned to its own home-ground through its reentry into the field where all things are manifest. This is why the "natural light" within us was spoken of earlier as the light of the things themselves coming to us from all things. The light that illumines us from our own home-ground and brings us back to an elemental self-awareness is but the nonobjective being of things as they are in themselves on the field where all things are manifest from their own home-ground. It is also the reason why we could say, with Dōgen: "To practice and confirm all things by conveying one's self to them, is illusion; for all things to advance forward and practice and confirm the self, is enlightenment"; and with Musō Kokushi: "Hills and rivers, the earth, plants and trees, tiles and stones, all of these are the self's own original part."

The field of śūnyatā is a field whose center is everywhere. It is the field in which each and every thing—as an absolute center, possessed of an absolutely unique individuality—becomes manifest as it is in itself. To say that each thing is an absolute center means that wherever a thing *is*, the world *worlds*. And this, in turn, means that each thing, by being in its own home-ground is in the home-ground of all beings; and, conversely, that in being on the home-ground of all, each is in its own home-ground. (As I have stated repeatedly, this relationship is inconceivable except in the nonobjective mode of being of things where they are what they are in themselves.)

To claim, then, that a thing is such as it is, and is really itself, is no different from saying that all things are essentially one with one another and gathered together as a world. This is the "One and All," not as it is contemplated on the field of reason, but as it is comprehended on the field of śūnyatā. This is, as noted earlier, not simply "being," but being at one with emptiness; and, consequently, it is not an absolute unity abstracted from all multiplicity and differentiation in the world, but an absolute unity on the field where multiplicity and differentiation are absolutely radicalized. It means that an All that is nothingness-*sive*-being, being *sive*-nothingness is One; it means that on the field of śūnyatā all centers, each of which is absolutely independent, are essentially one.

In the nonobjective, "middle" mode of being where each thing in itself is concentrated in itself, all things of necessity concentrate themselves into one. For in the middle mode of being, it is necessary to the very essence of being that a thing be in the home-ground of every other thing in being in its own home-ground. Moreover, for the field of śūnyatā to open up in the return to our own home-ground, our self—in which the possibility of the world and of the existence of things takes hold—has to be what we termed above a self in itself: a self that is not itself in being itself, a self that is not a self.

We spoke of the selfness of things as the mode that we see, for example, in fire not burning fire, in the eye not seeing the eye, and so forth; and that can only be expressed paradoxically in statements such as, "Fire is not fire, therefore it is fire." Borrowing a term usually reserved for a state of mental concentration, we called this samādhi-being.

Now the same can be said with regard to the self that was spoken of as "confirmed by all things" in that mode of being, namely, the self that is not a self. The mode of being of the self that I have in mind in saying that emptiness is self, or that the self is not self because it is self, can also be expressed as what the ancients called "emptiness samādhi" or the "samādhi of non-mind Form." Samādhi is not simply a psychological concept but an *ontological* one. The point at which the non-objective mode of being of things as they are in themselves takes hold of its ground lies at the home-ground of our self ("in hand" and "underfoot"). In its own home-ground, the being of the self is essentially a sort of samādhi. No matter how dispersed the conscious self be, its self as it is in itself is ever in samādhi. Indeed, when we look back at it again from its home-ground, that dispersed mode of being, such as it is, is in samādhi.

I have called this nonobjective mode of being of things as they are in themselves—namely, the mode of being wherein things rest in the complete uniqueness of what they themselves are—a "middle"; I cited the saying, "If you try to explain something by comparing it with something else, you fail to hit the middle." If we grant that the field of śūnyatā, on which the possibility of the existence of the selfness of things takes hold of its ground, opens for us only when we return to our own home-ground, these words would apply in their most original sense to our own self in itself. Our self in itself is most elementally "middle." It resists all explanation because it is a being in unison with emptiness; because it is a being united with emptiness in a self-awareness according to which emptiness is self; and because, by virtue of that self-awareness, which is nearer to the elemental than anything else, it precedes the world and all things. Every human being in its selfness contains the field of that force by virtue of which the selfness of all things are gathered into one as a world. This field contains a roothold for the possibility of all things that become manifest in the world. And yet each human being, as such, is but one illusory thing in the world among others.

When we say that our self in itself is most elementally "middle," we are not thinking in terms of the "middle" that Aristotle, for instance, spoke of as the "mean" between too much and too little. Nor are we thinking of the role of go-between that Hegel attributed to reason as a "mediation" between contradictories. Whereas these are both "middles" projected on the field of reason, the "middle" seen as a mode of being on the field of emptiness cannot be projected on any other field whatsoever. It is immediately present—and immediately realized as such—at the point that we ourselves actually are. It is "at hand" for us and "underfoot." Just as no one else can see for us or hear for us, so too *none* of our actions can be performed by proxy. All actions imply, as it were, an absolute immediacy. And it is there that what we are calling the "middle" appears.

Now this insistence that we do not hit the "middle" of the self when we come at it through some other thing may seem to contradict the words cited earlier about hills and rivers, grass and trees, and so on being the self's original part. But this difficulty stems from the fact that hills and rivers, grass and trees, as well as the self itself, are being represented in a merely objective manner. On the field of the opposition between the subjective and the objective, the subject is still represented in a self-conscious manner such that it can never be objectified. But at a deeper level we find a relationship in which all things are in our home-ground and we ourselves are in the home-ground of all things. What we have in mind here is not a unification of subject and object, but what we called before a circuminsessional relationship. Therefore, even though we speak of hills and rivers as the self's original part, hills and rivers are here hills and rivers in *not* being hills and rivers, just as the self is the self in *not* being the self. And yet it is only here that hills and rivers are real hills and rivers in their suchness, only here that the self is the real self in its suchness. It is on this field that our self is the "self-presentation" of the most elemental "middle."

The same *Muchū mondō* that speaks of hills and rivers, grass and trees, and so on as the self's original part also contains the following example:

> The ancients tell us that every man possesses a spiritual light. When the *Sutra of Perfect Enlightenment* speaks of the samādhi of the Storehouse of the Great Light, it means this spiritual light that belongs to the nature of all sentient beings. What is called the body-light, the wisdom-light, and the miracle-light of all the Buddhas, all are born out of this Storehouse of the Great Light. Down to the ordinary man's distinguishing of east from west and black from white, there is nothing that is not the marvellous work of that spiritual light. But fools forget this original light and turn to the outside in search of a worldly light.

We noted earlier that the "natural light" is not the light of reason but the light of all things. What is here called "spiritual light" does not mean the light of the "soul" or the "spirit" in the ordinary sense of those words. It is rather a "samādhi of the Storehouse of the Great Light" out of which the light of all things (namely, the being itself of all things) is coming to birth; it belongs to the nature of every human being. When we say that our self in itself is the original and most elemental "middle," we are pointing to nothing other than just this.

5

ŚŪNYATĀ AND TIME

I

In previous chapters I touched on the problem of nihilism in connection with the standpoints of nihility and śūnyatā. This is not to say that the awareness of the abyss of nihility found in nihilism appears only in the West. Quite to the contrary, it has been present in the East, particularly in India, since ancient times as a perennial and fundamental issue. As we shall see presently, the central role that the problem of birth and death has played in the East illustrates the presence of this awareness.

But the advent of nihilism as a problem of deep significance, particularly for the modern Western world, was an historical, existential event that rose to awareness from the depths of history as a "European nihilism" and subtly foreshadowed the ground-shattering collapse of European civilization as a whole. The questions brought up by nihilism, at first heeded by only a few gifted thinkers, have since come to haunt us in modern life.[1] In Nietzsche, and in more contemporary figures like Heidegger, for instance, nihilism is dealt with on the horizon of the so-called "history of being."

This sort of situation does not exist in the East. Still, the East has achieved a conversion from the standpoint of nihility to the standpoint of śūnyatā. Given this achievement, it seems a matter of course that we be driven to pursue as a modern question the relationship of the standpoint of śūnyatā to historicity: the modes in which historicity *has* appeared on that standpoint in the past and *ought to* appear there today.

The Sanskrit term "*samsāra*" has been rendered as "birth-and-death" and also as "transmigration." It refers to the world view according to which the forms of life and existence found among all that lives, including man—collectively called "sentient beings"—as well as the fields of existence proper to each of these forms, are divided into "six ways" along which sentient beings are thought to migrate, alternating between birth and death like an endlessly rotating wheel.[2] In other words, it signifies the being-in-the-world that is apparent in all sentient beings. In Buddhism, this being-in-the-world as samsāra is grasped in a keenly existential fashion. Buddhist teaching speaks, for instance, of the "sea of samsāric suffering," likening the world, with all its six ways and its unending turnover from one form of existence to another, to an unfathomable sea and identifying the essential Form of beings made to roll with its restless motion as suffering.

Similarly, when the abyss of nihility arose existentially to self-awareness in the nihilism of modern Europe, the Existenz suspended out over that abyss could not help but awaken to itself as something pervaded by a Great Suffering (*Leiden*). But Buddhism goes a step beyond the existential self-awareness of suffering to speak of a "universal suffering" where "All is suffering," and to recognize in suffering a basic principle. It might not be wide of the mark to suggest that Buddhism's explanation of suffering as one of its Four Noble Truths— the "Truth about Suffering"—be regarded as an advance beyond the existential *awareness* of suffering to an existential *interpretation* (in Heidegger's sense) of being-in-the-world.

Be that as it may, contained in the awareness of an existence tossed about in the sea of samsāric suffering is the awareness of an unfathomable nihility and "nullification." The turnover of birth-and-death—that incessant becoming that is the essence of our being—occurs as a result of our own acts (the three karma of thought, word, and deed which constitute our voluntary actions of body and mind) and the "worldly passions" that accompany them. Since our Dasein, determined by the karma of an unlimited past, in its turn determines the karma of an unlimited future, the essence of our present voluntary actions (karma) comes into perspective against the backdrop of a causality of fate without end. We say "fate," but seen from the viewpoint of endless transmigration in the world of birth-and-death, it means fundamentally that everyone without exception reaps only the fruits of his own acts. Existence seen as suffering is able to clarify its true Form only by "taking hold of" its own acts. One may explain this as a deeply existential prehension of being lying beneath the surface of this way of looking at birth and death in terms of samsāra.

The finitude of man's being-in-the-world is here grasped as un-bounded and unending in its essence. The finitude of human existence is essentially an *infinite finitude*. Now to be infinitely finite, or in other words, for the finite to continue on infinitely, is "bad infinity" (*schlechte Unendlichkeit*, as Hegel calls it), a concept that logic usually treats as a stepchild. On the one hand, for a logic of *Verstand* ("understanding"), which takes its stand on a discursive thinking that is at bottom incapable of prehending anything but finite things, to be infinitely finite is a sheer contradiction. Such thinking can only land one in antinomies. On the other hand, in a logic of *Vernunft* ("reason"), which relies on an intuitive thinking that grasps the whole at a single stroke, the representation of infinity in the shape of an interminable finitude is not the notion of a true infinity. In either case, no valid concept emerges from our talk of an "infinitely finite" or an "interminable finitude." These things remain, as a whole, meaningless.

When man takes the standpoint of Existenz as his own, however, and becomes aware of his own finitude as "infinitely finite" in its very essence, something is implied that cannot simply be dismissed as logi-cally meaningless. The logical contradiction here of something being infinitely finite rather brings out the fact that finitude has been revealed as a radical finitude. It signals a revelation of the essence of finitude *qua* finitude. This revelation of essence is impossible for a conceptual way of thinking about finitude; only an existential self-awareness directly con-fronting its own finitude can bring it about.

On this standpoint of Existenz, the essence of finitude is not finite. In conceptual thinking, it is a self-evident tautology to say that finitude is finite; in existential self-awareness, for the finite to grasp itself purely and simply as finite is for it to grasp its own finitude nonexistentially, that is, "contemplatively" or, rather, "representationally." One's own finitude is represented as finite, as something that will one day cease to be.

It is much the same with our ordinary way of considering death: on that day in the years ahead when I die, death will, along with me, cease to be. This representation of death is altogether different from what we spoke of before as existentially realizing the essence of death together with the essence of life from the midst of one's own lived existence. If one starts from a prehension of self and death according to which one's own death also means the death of one's own death, access to a way beyond birth-and-death, passage to a field that has cast off birth-and-death, is blocked. It is not that a passageway beyond birth-and-death does not exist, but only that man bars himself from it and commits it to oblivion. (This is the true form of indifference to things religious.)

In brief, the statement that the finite is finite, while quite valid in terms of conceptual thinking, is in error from an existential standpoint. It misses the essence of finitude, and because it is prehended from a standpoint that does not face up to existential finitude existentially, it fails truly to reveal finitude. From the standpoint of Existenz, not only the logic of discursive understanding but also the logic of speculative reason fundamentally entails such an omission. Indeed, it was just such an insight that called forth Kierkegaard's confrontation with Hegel.

The claim that the essence of finitude is not finite, however, carries meaning as a *ratio* of a stamp and scope altogether different from that of discursive understanding and speculative reason. We find an outlook of such scope in our own time, for example, in the development of what is called a phenomenological standpoint. Blossoming out of Husserl's "intuition of essence" it developed further in the "existential interpretation" of Heidegger's existential phenomenology. Within such a perspective, a *ratio* completely different in character from the *ratio* of logic comes to light.

Now what sort of *ratio* of what sort of Existenz is meant by saying that finitude is seen as infinitely finite in its essence, and that this is a radical revelation of finitude? It consists in man's grasp of his own finitude on a dimension of transcendence—of "trans-descendence," so to speak—that breaks through the standpoint of discursive understanding and speculative reason to the depth of his own existence. It is an awareness that the finitude of Dasein, as well as finite Dasein itself, becomes manifest from such a field of transcendence. It is, in other words, the *ecstatic* awareness of Dasein.

In comparison with this transcendence-as-ecstasy, even the absoluteness of Hegel's speculative reason remains immanent. From his standpoint of absolute Reason, where the most profound internal continuity between God and man may be said to have opened up, all phenomena whatsoever are absorbed into the self-development of the rational order of Reason and become part of the process whereby the thinking of Reason reverts back to itself.

The dimension of transcendence, or field of ecstasy, in comparison with which even this circular process of absolute Reason is still immanent, is the field where the *essence* of finitude reaches awareness. It is the field where birth-and-death is seen as an endless "wheel of becoming" (κύκλος γενέσεως or samsāra); or, we might say, the circular process of finite existence itself. To confront finitude existentially is to confirm through insight the essence of actual existence as a being-in-the-world, and to do so directly underfoot of actual existence itself, on such a field of trans-descendence. In other words, for actual existence and its finitude to be confronted directly underfoot as what becomes manifest from a field that lies beyond even the dimension of reason is the revelation of the essence of finitude. The essence revealed in this way is entirely different in character from the so-called essence that is grasped conceptually on the dimension of reason. It can only be investigated existentially.

But if the possession of reason in general is the distinctive trait of mankind, and if man be definable as *animal rationale*, then it follows as a matter of course that the existential investigation of human existence just spoken of and its existential interpretation lie beyond the scope of the "human," as something on the dimension of an ecstatic transcendence. The essence of finitude or birth-and-death may be revealed in man's existential investigation of his own existence, on the field of ecstasy on which that essence arises to awareness as an infinite finitude, as an endlessly revolving finitude or as the circular process of finitude itself. Still, a perspective that goes beyond the scope of the merely human is required for the revelation of that essence. For a fundamental investigation of human existence, the man-centered point of view, the kind of outlook in which man sets himself at the center, has to be broken through. To look on the birth-and-death of man—namely, the finitude apparent in the "species" called man—as a transmigration along the "six ways," from a total horizon that embraces the other forms of existence and types of species within the world, in fact points to a true prehension of the essence of the life and death of man himself. It signals a radical and direct confrontation with birth-and-death, one that has penetrated all the way to the field of ecstasy. There birth-and-death is truly grasped as birth-and-death.

We have two perspectives: one looks on the essence of birth-and-death as unending, the other as falling within a total scope that embraces man and the other species. In direct existential confrontation, they are fused together. If infinite finitude be said to constitute the temporal facet of the essence of birth-and-death in being-in-the-world, the total horizon can be called its spatial facet. The endless rotations of finitude, the circular process of finitude itself, is an endless pilgrimage of finite existence on a horizon embracing the forms of human existence and the existence of other species. The same correlation between temporality and spatiality is also seen in the way that man grasps the samsāric suffering of his being-in-the-world, against a background of "transmigration along the six ways," as "universal suffering." This Buddhist doctrine can also be seen as one expression of an existential investigation and existential interpretation of human existence.

Needless to say, in terms of its representational content, the notion of transmigration is "mythical" and can easily be criticized as prescientific fantasy. And as far as content goes, such criticism is well taken. But matters are not quite so simple. In general, scientific criticism against the mythical is quite correct to point out the limits of prelogical thinking involved in the representational content of myth. But it is quite incorrect to pass over the existential elements that compose the core of myth: the direct existential confrontation with being-in-the-world and the unique *ratio* this reveals, as we see these embodied in the mythico-religious aspects of human existence in prescientific societies. Here again, intellect is prone to throw out the baby with the bath: somehow the baby in the tub seems to elude the eye of intellect. The field that has broken through the dimension of intellectual knowing does not enter the field of vision of intellect.

We say "intellect," but in fact matters are not so simple here either. There is intellect on the standpoint of science and intellect on the standpoint of philosophy. Even when philosophy first came to being as a *logos* or "science" (though opinion is divided on this question), it did so as a *demythification*—or, if you will, a *logification*—of the mythical world view in which it, nonetheless, remained firmly rooted. We may even go so far as to say that the underlying root of the *mythos* hidden deep beneath Greek philosophy has remained intact throughout the whole of its development, and that this accounts in part for the depth and richness of its *logos*. While it may be called a *de*mythification of the mythical through the logical, it was not a pure and simple negation of the mythical. That sort of negation begins with the standpoint of science proper, or rather, "scientism." Science grasps the mythical on the dimension of its outer shell of representations, which it banishes as unscientific. Philosophy, for its part, recognizes in the same representations symbols of *logos* which it then restores to the dimension of *logos*.

But neither the negation of myth by scientific intellect nor its transmutation into *logos* by philosophic intellect can exhaust the essence within myth. The mythical has to be restored to the existential whence it originates in an elemental sense and within which the core of the content of its meaning can be accorded anew an existential interpretation on the dimension of Existenz. The positive significance in myth will truly be revealed only through what Bultmann speaks of as *existentielle Entmythologisierung*. The same applies to the notion of transmigration.

The dynamic of demythification in this sense has been at work throughout the history of Buddhism. Indeed, from the very time that Buddhism first came to being, from its inception as a religion, this dynamic was already present, such that it may even be taken as the unique feature of Buddhism, distinguishing it from other religions.

The notion of transmigration taken up into Buddhism has time and again in the history of Buddhism been drawn back to the problem of the essence of Existenz. The "meaning" of transmigration has been drawn from an existential interpretation of human existence. It was, in a word, the essence or true Form of finitude within human existence: the infinite finitude that is true finitude. Though a bottomless nihility at the ground of human existence, it was opened up existentially. Though a nihility so abyssal as to nullify everything that has being in the world (called collectively "the three worlds" in Buddhism), it came to actualize itself in the Dasein of man even as it nullified the being of Dasein.

In such a *realization* of nihility, man takes possesion of birth-and-death in its suchness, that is, he takes possession of the original Form of his own Dasein and the original Form of things in the world such as they are. What we have here, in short, is an existential encounter with nihility. Nihility can only be known existentially. If we stray but a step from the path of Existenz, nihility can only seem an utterly meaningless notion, devoid of reality. In fact, a great many philosophers, from a great many points of view, have come to that very conclusion. It is like a radio that has not been tuned in properly and picks up only senseless static that totally blocks out the real sound of the broadcast. For only in the existential confrontation with nihility do we see the earnest life-or-death struggle for the transcendence of birth-and-death, escape from the unending causality of karma, and attainment of the "yonder shore" beyond the fathomless sea of suffering. It is, in other words, the struggle for *nirvāna*.

II

It is only in breaking through to the field of ecstatic transcendence (or trans-descendence), then, that the awareness of birth-and-death as "transmigration" comes about. This ecstatic trans-descendence appears in the endlessness of finite life and in the totality of the horizon that embraces the mode of being of man along with that of the other species. Nihility opens up only in this transcendence. The nihility encountered in the nullification of all that is or might be constitutes the existential meaning contained in the notion of transmigration. In a universality that embraces all possible forms of existence (the six ways), and in the infinity of birth-and-death migrating through all these forms of existence, this nihility represents the final ground of being-in-the-world.

.   In this nihility, the "limit-situations" of human existence are pushed beyond the field on which they are usually considered to the field of ecstatic trans-descendence. The limit-situation that rises to awareness here is set against a horizon of worldliness that goes beyond the perspective of the merely "human" and stops to rest on a field rid of a mode of being determined by a "human" ego that falls within the determined span of time from birth to death. The real Form of our existence in the world (in other words, the essence of actual existence or the meaning of being-in-the-world) is revealed at its ground only on a field that has gone beyond the scope of a man-centered outlook and taken leave of a subjective, "egoistic" mode of being.

The limit-situation we meet on that all-encompassing field of transcendence as an infinite finitude marks the point of a self-awareness that has pierced through human existence to its very bottom. There, directly beneath the Dasein of man, the real Form of his existence rises to self-awareness at one with the real Form of all other things in the world. There the essence of human being-in-the-world is revealed as a being-in-the-world in this sort of all-encompassing infinity (infinite finitude) and thence in its own selfness as well.

For this reason, at the outer limits of human existence, the essence of human existence is no longer merely "human." It belongs to the class of all sentient beings in the sense that it embraces every other form of existence. Freed of the determinations of the human, it is, as it were, a naked being-in-the world *as itself*. It is sheer being-in-the-world in its straightforward sense, existentially more essential then being-in-the-world *as man*. The existential self-awareness of existence as human existence is only able to be truly essential when it progresses to a being-in-the-world in such a straightforward sense, and from there goes on to become an awareness of "human" existence.

This is what was meant by the claim advanced earlier that existential self-awareness can only open up on the field of ecstatic transcendence where the framework of the "human" self has been broken through in an abyssal nihility that nullifies at one and the same time the existence of man and of all things. Abyssal nihility is the point at which being-in-the-world is encountered as sheer being-in-the-world, rid of all its possible determinations. It is the point at which all existing things are stripped of all forms of existence found on the "six ways," be they godly, human, animal, or whatever; and are pushed to the pure and simple form of merely having being in the world.

Now the ecstatic trans-descendence we have been speaking of is that of an existence through and through within the world and striking against its own bottom. To that extent, it remains thoroughly inner-worldly. This sheer being-in-the-world rid of all determinations does not of itself represent a transcendency from the world. Nor is it a departure from the "three worlds." On the contrary, it reveals the ultimate form of being in the world and the essential form of the existence of all things that have their being in the world. This essential form is, as noted above, interminable finitude, birth-and-death as "transmigration." It signals an advance to the final frontier on the field of sheer being-in-the-world at which man surpasses the determinations of the human. It is man's collision with the essential barrier of his own Dasein. This is the so-called brink of despair, and yet also the ultimate form of man's being in the world.

Despair is the truly real Form of existence: it makes its presence felt as something that allows for no skepsis. Whereas skepsis is a matter for the dimension of reason, despair belongs to the dimension of transcendence. It is the Form that existence itself assumes in the nihility that has opened up. This is the same sense in which we spoke earlier of the "self-presentation of the Great Doubt," the "doubt without doubt" that emerges as human existence itself on the dimension of transcendence.

In Buddhism, true transcendence, detachment from the "world" of samsāra as such, has been called *nirvāna*. If existence in the world rests essentially on nihility, as something being nullified; and if life, subjected to the cycle of birth-and-death, be in essence a death; then nirvāna, which means dying to this "life" of birth-and-death and hence dying to "death" in its essential sense, is a "life" in its essential sense. Or again, if the essence of being-in-the-world be taken as a "being-unto-death" (to adopt a term from Heidegger), then nirvāna points to an essential conversion away from it, a breaking through this being-unto-death. It is the essential conversion from true finitude to true infinity, that is, away from finitude as "bad infinity" in Existenz to infinity in Existenz. As a taking leave of the endless cycle of birth-and-death, nirvāna is a rebirth to true life. It is new life. And here, for the first time, true infinity appears.

Infinity, as a reality, is cut off from the prehension of reason. No sooner do we try to grasp it on the dimension of reason than it turns forthwith into something conceptual. True infinity as reality refuses to be encountered anywhere but along the path of Existenz. This infinity itself arises to awareness only in becoming present within human existence, even as it effects an essential conversion in that existence. To take possession of infinity is for infinity to become reality as life; for it to be *really* lived.

The Existenz that connotes such a new life is nothing other than nirvāna, and such true infinity is śūnyatā. In the departure from samsāra to nirvāna, a conversion from nihility to śūnyatā takes place. It is an essential conversion from "death" in its basic sense to "life" in its basic sense, from true "finitude" to true "infinity."

III

Passage from the world of samsāra to the far side of the "yonder shore" means an essential (ontologically speaking, an "existential") conversion in Existenz. But in Buddhist teaching the existential investigation into self-being and self-awareness does not stop there. The return of Existenz to its own home-ground and the quest of the self for the *original self*, the self as it is at bottom, still harbor the possibility of a final great conversion. The openness of existential transcendence has to advance a stage deeper in its development. I spoke earlier of nihility as the truly real Form of birth-and-death, and of true finitude as nihility; moreover, I spoke of nirvāna as true life, and of true infinity as nirvāna or śūnyatā. But is this in fact the case? Even if this all be granted as sound truth for the process of existential inquiry into existence that begins from the fact of being within the world of life-and-death, can the same still be said after the conversion from the world of life-and-death to its far side? In the previous chapters mention was made of how the absolute far side becomes an absolute near side on the standpoint of śūnyatā. But what actually takes place there on that standpoint? Is true finitude and the true form of birth-and-death indeed nothing but nihility? Do true infinity and true life really come down only to nirvāna?

It is a widely known fact in the history of Buddhism that with the development of the Mahāyāna teaching, an entirely new standpoint appeared on the scene: a standpoint referred to as a "non-abiding in nirvāna" or as "samsāra-*sive*-nirvāna." We find this expressed clearly and simply, for instance, in Dōgen's well-known words from the *Shōbōgenzō Shōji*: "Just understand that birth-and-death itself is nir-vāna. . . . Only then can you be free of birth-and-death." And later: "This present birth-and-death itself is the Life of Buddha." This is Existenz on the standpoint at which "birth itself is non-birth" and "extinction itself is non-extinction."[3]

We may perhaps see in Dōgen's admonition to "understand" sam-sāra-*sive*-nirvāna that Existenz-as-"realization" of which we have just spoken. This "understanding" is the realization (manifestation-*sive*-apprehension) of the proper point at which samsāra is nirvāna and nirvāna is samsāra; and, hence, where samsāra and nirvāna are *not* samsāra and nirvāna. It is the realization of a reality that is neither samsāra nor nirvāna, of what is intended, in short, by the copula "*sive*" in the formula, samsāra-*sive*-nirvāna. The essence of this reality that becomes manifest in its suchness—or, in Buddhist terminology, the "mind" of the Tathāgata or "Buddha-mind"—*projects* itself (in the double sense of a reflection and a transference) into the essence of human existence, into the "mind" of man, bringing about its conver-sion; at the same time, the essence *projects* that reality back into itself. As the well-known Buddhist simile goes, it is like two mirrors reflecting off of one another without any intervening image. The mind of the Tathā-gata and the mind of man reflect each other in such a way that the very same light (the so-called light of the mind) transfers from one mind onto the other, and vice versa. This is the sense of the word that Dōgen uses for understanding, a word that means literally "obtaining the mind of."

In Japanese, the "meaning" of a given *koto* (a term signifying either "matter" or "affair," as well as "word") can also be called its "mind," or *kokoro*. In solving a riddle, for instance, we say that we have "obtained its mind" when we have understood what it means.[4] To "obtain the mind" of the "meaning" of a given *koto* ("matter"), to apprehend its *ratio* or *logos*, is for the reality that has become manifest as that *koto* ("matter and word") to transfer essentially, just as it is and in its suchness, into the man who understands it; and for the man who understands it to be transferred into that reality. In other words, the mind of the matter at hand (or the very reality become manifest in the *koto*) reflects into the mind of man, and the mind of man reflects itself onto the mind of the *koto*. This living transmission of minds being projected onto one another just as they are, and the obtaining of mind that this effects, is the elemental mode of the understanding of meaning. It is not, therefore, that the "meaning" of a certain thing first exists somewhere and then we come along to grasp it. Rather, the obtaining of mind (understanding) is aboriginal as the sort of realization wherein a *koto* takes possession of us and transfers into us, even as we in turn really transfer over into the *koto* so that our mind becomes and works as the *koto*.

"Meaning" is something abstracted from out of this living co-projection between mind and *koto*: an abstraction in which mind and *koto* stand in some conceptually "ideal" correlation. At the bottom of the dimension that sees the emergence of the meaning we ordinarily speak of understanding by means of intellect and the emergence of the objects of intellectual cognition, there lies the dimension of the elemental encounter with *koto*. It is here that meanings and intellectual cognition are constituted. Intellectualism, faced with deciding whether or not any given *koto* is meaningful, operates with a blind spot at its ground in virtue of taking a stance that assumes as its criterion this sort of "meaning." It forgets to ask in the first place after the meaning of the "meaning" that it sets up as its criterion. A *koto*, as some matter seen objectively or as the spoken word, is, along with its *ratio* or meaning, already divorced from reality. We have merely a mirror image of reality projected onto the dimension of the intellect.

With respect to the *koto* of samsāra-*sive*-nirvāna, I have said that its meaning is apprehended existentially in such a way that the mind of the Tathāgata projects into the mind of man, and the mind of man projects into the mind of the Tathāgata. I also spoke of this co-projection as the realization of the reality of the *sive*. But what does all this amount to for us after all? We recall that Dōgen said it is only through "understanding" of this sort that we may free ourselves from birth-and-death. That is, only in an Existenz of samsāra-*sive*-nirvāna is there true emancipation from the transcendence of birth-and-death.

I would underscore the use of the word "true" here, since it has been our focus all along to find out just what that word means. In this regard, it was noted earlier on that in the orientation to ecstatic transcendence in human existence, nirvāna (the transcendence into emptiness), rather than transcendence into nihility, is the *true* transcendence. Again, we also spoke of *true* infinity in nirvāna in contrast to *bad* existential infinity in nihility. But now I say that the "true" referred to there is not yet *truly* true. It is not so-called nirvāna, but rather a non-abiding in nirvāna, samsāra-*sive*-nirvāna, that is truly *true* transcendence, *true* infinity, and, in this sense, *true* nirvāna.

Once again, we are faced here with a situation in which nirvāna is nirvāna only when it is not nirvāna. When we persist in our pursuit of what is *truly* true, among the things that are true, the *truly* true appears in the mode of paradox or absurdity, under conditions ordinarily considered as altogether contradictory to truth. Where *ratio* is pushed to its true extreme, the "irrational" shows up. Where meaning is pushed to its extreme, "meaninglessness" shows up. And yet what thus appears as paradox, irrationality, or meaninglessness, is truly absolute reality. It is the living vitality of "life" itself. To say here that life as such is meaningless is to say that life is truly living itself. It is, in other words, a point where life transcends all meaning, albeit a point where all meaning is able to be constituted as "meaning" only in relationship to that point. It is the point that Meister Eckhart calls *Leben ohne Warum* ("life without a reason why"). It is the same with the claim that paradox is the "truth" and that irrationality is the *ratio*.

The field of nirvāna appears, therefore, only when one does not cling to nirvāna and when nirvāna is turned around so as not to be nirvāna. It was remarked earlier that nirvāna is essentially "life" because it is a dying to samsāric life, which is essentially a "death." But when we pursue the *essentiality* of this essential life to its very end, non-essential life appears where essential life reaches its outer limit, its point of consummation, where it is, as it were, on the point of being totally consumed. In other words, true nirvāna appears as samsāra-*sive*-nirvāna. Here life is sheer life and yet thoroughly paradoxical. We can speak, for example, of essentiality in its true essence as a non-essentiality. If we could not speak in such terms as these, life would not truly be life. It would not be life at once truly eternal and truly temporal.

Therefore, it is not enough to say that birth-and-death is essentially "death." It is essentially life while remaining essentially death. As Dōgen says, "Birth-and-death is itself the Life of Buddha." Samsāra is truly samsāra as samsāra-*sive*-nirvāna, "Samsāra is not samsāra, therefore it is samsāra"—this is its truth. This *sive/non* in samsāra, along with the *sive/non* in nirvāna mentioned earlier, mingle into one. Samsāra-*sive*-nirvāna is true samsāra and true nirvāna. It is true time and true eternity. Samsāric life as such, at every moment coming into being and at every moment passing away, its every moment but a transitory node of the no-more and the not-yet, must be the very place that the bliss of nirvāna makes itself present. What is brought to awareness as the essence of Dasein in this world of birth-and-death (namely, the interminable finitude of "being" that embraces all possible forms of existence on the field of what is called the "world") and the history of "karmic" causality trailing off into an endless future (as the Zen saying has it, "Out of the ass's womb and into the horse's belly"), these things, just as they are, make up the Life of Buddha. In Dōgen's words, "Birth itself is non-birth; extinction itself is non-extinction."

I said that interminable finitude in birth-and-death is true finitude, but in fact this still falls short of truly true finitude. Truly true finitude is the finitude of birth-and-death on the level of samsāra-*sive*-nirvāna. As the negation-*sive*-affirmation of birth-and-death, nirvāna becomes that which makes birth-and-death to be truly birth-and-death. Nirvāna becomes the real suchness of birth-and-death, its *reality*, its bottomlessness. The birth-and-death that thus becomes bottomless in samsāra-*sive*-nirvāna, the finitude of birth-and-death that there becomes bottomlessly samsāric, is true finitude.

Here each and every moment of time that becomes manifest in its bottomlessness, the life of each and every moment of time of Dasein in birth-and-death, is *realized* (manifested-*sive*-apprehended) as the Life of Buddha. In such an Existenz, we are at each moment of time bottomlessly "in time." In bottomlessly embracing the endless past and endless future, we bring time to the fullness of time at each and every moment of time. On the field of the absolute near side, where transitoriness as such is nirvāna, time is at all times arrived at the fullness of time. Every moment is a "good" moment for us. "Every day, a good day," says Ummon. And Dōgen, referring to this way of Existenz, says "Body-and-mind dropping off, dropped off body-and-mind."

We said above that "understanding" in the sense of a realization—that is, as the apprehension of a reality that has become manifest essentially, "just as it is"—means that the mind of the Tathāgata is *projected* into the mind of man, and vice versa. Even if we substitute "life" for "mind," there is, of course, no change in meaning. For the "mind" we are dealing with here is not the mind we ordinarily envisage as consciousness or intellect. At least it is not consciousness or intellect on a field where they grasp themselves (and are thereby, instead, caught in their own grasp). It is not the discerning mind that is discerned only by the discerning mind itself, since that was already broken through in the ecstatic transcendence to the field of nihility. Nor is the discerning mind the mind of existential self-awareness on the field of true emptiness, of true nirvāna as samsāra-*sive*-nirvāna.

The mind we are speaking of here is the non-discerning mind that is the absolute negation of the discernment of consciousness or intellect. This is non-discernment: "Do not be anxious about tomorrow, for tomorrow will be anxious for itself" (Matt. 6:24). As the Japanese proverb has it: "Tomorrow's wind will blow tomorrow." We noted above that true life is beyond all meaning, and yet all meaning is constituted in relationship to it. This *meaning*less character of "life" corresponds to the non-*discernment* of "mind" spoken of here.

Now this meaninglessness and non-discernment are not the same as we find them on the standpoint of nihilism. Here non-discernment is the bottomlessness of the discernment that takes place on any given occasion, its reality, its true suchness. It is what makes every discernment a discernment in the true sense of the word. It is a *discernment of non-discernment*. It is like the words of the gospel: "Do not be anxious, saying, 'What shall we eat?' or 'What shall we drink?' or 'What shall we wear?' . . . Let the day's own trouble be sufficient for the day" (Matt. 6:31,34). The anxious, petty troubles of daily life (ἡ μαμία) are sufficient to themselves from one day to the next. The karma of deed, word, and thought in the world of birth-and-death, with its accompanying worldly passions and discernment, is complete in itself from one day to the next. That is what we call the discernment of non-discernment that is an essential element of true life and true mind. Here, in the discernment entailed in our preoccupations with workaday trifles, lies the bottomlessness of non-discernment. In Christian teaching, this bottomlessness seems to open up to the Kingdom of God and his righteousness (Matt. 6:33). In Buddhism, it can be said to open up to the absolute state where, for instance, "Every day is a good day."

In any case, the non-discerning mind at issue here is not something subjective in the manner of what is ordinarily called mind. It is a field that lets the being of all things be, a field on which all things can be themselves on their own home-grounds, the field of śūnyatā that I have called the field of the elemental possibility of the existence of all things. This emptiness—where it is said, "form (or a given thing in its determined, definite form) is emptiness, emptiness is form," and where something similar can be said of the other *skandhas* (namely, perception, imagination, volition, and recognition)—is the mind of non-discernment. In terms of objectivity, this mind is more objective than anything "objective." In terms of subjectivity, it is more subjective than anything "subjective." While itself transcending determinations of objectivity and subjectivity, it yet bestows objectivity upon whatever is said to be objective and subjectivity upon whatever is said to be subjective. This "mind" is not an object of contemplation; it is only *realized* (manifested-

sive-apprehended) existentially. Here, even contemplation is transformed into Existenz.

In the *Heart Sutra* we read:

> At the time Avalokitesvara Bodhisattva engaged in the observance of deep prajñāpāramitā, he saw with illuminating insight that the five aggregates [skandhas] were all empty and delivered sentient beings from all their suffering.

The "observance" and "time" alluded to here are matters of Existenz. For this reason, the "illuminating insight" does not stop at mere contemplation. It is integrated with the deliverance of all beings in time from the universal suffering of the world. When this mind is realized, it is realized as something like a reality through which alone all things real are rendered real, as "True Emptiness, Wondrous Being," a phrase usually acknowledged as expressing the core of Mahāyāna Buddhism. This is more real than anything that is real. When it is called "mind," it is not that it is being conceived of merely in terms of an analogy drawn from subjective consciousness. Quite to the contrary, each of the activities of our subjective consciousness and intellect, as in truth a discernment of non-discernment, proceeds forth from the mind referred to as "True Emptiness, Wondrous Being."

In general, our true self is a self only as that "self that is not a self," which I spoke of earlier. The self-conscious, self-centered self we usually take for the self—namely, the "ego"—is not grounded in itself. The *original self* within the ego as the home-ground of the ego is, at bottom, ecstatic. The essence of the ego is not of the ego. That which emerges into the nature and disposition of the ego is the negative of ego: the self as non-ego. The reason ego can emerge at all can only lie in the essential nature of ego itself, and yet in its emergence that same ego always comes to appear as something that obscures its own ground of being and its own true nature.

It was noted earlier on that the self is laid bare when "in the Great Death heaven and earth become new," and where the world *worlds*. This original self is invariably already present in each particular operation of the ego, albeit in the sort of mode we referred to in saying that "The eye does not see the eye." But, on the other hand, the ego can never make itself present to the original self. Insofar as ego is ego, the continued presence of the original self in the ego is forever hidden from the ego. So much for the "mind" as the discernment of non-discernment.

The same can properly be said of what we have been calling here "life." But this should not be understood simply on the basis of life as we are used to thinking of it, in terms of life-and-death, as if Dōgen's words were merely an expression of that ordinary life by means of conceptual (or, at best, metaphysical) analysis. From such an approach, life as such could not be conceived of as the Life of Buddha. It would be putting the cart before the horse, viewing discernment from without, aloof from Existenz. To say that birth-and-death is the Life of Buddha would be, in a word, an utter falsehood. It would mean turning on its head the way of looking at birth-and-death as well as the way of looking at the Life of Buddha, with the result that both would cease to be right "understanding" as Dōgen speaks of it. It is only on the field of samsāra-sive-nirvāna, on the field of "release from birth-and-death," that it becomes possible to speak of samsāric body-and-mind as such as being the Life of Buddha.

Hence, when we say "mind" and "life" here, we mean mind and life on the field where body-and-mind "drops off," and where the "dropped off" body-and-mind is present in full self-awareness and openness to the vitality of life. This "body-and-mind" does not refer simply to "thing" and "consciousness" in their ordinary senses. Nor is this body-and-mind on a field where it can become an object of study for physics, physiology, psychology, and the like. As Dōgen puts it, "The dropping off of body-and-mind is neither form [thing] nor consciousness."

IV

The phrase, "body-and-mind dropping off" expresses the characteristic feature of Dōgen's Zen as it was imparted to him by his Chinese master Ju-ching (1163–1268). It also affords us a glimpse into one refined configuration of the religious Existenz found in Buddhism in general.

We ordinarily regard our own body-and-mind as our "self." We fix it as the cardinal point within us, so to speak, on which all our seeing and doing hinges. But, as was said before, the true form of the original self only appears when this structure is broken down and we have become disengaged from our fixation on body-and-mind. Dōgen tells us that when he was studying and practicing Zen under Ju-ching, he attained the Great Enlightenment in a flash upon hearing Ju-ching say,

"To practice Zen is to drop off body-and-mind." In the same context we find such statements as: "The practice of Zen is the dropping off of body-and-mind: it is *just sitting*"; and "Dropping off of body-and-mind means sitting in Zen meditation. When we are *just sitting*, we free ourselves from the five desires and rid ourselves of the five hindrances."

The dropping off of body-and-mind and *just sitting* are one and the same thing here: they emancipate us from the five desires (the desires that tether us to the external world through attachment to the objects of our five senses) and from the five hindrances (the worldly passions that tie us to ourselves by knotting up our minds and keeping our true mind covered over). And this emancipatory dropping off of body-and-mind sets us free of those ties and fetters, and, hence, from the world of suffering and birth-and-death as well as from ourselves. It means that our true mind, once stripped of its hindrances, is laid bare as an ecstatic openness and passes out of the world. It is Existenz that stands upon the field of transcendence even as it opens the field up. And all this, again, is nothing other than "to practice Zen."

The practice of Zen is said to be the dropping off of body-and-mind, and the dropping off of body-and-mind is said to be sitting in Zen meditation (zazen). But Ju-ching tells us to take leave of the fundamental darkness of ignorance (*avidyā*) that constitutes the ground of the five hindrances by *just sitting*. In his words:

> Descendents of the Buddhas and the patriarchs first rid themselves of the five hindrances, and then rid themselves of the six hindrances. The six hindrances consist of the five hindrances plus the hindrance of the darkness of ignorance. If we only eliminate the hindrance of the darkness of ignorance, we thereby eliminate the five hindrances as well. Although we get free of the five hindrances, if we do not get free of the hindrance of the darkness of ignorance, we cannot attain to the practice and realization of the Buddhas and the patriarchs.

The hindrance of the darkness of ignorance in question, the so-called fundamental affliction, is, it seems to me, the form proper to sheer being-in-the-world that I spoke of earlier as the basic mode of being in the samsāric world. It is said here that we take our leave of the darkness of ignorance exclusively by means of *just sitting*.

Elsewhere in the same work Dōgen reports receiving the following instruction from Ju-ching:

> What you have been striving for until now is nothing other than a means for release from the six hindrances. . . . Through working out a resolution in just sitting,

body-and-mind comes to drop off. This is the technique for release from the five
desires, the five hindrances, and so on. Aside from this, there is no other way.[5]

Therefore, the point at which man takes leave of the darkness of
ignorance is the point at which the true mind is thrown open. It is the
point where, as Dōgen has it, "body-and-mind drops away naturally,
and the original countenance becomes present."[6] This "original
countenance" Ju-ching calls "supple mind": "To discern and affirm the
dropping off of body-and-mind of the Buddhas and the patriarchs—
that is the supple mind. This we call the mind-seal of the Buddhas and
the patriarchs."[7] The "supple mind" that hits the mark in its discernment of the dropping off of body-and-mind in the Buddhas and the
patriarchs and affirms it, is itself the dropping off of body-and-mind,
and the attestation to a new life animated by the "Life of Buddha." This
Life of Buddha, however, cannot exist apart from birth-and-death. It is
only by "obtaining the mind" of samsāra-*sive*-nirvāna that one can share
in this release from birth-and-death. In an old commentary on the *Shōji*
("Birth-and-Death") chapter of the *Shōbōgenzō*, this is described as becoming "the solitary one laid bare amidst the myriad phenomena."[8]

At any rate, Existenz on the field of samsāra-*sive*-nirvāna is a
dropping off of body-and-mind, the original countenance of the "supple mind." And just as Ju-ching speaks of "body-and-mind dropping
off, dropped off body-and-mind," the field of release from birth-and-
death lies directly beneath the body-and-mind of birth-and-death. For
this reason, after citing Ju-ching's words to the effect that the practice of
Zen is the dropping off of body-and-mind that is attainable by *just
sitting*, Dōgen remarks that the body-and-mind sitting in meditation as
such is the King of Samādhis Samādhi, "plucking out the eye of the
buddhas and the patriarchs and just sitting in its hollow."[9] Here we see
how the "just" of *just sitting* implies the single-mindedness of self-
concentration (samādhi) in the practice of zazen.

The character of *just sitting* is further spelled out in another passage:

> Now we know, without any doubt, that sitting cross-legged is in itself the King of
> Samādhis Samādhi. It is entering into realization. All samādhis are subordinates of
> this King of Samādhis. Cross-legged sitting is the body of suchness, the mind of
> suchness, the body-and-mind of suchness, the buddhas and patriarchs in their
> suchness, practice-realization in its suchness, the crown of the head in its suchness,
> the Dharma lineage in its suchness.
>
> Bringing this present human skin, flesh, bone, and marrow together, one forms
> the King of Samādhis Samādhi.[10]

Elsewhere, Dōgen terms *just sitting* a "self-joyous samādhi." His *Shōbōgenzō Bendōwa* begins with the well-known words:

> Buddha-tathāgatas all have a wonderful means, which is unexcelled and free from human agency, for transmitting the wondrous Dharma from one to another without alteration and realizing supreme and complete awakening. That it is only transmitted without deviation from Buddha to Buddha is due to the self-joyous samādhi, which is its touchstone.
>
> To disport oneself freely in this samādhi, the right entrance is proper sitting in zazen. This Dharma is amply present in every person, but unless one practices, it is not manifested; unless there is realization, it is not attained. It is not a question of one or many; let loose of it and it fills your hands. It is not bound vertically or horizontally; speak it and it fills your mouth. . . .
>
> Patriarchs and Buddhas, who have maintained the Buddha Dharma, all have held that practice based upon proper sitting in zazen in self-joyous samādhi was the right path through which their Enlightenment opened.[11]

Samsāra-*sive*-nirvāna, or samsāra-*sive*-Life of Buddha, comes down more or less to the Existenz of the dropping off of body-and-mind, in this sense of the King of Samādhis Samādhi, or the self-joyous samādhi.

Again, in this same sense, Dōgen notes in another context: "The dropped off body-and-mind is not form [thing] or consciousness. Do not say it is Enlightenment or illusion. How can it be any thing or any Buddha?"[12] This claim, that the dropped off body-and-mind does not belong to the field of illusion or the field of enlightenment, that it is not a thing or a Buddha, is noteworthy in that it expresses the culmination of Zen.

In this case, however, the supple mind seen as the dropping off of body-and-mind contains another aspect that Ju-ching points to and that we would do well to bear in mind:

> The zazen of the Buddhas and the patriarchs, already from the first steps of the religious mind, is a vow to gather in the Dharmas of all Buddhas. Therefore, in their zazen they do not forget any sentient being, they do not forsake any, even down to the smallest insect. They give compassionate regard at all times, vowing to save them all and turning over to them every merit they acquire. That is the reason that Buddhas and patriarchs always dwell in the world of desire and negotiate the Way in zazen.[13]

After Dōgen returned home from China, the first lecture he gave his students in the meditation hall of his monastery went as follows:

> I had not gone around to very many Zen monasteries. I only happened by chance to encounter my last master T'ien-t'ung Ju-ching, and readily apprehended that eyes are horizontal and nose vertical. Totally free from any deception by others, I

returned home with empty hands. Therefore, I do not have a single strand of the
Buddha's Dharma. I now while away my time, accepting whatever may come.

> Every morning the sun ascends in the east,
>   every night the moon descends in the west.
> Clouds retreat, the mountain bones are bared,
>   rain passes, the surrounding hills are low.
> How is it after all? [Pausing a while, he goes on:]
> We meet a leap year one in four.
> Cocks crow at four in the morning.[14]

These words may also be said to point to the "dropping off of
mind-and-body, the dropped off mind and body." "Eyes horizontal,
nose vertical" refers to body-and-mind on the field of the King of
Samādhis Samādhi, where one is said to "pluck out the eye of the
Buddha and just sit in its hollow" or on the field of "penetration in
realization," or again, the dropped off body-and-mind that, as we noted
before, is not Form or consciousness, not thing or Buddha. It is the
original countenance.

It is also called the practice of Zen held up by Dōgen as the "right
entrance" to "free and unrestricted activity in the self-joyous samādhi."
"Eyes horizontal and nose vertical" is Existenz on a field beyond birth-
and-death, where birth-and-death as such is the Life of Buddha. It is in
the Existenz of the "solitary one laid bare amidst the myriad phenomena." Insofar as it is Existenz in self-joyous samādhi, where the self can
be absolutely itself; and insofar as all things—in Pascal's phrase, the
infinitely great as well as the infinitely small—are truly the "treasures of
one's household"; there, in the vast expanse of our home-ground the
self's dropping off of body-and-mind falls to no one else's charge, not
even to the Buddhas and the patriarchs. Only as an independent
follower of the Way of the Buddha, relying on nothing and "immune to
guile" (even where relationships to the Buddhas and the patriarchs are
concerned), does this Existenz become a samsāra-*sive*-Life of Buddha.
For the essence of the Life of Buddha does not appear except as an
Existenz like that described above as the self-joyous King Samādhi.

The point of absolute nonobjectifiability—where the eye does not
see the eye, fire does not burn fire, and water does not wash water,
where the willows are not green and the flowers are not red, and yet, for
this very reason, where the eye sees things, the fire burns things,
willows are green and flowers are red—is a point that withdraws
beyond all reason and *logos* and can only open up in the Existenz of the

dropping off of body-and-mind. Where fire, as something that does not burn itself, *is* fire (or is in the mode of being of fire), where the green of the willows *is* green (or is in the mode of being of green) in not being green, is what I have called "samādhi-being" or "position." This is the nonobjectifiable mode of being of a thing as it is in itself. Samādhi-being is, after all, nothing other than the appearance of the King Samādhi, and, therefore, as such is a self-realization of the Existenz of body-and-mind dropping off or of the Existenz of the absolutely independent solitary one laid bare amidst the myriad phenomena. Every mode of samādhi-being is a so-called dust-samādhi,[15] which is, after all, the "King of Samādhis Samādhi." There alone is the point where the true marrow of the Life of Buddha becomes apparent.

Dōgen's "eyes horizontal, nose vertical" and "coming back home with empty hands" also point to this "true marrow." Coming back home refers, of course, to his return from China to Japan, the land of his birth. At the same time, his statements that "being born is being unborn, dying is not-dying" and that "in the Buddha Dharma birth is said to be at once unbirth" suggest that this return to the homeland of his birth and to the homeland of his unbirth come together in his "coming back home with empty hands." There is a familiar Zen saying that goes: "Bodhidharma did not come to China, the Second Patriarch did not go to India." Dōgen crossed over into China and returned to Japan on a field where we can say that he never crossed into China nor returned to Japan. There, birth-*sive*-unbirth comes to be continually in time, in that "moment" that Kierkegaard referred to as the "atom of eternity" in temporality. It is the life of the dropped off body-and-mind that is neither mind nor consciousness, neither thing nor Buddha. Here each "time" is time because it is not time, because it is but an atom of eternity in temporality.

The words of Dōgen's lecture, "I now while away my time, accepting whatever may come," refer to just such a time. Because the dropped off body-and-mind is there "neither mind nor thing nor Buddha,"[16] but "this human skin-flesh-bone-and-marrow body" now cross-legging the King Samādhi, one marks time, without so much as a single strand of the Buddha's Dharma, just taking things as they come—as they are fated to come—consigning oneself to the destiny of circumstances. This is simply daily life with the sun rising every morning and the moon rising every night: the daily life of King Samādhi, which is altogether different from any sort of fatalism or resignation.

A noted Japanese priest of the Tokugawa Period named Genkō
Dokuan (1630–1698), who belonged to Dōgen's line of Sōtō Zen, wrote
as follows:

> "Eyes horizontal, nose vertical" is Master Dōgen's realization of confirmation in
> the Dharma. His testimony to the Dharma is a non-testimony. It lays waste heaven
> and earth right on the spot, and hurdles an infinity of time in the flick of a finger.[17]

What he is saying is that within the daily life that is marking time and
taking things as they come we see the Existenz of King Samādhi
instantly wipe away the boundlessness of space and stride across endless *kalpas* of time. This Existenz is true time, the time that is time
because it is not time; or, rather, it is Existenz as true time come to the
fullness of time.

In this same connection, we find this body in its coming to be and
passing away compared to a diamond for its hardness, its brilliancy, and
the sharpness that enables it to cut through all things. The question was
once put to a Zen master, "Man's body [*rupa-kāya*] will ultimately
decompose; what is the indestructible Dharma body [*dharma-kāya*]?"
The master replied, "Flowers cover the mountainsides like brocade, the
valley stream deepens into an indigo-like pool."[18] Here again, we must
not stick to the literal meaning of the words by reading them in rational
terms and transforming them into *logos*, so that the mountain flowers
and valley stream, fleeting as they are, become appearances or symbols
of some kind of unchanging, enduring dharma body. We must not turn
the so-called logic of *sive/non* into a mere explanatory logic.[19] The logic
of *sive/non* is the logic of Existenz, or the Existenz of logic (in the sense
that Existenz is a "logic").

In the case of the sort of *koto* ("matter and word") being held up
here, we need to listen to it from the home-ground out of which it
proceeds, to weigh it well and affirm its *kokoro* ("mind" or "meaning") in
order truly to understand what it means (or what this matter "matters").
From this ground even the *koto* of the brocadelike mountain flowers and
indigolike water is imbued with a peculiar, inexhaustible meaning at the
very point that it is meaningless in terms of *logos*. And the flavor of the
inexhaustible beauty of that *koto* needs to be understood (its *kokoro*
obtained) as something proceeding from the same home-ground.

At any rate, the Existenz of the dropped off body-and-mind, also
called "the King of Samādhis Samādhi," is shown in the answer of the
master to be what we called Existenz as true time brought to the fullness

of time. What is termed "historical body" in the philosophy of Nishida must, after all, be something of this sort.

Toward the end of his opening lecture, we recall, Dōgen put the question, "How is it after all?" And the answer he gave to himself was, "We meet a leap year one in four / Cocks crow at four in the morning." In these two phenomena there appears an "order" or "law" (the dharma) that holds sway over the world of transitoriness. The modern scientist will most likely go a step further to see behind that dharma the not only more abstract and universal but also more exact and inexorable laws of science. In both cases, the existence of all phenomena and the changes they undergo are in accord with some definite rational order: phenomena *being* what they ought to be and *becoming* what they ought to become. In other words, all things are in the "ontological" order and under the control of *logos*: they are a "dharmic naturalness." Even what is seen as irrational or lawless from the viewpoint of human interests never departs so much as a single step from the dharma as far as its existence or change is concerned. In this sense, all things, just as they are, are dharma-like.

But now, what can it mean to say that this is the very point at which someone finds himself, "after all," returning home with empty hands, perfectly free of cares? Earlier it was observed of Existenz characterized as a coming home empty-handed that it is a birth-*sive*-unbirth of each moment in time; that it is the life of the dropped off body-and-mind that is neither mind nor consciousness, neither thing nor Buddha; and that it is nothing other than daily life as King Samādhi. It is, in a word, the standpoint of śūnyatā as samsāra-*sive*-nirvāna. But this standpoint is said, after all, to be the point at which all things are dharma-like.

To speak of the dharma that is in control within the existence and change of all phenomena, or, rather, of the dharma-likeness wherein things are just as they are, says that emptiness lets all phenomena be just what they are (or, what comes to the same thing, it lets them be what they ought to be). For in the elemental mode of being of all phenomena—which is what it means to be "in emptiness"—in the mode of being of things as they are in themselves, on their own home-ground, being just what they *are* is completely in harmony with their being what they *ought to be* . This is what it means to be dharma-like. (As I have dealt with this considerably in an earlier chapter from the point of view of the circumincessional relationship, I shall here forego any further discussion of the structural relations of his dharma-likeness.)

In short, Existenz as a "coming home with empty hands" and a birth-*sive*-unbirth is Existenz on the field of śūnyatā as saṃsāra-*sive*-nirvāna, the field of the birthplace that is self-identical with the unbirth-place. This field embraces all things on their home-ground, where they become manifest as they are in themselves. If the term "embrace" be thought to incline too much toward a spatial sense of unity, we may paraphrase it: that all things are severally what they are in themselves directly implies that they are all collected together. Such is the field of emptiness.

Existenz in King Samādhi, returning home empty-handed, is in-separably connected in its essence with the field of emptiness. It may be likened to the mode of being of the king, whose position as sovereign is inconceivable without a land for him to rule over. His land represents the political scope of his governing powers. It is a domain initially opened up and kept open by virtue of that power, for which his position as monarch is a sort of self-realization. A similar relationship obtains between Existenz in King Samādhi and the field of śūnyatā. On the field of śūnyatā each thing is given a position where it is what it is in itself, in that essentially nonobjectifiable mode of suchness referred to above as the mode of samādhi-being. This field of śūnyatā belongs intrinsically to the essence of Existenz-in-emptiness and participates in its basic structure. Only Existenz in King Samādhi throws open the field of emptiness existentially while at the same time taking a stand on that field as the dropping off of body-and-mind.

Existenz spoken of as "body-and-mind dropping off, dropped off body-and-mind" implies the infinite openness of the field where all things are severally in themselves. Or put in other words, the totality of individual things are collected together to form one and the same "world." It is the point at which all things are made to "be in the world." It is where Dōgen saw the standpoint of King Samādhi. It is a stand-point where, to borrow a phrase from Rinzai, "To be master wherever you are is for wherever you are to be true." Each and every thing, in being in itself on its own home-ground (dharma-like) is *originally* pre-served by such a master in the Existenz of dropped off body-and-mind, a master who has risen to a position of self-awareness in his own domain of boundless emptiness.

As noted earlier, things on their own home-ground settle into a *position* on that home-ground, which is their samādhi-being. In this sense, that all things are as they really are on their "dharma-position" means that in the dropped off body-and-mind they come under the supreme dharma of the King Samādhi. Or we might say that these things are subject to the law promulgated by him who becomes master wherever he is. All things, through the essential dharma inherent in their actual existence and hence also through their actual existence in dharma-likeness, are gathered into a "world" and maintained together there by the lordly Existenz of King Samādhi. It is an empty-handed, homebound Existenz. All things, including the whole of humanity and the rest of sentient beings, insofar as they are seen basically in their sheer being-in-the-world, constitute a world-unity in emptiness: a unity of basic, irreducible freedom and equally basic and irreducible regulation. It is free in the sense that each being there *is* in its own position as what it is in itself, and regulated in the sense that each being there is as it *ought to be*, in the position determined for it in the nexus of being-in-the-world. And the reality that makes all this possible rises to awareness in Existenz on the field of emptiness and becomes actualized through dwelling in the lordly Existenz of King Samādhi. Even as this Existenz becomes actualized as the dharma-like nature of all phenomena, or as all dharma-like phenomena, it is itself the master of all phenomena. This is why we speak of the dropping off of body-and-mind as a "solitary one laid bare amidst the myriad phenomena." Here the field opens up on which the leap year comes one year in four and the cock crows each morning at dawn.

V

We have used the terms *ontological order* and *logos* to characterize the law or dharma that manifests itself, for example, in the crowing of the cock at daybreak. *Logos* has traditionally been conceived of as the essential rational order inherent in the very existence of things, and is regarded in philosophy as the object of the cognition of reason or speculative intellect. When we move on to modern times, we find that it has also come to acquire the character of scientific law by virtue of having become the object of the discursive understanding found in science.

Again and again we have returned to the point that the selfness of any thing, no matter what it be, can never be grasped on the field of this *logos*. This would seem to contradict what was stated above regarding true Existenz as "dropped off body-and-mind." There Existenz was seen as maintaining a collective hold (*dhāranī*) over all phenomena in their home-grounds, that is, where they are in themselves as they are in their dharma-natures—which we might also describe by saying that it has in its grip all things in their *logos*. Still, there is no denying that the *logos* of existence comes to bear a qualitatively different significance according to whether it is seen from the standpoint of reason or from the standpoint of Existenz (the Existenz of the dropped off body-and-mind).

Logos also carries the meaning of "word" or "speech." On the standpoint of Existenz, it comes to bear the meaning of *koto* ("matter and word"). There the rational order of existence can be referred to as word or speech. Just as the promulgations of juridical law and order are a kind of voiceless speech that shows people the track their social lives should run on, so the rational order is in the grip of the King Samādhi, the voiceless speech of one who "is master wherever he is." The rational order is, as it were, his preaching of the dharma.

Of course, although we speak of the *preaching* of the dharma, this is not to suggest that we have words on the one side and the dharma on the other. The word uttered in preaching is the dharma itself, just as it is. The dharma is always preaching itself in and through the phenomena whose dharma it is. Hence this preaching may be called a preaching without words, a *preaching of non-preaching*.

Further, since dharma does not exist apart from the things of dharma, we can say that in the preaching of dharma, it is things that do the preaching. In being just what they are, things themselves show their own dharma. And while they are preaching about their own dharma, things can be said to be preaching about themselves. Of course, we can also say that the dharma preaches about the things whose own intrinsic essence it shapes. These four facets—that the dharma preaches itself in phenomena; that the dharma preaches about phenomena; that the phenomena preach about the dharma; and that the phenomena preach about themselves—come down to one and the same *koto* ("matter"). And the whole constitutes the meaning of dharmic preaching.

But then, there is a "master" here who without preaching himself makes things preach the dharma. He makes things reveal their own dharma while at the same time he lets them reveal themselves; he makes the dharma preach itself as well as things. After all, the dharma is nothing other than this master's preaching of non-preaching.

Now, in the mode of being of things as they are in themselves in emptiness, both "as they are" and "as they ought to be" are, as I have said, entirely one and the same. And in this oneness, logos as *koto* ("matter and word") appears. That is, the dharma-like nature of the being of those things appears. That *is* directly implies *ought* means that we have present here a character of compliance with order. It signifies a presence of some word of directive command (what Heidegger calls *Geheiss*). In the dharma-like nature of things that are as they ought to be, there is a quality of listening compliantly. This dharma-like nature is the imperative of the "master" with "body-and-mind dropped off." It is indeed his "categorical imperative."

In brief, here *logos* or *koto*, as rational order (where *ratio* and order are taken in an ontological sense), indicates the aboriginal mode of being of things on the very field where they in fact *are* manifest in their aboriginality (on the field of *Urständigkeit*) and, at the same time, implies that this is the mode of being that these things *ought* aboriginally to show. That things *are* means, aboriginally, that they express themselves; and that in expressing themselves they give expression, at the same time, to what it is that makes them be, pointing it out and bearing witness to it (in the twofold sense of clarifying and confirming). This is what it is for things to be in a dharma-like mode. The one aspect we referred to as things *preaching* the dharma, the other as their *obeying* its imperatives. Both are one in the dharma-like nature of existence.

It may sound strange to say that "things" preach the dharma or speak the *logos*. But everything we know of rational order is from things. It is what we hear from things. All our knowledge springs from and returns to the place where, in Bashō's words, we should

> From the pine tree
>   learn (the *koto*) of the pine tree,
> And from the bamboo
>   (the *koto*) of the bamboo.

The pine speaks the *koto* of the pine tree, the bamboo the *koto* of the bamboo. Our "knowing" rational order, or *logos*, always begins from and ends in the place where things speak of themselves, of their own *koto*. Its point of departure is where things are on their own home-ground, just as they are, manifest in their suchness. For, that things *are* as they really are and that they speak of their own *koto* are truly one and the same thing.

Now I said that in this dharma-like nature of theirs, things give expression and bear witness to (clarify and confirm) what it is that makes them what they are. What they clarify and confirm is nothing other than the Existenz of the "body-and-mind dropping off, dropped off body-and-mind" that opens itself up as the field of emptiness that makes things to be aboriginally (that is, as they are and as they ought to be). It is nothing other than the self in enlightenment pointed to in the previously cited words of Dōgen: "To practice and confirm all things [dharmas] by conveying one's self to them, is illusion: for all things to advance forward and practice and confirm the self, is enlightenment." This self in enlightenment is what makes itself "master" wherever it may be.

Therefore, when it was said that the dharma of things has at once the character of preaching the dharma and of obeying the dharma, what this dharma "bears witness to"—in other words, what makes the dharma preach itself and obey itself, and hence, after all, what preaches and commands within this dharma—is this very self in the sense just mentioned. It is the self as non-ego.

Just as the automobiles and pedestrians that stop and go according to the traffic signals demonstrate traffic law and hence also man as legislator (the juridical person), so too do such things as the leap year that comes one year in four or the cock whose crowing is heard at daybreak, in demonstrating the fact that all things are "naturally in accord with dharma," also demonstrate man as legislator. It is "man," impersonal and non-ego, yet personal and self.

In a word, in the home-ground of the Existenz of the dropped off body-and-mind, there appears the dhāraṇī ("collective hold") of the whole of rational order. Here all things, while being collected together within the hand of Existenz, become "things in the world." As Dōgen says: "Unless it is *one's self* exerting itself right now, not a single dharma or a single thing can immediately manifest itself . . . ."[20]

Thus, on the standpoint of Existenz, *logos* as the rational order of existence is no different from the dharma-like nature of the aboriginal mode of being of things where each thing is just as it is. It is no different from things laid bare as those things themselves. Here, logos is directly the dharma-like nature of things. It is a "likeness" or "suchness" in the sense we have used those terms before, always with a connotation of the "trueness" of a thing become manifest. *Logos* is the true suchness that, ultimately, is the "thusness" of the "Thus Coming" (Tathāgata).

As is well known, Heidegger interpreted "truth" as Ἀλήθεια (*Un-verborgenheit*) in the sense of a laying bare or unveiling of things just as they are. The logos of things in emptiness can also be said to be "truth" in this sense. And in this laying bare of things just as they are, the Existenz of the dropped off body-and-mind unveils itself directly as "the solitary one laid bare amidst the myriad phenomena." That is to say, absolute "truth" is there. There it is that the absolute truth is to be found.

Logos is in its fullest sense primarily on the home-ground of that Existenz. And the *logos* of speculative reason or discursive understanding develops from this primary point to the dimensions of reason or understanding. Insofar as it is seen only on those dimensions, *logos* is no longer a revelation of the suchness of things. In order to become such a revelation, *logos* that has thus developed must always be brought back to its primary point, to the home-ground of "empty" Existenz that opens itself up as the field of śūnyatā itself.

In this way, things like meeting a leap year one in four or hearing a cock crowing at daybreak signify the sort of field of Existenz that assumes (in its dharma-like nature) dhāranī over all phenomena within this world of transitoriness. It signifies a field of Existenz that gathers to its own home-ground, where it is a self that is non-ego, each thing as it is on its own home-ground. This being the case, the Existenz of dropped off body-and-mind also signifies a being truly *in* time, or rather a being truly *as* time. As a birth-*sive*-unbirth, this Existenz *is* bottomlessly in time, or as time that has bottomlessly arrived at the fullness of time. It *is* as time, in the sense that, to repeat what was said earlier, "Time is not time, therefore it is time." In the Existenz we are now speaking of, "being" is one with "truth" (being unveiled) of time thus become manifest. It is an Existenz living in the world where

> Every morning the sun ascends in the east,
> every night the moon descends in the west.
> Clouds retreat, the mountain bones are bared,
> rain passes, the surrounding hills are low.

It is an Existenz living in the world that is time, in the world-time, while at the same time it is the self as master and non-ego that brings time to the fullness of time, or in other words, brings its own self-being to fullness. There, in true Existenz, true being is one with the truth of time; "to be" means "to be as time." While living in the passing of time, one's life is at every step a birth-*sive*-unbirth. It is life in which one whiles away one's time, accepting whatever may come.

This Existenz, while always in time, is always at the beginning of time. While it is a life given through parents, it is yet "before the parents had been born." Of course, this *before* is not a mere priority of temporal occurrence. It is rather the "beginning" of the origination of time itself, the *before* of the origination of temporality.

When asked what God had been doing during the boundless stretch of time prior to the creation of the world, Augustine replied that time itself was created by God together with the world. In a similar sense, *before* the birth of the parents is the *before* of time itself, the beginning of the origination of time. And this "beginning" lies directly beneath the dropped off body-and-mind. It is before all temporal "before" (all temporally immanent beginnings) as well. The beginning of time itself is *before* all possible pasts. And it is likewise *after* all possible futures. Past events, no matter how far back they go, and future events, no matter how far ahead they reach, gather together at the home-ground of the beginning of time. Only as such do they come into being one and all. All the various possible events of past and future can be said to be originally maintained in dhāranī in the time that comes to the fullness of time from this "beginning."

Earlier, speaking of the idea of transmigration, we characterized the essence of birth-and-death as an infinite finitude. On the standpoint of samsāra-*sive*-nirvāna, this infinite finitude is not apart from the home-ground of the Existenz of the dropped off body-and-mind, for this Existenz is released from samsāra in the very midst of samsāric existence. It takes its leave of birth-and-death because, at any given time, it stands continually at the "beginning," where that time comes to the fullness of time, at the beginning of time itself.

Touching on the opening phrase of the *Heart Sutra*—"At the time Avalokitesvara Bodhisattva engaged in the observance of deep prajñāpāramitā"—it was noted that the "observance" and "time" referred to are matters of this Existenz. This Existenz is the Existenz of the self in the sense that all things "advance forward and practice and confirm the self." It is the Existenz of the self that lives in the world-as-time from the very beginning where time comes to the fullness of time and where the world *worlds*. Existenz in this sense does not differ from its essential time.

It is the same with observance. We have already cited Dōgen to the effect that the practice of Zen consists in dropping off body-and-mind. The home-ground of the Existenz of the dropping off of body-and-mind is the point at which the world *worlds*, where all things are collected together in their dharma-like nature, where things are just as they are. It is the point where the self is confirmed by all things (dharmas); where, as Dōgen says, the Buddhas and the patriarchs have all together "held that observance based upon proper sitting in zazen in self-joyous samādhi." It may also serve our purposes to repeat a passage of Dōgen's cited earlier:

> To learn the Buddha Way is to learn one's self. To learn one's self is to forget one's self. To forget one's self is to be confirmed by all dharmas. To be confirmed by all dharmas is to effect the dropping off of one one's own body-and-mind and the body-and-mind of others as well.

The dropping off of body-and-mind and the dropped off body-and-mind constitute the practice of Zen. That the self is confirmed by all dharmas, and that in such a way the world *worlds*, is what was called "cross-legging the King Samādhi." It is here that all dharmas come forward to practice and confirm the self. This is the sense in which the observance of deep prajñāpāramitā that the *Heart Sutra* talks of can come to mean the Existenz of dropped off body-and-mind.

As noted in the previous pages, this Existenz of the dropped off body-and-mind denotes "the solitary one laid bare amidst the myriad phenomena" and is the truth (Ἀλήθεια) of that Existenz unveiling itself absolutely. In bearing witness to this solitary one laid bare, each and every phenomenon is by far more itself than it is on its own home-ground. We can say that in the beginning where the world *worlds*, the world is more truly itself than it is in the world itself. That "all dharmas advance forward and practice and confirm the self" means that all dharmas return to a point where they are far more able to be "truth" than when they are in and by themselves, to the absolute truth, to what is unveiled in its full grandeur, solitary amidst the myriad of things.

Seen from this angle, what is described as all things coming forward to practice and confirm the self is no different from defining the dropping off of body-and-mind as being the practice of Zen. The dropping off of body-and-mind is self-presentation of the original countenance. This original countenance is present at the point that the world worlds, where "one's treasure-house opens of itself and one can use it at will."[21] It is the place of self-joyous samādhi. It is none other than the very place where the Buddhas and the patriarchs observe zazen. On the whole, this is the meaning of "observance."

Hakuin (1685 – 1768), commenting on the occurrence of the word "observance" in the *Heart Sutra*, notes in effect:[22]

> What about moving one's hands and feet, or eating and drinking? What about the moving of the clouds, the flowing of the rivers, the falling of the leaves, and the flowers scattering about in the wind? As soon as one tries to affix any Form to them,

however slight, the result is bound to be the same as in Chuang-tsu's fable about
Chaos: gouging Chaos out and putting an eyeball there in its stead, Chaos died.

If, as we said before, observance means the samādhi of self-enjoyment,
an absolute freedom of harmony or Order, then the point is well taken.
If there is nothing here that is not in "one's own treasure-house," and at
one's own disposition to use as one wishes, we have no cause to inflict a
wound on this Order by letting an act of reflective thought intervene,
by fashioning an eyeball for it. No sooner has the attitude of objective
representation come on the scene than "Form," as something outside of
the self, is generated; something that is not of one's own treasure-house
and not at one's own disposition shows up. Chaos dies. One has already
deviated from observance.

The moment one sees observance in a representative fashion, therefore, one has already attached to its Form. On the field where observance is truly observance, the man moving his limbs, the clouds floating
across the sky, the water flowing, the leaves falling, and the blossoms
scattering are all non-Form. Their Form is a *Form of non-Form*. To adopt
this Form of non-Form as the Form of the self is precisely what is meant
by the standpoint of observance.

Continuing on with the term "deep prajñāpāramitā" (the "wisdom
that has gone beyond"), Hakuin again refers to it as "gouging out
perfectly good flesh to make a wound." And regarding "time," he notes
similarly, "Here again, good flesh is gouged out." His meaning is the
same as before. He wants to say that when one deliberately speaks of
prajñā and time, and thinks of them as being particular things, it is
identical with inflicting a wound on the woundless flesh of Order. In the
Existenz of the dropped off body-and-mind, all prajñā and time must be
a non-Form. They are the Form of non-Form of that Existenz.

In the foregoing, I dealt with birth-and-death on the field of
samsāra-*sive*-nirvāna as the problem of time in the Existenz of the
dropped off body-and-mind (that is, of true emptiness). This Existenz
is a standpoint of absolute freedom. By means of its own dharma, this
Existenz maintains dhāranī over all phenomena in their dharma-like
nature, or suchness, within this world of transitoriness and uses them
for its own enjoyment. Hence, when the self as body-and-mind is born,
it is a birth that is an unbirth; and when it passes away, it is a passing
away that is a non-passing away.

It is, therefore, no different from time which comes to the fullness
of time from the before of all time, from the beginning of time as such.

But the question still remains how what we call "history" is able to be explained as a result of this sort of time. This is the problem of the *historicity* of time. No matter how things stand in relation to the standpoint of the dropped off body-and-mind, human history is a world of men whose body-and-mind has *not* fallen away, who wander about continually in illusion, ignorant of the true path. Man may be saved through religion, but that is an individual matter. Human societies come and go in history regardless of whether individuals are saved or not. In particular, we need to ask, then, whether the Buddhist standpoint of śūnyatā is not transhistorical and hence also ahistorical. This is how it is generally conceived to be. A consciousness of history in the sense it is currently understood remains largely undeveloped within Buddhist teaching. It is only natural to expect that somewhere in the course of the development of Mahāyāna Buddhism the problem of history would have been called into question from its standpoint of samsāra-*sive*-nirvāna and, in particular, in its discussion surrounding Bodhisattvahood. But this has not been the case. Where does the reason lie? It is surely an issue of importance for us today to retrace the causes of this failure, but this is not a task I can embark upon here. I will instead take up another question, namely, whether the various basic views of history that have so far appeared in the West do, in fact, exhaust the possible standpoints for looking at history, or whether the standpoint of śūnyatā offered here can contribute anything new.

VI

In his book *An Historian's Approach to Religion*,[23] Arnold Toynbee argues against the view that the gap between liberalism and communism represents the greatest cultural gap of our times. While the opposition between them is highly conspicuous in our day, it cannot be regarded as fundamentally determining the future course of mankind. When we look into the sources of these two movements, Toynbee goes on, we find that both of them belong to the same cluster of religious ideologies stemming from Western Judaic traditions. (The term "Western Judaic" is being used here to comprise a broad range of ideologies, including Christianity, Islam, and Judaism.) The confrontation that *is* deep enough to determine the problems of the whole of mankind, Toynbee asserts, is to be seen in the gap between Buddhaic thought and Western Judaic thought. (Here "Buddhaic" is used to include not only the Mahāyāna and Hīnayāna traditions, but also pre-Buddhist Indian philosophy and post-Buddhist Hinduism.) The gap between these two ways of thought also forms the foundation of every manner of economic and cultural opposition. Although it may not be so immediately conspicuous as the opposition between communism and liberalism, it is of greater consequence for the future of all of mankind. It is, for Toynbee, the authentic question for the future history of the world.

In Toynbee's view, Buddhaic thought as a whole demonstrates two characteristic features. First, the movements of nature and the cosmos are held to be cyclical. And second, that which rules over the cosmos and the world of man is conceived of as an impersonal order (dharma). This is the outlook that determines the view of nature and history found in Buddhaic thought. In contrast, according to the view of history of Western Judaic thought, historical time is linear, and the whole process is ruled over by a personal Being. History is basically characterized as something that can be determined and given meaning by intellect and will.

Here the Buddhaic mode of thought has one distinct advantage over the Western mode: the former contains the possibility of going beyond the self-centeredness that is innate not only in man but in all living things. To think that the rhythms of the cosmos are cyclic, or that the cosmos and the human world fall under the control of impersonal order, is to look at things from an angle that puts the stress on the universal rather than the particular of each individual thing. Toynbee interprets this as a standpoint in which the individual is, one way or another, dissolved into the universal. And this is how it gets beyond self-centeredness. But, in exchange, on this standpoint history is withal robbed of its significance. For in a world where everything is reduced to the standpoint of the universal, nothing essentially new can occur. The same things just go on repeating themselves in a circular motion of the same universal entities.

On the other hand, to the Western Judaic way of thinking, the history of the world of man is taken to be similar to the rhythms of the individual human life. Like a drama, it has its beginning, develops according to a certain plot, and draws to its close. In its course, all sorts of dramatic crises come and go with all sorts of ups and downs, but somewhere the plot eventually comes to an end. When history is conceived of in terms of such a drama or individual career, the controlling factor is the will. The divine itself is conceived of in this regard as a personal God whose will rules over all of history. And likewise every individual person moving through the world-drama does so by means of will and the variety of other *personal* forces. History is here set up as something that contains meaning within itself.

But, in exchange, given this standpoint, the self-centeredness of man casts its shadow over everything. Trying to elude this shadow is in vain. A remarkably clear illustration of this is the way that the religion of Israel is bound up with the consciousness of being a divine elect. Of course, within the religion of Israel, the self-centeredness of man as one who stands before God is to be rejected as sin. But men who have cast aside their self-centeredness before God, obeying him wholeheartedly and following his will compliantly, thereby regain a consciousness, in their relationship to other men, of being a chosen people. In short, self-centeredness appears once again, only this time on a higher plane: as the will of self backed up by the will of God. Although this standpoint of the will first enabled the world to be furnished with a meaning, the standpoint never surpassed its initial self-centeredness.

This, in rough outline, is Toynbee's thesis. And it seems to me to put its finger on the core of the matter. History is essentially bound up with the fact that the self, here described as self-centered, comes to act from within itself in a certain sense as a *personality*. This is in contrast to the world of "nature." That being so, what kind of significance does history come to possess when seen from the standpoint of religion?

Human self-centeredness is a permanent fixture in religions of the West. Once negated, it reappears, as in the guise of God's chosen people. Lurking beneath the concept of a divine elect is a direct projection onto God of the wish of the Jewish people that God be severe in his judgment with other peoples. Projected onto God is the unconscious demand of the self to condemn other people. Crudely put, what we have here is a *ressentiment* come forth in the guise of a self-centeredness that has passed through God so as to become religious. Complete self-abandonment and wholehearted humility (total *Demut*) toward God turns around of its own accord and lays the cornerstone of a superiority complex of the self vis-à-vis other men—and that only at the sort of prereflective and prevoluntary level that depth-psychology speaks of.

Be that as it may, we cannot but feel that in spite of any religious self-denial directed against self-centeredness, the roots of self-centeredness remain deeply entrenched. It is at that point that an unconscious reaction takes over to invert this self-denial back into an unconsciously disguised self-centeredness. This point has borne the brunt of attacks by a great number of modern critics of Christianity, in particular by Feuerbach and Nietzsche.

The fact that the possibility remains for such a reaction or inversion to go unchallenged, for the roots of self-centeredness to be left intact as an "unconscious" force, points to a certain lack of transparency in the self-illumination that is quintessential to the self of man. The self remains opaque and not yet penetrated to its core. In Buddhist terminology, the self still leaves the basic *avidyā* ("the darkness of ignorance") intact as the root of the self. If, therefore, it be true that history can be endowed with meaning only from a standpoint of the self or the so-called subjectivity that, even when equipped with the lofty name of "personality," cannot fail to imply the character of a self-centeredness, then it will also be the case that history is essentially a world of existence charged with avidyā, and hence also tied to the standpoint of karma and the fruits of karma. In fact, this state of affairs is the constant companion of history, following it around like a shadow.

Conversely, however, it is generally held that historicity tends to get diluted when oriented to a radical denial of self-centeredness through a process of the dissolution of the individual and the personal into the universal and the impersonal. This has long been the conventional view in the West. As we have seen above, even so eminent an historian as Toynbee is of this opinion. This opinion would entangle us in a dilemma involving religion and history. But is this really the case?

I should first point out that the interpretation of Buddhism just spelled out by Toynbee, and in particular his interpretation of Mahāyāna Buddhism is open to question. He seems to assume that the conception of time in Mahāyāna Buddhism is merely cyclical, and that all things are ruled by an impersonal dharma, thus introducing either an ambiguity into the meaning of history or a lack of historical consciousness. Looked at from the Western idea of history, this may be the way it appears; but things are not quite so simple. Here at last we come up against the final problem.

With regard to the so-called cyclical nature of time, all religions that can be characterized in terms of *mythos* share the view in common that time is recurrent and ahistorical. Even within philosophy itself, where deliverance from mythical modes of life and thought is supposed to represent a distinguishing feature (a matter touched on earlier in speaking of the character of ancient Greek philosophy), there are any number of instances in which time is regarded as cyclical. This notion of time becomes fitting enough when we look at the universe or all things in the universe from the point of view of nature. In the world of nature, the four seasons follow upon one another periodically, and the blocks of time we call months and years keep on recurring. Nature's "time," including astronomical time, returns without fail to its starting point, time after time, following the same circuit.

The life of man can be thought of as similarly fashioned according to such recurrent time, even in terms of its contents. In ancient Japan, for example, at the time of the harvest of the new rice, new wine made from the crop would be offered in the royal palace to the deities of heaven and earth. Then the emperor and his subjects would drink the wine together in celebration. In ancient times this thanksgiving ceremony is said to have taken place every year. It was probably performed on the strength of a belief that this wine was possessed of a mana-like quality. When a man drank wine made from new rice, the spiritual force inherent in rice gave new guarantees to his life and new certainty to his existence.

Rice is also tied up with the generative force latent in the native soil. This force in the land works to uphold the existence of man. By the emperor and his subjects drinking of the same wine, the relationships of ruler and ruled among men that enable political cohesion and constitute the state are also renewed. What is more, all of this is based on a relationship between man and the gods. In other words, the relationships between man and the gods, the gods and the land, man and the land, and man and man form as one totality a socially and politically unified nexus the wholeness of which is renewed once each year. For this purpose a yearly festival is held without fail at a fixed time. If it were not observed, life thoughout the following year could not proceed on a firm basis. By observing the festival, life during the year that intervenes until the next festival time comes around, the existence of man, the existence and sociopolitical nexus of the state, the production of rice, and other economic activities throughout the year are once more guaranteed and regenerated. Since everything becomes old after one year has elapsed, it must be regenerated anew at the end of the yearly cycle. That total nexus must be put back in order and solidified by means of the same vital force granted by the same festival rites. That is what it means to say that life is *cyclic*.

Here, the character of history in its original sense does not come out clearly. The natural world and the human world move *pari passu* according to a definite "arrangement." Human life in its various phases has its own "conventions" and runs according to their norms. Conventions that have become a part of everyday life while maintaining their basis in religion have been with us from the beginning of history—or, in the example just cited, from the beginnings of the constitution of the state. In other words, history is conceivable only in terms of the repetition of something recurrent. Every deviation from this circuit is condemned as sin or defilement. Evil and sin in the ethico-religious sense mean straying from the norms of life, that is, from the mold that has been in effect since the beginnings of history. Simply put, religions that have their base in myth yield such a standpoint. At the same time, I think it worthy of note that in the Japanese myth of the birth of the nation, the beginnings of the constitution of the state are placed in a once-and-for-all, nonrecurrent event: the descent to earth of the heavenly grandson of the Sun goddess.

In several respects, the claim that historical consciousness originated with the Jewish people contains serious problems. Historical consciousness has since seen remarkable developments in the West. Particularly in the modern age, human life itself gradually came to take shape through the historical self-consciousness of man. But what is involved in such a development?

No doubt in Christianity, too, as in ancient Japan, righteousness was regarded as living in obedience to a divinely ordained scheme of things. But in Christian teaching, man is from the very outset viewed as having rebelled against the will of God and having broken the divine order. Sin becomes the most essential factor in the Christian view of man in history. In the concept of original sin, man's consciousness of sin, that is, of his separation from God, is intimately connected with the consciousness of man's existence as an autonomous, independent being. The implication of consciousness of sin is acknowledged as part of man's very subjective awareness of existence.

And at the same time, the consciousness of freedom that is absent in the standpoint of cyclic recurrence found in mythical religions has come about in Christianity in unison with the awareness of individual self-being. We can also say that only here has time ceased to be recurrent, so that every step of human life becomes part of a drama and every moment of time becomes something new and creative out of which new things may emerge.

In a word, awareness of self-being in man has come about in connection with three factors: the awareness of original sin, the awareness of freedom, and the awareness of the once-and-for-all nature (*Einmaligkeit*) of time. The consciousness of history is connected here with an awareness of existence turned in the direction of self-centered-ness. And since salvation is seen in an historic event through which this self-centered mode of being founded on original sin is conquered, and a reconciliation with God effected, religion is ultimately constituted with human freedom and historicity as its foundations and original sin as its cornerstone. This kind of religion rests on a standpoint more deeply grounded than the mythical one. When we pursue the problem of history, therefore, we inevitably encounter a standpoint bound up with the problem of the self-awareness of man and, along with that, the problem of sin and freedom and the historicity of time. This standpoint runs like a single thread throughout Christianity and its forerunner, the religion of the Hebrew prophets.

What kind of problem does this state of affairs imply for Christian-ity? Here I cannot enter into a detailed consideration of that issue; I can but touch upon it to the extent that it has bearing on our present concern, the problem of the historicity of the standpoint of śūnyatā. Within those limits, it seems to me that the problematic points con-tained in Christianity are tied up with the three factors referred to above as implicit in the Christian awareness of the self-being of man: the awareness of sin, the awareness of freedom, and the awareness of the once-and-for-all nature of time.

The first point at issue has to do with the self-centered character that appears within the self-awareness of religious man. As stated above, in Christianity, where the beginnings of *history* are thought to involve sin, the coming to be and development of history on the one hand and the self-centered existence of man on the other are essentially tied up with one another. (In this regard, Kant has noted that evil was taken to be the origin of history.) Further, the conquest of this self-centered existence, namely, the salvation brought about through atone-ment for original sin and reconciliation with God, is assumed to be an historical event *within history*, prepared for through the course of history according to a divine plan. The incarnation of the Son of God in Jesus Christ and the atonement of sin through his death on the cross are regarded as having opened up the field for man's salvation in history, that is, to have revealed the *agape* of God into history—the emphasis falling here on historical facticity. God's *agape* is revealed into history: it proceeds from the side of God and toward the self-centered human being who bears the burden of original sin. Repentance and faith, on the side of man, are related to this historical revelation, that is, to Jesus Christ as an actual historical reality.

Now the religious standpoint thus given rise to, carries with it a

character of exclusive absoluteness that leaves no room for any com-
mensurability with other religions. For the historical facticity of any
factum or actual reality is absolutely incommensurable as such, as it is
here where the character of historical facticity belonging to the objects
of religious faith is being stressed. In a case like this, the absoluteness
generally demanded of religious truth combines with the once-and-for-
all nature of historical fact, with the result that this standpoint of faith
cannot but demand exclusive absoluteness for itself. At this point
intolerance inevitably raises its head. Like the consciousness of being a
chosen people that appeared in the religion of Israel, we have here
another case of the self-centeredness on a religious dimension which
Toynbee was speaking of.

Intolerance here is essentially bound up with the fact that faith
comes into being here on a *personal* standpoint: the standpoint of a
personal relationship with a personal God. This is so because, in the last
analysis, in religion the personal contains some sort of self-centeredness. Consequently, the faith of Christianity could not help setting off
antagonisms from time to time between this self-centeredness and the
other element of *agape*, namely, the love of neighbor. The battles for the
conquest of heathendom that we see toward the end of the ancient
period, throughout the Middle Ages (as in the Crusades, for instance)
and the modern era, the persecution of heresy, the Inquisition, the
religious wars within the Christian world—all of these and the intolerance displayed, along with the similar phenomena found in Islam, are
all but absent in the history of Buddhism.

The second problematic area I should like to take up in connection
with the Christian view of history is its eschatology. It is not uncommon
in mythical religions to find a recurrent eschatology according to which,
at the end of its periodic cycle, the world perishes in a great conflagra-
tion and a new world rises up out of its ashes. In Buddhism, too,
thought is given to the coming into being, existence, destruction, and
emptiness of the world. There is no such cyclical character to Christian
eschatology, but, as is well known, the *eschaton* that will burst forth
from God upon the world without warning and bring history to its close
is connected with the second coming of Christ and the final judgment.

Now it seems to me that there are problems with this notion of the
end of history. Consistent with the demands of Christian teaching, the
final judgment is considered as an historical fact expected actually to
take place in the historical world. The epiphany of something transhistorical that will bring all previous history to a close is represented

here as a once-and-for-all affair that belongs only to the dimension of historical fact. This is what I find questionable. The history of Europe records any number of cases of people who, taking the eschaton literally as historical fact, went into panic thinking the end of the world to be at hand. It is no longer possible for us today to take seriously the notion of an end to history on the dimension of historical fact taken in such a literal sense, as something immanent within history itself. Contemporary theology takes eschatology seriously enough that it may yet prove possible to find new meaning for the notion, as for instance, in the so-called existentialist interpretation. But even in this case, it would still be difficult to think of the eschaton as something within the world of historical fact.

To sum up, then, in Christianity consciousness of the once-and-for-all nature and historicity of time was established and the recurrent nature of time in mythical religions discarded. Along with that, an eschatology of recurrence in mythical religion shifted over to an eschatology within history. The eschaton then came to be considered as bringing to a close, on the dimension of historical fact and as a once-and-for-all historical event, the whole of the previous history of mankind. In this way the whole of the previous history could be made into a "pre-history," as is the case even with modern thinkers like Marx and Nietzsche, or as the "in-between time" that Christian theologians speak of.

Although I would grant that the establishment of historical consciousness was an epoch-making event, I still find this consciousness problematic as it is intertwined with such a brand of eschatology and such a representation of the end of history. (All of this is tied up with the Christian view that sees the beginnings of history in original sin, a matter we shall have occasion to touch on later.)

Ever since the establishment of modern historical consciousness and the constitution of history as a "science," eschatology has by and large ceased to figure in the view of history of those who make historical fact the subject of their study. At the dimension of immanent historical fact, an eschaton coming into history from without is simply unthinkable. At that dimension, it is, of course, altogether possible to conceive of some orientation or some aim immanent in history, albeit not as something that comes to an end. One of the most simplistic expressions of this is to be seen in the idea of "progress" characteristic of the eighteenth-century Enlightenment.

The idealistic notion of mankind advancing onward and upward endlessly in history stands diametrically opposed to the eschatological view of history. Yet even this one-sided outlook contains an undeniable element of historical consciousness to it. Progress is certainly an aspect of history. In defiance of the notion of a last day on which everything will be subjected to divine judgment, the historical world reveals its aspect of unceasing progress through the unfolding of ever new developments. Even in our own day, those who take a firm stance on the notion of progress do so fundamentally with such a view of history.

In terms of its genesis, this view of history came about in resistance to the Christian faith and its intolerance. This view of history is based on trust in human reason. This emphasis on reason got its start amidst the bloody struggles within the Christian world, as the will to find a common standpoint apart from dogmatic faith. Hence, this rational standpoint was, in principle, born of a spirit of tolerance. This led, on the one hand, to the efforts of deism to reinterpret the Christian doctrines from a viewpoint of reasonableness. Later, it developed into the standpoints of the philosophy of religion and the science of religion, this latter branching out into psychology, sociology, anthropology, history (as the "history of religions"), and so forth, permeated with and governed throughout by an attitude of religious tolerance. On the other hand, the rational standpoint developed in the direction of a scientific approach to history and society in which the dominant tendency was critical of religion or outrightly opposed to it. The view of history as progress followed, as a whole, this latter orientation.

All of this already has some bearing on the third problematic, which points to another facet involved in human subjective self-awareness that cannot be exhausted merely in terms of original sin: I refer to the fact that both the standpoint of reason and the demand for rationality in the domains of knowledge and praxis are involved in this self-awareness. At a fundamental level, this standpoint of reason comes down to the freedom of man as a rational being. Human freedom contains at base not only the aspect of *sin* in the relationship of man to God, but also an aspect of man's relationship to himself that can be seen as *reason*. Herein lurks at one and the same time the discord between faith and reason and the discord between tolerance and intolerance, which Christianity has never been without during the course of its entire history.

Of course, we cannot think of history only as progress in the illumination of human reason. It is significant, for example, that a contemporary historian like Butterfield treats the notion of "judgment" not as a dogma of faith but as a category through which to elucidate history.[24] In addition, the appearance of things like the nihilism of Nietzsche, with its claims that "God is dead," means that the Christian notions of eschatology and divine judgment have lost their power to give direction to the human spirit. At the same time such appearance implies a critique aimed at the "God-slayer": that superficially optimistic rationalism with its optimistic idea of progress. Nietzsche's was a two-edged sword of radical skepticism turned against both these conflicting points of view. The idea of progress, therefore, can no longer serve as the sole category through which to elucidate history. But even so, the problem of modern historical consciousness that is taking shape around the idea of progress can hardly be resolved merely by returning to an eschatological view of history.

In this section I have tried to trace the kind of problems involved in the simultaneous occurrence in what Toynbee calls Judaic Western religions, particularly Christianity, of man's awareness of his subjective existence, on the one hand, and historicity in its twofold sense of historical consciousness and of history become conscious, on the other. The three problems we dealt with are basically bound up with one another and reach back, if we follow them, to the notion of a divine personality and hence also a human personality.[25]

VII

Although the views of history found in Christianity and in the Enlightenment represent diametrically opposed points of view, they both concur in recognizing a meaning in history. From its standpoint of *theocentric* faith, Christianity sees a divine providence or divine administration operative in history; the Enlightenment, from its *anthropocentric* standpoint of reason, locates the *telos* of history in the consummate rationalization of human life. In contrast to both of them, the world view of modern nihilism goes back to an abyssal nihility in which not only history but also all world processes are ultimately transformed into meaninglessness. As one possible ecstatic transcendence of human being-in-the-world, it expresses the awareness of Existenz at its limit-situation which we spoke of earlier.

With Nietzsche we find a turnabout on this nihilism that results in the standpoint of Eternal Recurrence as a disclosure of the Will to Power. This Eternal Recurrence of his is different from the recurrence of world processes found in mythical religions in that it is a recurrence of the world which includes the totality of all processes that can be regarded as new creations in history. It cannot, accordingly, simply be characterized as ahistorical. The nihilistic standpoint itself was already an historical event rising up out of the depths of Western history as a kind of uncompromising self-reflection. Hence, the standpoint of the Will to Power, which represented a conversion from nihilism, came also to be essentially bound up with the problem of history. Nevertheless, insofar as the Will to Power comes down in the final analysis to a world view of Eternal Recurrence, it is my view that the meaning it gives to history at its last and final ground, on the field of ecstatic transcendence, is based only on a negative pole.

Yet we must not overlook the positive pole in Nietzsche's thought. Within the perspective available from the standpoint of the Will to Power, all meaning in history which had been transformed into meaninglessness in nihility was tentatively restored in an affirmative manner in conjunction with the reaffirmation of all "world interpretations" as attempts of the Will to Power to posit values. The standpoint of the Will to Power and Eternal Recurrence is a standpoint of Great Affirmation, which could only appear after a nihilistic Great Negation. All the meanings that had been imparted to history on the dimension of history in its usual sense (as historically immanent)—even those meanings that human reason gives to history in making itself the principle of meaningfulness—were transformed into meaninglessness in nihility and then recovered once again when the Will to Power, as a standpoint of ecstatic transcendence, transformed them into its own perspective. But if the Will to Power, as the ecstatic basis on which all those meanings are restored, only opens up a field of the Eternal Recurrence of the same world-time, then history is ultimately merely restored in such a fashion that it cannot discharge its true historicity. So long as the view that something absolutely new is being created in time cannot radically be carried through, history is always deprived of its true meaning.

On this point, Nietzsche's view of Eternal Recurrence encompasses a problem that is the exact opposite of that found in Christian eschatology. As we have seen, Christianity broke down the cyclical character of mythical time and imparted historicity to time. But at the same time, it also supplied the mythical end of time with historicity, with the result that the eschaton was expected to descend from a transhistorical dimension and appear on the dimension of history in the once-and-for-all event of the second coming of Christ and the last judgment: an historical event to bring all history to its close. Thus, the historicity of history was brought to fulfillment by means of the historicity of eschatology, in such a way as to pen a final period to actual history itself. No such final punctuation marks Nietzsche's view of the Eternal Recurrence, where actual history is propelled in the direction of an immanent goal (called, from the viewpoint of the present, the "Overman"). But while history is exempt from being predestined to an abrupt end by virtue of being the field of recurrence as its ecstatic (and in this sense transhistorical) last and final ground, the guarantee of this endlessness is secured only at the cost of history's inability to discharge its full historicity.

Therefore the final question amounts to this: How is it possible for what we call history to carry its historicity through to its last and final transhistorical base without thereby being terminated as history at the hands of the transhistorical? In other words: How is it possible for history to become radically historical by virtue of its historicity being carried through to a transhistorical ground? The question leads us inevitably, I think, to the relationship between history and the standpoint of śūnyatā. It remains to be shown how.

The problem of eschatology has nothing to do with the end of history in the sense, for example, that the earth might cool off and annihilate mankind. It has rather to do with the question of a transhistorical dimension that is unveiled through the awareness of human historical existence. That is, it is the problem of the end of history in a *religious* sense. Particularly in Christianity we find the claim that the way of salvation for historical man was handed down to history from a transhistorical dimension in the historical event of the incarnation of Christ. The incarnation is the initiation of the eschaton, so to speak, which will be brought to its completion through the future historical event of the second coming of Christ.

Now the notion of the *end* of history corresponds with that of the *beginning* of history; the idea that history will come to a finish is in concert with the idea that it had a start. This start is spoken of as the fall of Adam. The incarnation of Christ took place in order to bestow salvation upon man, who is in a state of original sin due to the fall of Adam, that is, in order to put an end to the history that began with Adam. History starts with the sin of Adam and finishes with the second coming of Christ. Or, we might say, it begins with the punishment of God and ends with his final judgment. Since the fall, the incarnation, and the second coming are once-and-for-all historical events, as seen from within history, religion is essentially located on the field of history;

and conversely, history is essentially located on the field of religion. The history of salvation and the history of judgment as such *are* religion.

As we have seen, however, there is a problem for modern historical consciousness with the representation of the end of history as itself an historical event. On that point, eschatology falls back on the idea of the end of the world found in mythical religions. We see a regression to a dimension where, for instance, people conceive of the cooling off of the planet as a fate meted out by the "will" of nature or see the punishment of God at work in natural catastrophes like floods and earthquakes. But, to repeat, modern historical consciousness as it is expressed in the constitution of history as a science or branch of study, unfolds at the very point that this sort of eschaton ceases to have any relevance to its view of history: namely, at the point of its commitment to reason. The same can be said of the beginning of history as of its end. I would suppose that hardly anyone in the contemporary world believes any more that the history of mankind literally began with the fall of Adam.

That history has a beginning and an end must be flatly denied from the viewpoint of historical consciousness. And this immanent view, the view that unfolds into the science of history, is no less essential to history and no less indispensable to one's historical consciousness and approach to history than is the transhistorical view that unfolds into a religious prehension of history. Therefore, the idea of the beginning and end of history that runs throughout the long tradition of Christian teaching clashes with this point of view and, to that extent, leaves a problem still in need of a solution. It is a problem of the way the meaning of those notions is to be understood, a problem of interpretation which, in traditional Christianity, still remains confined to the framework of the old mythology.

How did things get to this point? In reply, we cannot but point to a view of God that conceived of the divine as a *personal* Being possessed of a conscious "will." The beginning and end of history are thought of in terms of divine punishment and divine judgment. History is interpreted as a history of judgment, or a history of salvation, through God. Back of history there stands a God who administers the world with wisdom and will, or with good will and provident wisdom. And it is only through the will of God that history started off and only through his will that it will draw to its close. These events are revelations of the divine will. The view of history according to which history has a beginning and an end is essentially connected with the fact that God is conceived of on a transhistorical dimension as a personal—that is, self-centered and in this case God-centered—Being possessed of will. In the last analysis, God is a "being."

There is no denying that the image of a personal God, a God of judgment or justice, or a God of love has, by bringing human beings before the "sacred" as a living subject, before a God no doubt beyond compare in the sacredness of his majesty and grace, drawn the conscience and love of man to special depths and thereby elevated the human personality to remarkable heights. And this alone, should the problematic as we have laid it out above in fact be the case, makes it all the more desirable that its solution unfold in the future from within Christianity itself. This seems to me to be necessary not only for the purpose of constructing a proper view of history suitable for future mankind, but also in order that Christianity itself may successfully confront the secularized view of history in the modern world.

With regard to Nietzsche's Eternal Recurrence, let it be said that as far as the term "eternal" goes, there is neither beginning nor end; and as far as the term "recurrence" goes, the same beginning and the same end always repeat themselves. The two are here one and the same.

This unbounded meaninglessness, surrounded by an aura of nihilism, is overcome through a turnabout wherein the standpoint of the Will to Power is forged out of this meaninglessness and the world becomes the epiphany of this Will. On this standpoint, all world processes become permeated with a "will to will" and turn into "play" in perfect abandon and high spirits on the field of the fresh purity of the "Innocence of Becoming" (*Unschuld des Werdens*). It is what we might call a "voluntaristic," modernized version of Heraclitus. It might also be interpreted as one of the currents of Western thought to come closest to the Buddhist standpoint of śūnyatā. We seem to be breathing here the same pure mountain air that we felt in approaching the standpoint of Dōgen through the words: "We meet a leap year one in four. / Cocks crow at four in the morning." And again: "I do not have a single strand of the Buddha's dharma. I now while away my time, accepting whatever may come."

But in spite of all of this, Eternal Recurrence does not make time to be truly time. Nietzsche, too, speaks of the "moment" as the twinkling of an eye (*Augenblick*), but it is a moment standing against a background of Eternal Recurrence and hence does not possess the bottomlessness of the true moment. Hence, it cannot signify the point where something truly new can take place. As remarked earlier, the historicity of history cannot here be fully discharged.

And how did things get to this point? Here, too, it must finally be said, some sort of "being" such as the Will to Power is being conceived of on a transhistorical plane. Of course, it is not an entity like the God of Christianity. It is not the *absolute ground of being* but the *principle of absolute becoming*. Nor is it seen as something objective. It is our own self as such that is an epiphany of that Will. At its foundations the standpoint of the Will to Power may perhaps be likened to the mystical union of *Brahman* and *atman* that we find in the ancient Indian expression about *Brahman*: "That art thou" (*tat tvam asi*). If the likeness is valid, it is certainly an important step forward. And yet insofar as what is here at issue is a "will," that is, something conceived of in the third person as an "it," it has yet to rid itself of the character of a "being."

Although, from Nietzsche's stance, we can say that our self is, in fact, "that," we cannot yet say that "that" in itself is, in fact, our self. In other words, although one can speak of a "self *that is not a self*," one cannot yet speak of a "*self* that is not self." This brings us to a fundamental difference between the position of Nietzsche and the position of Zen which speaks, for example, of the Existenz of "body-and-mind dropping off, dropped off body-and-mind," as the King of Samādhis Samādhi of one's self as such, with eyes horizontal and nose vertical.

That the Will to Power involves within it something that is not yet completely reverted back into the "self" indicates that it is still being represented as a "being" that "is." If it had been completely so reverted back into the self, we should not find so much as a single strand capable of representation as a "being" left on the ecstatic transhistorical dimension of Existenz in the King Samādhi. Then the original countenance of time would be unveiled in time originating as truly bottomless time; and the original countenance of history would be unveiled in the complete and radical discharging of its historicity.

The standpoint of this self, this time, and this history is the standpoint of body-and-mind dropping off, dropped off body-and-mind; of samsāra-*sive*-nirvāna; in a word, the standpoint of śūnyatā. It is the standpoint of real and complete actuality. In contrast, the standpoint of Nietzsche, substituting as it does the life-giving power of the Will for the God of Christianity, could not but display along with its keen sense of modernity a regression to *mythos*. Such concepts as Eternal Recurrence and the Dionysian point to such a regression. This has robbed

Nietzsche's image of time of both its historicity and its actuality.

In speaking of the notion of time found in the *Heart Sutra*, Hakuin remarks that "this, too, gouges out perfectly good flesh" and then appends three comments:

> Before all the kalpas [world-times] past and after all the kalpas to come.
> A marvellous spiritual light glints with austere chill in the sheath of a hair-splitting blade.
> A round gem, shining in dark night, is brought forth on its tray.

To these he adds a Zen verse:

> Yesterday at dawn I swept the soot of the old year away,
> Tonight I grind and knead flour for the New Year's sweets.
> There is a pine tree with its roots and an orange with its leaves.
> Then I don new clothes and await the coming guests.[26]

Hakuin's words are enough to give us a glimpse of how radically *actual* time is in Buddhism and on what standpoint so radically realistic a view of time is able to come about. Earlier I suggested that it is on the standpoint of śūnyatā that historicity is able to realize itself radically. I should like to return to this matter in the concluding chapter.

6

ŚŪNYATĀ AND HISTORY

I

To begin with, I will return to my earlier misgivings about Toynbee's view that the Buddhist concept of time is merely cyclical. A recurrent world process, as a cyclical movement, implies infinity to the extent that it lacks beginning or end. But to the extent that it does arrive at an end, in a sense, by going back to its beginning, its recurrent character signals a finiteness. It thus possesses, as it were, an infinite finitude, or, we might say, a finitude of a higher order. Only in connection with the repetition of recurrent movement running the same course over and over again without end does this higher order finitude get to become an infinite finitude of a higher order—what has been called Eternal Recurrence. But since this endlessly repeated recurrence is an Eternal Return of the same sorts of events and phenomena, its endlessness is a complete abstraction. It is, when all is said and done, a meaningless endlessness, nothing more than the *umsonst* ("in vain") that Nietzsche speaks of.

Might not what Buddhism points to in the phrase "since time past without beginning" belong to a different dimension? It is true, the *kalpa* is thought of in terms of a closed temporal system complete in itself. And from a succession of these kalpas a formal system of a higher order is conceived, leading in turn to still higher and more encompassing systems. From an accumulation of smaller kalpas, a greater kalpa is conceived, and from their accumulation, a still larger one, and so on without end. In this case, however, all the time systems imagined one after another in ever more encompassing spheres are all simultaneous. Consider the rotation of the earth about the sun within the solar system, the whole of which, in turn, moves about some other center. And then imagine an ever-widening circle of such patterns continuing on out into infinity. It makes sense to speak of the earth's involvement in all those movements simultaneously at each moment of time, at each "now." So it is with the kalpas.

What I am speaking of here is something other than the endlessly recurring system of identical time, in which the same world process returns again and again in Eternal Recurrence. In Eternal Recurrence, a before and an after are imagined in the successive repetitions of the same world-time; in that recurrence, time is represented purely and simply as a straight line without beginning or end. But in Buddhism, time is circular, because all its time systems are simultaneous; and, as a continuum of individual "nows" wherein the systems are simultaneous, it is *rectilinear* as well. Time is at once circular and rectilinear.

The idea of a stratified formation of simultaneous time systems necessitates the idea of an infinite openness at the bottom of time, like a great expanse of vast, skylike emptiness that cannot be confined to any systematic enclosure. Having such an openness at its bottom, each and every now, even as it belongs to each of the various layers accumulated through the total time system, is itself something new and admits of no repetition in any sense. The sequence of "nows" is really irreversible. Accordingly, in the true sense, each now passes away and comes into being at each fleeting instant. It is, in other words, something *impermanent* in the fullest sense of the word. As such a succession of nows with an infinite openness beneath it, time must be conceived of without beginning or end. Conversely, only when so conceived is it possible for every now to come about as a new now and as impermanent. Moreover, in time this newness and impermanency are tied to one another inseparably. In that interrelation, as I will explain presently, there appears an ambiguity essential to time.

To think of kalpas—to which the name "Aion" may also be fixed with its twofold meaning of time and world-time—as a great, manifold time system suggests a mythical representation of time. But the "meaning" of this representation can be interpreted as a recognition of an infinite openness at the bottom of time. Likewise, the phrase "since time past without beginning" is a vague and crude way of thinking, which belongs to a period previous to Kant's reflection on the antinomy implied in the question of whether time had a beginning or not. Yet this is not to say that we cannot all the same see the true Form of time appear here. The true Form of time may be called its essential ambiguity. One aspect of that ambiguity has been pointed out as the inseparable connection that obtains between the sense of newness and the sense of impermanence found in the now. But this ambiguity extends to all aspects of time.

To repeat, only as something in infinite openness without beginning or end does time become something perpetually new at each now. But this newness has a double meaning. The constant origination of new things, on the one hand, has the positive significance of genesis or creation. In that sense, time is a field of unlimited possibility in creative freedom, or, rather, it is that very possibility itself. A time without beginning or end within an infinite openness displays an infinity of possibility. It enunciates the character of indefiniteness maintained by the possibilities we have within our nature as time-being (or being-time).

On the other hand, this same constant origination is not something we could put a stop to even if we wanted to. It gives us no rest, but pushes us ever forward. It makes us do things and tugs at us from within to keep turning us in new directions. This obligation to unceasing newness makes our existence an infinite burden to us. It means, too, that time itself comes to appear to us as infinitely burdensome. It is in the nature of time and our very existence, so to speak, that from the start both are saddled with an inexhaustible debt. It is in the nature of our existence that we are unable to sustain ourselves except through being engaged without intermission in doing something. Or put the other way around, our life is such that we must work without pause to pay back the debt that lies heavy upon our shoulders.

Essentially, then, *time* and *being* take on the quality of a liability for us, as evidenced by our need to be continually involved in doing something. What is more, anything we do invariably results in a new liability and imposes the obligation of doing something else. In the very act of working constantly to pay off our debt, another obligation is added on. The dissolution of one debt becomes the seed of another. In this causal nexus we see the infiniteness with which our being and time become for us an interminable burden. In any case, having always to be doing something, or planning to do something, belongs to the essential form of our life. In its essence, our actual existence can be called a "project" (*Entwurf*). And here, it hardly bears mentioning, even doing nothing at all—as, for instance, when we are resting—is in essence already being at work, already being entangled in the net of causal conditions. It is a *samskrta*, a "being-at-doing." Indeed, our own being and time lay bare their burdensomeness most clearly precisely when we are doing nothing at all—a point that has often been made in connection with the phenomenon of *ennui*.

To sum up, then, that we *are* in time means that we are condemned to be *doing* something incessantly, and in that constant doing our being constantly comes about as a *becoming*. That is, existence in time occurs as a constant "incessant becoming."

The problem here, though, is the infinity implied in the burden we spoke of. The ineluctability or intrinsic inevitability of our having always to be engaged in doing something or other has the character of a burden by its sheer interminableness. It rises to self-awareness with our Dasein itself as an infinite, restless, forward drive within. Our life is finite, but the essence of that life reaches our awareness as this sort of *infinite drive* spurring us endlessly on from our inward parts. The finite aspect of our life displays its essence as an infinite finitude. (It is here, as noted before, that the original sense of the mythical notion of transmigration is to be seen.) Our existence and time appear to us here as burdens.

This infinite drive has since ancient times been taken as "greed" or "lust" (*cupiditas* and *concupiscentia* being the Western equivalents). Being so driven by an infinite drive and unable to refrain from constantly doing something new—the mode of being that constitutes the essence of our life or being-in-the-world, together with the causal nexus it implies—led to the idea of karma. The term "karma" expresses an awareness of existence that sees being and time as infinite burdens for us and, at the same time, an awareness of the essence of time itself.

To recap the main point, in newness without ceasing, we see two simultaneous faces of time: one of creation, freedom, and infinite possibility, and one of infinite burden, inextricable necessity. Newness is essentially equivocal; thus, so is time.

As noted, only by coming to be without beginning and end in infinite openness can time express its twofold meaning of an ever new now and impermanence. But this impermanence contains an ambiguity of its own. On the one hand, it indicates the volatility of time, in which each now, ultimately containing an infinite openness at its bottom and thus having no base on which to stand safe and secure, comes to be at one fleeting instant and passes away at the next. In this sense, every now represents time continually vanishing into thin air, as it were. Hence the expressions of the swiftness of fragile, transitory existence that liken it to a flash of lightning or a horse seen galloping by through a chink in the door, or that compare all things in the world to floating phantasms or dewdrops in the morning sun.[1] Time is at all times on the verge of vanishing, and all things show the frailty of being that keeps them ever poised on the brink of collapse. Time and being display a constant pull to nullification from beneath their very ground. That is impermanence.

But at the same time, from another angle, impermanence is the negation of "permanence" in the sense of being hitched to some particular determination or other. To say that impermanence is a non-permanence means that a determinate mode of being does not become a hindrance for the being so determined itself. Here time and nothingness as the nullification of all things signify the freedom and effortless flight of a bird gliding across the sky without a moment's hitch, unburdened. Like the bird that leaves no tracks along the path of its flight, impermanence here means the non-hindrance of being free of the encumbrances of one's past and of restrictions stemming from former lives. Therefore, just as in the case of the being and time implied in newness, so also in the case of impermanence, and the nothingness and time it implies, the meaning of impermanence and nothingness (or nullification) is ambiguous. And so, too, is the meaning of time.

Lastly, we said that time only comes about in virtue of having an infinite openness at its bottom. This infinite openness also contains an ambiguity of its own. In a word, it can mean both nihility and śūnyatā in its original sense. According to the meaning it takes on, time and all matters related to time will assume meanings fundamentally opposed to one another. The true Form of time consists in the simultaneous possibility of these opposing meanings. The essential ambiguity in the meaning of time means that time is essentially the field of fundamental conversion, the field of a "change of heart" or *metanoia* (*pravritti-vijñāna*).

II

In the preceding section we saw how time, seen as containing an infinite openness at its ground, exhibits the quality of "since time past without beginning." Time comes out of a past that can be traced back interminably and goes further into a future that can open up interminably. And concerning our existence in time, we spoke of the infinite drive of karma.

Time is inextricably linked with all things existing and originating

into existence in this "world." It encloses their being (and, consequently, also their nothingness) in the deepest of enigmas. The question
of the home-ground of our Dasein itself (Where do we come from?
Where are we going?) is shrouded in mist. This creates an uneasiness
within us regarding our own existence. It means that our existence is
essentially tied up with groundlessness and anxiety. The awareness of
this our existence lays bare the enigma and anxiety in the best possible
relief at the very point that time is seen as something *without beginning or
end*. My birth stems from my parents, just as theirs does from their
parents, and so on interminably into the past. If we continue our
pursuit, eventually we will go back to a point before the appearance of
the human race, before life, before the emergence of the earth and the
solar system, and so on without end. In like manner, we can continue on
indefinitely into the future, from father to son to grandson, and so on
until we come to the disappearance of the human race, of living beings,
of the earth and the solar system—until all is lost in the vast expanse of
an endless future.

But there is more at issue here than mere chronological or *vertical*
relationships. I have brothers, sisters, and relatives, just as my parents
and their parents had. When we pursue these *horizontal* or spatial
relationships in conjunction with the chronological ones, we find them
eventually spreading out in all directions into a web of relationships
beyond measure. My existence stands against the backdrop of such a
network of relationships whose beginning and end are beyond comprehension, and comes into being from out of its midst. From this perspective, questions regarding the source of my existence remain ultimately
unanswerable. No matter how much progress is made in the scientific
explanation of the "history" of animate beings on the earth and the
history of the universe as a whole, such history can only step backward
endlessly into the past and open up endlessly into the future, without
ever being capable of learning the secret of the beginning or the end.

Even so, the unshakable fact remains: I am actually existing here
and now. Let time be without beginning or end; this being that is
present *is* actually present. Its presence is beyond doubt. And, as
mentioned before, even the fact that time reveals itself as without
beginning or end is only possible because in the awareness of existence
that occurs within this actual presence, what may be called an infinite
openness comes to awareness from the bottom of that present time. The
revelation of time as without beginning or end is inseparable from the
revelation of the infinite openness lying at the ground of this actual

presence. Only in that infinite openness does time appear as an infinite regression and an infinite progression, as something without beginning or end.

Therefore, although it is a contradiction and an impossibility to ask about the beginning or the end of time (or about the beginning or end of our "being" as actual existants) within a time that has neither beginning nor end, the beginning and end of that time in itself can be sought within this actual presence itself. This is the quest for the beginning and end of time and being at a more elemental level, one that draws closer to the elemental home-ground and asks about the essence of time and being.

While the beginning and the end of time in itself without beginning or end can be sought within this actual presence, that presence itself implies something that remains out of reach, no matter how far back or how far forward we go. It involves something of another dimension, as different as a solid body is from a flat plane, something like a true infinity that can never be attained no matter how much something finite is enlarged. Seen from this perspective, it stands to reason that the beginning and end of time and being are not to be found within time. In the same way that a three-dimensional solid can never be reduced to a two-dimensional plane (for example, the angle of vision at which a mountain top is viewed by someone standing on the plain below never reaches zero, no matter how far one distances oneself from the mountain), we never encounter the beginning or the end of time, no matter how deeply we step back into the past or how far ahead we reach into the future. For this, at bottom, is the essence of time.

The beginning and end of time in itself lie directly beneath the present, at its home-ground, and it is there that they are to be sought originally. To look for the home-ground of time (or being) by tracing time interminably backward or pushing it interminably ahead is to fall victim to a sort of optical illusion, a confusion of dimensions. It is an error of orientation in the pursuit of the home-ground.

There is also good reason here for Christianity to consider time itself as a creation of God, and to consider the beginning and end of the time of the history of mankind, in particular, in terms of divine judgment and punishment, that is, as the will of God. It is also quite natural for Christianity to regard divine creation and punishment as still at work in the home-ground of the present and to regard the coming judgment, too, as already at work in the home-ground of the present.

Similarly, it is not without cause that Nietzsche arrived at his idea of Eternal Recurrence through the intuition, in a kind of philosophical vision, of time retreating endlessly backward into the past and time marching endlessly forward into the future meeting at their outer limits, which led him to proclaim that time "bends." In this vision, too, the meeting of time past and time future, as well as the disclosure of world-time (Aion) as an Eternal Recurrence, must take place directly underneath the now of the present moment, as Nietzsche himself points out in *Zarathustra*.[2]

In both cases, the optical illusion we spoke of is provisionally resolved. Only, as we also indicated, the respective orientations to transcendence run counter to one another, and therefore the problematic involved comes to appear in diametrically opposite fashion.

In Christianity, the will of God bestows a beginning and an end to the time of the world and the time of man, controlling those times from their home-ground and remaining at work in the home-ground of the present. The optical illusion that results from the tireless pursuit of time backward and forward in search of the home-ground of time and being is broken down from the start. Then, too, in locating the origin of historical time elementally on this transhistorical dimension, historical time becomes historical in an elemental sense. And the religious things that are joined to the transhistorical dimension of the relationship between man and the will of God all become historical events.

But the other side of the coin is that general, secular history, which requires an immanent understanding of history, cannot but be drawn completely into the framework of a beginning and an end posited by the power of an absolutely surpassing God. As explained in the last chapter, the secularization of the concept of history, that is, a view of history based on the idea of "progress," or the secularization of historical actuality itself, originated in revolt against this view.

In the atheistic nihilism of Nietzsche, on the contrary, any beginning or end posited in history from a transhistorical dimension is disallowed, and in its stead history is allowed to execute its own evolution everywhere and without limits. The secularization of the view of history is here presupposed from the start. Consequently, the standpoint of the optical illusion, which, as I shall explain presently, is essentially linked to the process of secularization (for example, in the idea of progress), is also accepted more or less as is.

But when time spoken of in terms of an unlimited past and an unlimited future becomes a single, circular whole; when this circle of time is depicted as a meaningless repetition on the canvas of nihility;

and when all being in time is nullified from the ground up and turns into an endless, pure becoming; then the optical illusion or confusion of dimensions that tries to ask about the home-ground of time and being with time, is awakened from its illusion and refocused on what Nietzsche calls a "radical nihilism." There is no home-ground at all to be sought in the world of that pure becoming, that circular world-time turning eternally within itself. And where all things are to be repeated endlessly in exactly the same fashion, where everything is nullified and rendered meaningless, any search at all for the elemental loses its significance.

Science, which everywhere goes backward in time to look for the "causes" of present phenomena, scientistic philosophy and its positivism, and the idealism of progress, which is an antipode to that positivism in turning to the future in search of its ideal as a *telos*—all are robbed of the ground of their meaning, uprooted by a radical (elemental) nihilism. It is the same, at a more elemental level, with Platonic contemplation, which, in its search for the home-ground of temporal things, goes back to a transtemporal past ("preexistence") to "recollect" the eternal Ideas contemplatively back into the present; and also with Christian faith, which, in its quest of the same home-ground, turns to a transtemporal future ("eschaton") to "await in hope" the coming of the Son of God. In the eyes of nihilism, these, too, are to be rejected. Each in its own way, then, all the standpoints mentioned here are reduced eventually to nothing more than some type of optical illusion. Since this radical view seems to me pregnant with a grave problem, I should like to examine it in a little more depth.

The natural sciences, social sciences, and historical sciences represent the standpoint of positivistic theory in their persistent turning to the past in search of "causes," or of a home-ground in the sense of a "beginning." The standpoint of progress represents the standpoint of idealistic praxis in turning persistently to the future in search of a *telos*, or a home-ground in the sense of an "ending." Their common foundation, however, lies in the self-affirming independence of intellect and will within human reason or, in other words, in the "secularization" of that reason. But seen more basically, deep beneath this "becoming independent" there lies within man the drive of existence to achieve autonomy: to push forward and stand on its own feet and as its own master. And again, at the deepest ground of this drive, is the will to persist in being itself in spite of everything, a will that forever wills to see its own way through. It is, in that sense, a "self-will," or, as

Heidegger called it, "a will to will." As a phenomenon, it appears in the achievement of independence, or secularization by human reason.

Indeed, it is a "secularization" in the preeminent sense of the word. By this we mean that it is a standpoint that looks only within time for the home-ground of all that exists and originates within time. It tries to construct the necessary causal relations, whether mechanistic or teleological, between actually existing things and their home-ground, solely within the confines of time. It has no regard whatsoever for any home-ground beyond time. This standpoint makes "sense" in its own way; but it has failed to realize yet that the time that provides it with its field, a time unrestrictedly open to both past and future, can only come about by virtue of an infinite openness lying at the ground of the present. This total lack of eye for any ground beyond time belongs to secularization in its preeminent sense and is characteristic of an age and a world dominated by science and technology.

It is in this sense, then, that the standpoint of natural science, sociology, history, scientistic philosophy, positivistic realism, and the idealism of "progress" all essentially contain the potential for optical illusion. When they become self-satisfied, each for its own scientific, positivistic, rational, or progressive reasons, and then go on to absolutize their "secularization" and to reject every quest of religion and metaphysics for a transtemporal ground as so much empty fantasy—in sum, when they fall headlong into the conceits of a "man-centered" attitude—the latent potential for optical illusion becomes an actuality. In either case, though, from a standpoint where the infinite openness of time has been radicalized all the way to nihility, from a standpoint that arrived at ecstatic transcendence in the ground of time, these various secularized standpoints cannot avoid facing up to questions regarding the roothold of the "sense" they make.

By way of contrast, Christian teaching and the metaphysics of which Platonism is representative conceive of the home-ground of temporal things as something having being in an eternal immutability beyond time. The Christian God is even the home-ground of time itself. Things of this world do not possess the roothold of their own existence within themselves. Their being takes hold of its ground in a transcendent Being somewhere on the "far side," beyond this world. No temporal thing as such can have any meaning or value of its own; meaning and value are granted only from what is transtemporal.

In modern times particularly, however, science is committed to finding the causes of temporal things strictly within the temporal things themselves, while ethics and culture are committed to pursuing the aims of secular life exclusively within secular life. The things of "this world" have recovered the roothold of their own existence, as well as their own meaning and value, solely from within this world. As pointed out earlier, due to its intolerance and, above all, its internal divisions and conflicts, Christianity has been made to relativize its own demand for absoluteness. Along with that the authority of the transcendent Being has beaten a gradual retreat; in its stead, secularism in its pre-eminent sense has become dominant.

In short, the standpoint that Nietzsche dubbed as "Platonic-Christian" sought the home-ground of time and being within time in a transcendent Being, and for that reason could not manage to allot its proper place to the open-ended view of secularized time in which time is allowed to stretch back endlessly and to open up endlessly ahead, to possess an infinite openness in both directions, and to contain in itself a kind of infinity (or rather, an infinite finitude). As a result, by virtue of its intrinsic infinity, time became independent of eternity, so to speak, and temporal things, the "things of this world," were able to be considered from within the confines of this world.

As I said earlier, though, the standpoint of secularism for its part loses sight of the orientation of time to transcendence, or even ignores it altogether. This it does in spite of the crucial fact that while the standpoint of secularism rests on the time of this world, the distinguishing feature of that time, the infinity (or infinitude finitude) opened up in both directions, is in reality only a projection of the transtemporal infinite openness (or emptiness) opening up directly beneath the present and can appear only on such a "supposition" (in the sense of an underlying ground).

Thus it can be said that the *theocentric* standpoint, as represented by Christianity, and the *anthropocentric* standpoint of secularism both find themselves currently at the brink of mutual elimination with regard to the problem of time. Nietzsche's philosophy could not have come to birth without a footing on such a brink.

III

"God is dead" means that all is dead. It means that the elemental ground of all things has turned to nihility, that the being of all things has been nullified from its elemental ground. Their unity and transcendent center lost, with no home-ground to return to, things scatter with the four winds in a time whose boundaries have been wiped away. This nullification of being transforms all things into transitoriness. At the same time, the roothold where the meaning of all existence takes hold is swept away, transforming the whole into a mass of meaninglessness.

But so thoroughgoing a death as to include even the death of "God," that is, so radical a radical nihilism, is at once the point of a conversion to life. The vision of Eternal Recurrence implies such a meaning. On the one hand, with world-time assuming the character of an Eternal Recurrence, "becoming" comes to be an utterly pure and transparent becoming. The impermanence of time is radicalized into pure impermanence, and the meaninglessness of time into an *Ungrund* of meaninglessness. It is the outer extreme of nihilization that we speak of here. At first blush, all of this might seem idle fiction. But in fact, if the whole, with all its consequences, is raised to the dimension of a *Weltanschauung*, it proves by and large inevitable that a secularized world and a world-time both of which leave God out of the picture should take shape in this way.

On the other hand, when both extremes of time infinitely open in both directions meet once again, when time becomes a circle, then time returns to the home-ground of the now, that moment wherein time itself is always present as a single whole. Then all beings scattered limitlessly throughout time are gathered together again into one, even as the pure becoming they are, and appear in the home-ground of the present. The vision of world-time as an Eternal Recurrence is inseparable from a return to the home-ground of the present.

And this means, as I have been saying, that at the home-ground of the present—directly beneath the present that penetrates vertically through the stratified accumulation of endless numbers of lesser and greater cycles of time—nihility opens up as the field of the ecstatic transcendence of world and time. It means that the abyss of nihility on which this endless recurrence takes place appears as an infinite openness directly beneath the present.

For example, when Nietzsche speaks in *Twilight of the Idols* of the fact that *es gibt Nichts ausser dem Ganzen* ("there is nothing outside of the whole") as a Great Liberation, he is saying, of course, that outside of the world as a whole there is no God, no world beyond on a far side, that nothing is to be found outside of this world, "the whole." But at the same time, he is saying that the field of nihility (the *Nichts*) opens up as a field of Great Liberation. This opening up means that nihility comes to participate in time, as a participation occurring at all times on the home-ground of the present. It brings "the whole" back to the home-ground of the present. The "nothing outside" and the "whole" appear at one and the same time in the home-ground of the present. And this signals a Great Liberation.

When time becomes a circle and the world becomes an Eternal Recurrence, this world-time (or time-world) becomes present in the home-ground of the present, opening up the abyssal nihility directly beneath it. In this case, too, infinite openness as transcendence beyond world and time takes on the character of eternity. It is not, however, the eternity of a transcendent *being*, but something that might be called the eternity of a transcendent *nothingness*, or the eternity, so to speak, of Death itself. It opens up directly beneath the present—there and only there can it open up. When the field of eternity, that is, the field of transcendence opens up—when it is given (*es gibt*) as giving to world and time the possibility of presenting themselves as world-time—it does so only in such a manner that world and time return as a single whole to the home-ground of the present. This return then means that the home-ground of the present directly underfoot is, as it were, cut through and cleared out; that the present at its own home-ground opens itself to infinite openness, to the field of eternity; in brief, that the present returns to the home-ground of the present itself.

Seen from the perspective of the awareness of our own existence in the present, all of this indicates that what we have called abyss of nihility, or the eternity of death, comes forth and makes itself present from the home-ground of our existence. It becomes our own utter death. We make the general statement that the field of eternity or transcendence can in each case only be opened at the bottom of the present, because what is called eternity or transcendence can neither be truly inquired into nor truly opened up except as our own *koto*. It is the same with nihility and death. When we say that the elemental source of beings one and all is transformed into nihility, or that the world is transformed into a world of death, we are not pointing to a merely objective *koto*. It is not "somebody else's affair." Instead, as noted earlier, all things in the world, together with the self, turn into nihility as one, and the Great Death presents itself out of the bottom where world and self are one. It is the *koto* of being-in-the-world itself. It is "our own affair."

But then, this is not our own affair in the sense of something that can be considered from a contemplative standpoint as if it were some-body else's affair. This *koto* is not some matter to be pondered over or discussed in terms of *logos* on a rational dimension. It is a *koto* that makes itself present only where an actuality is actually actual. It is the *koto* of our own self as Existenz. It is also for the sake of the same *koto* that the "eternity of nothingness" presenting itself from the home-ground of the world as the Great Death becomes, in turn, the existential self-aware-ness awakened in our Dasein. Talk of the infinite openness of nihility appearing beneath the present means no less than the return of the present to its home-ground. It is another way of expressing this exis-tential self-awareness.

We find something similar in Nietzsche's vision of Eternal Recur-rence. This vision, inseparably connected with the moment we call "now" and emerging from directly beneath it, bears the mark of a present and moment-to-moment existential awareness, an awakening to the "eternal" presence of the whole world-time, and with it the field of nihility. The appearance of the world-time as an Eternal Recurrence can also be referred to as the nihility that constitutes its field, or as the eternity of death become revealed in existential self-awareness. Thus, Nietzsche's Eternal Recurrence means that we are led to the Existenz of a Great Death, as great as the world itself. The Eternal Return of world-time means the *realization* of that Great Death. (What we are saying here is related to a problem that runs, for instance, beneath the surface in *Zarathustra*, beginning with the section entitled "On Great Events" in the second part and continuing on to the end of the third part.) This nihility becomes manifest as such an existential death, as our own Great Death. It occurs en route to what Nietzsche has in mind when he says, "When you gaze long into an abyss, the abyss starts gazing back into you." That is the self-presentation of nihility, what has been called above a participation in nihility.

Only when such an extreme is reached, however, is the funda-mental conversion able to occur. It is the turnabout from the Great Death to the Great Life. It is something of which we cannot ask why. There can be no conceivable reason for it, and no conceivable basis for it to take hold of. That is to say, this conversion is an event taking place at a point more elemental than the dimension on which events occur that can be spoken of in terms of reasons and bases. If a reason is to be sought, it can only be as the traditional religions have all sought it: on the "other" side, in God or in Buddha, in something like Divine Providence, Love of God, or the Original Vow of Amida Buddha. But a reason that is on the side of God or Buddha is not the sort of reason man is after when he asks why. (The *Book of Job* cuts deeply into this state of affairs.) After all, we can do no other than to say: it is so. There is no room for *what* or *why*, not even the *what* or *why* issuing from an Hegelian absolute Reason. All that is left is *that* or *thus*. All we can say is that such is the way Existenz is. And so it is indeed; as Kierkegaard, the first apostle of existentialism, said, only a leap and a "qualitative dialectic" are possible.

For Nietzsche, it was the Will to Power that appeared in the conversion from the Great Death to the Great Life. There everything that has so far shown the elemental Form of death now shows the elemental Form of life. The field of ecstatic transcendence from world and time, the field of eternity, now appears in its original Form as the field of the Great Life. And the Will to Power that opens up this same field of Life as its own becomes manifest in that field, or *as* that field. We might compare it to something radiating light, and thus creating a field of light around itself, in its very act of appearing there as itself the center of its own circumference.

The eternally recurring world, in its *Unschuld des Werdens* (in the undefiled and artless innocence of its becoming) is the revelation of this Will. Eternal Recurrence is its innocent play, its aimless (or transteleological) activity. This Will is immanent in the world as the driving dynamism immanent in the infinite movement of the world. It is also immanent in all things in the world as their essence or "selfness." There is nothing that is not a revelation of the Will to Power.

Such a standpoint seems a clear and striking antithesis to the standpoints of secularism and Christianity, which have been treated together above. In contrast with the man-centered approach of secularization and its declaration of the independence of human reason, man is here something to be "overcome." In secularization, man became man-centered and slayer of God. Nietzsche says in his *Joyful Wisdom* that we are drifting about in an infinite nihility, that we are a race far from worthy of the sublimity of the deed of deicide. Man, to be truly himself, has to rid himself of the merely "human" or "man-centered" mode of being. He has to turn toward the field of the Will to Power and there to overcome himself ecstatically. He must die the Great Death in the abyss of nihility and come back to Life again. In so doing, he divests himself of existence in the *eidos* of a human being, of the human mode of being itself.

The world view of Eternal Return which was, as we shall see later, the culmination of Nietzsche's nihilism, is a sledgehammer smashing the optical illusions of man. The man-centered illusion is no exception: man in the age of secularization must be tempered by the blows of that hammer. Seen from the standpoint of the Great Will, human reason, the principle of secularism, is nothing more than an instrument of the flesh; or, rather, the flesh itself is the Great Reason. For the flesh is more elemental than reason and, as such, belongs to the whole man.

The contrast of the standpoint of the Will to Power with that of Christianity is clear enough and does not require much further explanation. It was remarked earlier that the fall of the transcendental dimension into oblivion belonged to the essence of secularism, where there was an optical illusion to be seen. But there seems to be an optical illusion essential to the Platonic-Christian standpoint as well, albeit in an opposite configuration. In lieu of a *nothingness* transcendent with regard to the "world" of pure *becoming*, this latter standpoint conceives of a transcendent *being*; that is, it conceives of a world on another shore beyond this world and of an eternal transcendent God, so that this world is depreciated to a world of sin and death and impermanence. But from the standpoint of the Will to Power, which looks at this world and sees the innocence of becoming instead of sin, and instead of death and impermanence, "this life, this eternal life," the Christian view is nothing but an optical illusion. Not only the man-centered but also the God-centered mode of being has to be smashed, Nietzsche would claim, by the sledgehammer of the idea of Eternal Recurrence. Only when every sort of optical illusion has been demolished through this "transnihilism" does the standpoint of the Great Affirmation of the Great Life come to light.

All such optical illusions have their origin in weakness born of an inability to stand firm in the Will that is the true essence of the world and the self, of an inability to give up one's mind to quest with undaunted Will after the standpoint of the Will to Power, the standpoint of the self affirming itself. Looked at from another angle, this weakness is the fear of all the various negations and self-negations required in the willful carrying through of this Will as the self itself, that is, the fear of all the various "deaths" that one must die. Because of this weakness, man sets up all sorts of ideals outside of himself after the manner of an "other" where he can turn for support, someplace he can rely on. They are all products of aspirations spawned of that essential weakness of will that does not persist in seeking to be and to become the self itself.

Consequently, in this sense any sort of optical illusion is in essence an unconscious self-deception. And the collapse of these illusions through the idea of Eternal Recurrence means a demolition of all those aspirations that divert man from the will to be and become himself through and through. This demolition is man's self-overcoming and his self-tempering. It is an awakening from all aspirations with their delusions and unconscious self-deception. It is the return to the essential will of the self.

From the standpoint of the Will to Power itself, all things are appearances of that Will. In their essence, of which they are unaware, even the aspirations stemming from the weakness of Will just spoken of and the products of those aspirations have the Will to Power at work within them. For example, should one be able to live in peace and assurance only in passive dependency on an absolute, inasmuch as this life of assurance implies a sense of life consenting to itself, it is in effect an expression of Will pursuing itself as the Will to self-affirmation. Only here—and this is the special feature of this case—the Will appears indirectly, making a detour through an Absolute Other. Looked at in this way, all optical illusions and self-deceptions are, in their essence, of which they themselves are unaware, appearances of the Will to Power. As mentioned earlier, all evaluative interpretations of the world come to be seen as so many perspectives opened up from within the Will to Power itself. The various interpretations of the world smashed under the sledgehammer of the idea of Eternal Recurrence are granted a reinterpretation from the standpoint of the Will to Power. From a standpoint that sees all historical processes of the world as an attempt by the Will to Power to return to itself, they are all incorporated into the process of that Will to Will.

But while granting the profoundness with which Nietzsche's "philosophy" exposes the fundamental barriers that man comes up against in modern times and tries to open one possible path to break through them, I have to repeat what was said before: Nietzsche's standpoint of Eternal Recurrence and the Will to Power was not able fully to realize the meaning of the historicity of historical things. And the fundamental reason for this lies in the fact that the Will to Power, Nietzsche's final standpoint, was still conceived as some "thing" called "will." So long as it is regarded as an *entity* named will, it does not completely lose its connotation of being an *other* for us and thus cannot become something wherein we can truly become aware of ourselves at our elemental source.

There is no need to elaborate on this now. What I am concerned with here is that in all the Western standpoints referred to, "will" is made into the foundation, and that this is essentially linked to problems such as time and eternity, the historical and the transhistorical. I have on several occasions argued that the Will of God in Christianity and the Will to Power in Nietzsche are inseparably connected with the problems of time, eternity, history, and the like. Even on the standpoint of secularism found in the view of history as progress, the way of looking at time and history is essentially linked to the idea of man as will. This is because at the bottom of the elevation of human reason to independence—which serves as the basis for the great conversion to secularization that begins with a world where God is taken out of the picture—and extending throughout all the things of culture, society, and man himself, we find hidden an important event: man's grasp of his own being as will, and of his own will as self-will.

In touching on the subject of modern secularism in the previous section as secularization in its preeminent sense, it was noted that at the ground of the independence effected in human reason lies what could be called the drive of existence itself to become autonomous, and, moreover, that in the deepest ground of that drive, self-will—what Heidegger called the "will to will"—is at work. In early Christian theology this was considered to be the mode of being of the human spirit that tried to usurp the throne of omnipotence from God and fell victim to the wiles of the devil's seductions. Modern scholars have called this the *daemonic*. Of course, to speak in this way of the standpoint of secularism is not to imply that that standpoint itself has been aware of all of this. I merely wished to point out that within secularism in the modern age, within secularization in its preeminent sense, the life of man completely freed from a divine world order has come to show in its every facet something that may be called an infinite drive. May we not say that in such realms as the study of nature in science, the technical revolutions of technology, the pursuit of social progress, and even the areas of sexuality, sports, and the like, a driving dynamic oriented to the infinite has come to the fore? In all of these realms of life, there slumbers a particular "heat" or "passion." And this means that along with secularization, each of the various facets of human existence becomes *autotelic*, each as it were becomes *autonomous*. Each begins to contain a kind of infinity, an infinite finitude.

In thus becoming autotelic, all the fields of human endeavor became *aimless*. They ceased to be subordinate to anything higher than themselves, to make it their own end, and to serve as its substratum. Along with the collapse of the teleological system of a divine world order, the hierarchy of values it implied also collapsed. Subsequently, the various occupations of man scattered, each becoming an end to itself, autotelic and autonomous, transformed into something unchecked and unlimited. In other words, the infinite drive appeared as something aimless, *a-telic*. This corresponds to the situation in a world devoid of God where time became open-ended in both directions. The time that lost the beginning and the end it had through the Will of God is the time of the world in secularization. Within that time, every function of life, as something that is autotelic and therefore aimless, is given over to the unrestricted pursuit of itself. It is here that the infinite drive, or what may be termed "self-will," is to be seen.

In the West, then, the problems of time and eternity, of the historical and the transhistorical, in the end always come to be combined with the concept of will. This is probably because the problem of the existence of the world and man, or rather the problem of being-in-the-world, is one which must ultimately be considered, not *sub specie aeternitatis*, but *sub specie infinitatis*. To shift our viewpoint, being-in-the-world is invariably involved with what is implied in such concepts as providence, destiny, fate, and the like. None of the standpoints discussed so far—the Will of God, eschatology, Eternal Recurrence, Will to Power, time without beginning or end, infinite drive, and so on—has looked at being-in-the-world simply under the Form of eternity. Instead, they originated from viewing it in terms of the dynamic Form of infinity, from the point where time and eternity, the historical and the transhistorical, intersect. From there, the meaning of fate and the like flows naturally into the question of being-in-the-world. With this it becomes understandable how will comes to be regarded as the essence of existence.

We are reminded here of a similar characteristic to be found in the Eastern notion of karma. It would seem that in karma, too, being-in-the-world is viewed under the Form of infinity in the dynamic sense just alluded to, that a sense of fate appears along with it, and that the essence of existence is grasped as a thing of the will. Moreover, the greatest problem here is that karma is considered on the field of a time without beginning or end, as we see it in such expressions as "karma since time past without beginning or end."

As noted before, in the West the notion of time without beginning or end grew out of the establishment of the standpoint of secularization, in its preeminent sense in modern times, and continues to be influential. Although the essential limitations of this standpoint have been critically exposed from any number of angles, especially and most fundamentally

from the viewpoints of Christianity and radical nihilism, its true sublation (*Aufhebung*) remains yet to be achieved. The standpoint of modern
secularism, we then went on to show, conceals an infinite drive at its
ground, even though secularism itself be not aware of the fact. When it
does rise to self-awareness, the standpoint of secularism begins to
crumble.

The standpoint that belongs to the notion of karma, on the contrary, *implies* this self-awareness. Time without beginning or end and
infinite drive are characteristic elements of karma from the very outset.
This means that in karma, being-in-the-world within modern secularization only appears after it has already passed through reflection under
the Form of infinity. At least, it seems possible to say that in essence the
idea of karma includes a "meaning" that allows of such an interpretation. So explained, this timeworn, almost mythical idea appears,
somewhat unexpectedly, to have a bearing on our contemporary problem. With this, we wind our way back at long last to the starting point of
our inquiry.

IV

At this point there is no need to go into the whole range of ideas that
have developed around the notion of karma throughout the history of
Buddhism. What we need is the basic content of that idea as it is found,
for example, in the Buddhist *Verse of Repentance*: "All the evil karma
wrought by me from long ago stems from a greed, anger, and folly
without beginning. It is all born of my body, mouth, and mind. I now
repent of it." It is in this basic sense that the idea of karma comes to have
a bearing on the contemporary problem as it was explained above.

Two points have been emphasized in connection with the time
without beginning or end implied in the expression "from time past
without beginning." First, time without beginning and end bestows on
existence at one and the same time the character of a burden or debt,
and the character of a creativity or freedom, while in the background a
kind of infinite drive is seen to be at work. Secondly, time without
beginning or end can come about only if it contains at its ground the
presence of an infinite openness.

In the compulsion to be engaged incessantly in doing something, I
further noted, our being and time bears for us the marks of an infinite
burden. The sense of a "project," a throwing-forward (*entwerfen*), essential to human Dasein means that our own existence is a burden unto

itself. That time is infinitely open in both directions, without beginning or end, makes time itself, as well as our existence in time, an infinite weight saddling our existence. Or, seen from within, it means that we are impelled to constant new becoming and incessant change within a time in which we come to be and pass away from one fleeting instant to the next. An infinite drive urges us on without a moment's rest. At the same time, however, this infinite drive signifies the unrestricted and boundless nature of the possibility we contain within ourselves. Thus, working at perpetually doing something—the karmic activity of "body, mouth, and mind"—irrespective of its inner necessity already appears as our freely working to create something new.

Time that is in such a sense without beginning or end, together with our existence in that time, cannot be thought of apart from the totality of relationships that make up the world. As mentioned earlier, our existence comes about from within an infinite nexus, reaching back into the past from our parents to their parents, back before the appearance of the human race, the constitution of the solar system, and so on *ad infinitum*, even as it extends equally without limit into the future. This temporal nexus, bound up with an infinitely large nexus of spatial relationships, makes up our world. Accordingly, all we are engaged in doing in time without beginning or end, that being-at-doing (samskrta) of each moment seen as the becoming of time itself, comes down in the last analysis to the intersection of two movements: *vertically*, it grows out of the whole nexus of relationships present "since time past without beginning" at the background of our own being in the world and time; and *horizontally*, it occurs in connection with all things existing simultaneously with us. The existence in which we have our being at constantly doing something comes about from a dynamic, limitless *world-nexus*. Time without beginning or end and being in such a time, or what we have called infinite drive, have to be seen from such a perspective. This is what is meant by saying that being-in-the-world has to be seen "under the Form of infinity." The same perspective appears in the *Verse of Repentance* as the confession that all evil karma issues from body, mouth, and mind (deed, word, and thought), and that, moreover, this karma springs from "a greed, anger, and folly without beginning." But whatever can all of this mean?

Time without beginning or end, together with our being in that time, presents itself to us, then, with the character of an inexhaustible task that has been imposed on us, which means that we can maintain our existence in time only under the form of constantly doing something. *Being* in time consists essentially in being obliged ceaselessly to be *doing* something. It is like the feudal serf compelled to toil year in and year out to meet his quota, or like the inmate in a penitentiary serving at hard labor to pay off his debt to society and expiate his guilt. To assure our own existence, we have to work off the burden imposed on it. The only difference between us and the serf or convict is that the debt weighing on our existence cannot be attributed to someone other or something else. It is from the very beginning part of the essence of an existence that "is" in the world of time.

Of course, when we seek the origin of that mode of being in time, an answer might be conceived of in terms of a punishment meted out for sin by an other. This is the case, for instance, with the "original sin" of Adam, which is seen as the origin of being in time, that is, being as something that is born and dies, something that must "work by the sweat of its brow." This is one of the mythical representations of fate according to which human existence has been understood under the Form of infinity. The idea of the debt or guilt of existence appears often in ancient myth. When it comes to the essence of human existence, one could say that man the mythmaker saw things that man the intellectual has failed to see.

Now to see this "debt" as an essential part of being-in-time, means that it entails an inexhaustibility. While there are limits to obligations imposed by social or legal regulation, the debt essential to existence is as elemental as existence itself. It is infinite because in doing something, that is, in the very act whereby we exhaust our debt, we sow the seeds of a new debt. The very work through which we make things lighter for ourselves and unburden ourselves, in the very work of freeing ourselves of the "existence" that weighs heavy upon us, in a word, through our own "free" work, it is simply our own existence that we are preserving in the process. (As we shall see later, however, this is a freedom that comes forth from the infinite openness of nihility at the ground of the present.) The interminable payment of this debt creates a new debt through the samskṛta of the payment, and in this process we see the functioning of the basic pattern of karma. This samskṛta mode of being condemned to be continually engaged in doing something, contains in its essence this sense of the infinite or the inexhaustible. The home-ground that gives birth to the debt is the home-ground of the karmic activity that works to dissolve it. Each of the deeds that remove the debt invariably return to the home-ground of the debt, in each case reinstating the debt. And this return to the home-ground is, at the same time,

the springboard for new karmic activity to work off the new debt. So it
is that our Dasein, even as it endlessly steps outside of itself, by that
very act never departs its own home-ground but keeps itself shut up
perpetually within itself. The self is at all times, unendingly, itself,
permanently tethered to itself. This self-contradictory dynamic of
"tying oneself up with one's own rope," so to speak, is the essence of our
existence.

The "Consciousness Only" school (*Vijñapitamātratā*) spoke in this
connection of a "store-consciousness" (*ālaya-vijñāna*), on the basis of
which it conceived of a dynamic nexus wherein "seeds" give birth to
"manifest action" in deeds, words, and thoughts, which in turn "per-
fume" the seeds with a lingering aroma (*vāsana*). While the thought
developed around this conception may be rich in insight, we cannot
pursue it further here.

The essence of our being within time has thus come to be conceived
in a dynamic, spontaneously self-developing "causal" framework, infinitely open in both directions of time. The conception of time as
without beginning or end is essentially inseparable from such a prehension of being-in-time.

As a being-in-the-world, the essence of our Dasein lies within the
infinite world-nexus described above. The indebtedness of our existence and the karmic character of our activities come about only under
the conditions of that world-nexus. This conditioning is an essential
moment of our samskrta mode of existence. The world-nexus is woven
deep into the stuff of the spontaneous self-development of our being-in-
time (or our being *as* time). It is part and parcel of the being of restless,
incessant becoming which seems to be spurred on from within by an
infinite drive. When our *being* comes about as an incessant *becoming*
brought about by its being destined to a constant *doing*, this doing can
only come about as a doing *something* and this, in turn, cannot come to be
without this world-nexus.

In general the two aspects of determining the self and being determined by an other are inseparable in existence within time. In other
words, existence invariably comes about as a co-determination. Basically, for an existence to be determined by an other means that it
determines itself as a being that is so determined. Each case of determination at the hands of an other is a mode of being of the self, and as
such a self proceeds in turn to determine the other. It can receive
determination by the other only as a self-determination. To take an
expression from the ancients, it is a "causal kinship" (*hetu-pratyaya*) set

up in the world-nexus woven of inner and outer causes, such that all beings in the world come to be by virtue of this causal kinship.

If we grant that the fact that I "am" in time, that I am myself, comes about as a constant becoming through a constant doing something (becoming I myself who am determined from one moment to the next), in this existence of mine the whole world-nexus, linked together in mutual reliance and cooperation through causal kinship, is at all times coming to light. While determining my Dasein to be the Dasein it is, this infinite nexus is bound to it in causal kinship. This makes it necessary to consider the whole of mankind, the whole of living beings, the whole world, as "destined" to form a single whole with my existence and my work. At the home-ground of my Dasein, directly beneath my work, this whole labors to make this Dasein what it is, that is, to determine it. My own labors all become in each case one with the ebb and flow of the whole nexus since time past without beginning. They become manifest, as it were, as a focal point of that total ebb and flow. They can all be seen as having appeared from out of that unlimited whole that lies behind them. When being as a being-in-the-world becomes itself through its being condemned to do something, it does so at all times in this fashion.

In this regard, however, we ought not neglect to make mention of the second element alluded to at the opening of this section: the infinite openness that constitutes the field of freedom in doing things, the *nothingness* that is at one with being within incessant becoming in time. I shall defer discussion of that question for the moment, however.

Even though being-in-the-world be viewed in this way within an unlimited world-nexus in terms of its causal kinship with the whole "all in all" world-nexus, this is not to say that it is being viewed from a standpoint of theoretical speculation or metaphysical contemplation. Here, the being and becoming of being-in-the-world cannot be separated from doing; they cannot be thought of apart from the karma of body, mouth, and mind. But the main point is that the works of deed, word, and thought come to awareness on the field of time without beginning or end, and within the unlimited world-nexus, as something engaged without end in weaving the web of causality that makes up the world.

We have already seen how the karmic activity of doing, each act of dissolving the debt that is our very being, invariably returns to the home-ground of this debt, thereby resulting in its reinstatement. At this home-ground, every activity gauged to settle one's obligations determines one in turn to new obligations. *Doing* determines *being* anew: *does* being; it *becomes* being and thereby re-creates being in time. In other words, doing renews and reestablishes being in time. But then the karmic activity that will re-return that being, already reinstated once as a debt, back to its home-ground—namely, the doing that dissolves the debt—has already set out again from that home-ground. Thus, this Dasein of ours that is constantly doing something is an incessant becoming *in* time and *as* time. Dasein is constantly taking off from its home-ground and at the same time constantly going back there. Even in ceaselessly ridding itself of itself, it is ceaselessly ending up back at its home-ground.

And so it is that we have our being in constantly doing something, relating to what is other than ourselves, and thus transitorily becoming within time. Or rather, let us say that we *are* because we produce time ourselves as the field of our transitory becoming. To that extent, our being can never be rid of itself. A debt that we must constantly pay off and an infinite burden that we must constantly lighten, our being is yet endlessly reborn out of our own home-ground. In this way, an infinite drive rises to self-consciousness at the ground of our own being and doing, at the home-ground of our Dasein.

At the home-ground of Dasein, where we find the wellspring of that infinite drive, we become aware of an infinite self-enclosure, or what Toynbee calls "self-centeredness." The ancients took this elemental self-enclosure, this self-centeredness that is the wellspring of endless karmic activity, as the darkness of ignorance (avidyā) or "fundamental darkness." In it the karma of all our behavior, speech, and thought is seen under the Form of infinity, as something existing on the field of a time infinitely opened in both directions and infinitely formative of the causal nexus. Being obligated to the infinite drive from the home-ground of the self itself to be constantly engaged in doing something and consequently being obligated also to keep entering into relation with others and co-determining the self with others endlessly, but yet remaining forever incapable of taking leave of the self that presses onerously down upon us—this, it seems to me, is by and large the state of affairs that has arisen to awareness through the concept of karma. It might be termed a self-awareness of the essence of existence in time, conceived as a dynamic nexus of being, doing, and becoming.

The notion of karma is usually linked to the notions of transmigration and metempsychosis. And along with this goes talk of such things as a "former world" or "former lives" before one was born, and an "afterworld" or "afterlife" that begins at death. In addition, various theories have been proposed from a number of different angles (even the biological) regarding the causality of karma as it extends over the "three world-times" (the third being the present). The explanation for this is not hard to come by. Our being-in-time is essentially tangled up with an infinity in such a way that we, as inmates of the world-nexus, are endlessly driven to be doing something and to be entering into relation with others. What is more, we come to the awareness that, even within this infinite causal kinship, we can never take leave of the basic home-ground of the self itself. It follows as a matter of course, then, that this awareness of existence, by partaking of that infinity, will naturally go beyond the short-term framework of the life of this world to embrace the unlimited openness of the before and the after as well.

Speaking in an earlier chapter of the concept of transmigration, we remarked that the essential meaning of a mythical representation can only be grasped when we interpret it so as to bring the content of that representation back to the home-ground of our existence in the present. In fact, mythical representations in general are born of the wish to ask after the home-ground of human Dasein; they contain a kind of intuition of the essence (*Wesensschau*) of being-in-the-world. In interpreting the existential meaning of transmigration, we saw further that the finitude of man is existentially grasped as an infinite finitude; that it is grasped in the horizon of a world that also embraces species other than man; and that it is grasped at the most basic level of sheer being-in-the-world, stripped of all specific differences whatsoever.

It is the same with the idea of karma in the "three world-times." The essential significance of that idea lies, first, in the fact that our work as human beings is grasped in the home-ground of the present—and from the point where it has dropped off even the *eidos* of the human—as an infinite finitude. It means, further, that our being is grasped as something that, even in its being present as human, extends its roots limitlessly throughout the world-nexus. And finally, it consists of the fact that our being-doing-becoming in time is grasped at one with the world-nexus and in the mode of a causal kinship, the reciprocal relationship of all inner and outer causes. This mode of grasping Dasein at the home-ground of the present, as noted earlier, means taking Dasein back deep within its own home-ground. It means that Dasein returns to the home-ground of Dasein itself.

When the causality of karma is conceived as extending over "three world-times," when within the spectrum of former, present, and after lives a transmigration of human being is so conceived as to suggest that we might possibly have come from and be going to another mode of sentient being, this means that the home-ground of present karmic activity has been fathomed, directly beneath the present, down to just such a depth and range of perspective. And when that causality is viewed in the perspective of the openness of time without beginning or end, wherein one dies and is reborn interminably on the "wheel of transmigration," this means that the home-ground of present karmic activity is sought for and recovered directly beneath the present in an orientation to an infinite openness beyond all time, in an orientation to the openness of nihility. It means, that is to say, an elemental deepening of self-awareness of existence in the present.

V

This brings us to the second point mentioned above in connection with time without beginning or end: that this time comes about in cooperation with the appearance, from the home-ground of the present, of an infinite openness beyond all time.

Openness appears here as a nihility beyond existence and all its forms. We might entertain the mythical idea of an unending transmigration along with that of the "kalpas" and "great kalpas," or Nietzsche's notion of Eternal Recurrence, or the idea of countless worlds succeeding one another in time or coexisting in space, or whatever: all these worlds come about within the openness of the field of nihility. This field lies forever open directly underfoot of our Dasein. In fact, without this *nothingness*, what we have been speaking of as *being*-in-time would not be possible. That this being consists in being engaged ceaselessly in doing something means that the doing, which is impelled from within by an infinite drive, is at the same time a totally free doing. It is karmic activity creating hitherto nonexistent being. It is our existence receiving a completely new determination.

In the foregoing, these determinations have been considered as coming about in the manner of a causal kinship, that is, at one with the world-nexus where our being sends out its roots limitlessly. But the fact that these determinations always constitute a new mode of being for the self itself, and must accordingly be *self*-determinations, means that the freedom of karmic activity has a share in that process of determination. When our being within time consists of a constant doing, this doing must needs take hold in the infinite openness of nihility which transcends being in general and all the ties of causal kinship in the world-nexus that form its determinations.

Of course, this does not mean that there is some "thing" called nihility. In order for being constantly to come about anew in time, for existence constantly to come about in the form of a new becoming, it is necessary that there be the freedom to render such new determination possible. In other words, in order that being not freeze into permanent immobility, there must be an impermanence, a transiency unhindered by being. And this is possible only if doing, being-at-doing, is grounded in nihility. Only then can being-in-time, as an essentially unending and constant new becoming, and time without beginning or end—both of which share in the character of infinite finitude—be constituted at one and the same time. Samskrta is in essence bound up with nihility.

From that viewpoint, the world of karma is a world where each individual is determined by its ties and causal kinship within an endless world nexus, and yet each instance of individual existence and behavior, as well as each moment of their time, arises as something totally new, possessed of freedom and creativity.

Although the ebb and flow of the total nexus "since time past without beginning" is conceived as an infinite chain of causal necessity, its having no beginning implies, conversely, a *before* previous to any and all conceivable pasts. For such time to have no end means that it has an *after* that is future even to the most remote of possible futures. Any such before and after (beyond any definite before and after) lies in the present of every man and makes the present into free and creative activity.

The infinite openness of time in both directions is nothing other than an introjection into time of the transtemporal openness or ecstatic transcendence lying directly beneath the present, an introjection achieved on each occasion of karmic activity. When doing constitutes being-in-time, it constitutes that being *qua* becoming in each case as a being in time without beginning or end. And the karmic deeds that make manifest this restless, incessant becoming always return thereby at the same time to the home-ground of karma, to the home-ground of the present. In other words, doing opens itself up on each occasion to the openness of nihility and thus preserves the dimension of ecstatic transcendence.

This means that the self is at all times itself. Even as in my karma I constantly constitute my existence as a becoming *qua* being, in the home-ground of that karma I am ever in my own home-ground: I am always myself. This is why restless, incessant becoming within time is at all times *my* existence. Karma is at all times *my* karma. And this means that it is a free karma, that it implies an ecstatic transcendence to nihility.

Of course, although we call it freedom or creativity, it is not at this point true freedom or creativity. Freedom here is one with an inner necessity compelling us constantly to be doing something. It is in unison with that infinite drive and that infinite drive in turn is in unison with freedom. To be within the limitless world-nexus ceaselessly relating to something or other, and to be conditioned and determined in these relations by the world-nexus, is, seen from the other side, a self-determination. While the present karma is here the free work of the self, it appears at the same time to be possessed of the character of fate. Fate arises to awareness in unison with that freedom. Here the present karma reaches awareness under its form of infinity as infinite drive, in its "willful" essence.

The self's relation with something, seen as a self-determination, is the self's exercise of free will. Of its own accord, the self accepts a thing as good or rejects it as bad. But insofar as it is determined through causal kinship within the total nexus, this free will is a fate, a causal necessity, without thereby ceasing to be free will. To accept or reject something implies a simultaneous "attachment" to it. The karma that relates to something by lusting after it is at once voluntary and compulsory. The being of the self that comes about in that karma is at once a freedom and a burden. Here spontaneity becomes a burden and a debt. Moreover, the spontaneous, voluntary activity that absolves the debt enjoys itself in the process and so renews the original "lust." Within karma, joy and heaviness of heart (*Schwermut*) are intertwined as one. As noted earlier, existence in time is essentially ambiguous.

In the creativity we speak of here, the creation of something new means being constantly exposed to nihility. The being of the self in the world—the self itself along with the *koto* ("matters") that arise out of relations with things—implies essential impermanence, in which the self comes to be at one fleeting instant and passes away at the next. That is, our present karma consists in returning to the openness of present nihility. Our being-in-the-world, which comes to be out of being engaged constantly in doing something, is ever held in suspense over nihility and enveloped in constant nullification with nothing to rely on and nowhere to rest assured. Our existence is in constant danger of collapse.

Seen under the Form of infinity, our present karmic activity is constantly shadowed by spontaneous freedom, lust, the joy of living, and deep beneath everything the roots of attachment (infinite drive) and an equally elemental sense of the profound vacuity, the profound nihility and impermanence of things. It is the same ambiguity seen from a different angle.

What the Japanese call *mono no aware* ("the pathos of things") indicates the point where lust and joy are one with a sadness over the feeling of impermanence. In other words, the phrase signifies that where the being of man, as something bound to things in time, rises to awareness "perfumed" with the feeling of world and time and under the Form of infinity, there also the essential impermanence of all things, or sheer being-in-the-world, is *aesthetically* felt to the quick—in the Kierkegaardian sense of "aesthetic existence." It means that all the things of the world and the self itself are realized together aesthetically, in the original countenance of their manifestation.

Thus, when the workings of freedom and the fateful nature of determination become manifest in inseparable oneness within our present karma, the ultimate ground of self-being in time—what we called above the infinite self-centeredness or infinite self-enclosure—rises to self-awareness in unison with a transtemporal, eternal nihility as something located in nihility. Infinite self-centeredness is the fundamental avidyā. It is the fountainhead of the infinite drive lurking within the essence of being *qua* becoming and makes it a being *qua* becoming in unlimited time, or rather *as* that time. The infinite openness of time in both directions is an introjection into time of the openness of the *eternal* nihility opening up at the home-ground of the present. It is an introjection that occurs each time that a karmic deed—and every deed of the self is karmic—is performed. This is, by and large, the reason why the self-centeredness that is the elemental source of being within time is only constituted in unison with nihility, as something always located on *eternal* nihility.

All of this indicates how deeply rooted self-centeredness is. So deeply underground do the roots of the self extend that no karmic activity can ever reach them. The karma of the self at all times returns to its own home-ground, namely, to the self itself, but it cannot get back to the home-ground of the self as such. Karma can do no more than go back to its own home-ground in the self and there reinstate its debt-laden existence. In karma, the self is constantly oriented inward to the home-ground of the self; and yet the only thing it achieves by this is the constant reconstitution of being *qua* becoming in a time without beginning or end. To transit endlessly through time in search of the home-ground of the self is the true form of our karma, that is, of our being in time, our life.

The karma of "time past without beginning" is the true form of our life. It implies a sense of essential "despair." Karma is what Kierkegaard calls the "sickness unto death." Its despair rises to awareness from directly underfoot of the work of our present deed, word, and thought, from the fountainhead of time without beginning or end, and of being within that time, in short from our self-centeredness. We can see an awareness of that despair also underlying the confession of the Buddhist *Verse of Repentance*, which suggests that every sort of karma stemming from the body, mouth, and mind of the self is grounded in a greed, anger, and folly without beginning.

Thus, although the elemental source of being that has thus become one with nothingness, of self-centeredness so constituted at one with nihility, lies directly under human existence, it is there that the form of human existence is cast away. Since nihility is absolutely non-form, that is, since it represents the point at which all form returns to nothingness, being—at that elemental source where it is in unison with nothingness—is a being that has rid itself of all form. In the sense given above, it is a sheer being-in-the-world as such.

In its ultimate home-ground, the self-being of man is not human. Human Dasein may be said to emerge as the "con-formation" of the form of the human and the "trans-form" of being into a single whole. At the ground of our being human lies a level of *pure* being beyond any determination to the human. And being human, precisely in implying such a level, is also *concrete* being-in-the-world. That our existence is in *interrelation* through causal kinship with all other things in an unending world-nexus is due to the fact that, at the ground of the work we are continually engaged in as men, we contain a horizon of *intercommunication* with the being of all things of the world. Within this horizon we are a sheer being-in-the-world as such, rid of all particular determinations.

In other words, the being of all things is brought to the home-ground of our self-centeredness and there gathered into one. Even as existence in karma is constantly going outside of itself to be at the home-ground of the other and attach itself to the other within the web of its causal kinship to all things, at the same time in its essence and on the horizon of its sheer being-in-the-world, existence in karma is gathering the being of all other things to its self. This means that the self-centeredness of this being is also transforming the self into the center of the world. It was in this sense that we called the mode of being in the field of nihility an absolute self-enclosure or abyssal solitariness. This solitariness is most deeply abyssal for existence within the world (which has been the main focus of our discussion here) because its self-enclosure occurs on the horizon of the deepest intercommunication with every other thing.

Karma here comes to bear the marks of guilt and sin. In a certain sense, it takes on the character of original sin, namely, sin that is as equally elemental as the free work and existence of man. Karma is freedom determined by causal necessity within the whole infinite nexus, a freedom of spontaneity in "attachment" and, therefore, a freedom totally *bound* by fate. At the same time, having reduced the whole causal nexus to its own center, it is a freedom altogether *unbound*. In karma these two aspects of freedom and causal necessity become one. Consequently, as a freedom that derives entirely from the determining force of causal necessity, as a freedom chased out and driven away from necessity, karma binds itself in attachment to the other, while at the same time it remains an altogether unbound freedom, gathering every other into the center of the self. This freedom is in the mode of an original sin.

But self-being in its true sense, the self-centeredness of true self-being, is another thing altogether. True self-centeredness is a selfless self-centeredness: the self-centeredness of "self that is not self." It consists of what we referred to in an earlier chapter as "circumin-sessional interpenetration" on the field of śūnyatā. The gathering together of the being of all things at the home-ground of the being of the self can only come about in unison with the subordination of the being of the self to the being of all things at their home-ground. But in the self-centeredness found at the standpoint of karma, which in turn rests on nihility, the calling of the being of all things to assembly, at the home-ground of the self, is not possible except by way of bringing about a self-enclosure.

In that same context, the term "nature" was assigned to the force that acts to gather all things together and connect them to one another. In karma, nature in this sense can be conceived of as the elemental force by which the self connects all things while gathering them together into the self in the manner of a self-enclosure; and the force by which the self itself then enters into incessant becoming without beginning or end while so engaged in connecting all other things to one another. It may be thought of as the elemental force at work in a self-centeredness of a self become center of the world. At its elemental source, the karma of man's deeds of body, mouth, and mind, originates through the force of this same nature from the horizon of what I have called sheer being-in-the-world.

VI

What we have been saying about the standpoint of karma is a matter of the fundamental form of human life in the ordinary world of history. All of our work belongs to this world of history. Then, too, as has been pointed out, human life and the standpoint of karma in the modern secularized world essentially draw on one another. The man-centered mode of being that shows up in modern secularized man contains in its essence something I have called infinite drive or "self-will." Ever since the modern era, the essential nature of man has demanded to be seen under the form of infinity. And the idea of karma offers what may be interpreted as a clarification of man's secular mode of being as viewed from just such a perspective.

The standpoint of karma, however, has to be abandoned to reach the standpoint of emptiness, a disengagement that signals a conversion from the standpoint of nihility to the standpoint of śūnyatā. It is a conversion from the field of samsāra to the field of nirvāna, and thence to the field of samsāra-*sive*-nirvāna. In the course of our observations in this regard on Dōgen's "body-and-mind dropping off, dropped off body-and-mind," it was pointed out how the work of our everyday lives—the karma of deed, word, and thought—can become an occasion for absolute truth (truth as Ἀλήθεια) to appear.

From the standpoint of śūnyatā, everything that has been said regarding the standpoint of karma can be converted by way of absolute negation and given a new life. In any case, the Buddhist, especially the Mahāyāna, standpoint of śūnyatā possesses its own unique trait that locates it, unaffiliated, somewhere between religions centered on a cyclical world view wherein, according to Toynbee, history disappears (he includes Buddhism in this group), and the Judaeo-Christian religious tradition marked by a developed historical sense but forever unable in the end to rid itself of its self-centeredness.   ·

As such expressions as "non-ego" and "body-and-mind dropping off" would indicate, the standpoint of śūnyatā is the standpoint of radical deliverance from self-centeredness. It does not even leave room for the self-centeredness of religious consciousness, the so-called higher level of self-centeredness that we find, for instance, in the idea of being chosen or predestined by God for salvation. In more elemental terms, essentially implied in the standpoint of śūnyatā is an absolute negativity toward the will that lies at the ground of every type of self-centeredness. It implies an orientation directly opposed to that of will. As noted before, we can find the concept of will at the ground of all the most important Western standpoints regarding time and history. This is obviously the case with the Will of God in Christianity and the Will to Power in Nietzsche's atheism, but a human self-will, which can be called a kind of daemonic infinite drive, lies hidden even behind the man-centered reason of modern secularism. In the East, as we have noted, this infinite drive arose to awareness already very early on in the idea of karma.

Now the standpoint of śūnyatā is constituted only at a bottomless point beyond these standpoints of will, and in fact beyond all standpoints of any kind related to will, through absolute negation. It is in such a bottomlessness that the standpoint of śūnyatā is the standpoint of the Existenz of non-ego.

In the Existenz of non-ego, non-ego does not mean simply that self is not ego. It has also to mean at the same time that non-ego is the self. It must reach self-awareness as something come from the self's absolute negation of itself. It is not the case that the self is merely not self (that it is non-ego). It must be the case rather that the self is the self because it is not the self. Were it simply a matter of the self not being the self, the way would still be open to follow Nietzsche in taking the Will to Power as the true self, or the "selfness" of the self. It would be equally possible to take the Eastern notion of karma, or something like Schopenhauer's Will to Life, as the selfness of the self. Or again, the real self might be sought in the union with some absolute being like God, or the One of Western mysticism, or in the oneness of Brahman and self (*tat tvam asi*: That art thou) of Eastern mysticism. Yet in all of these, the standpoint of the true non-ego is still incapable of appearing in complete fashion. Only by going a step further does the standpoint of true non-ego appear in the reversal, "self is not self (self is non-ego), therefore it is self." This reversal is precisely that existential self-awareness wherein the self is *realized* (manifested-*sive*-apprehended) as an emergence into its nature from non-ego. It is Existenz as "body-and-mind dropping off, dropped off body-and-mind."

In this Existenz of non-ego, work from one moment to the next originates, as we have seen, from the beginning of time. It is a revelation of the beginning of time itself and, in that sense, is the emergence of that beginning into its nature. It is, so to speak, a moment of eternity appearing in time. Here, too, our life comes to be as a restless engagement in doing something. Our being preserves the form of ceaseless becoming in ceaseless doing. This being, as a being-at-doing (samskrta), is a becoming that comes to be and passes away at each moment.

But here our work is no longer an endless payment and reinstatement of a debt. Our existence does not become an endless burden to us. Our work, our karma of deed, word, and thought does not arise from the darkness of ignorance (the root of self-centeredness), which is the home-ground of the infinite drive; nor does it return to that home-ground. Each one of our deeds is no longer something that produces being in a time without beginning or end. No longer is it karma on the field of nihility, a karma that produces being at the same time that it nullifies it.

As an Existenz of non-ego, being, doing, and becoming in time all emerge into their nature on the field of emptiness which is their absolute negation. And on this field constant doing is constant non-doing. Constant coming to be and passing away is constant *non*-coming to be and *non*-passing away. To be constantly engaged in doing something is, as such, not to be doing a single thing. Being in a restless, incessant becoming, a turning on the wheel of transmigration, means not departing the homeland of unbirth. To return to a phrase of Dōgen's quoted in the former chapter, we could say that everyday life of body-and-mind with eyes horizontal and nose vertical is, as such, returning home with empty hands, whiling away one's time and taking things as they come.

On the field of emptiness, then, all our work takes on the character of play. When our doing-being-becoming, when our existence, our behavior, and our life each emerges into its respective nature from its outermost extreme, that is, when they emerge from the point where non-ego is self into their own suchness, they have already cast off the character of having any why or wherefore. They are without aim or reason outside of themselves and become truly autotelic and without cause or reason, a veritable *Leben ohne Warum*. At bottom, at the point of their original, elemental source, our existence, behavior, and life are not a means for anything else. Instead, each and every thing exists for their sake, and each gets its meaning from its relationship to them, while they themselves are their own *telos*. To the extent that they become manifest at that point of their elemental source, existence, behavior, and life assume the character of play.

The point of elemental source, however, is the point at which non-ego is self, which means that in fact even autotelism is still impure, not quite true. The autotelic form is not to be clung to; it is not to become a standpoint of autotelic consciousness. At the point that our existence, behavior, and life are authentically autotelic, their autotelism too is to be passed beyond. What is called for is samādhi. This point of elemental source is the "King of Samādhis Samādhi" spoken of at length in the former chapter. It is the point at which non-ego is self. Although samādhi contains no sense of serving as its own *telos*, precisely for that reason it *is* truly its own telos—which is why it is called non-mind.

The "play" we alluded to must be something with this sort of meaning. (Later on we shall have occasion to comment on the ethical significance of autotelism.) This play is not even autotelic, and that sets it apart in a fundamental sense from what we are used to calling play. In its ordinary sense, play comprises sports and other recreations that represent a break from everything in everyday life that is considered "labor." Play refers essentially to various temporary diversions or modes of relaxation. In contrast to labor, which invariably labors for some end or other, play is done for its own sake; it is autotelic, and thus serves as a release from toil.

In the sense in which we are using the word here, however, the *work* that we perform, without any discrimination between "labor" and "play," appears in the character of playfulness. Both labor that toils for the sake of something else and play that is divertissement for its own sake, each in its own way and such as it is, are play as activities we engage in.

Here *working* and *playing* turn back to the *doing* that takes place on the near side, prior to their differentiation; but at the same time, they come to appear as events emerged into their nature from the far side, beyond those differentiations. Both working and playing become manifest fundamentally and at bottom as sheer, elemental doing. This is what Buddhism calls "playful samādhi."

On the standpoint of śūnyatā, to which man "returns empty-handed," all doing presents that character of playfulness from one moment to the next within the passing of time without beginning or end. In other words, all being-at-doing (samskrta) as the dynamic nexus of being-doing-becoming takes the shape of a non-doing, of "taking things as they come."

To repeat earlier remarks, our being possesses for us the character of an obligation imposed on us, which our doing is constantly dissolving and working off. We are, so to speak, paying our debt off in meager installments. But then, too, our ceaseless doing directly generates a new debt in its very act of redeeming us from the old debt. The termination of debt creates debt. In this way, as a deed implying at once the passing away and coming to be of our debt, our doing comes to carry the sense of karma. Here freedom from being is at once a constitution of being that is a being in the process of *nullification*. Moreover, the escape from the nothingness of that nullification is at the same time a revelation of a nothingness that is a nothingness in the process of *beification* as debt. By virtue of this, our Dasein betrays the form of *incessant becoming*.

Now what was said about all doing displaying a character of playing on the standpoint of śūnyatā, and all samskrta directly assuming the shape of a non-doing, says nothing more than that the doing that brings the debt to life is, in that very act, *not* giving it life. Doing thus comes to be rid of the indebtedness that is its essence, resulting in a true dissolution of the debt and settlement of all outstanding accounts. Nevertheless, so long as it is a doing, the point is never reached where there is no longer anything to be borne. Only now, what is lifted up on one's shoulders to be borne is done so from a point where the debt has been absolutely absolved. So it is not that there is no burden, but that the burden is taken up again from the standpoint at which it had all been laid down. Shouldering the burden takes on the sense of play, and the standpoint appears from which we go forward bearing the burden spontaneously and of our own free will. The labor imposed, without ceasing to be an imposition, is transformed into play by arising spontaneously in an elemental way.

This elemental spontaneity is but the standpoint of samādhi and its standpoint of non-mind, or of non-doing, both of which were mentioned above. Elemental spontaneity, true spontaneity, comes into being on a field where non-ego is self, where self emerges into its nature from non-self. Freedom and spontaneity of will as usually conceived still belong to the standpoint of karma and its labors. They are unable to cast off the self-enclosure, or avidyā, of self-centeredness and to escape attachment. They do not offer a standpoint where labor is truly transformed into play.

Only when the shouldering of the burden becomes play is the burden truly (spontaneously) born. Debt is truly instated and truly apparent only when debt has first been perfectly absolved, that is to say, when doing becomes something that has truly (spontaneously) taken debt upon itself. The debt then comes to signify responsibility truly taken on by the self. The debt as one's apportioned *lot* then becomes one's own *task* in the sense of a self-imposed duty or vocation. (As we shall explain later, a debt that becomes a matter of self-responsibility from the point where the debt has once been completely canceled is a debt to one's neighbor, to every "other," a debt, as it were, that is not a debt. And in spite of being a "debt without debt," it is still a debt the self assumes as its own responsibility.)

To sum up, in the conversion from the standpoint of karma to the standpoint of śūnyatā, from the standpoint of the self-centered will to the standpoint of non-ego samādhi, all that we do is at once a true payment and a true shouldering of debt. As a result, our doing truly becomes manifest as doing. In the elemental spontaneity appearing through that conversion, doing becomes a true doing, ecstatic of itself. This doing implies a responsibility to every neighbor and every other; and, as we shall mention further ahead, it is something that has taken upon itself an infinite task. It is a doing on the standpoint of non-ego, of the "non-duality of self and other."

At the point that our work becomes play, it is at the same time an elemental *earnestness*. In reality, there is no more unrestricted, take-things-as-they-come sort of play than the emergence of self into its nature from non-ego; and, at the same time, there is nothing more serious and earnest. In the state of "dharmic naturalness"—of natural and spontaneous accord with the dharma—this is how it is with all things. That is why from time immemorial the image of the child has so often been invoked to portray such an elemental mode of being. For the child is never more earnest than when engaged in mindless play.

VII

An attempt has been made in the preceding to explain that our existence, our behavior, and our becoming all come about within a world-nexus that is unlimited not only with regard to time but also with regard to space. Already on the standpoint of karma as well, the Dasein of the dynamic nexus of being-doing-becoming comes about within time without beginning or end, while opening up the infinite openness of nihility directly beneath the present. But inasmuch as this dynamic nexus appears only as a perpetual relating to something, our Dasein, in being determined by that world-nexus, becomes one with it in "fate."

Dasein is always and at each occasion becoming manifest as one particular roll of the waves that gathers up into itself the whole ebb and flow of the world-nexus since time without beginning or end. Our doing in that context is free with the freedom of attachment determined by causal necessity within the total nexus and, at the same time, is also free with the arbitrary freedom that contracts the total nexus into the one center of the self.

That is why our doing is karma standing on nihility. In that doing, nihility, even as it becomes manifest from the ground where self and the world are one, nullifies the being of the self, sets the self adrift in transitory becoming, and transforms the self and all other things into a samskrta existence.

It was noted earlier in this chapter that *being-determined* in the world-nexus and *self-determination* are one. But on the standpoint of karma this self-determination makes the infinite drive that originates from the self-centered elemental source of avidyā its essence and becomes manifest in taking the form of will as attachment and control. And being-determined means being conditioned through causal necessity in that total, unlimited nexus.

Further, it was noted that the free exercise of will, consisting of attachment and control in its relations with any given thing, is in its very freedom a configuration determined by "fate"—which is after all what karma is. In this karmic mode of being, then, nihility becomes manifest from the ground where self and world are one. And the reason for this, as we went on to explain, is that avidyā, as an infinite self-enclosure elemental to karma, rises to awareness only in unison with the nihility in which it stands. In karma we can only have our being through being constantly engaged in doing something. That is, in order to *be*, we are obliged to *be relating* to something. This means that our being is a debt unto itself, and that our doing as a settlement of that debt is equivalent to the direct instatement of a new debt. This means, on the one hand, that our being is passing away and coming to be at every fleeting instant and that therein the nihility that is constantly nullifying our being is revealed. On the other hand, at the same point that the continuous cancellation of debt is a continuous reinstatement, there appears something that urges us on endlessly from within. In that infinite drive, our Dasein is never able to divest itself of its own home-ground, and our self within that dynamic nexus of being-doing-becoming is always itself—in incessant becoming.

Avidyā comes to awareness as the home-ground of the self, where the self is caught in incessant becoming and unable to take its leave, that is, as the outermost extreme of self-centeredness. As a result, in avidyā, the persistence of the self at being itself and emerging into the nature of a self-centered being, always comes about as a simultaneous whole with the disclosure of nihility in avidyā in its very process of nullifying the being of the self. The inability of the self to detach itself from the home-ground of its own transitory becoming—or, conversely, the self's being ever itself, while its being is nonetheless in constant change—also has its base here. That is what karma means. Dasein in the dynamic nexus of being-doing-becoming is but the being of the self being constituted directly beneath the present as an emergence from nihility into the nature of avidyā.

Now even on the standpoint of śūnyatā, which represents a conversion from that standpoint of karma, one thing remains unchanged: doing still comes about within the world-nexus through being related with other things. Only here this relation ceases to be dependent on attachment and arbitrary will. It comes about as a relation on the yonder side, beyond all standpoints of will with their accompanying self-centeredness. In other words, it is a relation on the field of śūnyatā. It is, moreover, a self-determination in its elemental sense of play, the emergence of the self into its nature from a point beyond the self-enclosing confines of avidyā, as well as from the point of non-ego where the resultant infinite drive has been renounced.

Here the nexus of being-doing-becoming which makes up Dasein possesses the character of non-doing. Here being is a *non*-self-nature. Neither rational nor substantial nor subjective with a will, it is what we explained earlier as a "selfness." In other words, it is a self that emerges into its nature where each and every thing is in itself and at its own ground (whereby fire is fire because it does not burn itself, the willow is green because it is not green, and time is time becauss it is not time) and is at one, in a manner of *sive/non*, with all of them.

This self that is not a self, the self emerging into ibs nature from out of non-ego, is the truly *original self*. The doing in non-doing is a doing that "does all day long without doing a single thing." In non-doing, becoming becomes the utterly free and spontaneous activity referred to earlier as "whiling away the time and taking things as they come." It is a true doing and a true becoming.

While the dynamic nexus that emerges into its nature on that field of emptiness is a yonder side with regard to all time and space and causality, still it comes into being in a oneness of *sive/non* with all other beings. As this dynamic nexus, Dasein is at one with the world-nexus in the manner of *sive/non* (in other words, as a selfness). Put in terms o- the circuminsessional interpenetration dealt with earlier, it is the point at which our Dasein is in the home-ground of all things, giving itself to all things and making each of them come into being in its respective selfness, at the same time as it gathers all things to its own home-ground, becoming their absolute center and master wherever it is.

Such is the standpoint of the self as a self on the field of emptiness emerging from non-self into its nature. In this manner, it comes about and has its being in an elemental sense as play. In Western thought, when thinkers like Heraclitus or Nietzsche conceive of the world as cyclical and see it as a kind of play, they, too, point in the same direction. As I have explained, for the world to be regarded as cyclical was for it to be envisaged intuitively as gathered into a single whole, and that intuition brought it back directly beneath the present moment to the home-ground of Dasein. So to return the world to the home-ground of Dasein is but to return Dasein to the home-ground of Dasein itself and to excavate its ground.

This is no doubt the reason that thinkers like Heraclitus and Nietzsche experienced life "leaping forth" from the bottom of the world and its myriad of beings by way of the ground of their Dasein as if it were a fire erupting from the bowels of the earth. From its very bottom, the life of the universe had, as it were, permeated their Dasein. And that, it seems to me, was connected essentially in the sense explained above with their intuition of world recurrence. May we not say that some such intuition and experience lay behind such concepts as Heraclitus' primal Fire (fire as *archē*) and Nietzsche's Will to Power? In any case, these philosophers likened the cyclical process of the recurrent world to the play of children, signifying thereby a doing of pure activity beyond the measure of any teleological gauge (as is the case, for instance, in Nietzsche's *Unschuld des Werdens*). It is the standpoint that views *homo ludens* as the highest mode of human being. It is the standpoint of the man who has returned to the home-ground of self-being by transforming the world process into spontaneous play. At the elemental source where the self emerges into its nature as self, the Dasein of the self is at play together with the world.

But then again, we recall, playfulness in its elemental sense was at the same time an earnestness in its elemental sense. Seen this way, play as a divertissement from labor is not true play, nor is the earnestness of labor distinguished from play a true earnestness. Again, only when the indebtedness essential to Dasein is removed on the standpoint of śūnyatā does the true debt appear. This debt does not mean simply that

Dasein, while being compelled constantly to be doing something, experiences itself as a burden. It is a debt that we assume of our own choosing in true spontaneity on the standpoint of elemental play, a debt that is constituted in the samādhi that emerges into its nature from out of non-ego and its accompanying non-mind. It is what we have called a debt without debt, where the burden imposed as one's lot (that is, Dasein itself) becomes a task and a vocation for Dasein itself. Dasein can be said to change from something imposed as *fate* to something accepted as *vocation*. Here earnestness means nothing other than the *sein* of Dasein.

In the conversion from the standpoint of karma to the standpoint of śūnyatā, Dasein achieves a true and elemental spontaneity, but this spontaneity is at once an earnestness in its elemental sense and a play in its elemental sense. Compared with that earnestness, the earnestness of any occupation on the standpoint of will prior to that conversion is mere time-killing divertissement, or *Zerstreuung*. However deep the concentration one invests in such occupation, to the extent that it is not performed in samādhi, the mind engaged in the doing is essentially distracted or "scattered."

Dasein itself, and all the activities that go with it, becomes a task unto itself and a vocation on the standpoint of non-ego and non-doing. This standpoint lies on the yonder side of the fundamental self-centeredness of avidyā, a field where the infinite drive called "covetousness" is cast off and karmic debt has been paid off. It is for that reason that the debt of Dasein that emerges into its nature on the field of emptiness is a debt without debt. It is thus a debt coming at the point of release from self-centeredness and the infinite drive that accompanies it. It is a debt to one's "neighbor," and to every "other." For our Dasein— involving all our being, all our behavior, all our becoming—to be embraced as a task and a mission is for that very Dasein to appear as something shouldering a debt to its neighbor and all other things.

When Dasein goes back to its own home-ground on the field of śūnyatā to become itself ecstatically (or in its suchness), its being is constituted as something that makes the debt toward all others its own essence. It does so, moreover, as something that is at bottom (originally) the sort of thing that does just that. The tasklike character that existence carries is at bottom essentially other-directed and other-centered.

In its mode of being as it is in itself at bottom, Dasein makes all things its master, follows all things, and gives to all things their being. This belongs to the essence of the existence in selfness that comes about in such a circuminsessional interpenetration. The tasklike character of the debt toward others belongs to the essence of the mode of Dasein on the field of emptiness. If Dasein on the standpoint of śūnyatā is an emergence into its nature from non-ego, all of this is quite natural and follows as a matter of course. Here "as it is" and "as it ought to be" are one and the same; the nature of the task of the *ought* is the other-directedness of the *is*. If this being exists, then, in a constant doing (which is here a doing as non-doing); and if, further, on the field of emptiness doing becomes manifest ecstatically as a true doing; then it follows that in us the doing in its elemental and original form comes to be as something that is directed toward all others and makes every other its master.

It bears recalling here, however, that this other-directedness or other-centeredness is an aspect of the mode of being of things in their selfness within the nexus of circuminsessional interpenetration. As such, it can only come about concretely in union with its other aspect, in which Dasein gathers all things to its own home-ground and becomes master wherever it is as the absolute center of all things. In other words, as explained in the last chapter, it keeps a collective hold (dhāranī) on all things in their dharma-like natures. Such is the self-directed facet, the self-centeredness of Dasein. I use the term "self-centeredness" here, but it is the self-centeredness of a self that is non-ego, of a "self that is not a self." It is *true* self-centeredness.

From this point of view, the character of the task belonging to Dasein means that Dasein forever realizes (actualizes-*sive*-apprehends) itself as itself in its suchness. It means that the self is forever becoming the self itself in its original sense. The task is to *actualize* existence as emerging into its nature from non-ego, and to disclose the "meaning" of such an existence, and in so doing to locate and *apprehend* that existence. In the light of what has been set forth in the former chapter, we may say that we "obtain the mind of" the nature of this task by adapting our own existence to its source.

What we have just remarked about the realization of Dasein as an emergence into its own nature from non-ego—as a realization of the existence of the self as a selfness—is no different from what was said earlier about "understanding" samsāra *qua* Life of Buddha in the Existenz of body-and-mind dropping off, dropped off body-and-mind. It is no different from the manifestation-*sive*-apprehension of the mind of the Tathāgata or "Buddha-mind." As for the self forever becoming itself, this is not merely a matter of the "will" of the self alone. It has to do rather with the "natural" mode of the self in its emergence into its nature from non-self, a matter of Dasein being at bottom and essentially a task unto itself.

When Dōgen says that the dropping off of body-and-mind is the practice of Zen, he seems to be suggesting the same thing. To practice or "observe" the Way of the Buddha is nothing other than the Dasein of the self on the field of emptiness. Here "doing" takes on the character of such a religious observance. Here *being* oneself is no different from *becoming* oneself or from *making* a self of oneself. For the vocational, tasklike character of our Dasein to be the shouldering of a debt without debt means that existence as such is religious observance. On the field of emptiness, the dynamic nexus of being-doing-becoming essentially implies that one is a task to oneself.

Although we speak of "practicing" Zen and "observing" the Way of the Buddha, this is not to suggest that showing the original countenance of existence in observance is a matter for Buddhism alone. It is implied in all true religious life. There are different interpretations of religious observance just as there are different ways of understanding karma, for example by the Self-power teaching (the so-called "Path of the Saints" exemplified by Zen), and the Other-power teaching (found in Pure Land Buddhist schools). Here, however, no firm stance is taken on any particular religious or philosophic view. My aim is rather to inquire into the original form of reality, and of man who is part of that reality, including as well the antireligious and antiphilosophical standpoints of which the nihilism of Nietzsche and the scientism found in secularization are examples.

If I have frequently had occasion to deal with the standpoints of Buddhism, and particularly Zen Buddhism, the fundamental reason is that this original countenance seems to me to appear there most plainly and unmistakably. A few paragraphs earlier, I located that original form of reality and man in Dogen's words, "samsāra *qua* Life of Buddha," there explained as the realization (manifestation-*sive*-apprehension) of the mind of the Tathāgata. That the self that radically becomes itself in this way shows us the natural emergence of the self from non-ego. But that same view is to be found in an advocate of the Nembutsu (the invocation of the name of Amida) from the school of absolute Other-power, Manshi Kiyozawa (1863–1903). In the opening words of his well-known essay "The Great Path of Absolute Other-Power," he describes the self as follows: "My self is none other than this being which is here and finds itself fallen into the present circumstances, 'riding on' and entrusting itself to the wonderful working of the absolute and infinite One, taking things as they come and living in accord with the dharma."[3]

Further back in history we hear echoes of this in Shinran, for example, in the passage that reads: " 'One who rejoices in Faith,' says the Buddha, 'is equal to Tathāgata.' The Great Faith is Buddha-nature; Buddha-nature is Tathāgata."[4] Or in another work: "The Nembutsu is the unimpeded Single Path."[5] The implication here is that the observance of invoking the name of the Buddha (or Nembutsu), while it is a human activity taking place on the Way of the Buddha, has nothing to do with the calculating discriminations of the observing individual himself. It is playful, unhindered "wandering." Such observance is no different from the "mind at play in the Pure Land" that Shinran mentions in his Buddhist hymns. Do we not see in this that same pointing to the original form of man and reality?

In any case, at issue in this essay is the investigation of that reality apart, for the time being, from any verdict on religious standpoints such as those of the Other-power and Self-power; and, for that matter, apart from any particular religious or philosophical point of view. This was also the intention behind pursuing the discussion of emptiness and karma. I have not been interested in them as doctrines confined to a merely Buddhist context. It was also on such a horizon that the question of the task of Dasein was dealt with.

To repeat, then, on the field of emptiness there is no difference between the self-directedness or self-centeredness of Dasein and that other-centeredness described above. They are one and the same task or vocation. This is quite natural and follows as a matter of course, in that the Dasein emerging into its nature on the field of emptiness is in the manner of non-ego, of a non-duality of self and other. From the viewpoint of other-centeredness, statements like that of Dōgen's, to the effect that before crossing over to the other shore oneself, one first takes all others across, seem no less to follow naturally and as a matter of course. For only by all others returning to the far side, the "other shore," to samsāra-sive-nirvana, where they are free of birth-and-death and thus are each in their own home-ground, can the self really return to its home-ground. Salvation for oneself consists only in the salvation of all others.

Conversely, we have a declaration like that of Rinzai:

If you meet a Buddha, kill him; if you meet a patriarch, kill him; if you meet a sage, kill him; if you meet your father or mother, kill them; if you meet your relatives, kill them. Only then will you obtain liberation and dwell in complete emancipated freedom, without getting emotionally caught up in things.[6]

From the self-centered outlook, this seems to follow naturally and as a matter of course. Here, in the self's becoming truly itself, the way by which every other returns to its own home-ground is disclosed as Dasein itself. That means that the Way of the Buddha, which exists for the sake of the salvation of all others, is grasped and sustained as Dasein itself. The field on which all others ought to find salvation (rather, the field on which they are at bottom saved but do not know it, and where their salvation is actualized when they do come to take notice of it) is one that opens up in Dasein. Coming to notice it is another way of saying that the self comes to trust in itself. And that means for it to entrust itself to the mode of being in that field and *as* that field. This is the "self-trust" of which Rinzai speaks as a self-trust that is, in its essence of self-benefit, at the same time essentially to the benefit of others. Behind the words of Rinzai, then, we see a profound natural compassion.

True self-centeredness means that through the absolute negation of the self that takes place in the conversion from the field of nihility to the field of emptiness, and from the field of karma to the field of non-ego, the self becomes an absolute center. I have described the field of emptiness, however, as a field whose center is everywhere and whose circumference is nowhere. At bottom, each and every thing among all things is such an absolute center. Moreover, in order to return to our own home-ground, we have to pass through a conversion away from our ordinary abode on the field of karma and nihility. We have to kill the self absolutely. And to do that is also to kill the Buddha, the patriarchs, and everything else, breaking through the field where self and other are discriminated from one another and made relative to one another. The self itself returns to its own home-ground only by killing every "other," and, consequently, killing itself. This could be called the self-centeredness of the formless self, or the self of non-ego that has cast off all so-called self-centeredness. The observance (and its Dasein) that sustains the "flesh and blood" of that self of non-Form, while realizing such a Way and such a field, is none other than the revelation of the Right Path for all others to follow back to their own home-grounds, by killing all others and thereby killing themselves.

This relationship of circuminsessional interpenetration harbors an elemental strife in the sense that Heraclitus speaks of strife as father of all. For each thing to be an absolute center portends a strife above all strife. Yet insofar as this comes about only on the field of emptiness and non-ego, this strife is at once an absolute harmony and an elemental peace. Any tranquillity that does not get to that point is tainted with strife, is not yet true tranquillity. On the field of emptiness, elemental strife and elemental harmony are essentially one. There strife is a strife absolutely without strife, a strife that is strife because it is absolutely free of strife, and thus a strife that is, as such, a harmony. The field of circuminsessional interpenetration is the field of just such a harmony. And at bottom, all things, in their elemental and original Form, become manifest on this field; and Dasein, when it emerges into its nature from non-ego, is the *realization* of this field. That is why self-centeredness only comes about at one with other-centeredness, and other-centeredness at one with self-centeredness. And this is quite natural and as it should be. That is, it is "dharmically natural."

In this sense, the words of Dōgen cited above must also be said to express this self-centeredness, which is at once an other-centeredness. Referring to the "King of Samādhis Samādhi," he tells us to "pluck out the eye of the buddhas and the patriarchs and *just sit* within its hollow." Referring to "self-joyous samādhi," he remarks: "To disport oneself freely in this samādhi is proper sitting in zazen."[7] Play is here the practice of Zen and the practice of Zen is play; this elemental play is elemental earnestness, and vice versa. It is the standpoint where non-ego is self, where the true self emerges into its nature from non-ego, the field of "body-and-mind dropping off, dropped off body-and-mind." It is also the standpoint where one takes others across before crossing oneself. Hence we find Dōgen remarking elsewhere:

> The zazen of the Buddhas and the patriarchs, already from the first steps of the religious mind, is a vow to gather in the dharmas of all Buddhas. Therefore, in their zazen they do not forget any sentient being . . . vowing to save them all and turning over to them every merit they acquire. That is the reason that Buddhas and patriarchs always dwell in the world of desire and negotiate the Way in zazen.

In the so-called King of Samādhis Samādhi, "the vow to deliver others to the yonder shore" is, as such, the play of "self-joyous samādhi." Zen practice is, as such, the standpoint of the debt without debt toward all other beings. Everything is a self-benefiting *sive* other-benefiting observance, what we have called the character of task in Dasein itself. Again, for this reason, the most solemn religious observance undertaken for the benefit of others is as such a playful samādhi; and totally free and unrestricted play that does not get caught up in anything else is, in itself, the most elemental earnestness.

Brief mention was made of the standpoint of elemental play found in Heraclitus and Nietzsche, but in the light of the foregoing, we are hard put to see those standpoints as having attained true playfulness. They do not contain the other-centeredness by which they become "empty" and make all others their master. The self-centeredness of their play lacks a meaning that persists in being at the same time a dharma-like observance. It lacks the character of observance on the standpoint of the King of Samādhis Samādhi that maintains all things in dhāranī in accord with the dharma (or *logos*). They cannot be said to have arrived at the authentic self-centeredness of absolute emptiness that holds all dharmas in its grip, that, master wherever it is, makes wherever it is true. However one looks at it, theirs remains a standpoint of "will," not the standpoint of śūnyatā.

VIII

If, on the field of emptiness, Dasein bears the character of task as described above, then what is important here is the infinity that this task essentially implies. Dasein is an essentially unlimited task unto itself. That it *is* itself, that it *makes* itself to be itself, and thus *becomes* itself, means that it owes itself an unlimited debt. And this in turn means an infinite debt with respect to all others. This debt can be traced back to the fact that Dasein exists within a world-nexus that is temporally and spatially infinite; that in relating to things it is constantly engaged in doing something; and that it originates in such a fashion within time.

Unlike what takes place on the field of karma, however, on the field of śūnyatā, Dasein breaks down the total self-enclosure of avidyā and goes back to its original Form of the non-duality of self and other. Instead of standing on nihility, it stands on non-ego. Breaking away from the infinite drive, it achieves a non-doing, that is, a doing that is free of the agency of the self.

In this sense, the field of emptiness is a field of absolute transcendence, a transcendence of time and place, of causal necessity, and of the very world-nexus itself. But this absolute transcendence is at the same time an absolute immanence. Samsāra-*sive*-nirvāna, it has been noted, is true samsāra and true nirvāna; but nirvāna, the absolute far side, only becomes manifest as samsāra, which is the absolute near side. The field of true emptiness becomes manifest only in unison with that dynamic nexus of being-doing-becoming in time, or rather *as* time. That is also the meaning of what was said before regarding true Dasein as a self emerging into its nature from non-ego. Dasein is in its very being-in-the-world a *not*-being-in-the-world; because it is a *not*-being-in-the-world, it is a being-in-the-world. As such, it is essentially free of any debt and, thus, also essentially shoulders a debt without debt.

On the field of emptiness, as a dynamic nexus that comes about at one with the unlimited world-nexus, Dasein can be considered under three forms. First, it is a samskrta (a being-at-doing) existence of infinite becoming within the world, coming to be and passing away from one fleeting moment to the next in time without beginning or end. It involves continually doing something.

Secondly, on the field of emptiness as absolute transcendence, a *before* is seen at the home-ground of the present that is before any past, however far back it be traced, and an *after* beyond any future capable of being projected. On this home-ground of the present, Dasein is eternal: standing at the beginning, and hence also at the end, of time, it goes beyond time, beyond the world and its causality (the "three worlds"). This absolute transcendence, however, becomes manifest only in unison with the absolute immanence held up as the first form of Dasein.

Therefore, in the third place, in the same way that we can speak of birth *qua* unbirth, and extinction *qua* non-extinction, every instant of time can be called a "monad of eternity." Here each point of time throughout a past that reaches infinitely back into antiquity and each point of time in the infinite future ahead that lies further than we can see is likewise simultaneous with the present instant. The present instant only becomes manifest as something that projects (reflects) in itself, as it were, every sort of possible past and possible future. Alternatively, the present instant only becomes manifest as something into which are projected (transferred) all pasts from the beginning of time and all futures from the end of time. The instant comes about as a dhāranī maintaining all pasts and all futures in the home-ground of the present. (This is why I have used the term "monad of eternity," rather than Kierkegaard's "atom of eternity.")

From a different perspective, in the present instant, the present is at the home-ground of all points of time past and future without ever taking leave of the home-ground of the present. For an instant is ever a present *now*; each point of time past and future, when it is constituted as time, can only do so as an instant. In this way, the present, while inexorably the present of time, is nonetheless simultaneous with each and every point of time past and future. The past never ceases to be *before* the present, and the future *after* the present; the order of before and after in temporal sequence is never abolished. That is, while each and every point of time is itself—the past inexorably as past, the future inexorably as future—they are also simultaneous with the present. In this simultaneity, the present encompasses all pasts and all futures and maintains a collective hold (dhāranī) over them. What is being so encompassed and so maintained in the present? It is not only what actually *did* occur in the past and what actually *will* occur in the future. There is also what did *not* occur in the past but *might have*. All those various possibilities that have been eliminated in the determination to actualization and have come to be buried away without ever getting beyond mere possibility also enter into the dhāranī of the present.

The field of reality as a circuminsessional interpenetration is at the same time, as a field of emptiness, a field of infinite indeterminateness or inexhaustible possibility. It is what the Zen phrase calls "the inexhaustible storehouse with not a single thing in it." And the Dasein that emerges into its nature on the field of emptiness does so as something maintaining a collective hold, in such an inexhaustible storehouse, on the home-ground of the present.

The idea of the present being simultaneous with every point in time past and future may sound rather farfetched at first. But if we bear in mind that the *beginning* of time is always in the present, and investigate the point thoroughly, we should find such simultaneity to follow naturally as a matter of course.

In everyday life, time is regarded as without beginning or end but also as irreversible. This, too, is an essential Form of time and the first form of Dasein given above. When, within the dynamic nexus of being-doing-becoming of Dasein, being as becoming emerges in the being-at-doing where coming to be and passing away overlap in the present instant, time comes to be seen as something spreading out endlessly before and after with the present as its point of origin. This infinity is, we have explained, the projection within time of the infinite openness that unfolds directly beneath the doing of the present and from within which the doing originates. And doing, as something that originates from this infinite openness, constantly nullifies being (or makes it impermanent). This nullification at the same time makes being into new being, so that being is constantly being constituted as what is becoming.

Insofar as this becoming is ever new, however, and doing is on each occasion something that is once-and-for-all, time cannot but be considered as irreversible. Seeing time as stretching out boundlessly before and after the present without beginning or end is tied up essentially with the fact that time is regarded as irreversible. Only of irreversible time can we speak of tracing ever back in search of a beginning and probing ever forward in search of an end. Conversely, one cannot speak of irreversibility except in terms of a time endlessly open in both directions from the present.

All of this is, indeed, an essential Form of time. Such things as newness or the once-and-for-all nature of the present are essential moments in the historicity of time. But when this one Form is considered in abstraction from the totality, it results in the standpoint of progress in the preeminent sense of secularization mentioned earlier: the standpoint of modern secularism. In its abstractness, however, this standpoint does not come to the awareness that the idea of time without beginning or end is only constituted in unison with an infinite openness in the present. This openness lies hidden, as the openness of nihility, beneath every single step of progress. When it does arise to awareness, the standpoint of progress can only collapse into nihilism.

Now this standpoint of nihilism already touches on the second Form of Dasein. For here, the beginning and hence also the end of time itself have already risen to awareness, and the horizon of eternity has already opened up, in the ground of the present. But this eternity reaches awareness as an eternal nihility, and on that field of nihility, the world is perceived intuitively as a whole—alluded to before in the sense that "there is nothing outside of the whole" (*Es gibt Nichts ausser dem Ganzen*). That is, here time becomes a circuitous time whose beginning and end are one, and the world process turns into a circuitous event, and as such, time and world are intuited as a single whole at the home-ground of the present.

Instead of a time without beginning or end, then, we have a time whose beginning and end are the same. Here time is not irreversible. Circuitous recurrence and irreversibility are mutually exclusive Forms of time. The recurrence of the same events implies an essential reversibility. While it is true that the presence of a beginning and an end to time in the home-ground of the present, and the opening up there of the horizon of eternity also constitute an essential Form of time (and of Dasein), yet the idea of a recurrent world-time is merely a standpoint that has abstracted this one Form alone. The present here is not a field where anything new in an elemental sense originates. Both time and the world process become but the same things repeated over and over. This repetitive world process was grasped in ancient mythical world views as the activity of *life* on the field of a so-called pantheistic nature, and in the world view of modern philosophy as the activity of the *will* on the field of atheistic nihility. But in neither case does the opening of the horizon of eternity in the home-ground of the present truly signify an essential moment of the historicity of time. They go no further than a mere dehistoricization of time.

We do not find in them, for instance, the sense of "moment" that Kierkegaard calls, in *The Concept of Dread*, "the synthesis of time and eternity." The form of eternity in the present can serve as the elemental Form of time (and, consequently, of Dasein) only in unison with the first Form. In his *Philosophical Fragments*, Kierkegaard, as is well known, gives the appearance of the "moment" in Christianity a decisive significance. And in any number of his works, he discusses "simultaneity with Jesus."

Leaving Kierkegaard aside, however, when our Dasein is seen at the home-ground of the present, at the point where time and eternity intersect, or when it is seen, as we have before, under the form of infinity, time at all times shows the form of simultaneity. In Christianity, for example, all creatures are conceived of as sustained at the home-ground of their existence by the power of God the Creator, and this is conceived, in a sense, as the ongoing creation of God. In modern philosophy as well, ever since Descartes, this relationship has been given all sorts of interpretations. But however it be interpreted, so long as it includes the sense of a synthesis of time and eternity at the home-ground of the present, the horizon of simultaneity opens up there. On the horizon of eternity, things that are before and after within time are projected (reflected and transferred) into the home-ground of the present, even as the present is projected into the past and the future.

For example, in the case of the "original sin" that marks the "beginning" of history, it is said that in the sin of Adam all men have sinned simultaneously, and, conversely, that the sin of Adam is still at work in the home-ground of existence as the inheritance of all men. We find the same way of thinking in the "judgment" that marks the "end" of history. The last day is considered to be already arrived in the home-ground of the present, or, conversely, the present is already on the field of the final judgment.

Such a view of time is no product of idle fantasy, but shows an awareness of Dasein that goes very deep indeed. The Will at work in the Creation and Providence of God is, from the side of the becoming of creatures, ever new, emerging as a sequence of once-and-for-all occurrences. But from the side of that Will itself, the whole must come about all at once. In a sense, the totality of time can only exist at a single instant. At the point in the home-ground of the present where the Will of God and creatures come into contact with one another, where time and eternity intersect, the things that occur as consecutive but once-and-for-all occurrences must be simultaneous. It is there that we have a field where irreversible time, without ceasing to be irreversible, becomes reversible. Repentance, the forgiveness of sins, resurrection from the dead, and the like, are inconceivable except on such a field.

I cannot enter into such matters here. Suffice it to recall what was said earlier regarding the problem raised for Christianity by the radically historical character in which time appears there, even though history itself is thought to have a beginning and an end; and also how the standpoint of secularism and its further turnabout to the standpoint of nihilism have emerged as a result.

The standpoint of karma has been viewed here as one which, like secularism, views time as without beginning or end and as irreversible, but which, unlike secularism, implies in its ground an awareness of nihility. Moreover, we have dealt with the standpoint of śūnyatā as a conversion from that standpoint of karma. It has been suggested that, on this standpoint of śūnyatā, the synthesis of time and eternity in the present instant means that all pasts and all futures are simultaneous with the present and maintained in dhāraṇī within Dasein. This means that the Dasein emerging into its nature on the field of emptiness does so within an unlimited world-nexus in a circuminsessional interpenetration with all other existents. Here all past and all future things maintained in dhāraṇī within the home-ground of the present—all things that appear in the world—become the liability and the task of Dasein as an unending debt (albeit, as a debt without debt). This task is in the manner of a "non-duality of self and other." It is other-centered *sive* self-centered, self-centered *sive* other-centered.

The original countenance of that Dasein is perhaps best revealed in the *Four Great Bodhisattva Vows:*

> However innumerable the sentient beings,
>   I vow to save them all.
> However inexhaustible the worldly passions,
>   I vow to extinguish them all.
> However immeasurable the dharma-gates,
>   I vow to master them all.
> However incomparable the Way of the Buddha,
>   I vow to attain it.

All are unlimited vows made in the face of unlimited realities. The original countenance of Dasein that emerges into its nature on the field of emptiness cannot be otherwise. It must express its essential nature of task.

The vow to save all sentient beings may be regarded tentatively as the other-directed aspect of that burden; and the vows to extinguish the inexhaustible worldly passions, to master the immeasurable dharma, and to realize the infinite bounds of the Buddha's Way, as the self-directed aspect. But both aspects—the traditional formula of "descending to save sentient beings" and "ascending to seek enlightenment"— are essentially interdependent and inseparable. Thereby, with all pasts and futures projected (transferred and reflected) into Dasein, and Dasein projected into all pasts and futures, Dasein is constituted within that circuminsessional interpenetration on the field of "the inexhaustible storehouse with not a single thing in it," on the field of simultaneity. (In contrast, on the standpoint of karma, we find within the concept of "karma from previous existences" a simultaneity similar to that found in the notion of original sin.) And just as, for example, the "dropping off of body-and-mind" was seen to be the practice of Zen, and the practice of Zen to be a playful "self-joyous samādhi," so here elemental earnestness is elemental play, and this play, for its part, is in earnest; and so, too, does everything become religious observance, and as such, totally unhindered.

Each moment of unlimited time without beginning or end is a "monad of eternity" that projects into the present the totality of infinite time; and the Dasein that emerges into its nature as such a time is itself, makes itself be itself, and becomes itself in unhindered "observance" that shoulders without limit all other things that appear within the unlimited world-nexus. This is a time of historical, causally conditioned being-at-doing, consisting of constantly new, once-and-for-all events, and is nevertheless an historical time firmly rooted in unconditioned non-doing. While Dasein comes about as this elementally new samskrta within an unbounded time and world, it is at the same time an absolute transcendence of time and world and thus, in mutual interpenetration with all pasts and futures, holds all the things of the world in dhāranī within the present instant. From there, Dasein as historical samskrta in the present emerges into its nature possessed of a historicity firmly rooted in the transhistorical.

While Dasein in the field of emptiness may thus be said to be finite to the core at each and every instant, it is also thoroughly rooted in the

eternal and hence is truly infinite. The unlimited vows taken in response to unlimited realities show the infinity in the home-ground of
the present, which is the infinite life of Dasein. In Buddhism, the
so-called Bodhisattva Path may be said to express the self-awareness of
such a life.

On the Bodhisattva Path, where each point of historical time
pierces through the field of emptiness, each time must be a time of
infinite solemnity. The most solemn moments of Christianity are perhaps the moment when God created the world, when Adam sinned,
when Christ was born and raised from the dead, and that moment at the
end of the world when the trumpets will announce the second coming
of Christ. Or perhaps it might also be said that it is when the self
experiences the *metanoia* to faith that represents the solemn moment
when the solemnity of those other moments is truly realized.

From the point of view of the Bodhisattva Path, the solemnity that
those special moments in Christianity possess is the very same solemnity that each individual moment of unending time possesses. We may
say also that while gathering all those times within the home-ground of
the present, Dasein realizes the solemnity of the present as a monad of
eternity, and thereby realizes all times in their true solemnity.

May we not say that a unique view of history comes about in all of
this? The three Forms of Dasein and time given above—let us call them
its forms of illusion, emptiness, and middle—are also one Dasein here.
This Dasein, although going in and out of these three forms, can yet
show its own totality within each of them. The freedom and self-sus-
taining of Dasein may be said to obtain here. And each of the three
forms becomes thereby something that reflects the three forms within
one. This one-*sive*-three, three-*sive*-one structure of Dasein and of time
is too multifaceted to investigate here.

The Bodhisattva Path is linked essentially with the question of
the so-called Great Compassion, or what is generally termed religious Love. It is the same with the vows mentioned above. I have
already spoken of the ground on which these come about. In what
follows, I should like to address myself to this question somewhat more
concretely.

IX

Having discussed above Kant's theoretical philosophy in connection
with the problem of knowledge, I would like now to say something
about his practical philosophy. Kant, as we know, stresses that the

"person" is an end in itself and may never be treated as a mere means. This person is the point at which the universal law of morality that goes beyond the arbitrary will of the individual and the true freedom of the individual actualize themselves as a unity; this point is both individual man himself as the original *subject* of behavior and individual man as the original *telos* to be actualized in that behavior. In this way, man's apprehension of the goal to be actualized according to the dictates of his own will (that is, as his own moral mode of being), invariably takes place within the self as the deepest expression of the subjective self-awareness of modern man, the revelation of the true meaning of human autonomy.

The standpoint of the person as autotelic and the concept of a "commonwealth of ends" formed by a community of such persons are not only clarifications of the most aboriginal base of ethics; they are also equivalent to the humanness of man reaching its apex of self-awareness. Indeed, the highest point man can achieve in ethics can only come through subjective awareness. But is the subject of behavior really encompassed fully by the self-awareness of such an ethical subject? Of course, the subject can only truly be subject as something having its roothold always and ever in itself, something that is, in its autonomy, self-sufficient. The mode of being of the subject cannot come about without this autonomy—or freedom to be one's own master. And the standpoint of the autotelic person is the supreme image of the essence of such a subject.

What I mean to ask here, however, is whether or not this standpoint of the self-sufficient subject that takes hold of its roots within itself does not rest on a still more fundamental ground. There is no doubt about the standpoint of the subject becoming manifest solely where the self finds self-sufficiency only in autonomy. But does the possibility of the subject becoming manifest in that way to begin with, does the roothold for the possibility of the existence of the subject, reside in fact in the subject itself? While autonomy is beyond doubt the essence of the subject, does this essence really belong only to the standpoint of the subject? Is it completely immanent to the subject?

Man is aware of the human within himself as his own essence. But can this essence—the fact that he is "man"—be exhausted by considering man solely from the standpoint of man himself? Does not the human existence that is thus aware of its own essence of humanness become manifest on a more fundamental field? In a word, the question is whether or not the person as an end in itself does in fact reveal the self-awareness of man at its most fundamental field.

From an ethical standpoint, it would no doubt be the final word on the matter to say that it does. But when we come to what religion calls Love (*agape*) or Compassion (*karuna*), something appears that has broken through the standpoint of person on which the ground of the subjective being of the self is seen only as autotelic in itself. Here the self is in no sense autotelic. Rather it is the negation of any such mode of being, even in its most sublime sense.

Of course, the standpoint of the person also presupposes a strenuous self-negation. It requires the will to refuse to be dragged along by the inclinations of desire and to follow the categorical imperative of practical reason, so that man's behavior may be in accord with a moral law. This self-negation, however, involves choosing one of the two orientations at odds with one another within the self and determining the self in that direction. That self-determination is the establishment of the person. And yet religious Love is absolute self-negation, a complete *renunciation* of the self as such. In that sense, it is fundamentally different from the standpoint of morality of the person, which is the standpoint of the self *prehending* the original self.

Even on the standpoint of the person, it is in a certain sense possible to speak of love. The person as autotelic cannot come about without at the same time acknowledging others as autotelic; for only through opening up within the self a field where others are also acknowledged as persons can the self also exist as a person on that same field. The standpoint of the person invariably implies a reciprocity that can only come into being through fashioning a community of persons—a commonwealth of ends. While this bespeaks a respect for the dignity of the person in oneself and in others, it can also be construed as a kind of brotherly love or "fraternity" in an eminent sense. The relationship between persons may be considered a religious Love of neighbor ("Thou shalt love thy neighbor as thyself") transferred to the realm of ethics on the standpoint of modern secularized man. It is as if religious freedom and equality had achieved their highest form of secularization in the freedom and equality of moral subjects in a Kantian personalism. But even though we can recognize a kind of fraternity in esteem and affection between persons, it is still fundamentally different from fraternity in the religious sense of Love of neighbor.

Kant's statement that the person is ever its own end and may never be treated as a mere means tells us that we are never to regard other people as *things*. When man's will is swayed by passion and greed, he always acts on the principle of self-love: others are approached as means (to gain happiness, for example), as if they were things. Morality comes about only through negating and passing beyond such a standpoint.

But even as the knowing of non-knowing that opens up the field that realizes the thing as it is in itself requires that the Copernican Revolution of Kant's epistemology make another fundamental conversion, so with the question of behavior, it is necessary that this standpoint of the person be radically inverted again. It is a complete conversion from the standpoint where the self is an autotelic person to the standpoint where the self is a means for all other things. The self that has returned to the original self, that (while taking a firm stand on the universality of moral law) finds its *telos* in the self itself, must break its way through that standpoint as well and revert to a self that finds its *telos* in all other beings. This standpoint, where the self returns to the home-ground of all other beings and finds its final "destination" in them, has to be opened up as a complete negation of any standpoint of subject or autonomy in any sense, even its authentic (ethical) sense. Here the self cannot in any ordinary sense of the term be an "end" unto itself. On the contrary, the self as person, including even its reason and will, the self such as it is in its totality, has to become a *thing* to all other beings. And this is possible on the field of emptiness as an absolute near side.

As remarked above, the self as subject is the self in itself projected (transferred and reflected) into the field of reason. This is so for the epistemic subject, but it is likewise so for the moral subject, on whose standpoint self-awareness as a subject comes most profoundly into view. When the self in itself is transferred in praxis onto the field of reason, that is, when the subject is subject as *practical reason*, it constitutes the most intimate and immediate projection (transference and reflection) of the self as it is in itself. It was also noted, however, that on the field of emptiness the being of the self in itself, as a being at one with emptiness, stands in a position that subordinates itself and makes all others its masters, constituting them as what they are and giving them their being. (Of course, this relationship involves a totally non-objective mode of being for both self and others.) Further, the self in itself was said only to be in its own home-ground and to become master by reentering into the home-ground of all things.

In such a circuminsessional relationship, absolute subordination and absolute autonomy come about in unison. Luther opened his essay *On the Freedom of a Christian* with two contrasting sentences:

A Christian is a free master of all things and subordinate to no one.
A Christian is subject servant of all things and subordinate to everyone.[8]

Of course, both statements amount to the same thing. Only he who returns in faith to the home-ground of God and receives freedom as master over all things can become the servant of all things, from the standpoint where his self is made into a "nothingness" and his auton-, omy as subject is negated. Conversely, only he who can be the subject servant of all things with a self become a nothingness can be the subjective master of all things while existing in the home-ground of God. Here we might discern the profound circuminsessional relationship between the self and all things.

For such a relationship to come about, the self must stand on a field of the mutual sublation of the standpoint of subject in the modern sense and the standpoint of substratum or *subjectum* ("that which is spread out underneath") of ancient philosophy. Such a standpoint is opened up by an absolute negation that makes the self into a nothingness in a return to the home-ground of God, and an absolute affirmation whereby one receives life in the Love of God.

This is how matters are formulated from a Christian standpoint, and an analogous situation pertains on the standpoint of śūnyatā. The following story is told of the T'ang Zen master Chao-chou (pronounced Jōshū in Japanese):

> A monk said to Jōshū, "The stone bridge of Jōshū is widely renowned, but coming here I find only a set of steppingstones and do not see the stone bridge." The monk said, "What is the stone bridge?" Jōshū said, "It lets donkeys cross over and horses cross over."[9]

This is the attitude of service and subservience to all things of the humble Sadāparibhūta Bodhisattva who appears in the *Lotus Sutra*, an attitude that someone speaking of Jōshū once described as "his practice of everyday life that follows in the footsteps of Sadāparibhūta, as low and modest as a bridge."

Now the standpoint on which one is able to lay oneself beneath the donkey's feet, beneath the questioner, and beneath all things, is no different from the standpoint where one is "master of all things." Jōshū's answer issues from such a standpoint. In this regard, Hakuin speaks of a "mind-master" in terms such as these:

> You must resolve to withdraw yourself this very day, to reduce yourself to the level of a footman or lackey, and yet bring your mind-master to firm and sure resolution. . . .

> When the mind-master stands firmly established, it is like a great immovable rock. . . like a range of towering mountains, like a vast and shoreless sea.[10]

Hence it appears that this autonomy, or "being one's own master," that comes about with becoming a *thing* and a means for all other things,

is a matter of a dimension altogether different from that of the autonomy of the moral subject. Here the absolute self-negation that sees the
telos of the self not in the self but in all things and the absolute self-
affirmation that sees the original selfness of the self in all things are one.
This is possible on the standpoint of śūnyatā. And looking back from
that vantage point, we are then forced to say that both the constitution
of the moral subject through locating its essence in autonomy and the
constitution of the person through locating it necessarily in a reciprocal
relationship are possible only by virtue of the elemental autonomy of
the self and the elemental circuminsessional relation of self and other.
All behavior becomes manifest at bottom from such an aboriginal field.
(This holds true, as noted earlier, even in the case of social praxis.)

Here, as we have said, the self, in being the self, is not the self; and
all our behavior, while it is invariably done by the self, is nonetheless
inadequately summed up by saying that "the self does it." As it is not
merely "the self," so it is not merely a "doing." Which is to say, it is not
simply something that originates spontaneously from *within* the self as
subject by freedom of the will. This does not mean that it must
necessarily originate from *without* the self, for instance from a material
relation of some sort or other. What arises of necessity cannot properly
be described as behavior *of* the self, or as something done *by* the self. In
their usual senses, neither the standpoint of freedom nor the standpoint
of necessity grasps behavior in its reality. Man's behavior is forever the
self's doing and, yet at the same time, forever not the self's doing. In its
inability to be expressed except through such paradox, it is true reality.
That is precisely why people in the past have spoken of it as the "action
of non-action." It is the free and unconditioned "non-doing" we spoke
of earlier.

On the whole, this is the kind of standpoint implied in what has
come to be called religious Love or Compassion. In Christianity, along
with the commandment to love God has gone the accompanying injunction to love one's neighbor as oneself. It seems to me that we have here
implicitly the very circuminsessional relationship that constitutes the
structure of all religious Love.

What does this "as oneself" mean after all? To begin with, loving
one's neighbor as oneself presupposes that men love themselves more
than anything else. But of course we are not being enjoined to love
others with the same degree of fervor with which we love ourselves.
Love of others is a negation of self-love. Moreover, the self-love of man
presupposed in such a commandment is grasped in its absoluteness as

something absolutely contradictory to man's love of God. Therefore, to love others must signify here the absolute negation of self-love. It is not a question of a superficial, quantitative comparison of loving others to the same degree as oneself. It has to do with the quality of the standpoint of the self as such; it is a matter of an essential conversion of the self at a point where comparison with others becomes irrelevant.

This is why Christianity holds that one can truly love one's neighbor only by loving God. In his *Works of Love*, Kierkegaard remarks apropos of the phrase "as thyself" that the injunction it implies penetrates unto the most secret recesses of a man's love for himself and carries with it the immediacy of severe negation characteristic of the eternal. It demands the absolute negation of self-love (and, consequently, of the self). It means making the self a "nothingness" and others the subject over against the self—making the self a servant and others its masters—so that every other is loved just as it is and where it becomes manifest as itself in its own home-ground. It means loving the other just as he is: loving him as a sinner if he be a sinner, as an enemy if he be an enemy. It is the non-differentiating love that makes the sun to rise on the good and the bad alike. Kierkegaard says that in his love for his neighbor, man resembles God and enters into unity with him.

But the standpoint of such non-differentiating love must be the sort of standpoint of *subjectum* or *hypokeimenon* ("that which is spread out under all the things of the world") mentioned above. The old metaphysics, in analyzing the nature of the existence of a thing, distinguished between its eidetic form and the matter that receives that form, referring to matter as a substratum (*hypokeimenon*). But here, of course, I am not using the word simply in that sense of an immanent moment in the constitution of the nature of the existence of things. *Hypokeimenon* is taken rather in the sense explained above of a field that makes each individual thing, with a totality beyond exhaustion by analysis, manifest in its mode of suchness. This field is not a moment immanent in existence but a field transcendent to existence. It is the field of the absolute *hypokeimenon*, which appears only through the self being made into a "nothingness."

To open up such a field in the self is to love one's neighbor as oneself with the non-differentiating love that makes one "like unto God." The non-differentiating nature of love, and the equality it contains, consists of all others, each and every one without exception, being loved "as oneself." Furthermore, "as oneself" means making oneself into a nothingness in order to return to stand on the field where all things become manifest just as they are. It is here indeed that the love of oneself is broken down even in its most secret recesses. But it is also here, and here alone, that the mode of being of loving all others as oneself can come about. When that takes place, this "as oneself" comes about where each and every "other" has its being as other, namely, at its own home-ground; or again, where all things are gathered into one circuminsessional interpenetration as a "world" and "All are One."

From the opposite point of view, we might say that the field of the world where All are One is also the field of the "transcendental apperception" of non-differentiating love where all others are loved individually "as oneself."

This state of affairs, in which each thing becomes really manifest just as it is in its own respective mode of being within a world seen as a circuminsessional system where All are One, is, in its original Form, what Buddhism calls "thusness" or "true suchness." But the field where this true suchness comes into its own forever opens up only in conjunction with the "as oneself." This is the original form whereby all things become manifest just as they are. To recall an earlier example, this true suchness appears when "a bird flies and it is like a bird." It is at once the very fact of the bird's flying itself together with a knowledge of its suchness. On that same field of emptiness, in the absolute negation of self-love, this "like" now becomes also the "as" of the "as oneself."

Such is the field where being is transcended. It is the field that serves as a roothold for the possibility of the existence of things as they are in themselves, for the possibility of the world. And as a field that brings all existences to manifestation, it is *before* being (in an essential, not temporal, sense). The opening up of this field in the self means that the self, in the absolute negation of self-love, becomes a *subjectum* lying beneath all things at their service, loving each thing "as itself" on its own home-ground. But it also means, at the same time, that the self truly returns to its own home-ground, where, having risen above all things, it becomes truly the self itself. It means that each one becomes "the self of the self," its own true self. All beings are here at the home-grounds of their own selves, just as they are in their selfness; and here as well, at those home-grounds, All are One. Hence the standpoint on which one sees oneself in others and loves one's neighbor as oneself means that the self is at the home-ground of every other in the "nothingness" of the self, and that every other is at the home-ground of the self in that same nothingness. Only when these two are one—in a relationship of circuminsessional interpenetration—does this standpoint come about.

If this is what loving one's fellow man as oneself is, it follows that the field where that love obtains is in fact not simply a field of the love of fellow man, a love between *men*; but must be a field of Love toward all living beings, and even toward all things. It must never cease to be a field where man himself can stand. And yet it is not a field given only to the human or to human relations. Here the self departs the standpoint of the autotelic person and takes up a vantage point where it can see its *telos* in all others and see itself as a thing (*Sache*) that is completely a means for all other things.

When St. Paul called himself an "instrument of God," he may not have been speaking merely metaphorically. His words express a mode of being that is, at ground, free of the merely human. It is the same mode of being that I have spoken of as the standpoint of the substratum (*subjectum* or *hypokeimenon*) underlying all things. When, in the old metaphysics, this was called "matter," this conception of matter was not the same as what we find in modern science. Yet they may have in common the character of being shapeless even as they constitute the foundations of things that have shape. Thus, matter is what things with shape return to upon dissolution or death. It can be called the outer limit of an existence seen as oriented to the death of things.

The *hypokeimenon* I have been speaking of in connection with religious Love, however, has a meaning altogether different from that employed in metaphysics. It is the field where the self is brought to utter "nothingness" in a religious sense, the field of the absolute negation or Great Death of the self. Here, where "we become dead men while living," is the field of absolute *hypokeimenon*. If we take matter or materiality, in either a metaphysical or scientific sense, merely as the end point of an existence oriented to the death of things, then the field of the religious *hypokeimenon* is a transcending of existence in an orientation to the Great Death of the self. Here the self, with body, consciousness, personality, and so on, intact, takes its place as a thing or as matter with the function of tool or instrument. In other words, without ceasing to be a human being, the self comes to a mode of being where it gets rid of the human. And that mode is none other than Existenz as non-ego, the Existenz of the "non-duality of self and other."

X

Granted that love of neighbor does come about on such a field, that field itself is not limited to the love of neighbor alone. The self is here at the home-ground of all things. It is itself a *home-ground* where every thing becomes manifest as what it is, where all things are assembled together into a "world." This must be a standpoint where one sees one's own self in all things, in living things, in hills and rivers, towns and hamlets, tiles and stones, and loves all these things "as oneself." And then, it hardly needs mentioning, the self is a self absolutely made into a nothingness.

Someone may object that it is not possible to love something other than a human being as oneself, since love in its original sense cannot obtain toward beings lower than man. And this is particularly so for religious Love, which is possible only between "persons"—an I and a Thou. The idea of loving all things "as oneself" might well be construed as a kind of pantheism.

In Buddhism, however, the religious Compassion extending to all living things is not merely a feeling of philanthropy or "universal brotherhood." It issues from the very essence of the standpoint of Buddhism as a religion. In the history of Christianity, we see something similar, for example, in St. Francis of Assisi who, it is well known, referred not only to his fellow men but to all things as his kin. When St. Francis addressed the sun, the moon, water, fire, and wind as his brothers and sisters in his famous *Canticle to the Sun*, he was not merely adopting a poetic figure of speech. That is how he in fact encountered them. I should think that for him every single thing actually *was* a brother or a sister, since each had been created, together with himself, by God. A field opened up where everything could be so encountered, because he had radicalized the standpoint where he spoke of "the little ones" (*minores*) so that he himself stood "smaller than anything," beneath them all. This standpoint opened up at the extreme point of his self-denial and self-dedication to God. Surely this is not a pantheism. The case of St. Francis may be rather exceptional in Christianity, but it serves us with at least one example of religious Love overstepping the boundaries of the human to reach out to all things.

In religious Love or Compassion, the highest standpoint of all comes into view. Aristotle, as we know, located the highest mode of perfection and happiness allowed to man in the "contemplative life." The self-sufficiency of that life, he held, is what brings man nearest to God: it is the life of the highest part of the human "soul," the part most akin to God. In that sense, it is the highest actualization of the character unique to man by nature and, at the same time, a life already higher than the merely human. But is this really the highest possible standpoint? Is such perfection and self-sufficiency, after all, true perfection or self-sufficiency?

Aristotle's ethics are based on his metaphysics. In that metaphysics, God, as the "thought of thought," exists in perfect self-sufficiency. As "unmoved mover," he is not moved by anything outside of
himself, but essentially takes all things of the world into himself in pure
contemplation. Conversely, all beings are essentially oriented in their
very being to God; they move while being moved by their *eros* unto
God. God is the "prime mover" in a teleological world. It is in this
self-sufficiency of God that man participates in the contemplative life.

Aristotle's grasp of the divine reality and its self-sufficiency, however, appears to be a one-sided abstraction to the transcendent aspect
alone. Self-sufficiency and perfection are not simply a matter of being
complete and sufficient in oneself (in immediate self-identity). Perfection must also include the field where things, however unfinished and
imperfect, and even things that work against perfection, such as sin and
karma, are brought into being in all their possibility and actuality. True
perfection comes at the point that Aristotelian perfection and its infinite
number of contraries and contradictories are one. It is the same with
self-sufficiency. When something is self-sufficient merely in an immediate self-identity, the "self" of that self-sufficiency, even though it be
the self of the one God who is *one* in himself and contains all things, still
retains a residue of individual ego. True self-sufficiency must not be
egoistic but rather a self-sufficiency of what we might call the "individual non-ego." It must be an "emptying" of self that makes all things to
be.

It is clear that the shift from Hīnayāna Buddhism to Mahāyāna
Buddhism implies such a conversion in the ideas of perfection and
self-sufficiency. It was here, of course, that the standpoint of the Great
Compassion appeared. The same could be said of the shift from the love
the Greeks called *eros* to the Love the Christians call *agapē*. Both bespeak
a conversion to a completely new view of God or Buddha, as well as of
man. But what relationship have these standpoints of Compassion and
Love to a world view?

Ancient Greek philosophy made a distinction between the form
(*eidos*) and matter of existing things and constructed a world view with
that form as its center. This philosophy conceived of a teleological
world with a hierarchical order of "being" as framework and God as
"prime mover." We have given as a common characteristic to the notion
of matter found in this metaphysic and that found in modern science the
extreme limits of an existence seen as oriented to the dissolution of
things with a shape, to the death of things. In contrast, in a teleological

world that comes about in an orientation to eidetic form, the contemplative life, including God as prime mover or "thought of thought," has been conceived of as the extreme limit of an existence oriented to the self-preservation of things, to the life of things.

In the new standpoint we have referred to, however, the world is viewed neither solely in terms of an orientation to death nor solely in terms of an orientation to life. What does appear on this standpoint is the orientation of the self being brought to a "nothingness" in religious Existenz, the orientation to the Great Death. It is the standpoint of death and rebirth implied in the phrase, "In the Great Death heaven and earth become new."

The world we have here is neither the mechanistic world of modern science nor the teleological world of the old metaphysics. It is a world on the yonder side of all such determinations, a world of *primal fact*, where each fact is bottomlessly on its own home-ground becoming manifest apart from all cause or reason or end, without How or Why or Wherefore: a world in which all things are truly "like" themselves and "such" as they are, and are encountered "as oneself" in their "suchness." The field of emptiness in which such a world comes about is none other than the field of the rebirth of the self—where heaven and earth are born anew in the Great Death. The self on that field is truly the "self" of the "as oneself."

The story is told of St. Francis of Assisi that, when he was about to have an infected eye cauterized, he turned and addressed the cautery:

> My Brother Fire, noble and useful among all other creatures, be kindly to me in this hour, because formerly I have loved thee for the love of Him who created thee. But I pray our Creator who created us, that He will so temper thy heat that I may be able to sustain it.[11]

And with that, he made a sign of the cross over the cauterizing iron.

It seems to be the usual practice to make the sign of the cross before a thing, either to ward off some threat it might pose or else to give it one's blessing. In this case, it was no doubt intended as a blessing. But in general how does it come that the sign of the cross takes on the significance of a blessing in the first place? What essential relation does it have to the fact that, with Jesus, death on the cross took on the significance of a love expiating for sin in the stead of mankind? If I may be allowed to hazard my own view on the matter: Could it not be that the sign of the cross made over the relationship between oneself and others signals the opening up of a field where self and others are bound together in divine *agape*, where both are made into a nothingness and "emptied out," and that this is where the encounter with others takes place? Does not the sign of the cross take on the significance of a blessing because in loving others "as oneself" in Christ, all men become one's brothers and sisters?

In any event, for St. Francis the purpose of making the sign of the cross was to solicit the love of his beloved brother, fire. This love occurred at the point that he emptied himself and consorted with the fire, and where the fire emptied itself (ceased to be fire) and consorted with him. When St. Francis made the sign of the cross in front of the burning iron, such a field opened up. And, in fact, the fire did not cause him any pain. As the doctor applied the cautery, drawing it from the earlobe all the way up to the eyebrow, St. Francis laughed softly, as a child feeling the caress of its mother's hand. And when the brothers who had fled came back, he chided them: "Oh cowards, and of little faith, why did you fly? In truth I say unto you, that I have felt neither any pain nor the heat of the fire."

We are reminded here of the Japanese saying, "Once you annihilate the mind, even the burning fire is cool." Of course, the fire *was* hot, and no doubt St. Francis *did* feel the physical pain. But the fire was not hot at the very point that it was hot, and the pain was not painful in its very painfulness. In the act of burning itself, the fire did not burn: it was not fire. In the very one that was feeling the pain, there was no pain: he was not himself. St. Francis and the fire consorted at the point that fire was not fire and he was not himself. Fire was indeed encountered as brother. In this encounter, the fire was in the home-ground of the fire itself, where "Fire does not burn fire" and where "Fire is not fire, therefore it is fire." And there St. Francis, too, was truly at the home-ground of his own self, as a "self that is not a self." When he blessed the fire with the sign of the cross, when he addressed not only the fire but water and wind, sun and moon, and all other things as brother or sister, was it not, in effect, an encounter on such a field?

In brief, in the circumincessional relationship a field can be opened on which contradictory standpoints—where the other is seen as *telos*, and where the self is seen as *telos*; where the self serves others and makes itself a nothingness, and where the self remains forever the self itself—are both radicalized precisely by virtue of their being totally one. It is the field of the "knowing of non-knowing" that we spoke of as no different from the "being" itself of things themselves. It is also the field of absolute freedom.

By freedom, we meant the true freedom that is not simply a matter of freedom of the will. When freedom is viewed as residing in the operations of will power that man is conscious of within himself, then it is already a freedom reflected on the field of self-consciousness and hence transferred out of the home-ground of freedom itself. Freedom as it is in itself is not simply subjective freedom. Subjective freedom, which is the cornerstone of so-called liberalism, is not yet rid of the self-centered mode of being of man himself. True freedom is, as noted earlier on, an absolute autonomy on the field of emptiness, where "there is nothing to rely on." And this is no different from making oneself into a nothingness in the service of all things. It is this that sets it apart from the freedom of atheistic existentialism expounded by Sartre and others.

The same applies to equality. True equality is not simply a matter of an equality of human rights and the ownership of property. Such equality concerns man as the subject of desires and rights and comes down, in the final analysis, to the self-centered mode of being of man himself. It has yet to depart fundamentally from the principle of self-love. And therein the roots of discord and strife lie ever concealed. True equality, on the contrary, comes about in what we might call the reciprocal interchange of absolute inequality, such that the self and the other stand simultaneously in the position of absolute master and absolute servant with regard to one another. It is an equality in love.

Only on the field of emptiness does all of this become possible. Unless the thoughts and deeds of man one and all be located on such a field, the sorts of problems that beset humanity have no chance of ever really being solved.

NOTES

1: WHAT IS RELIGION?

1. That the words "reality" and "real" are ordinarily used to denote something actually in existence might make it difficult to adopt them to refer to nihility, which is the absolute negation of existence as real. But then again, there are times at which we find ourselves saying, "It all came to nothing," and at such times we may well say that nihility has made itself *really* present. If we use "reality" in this sense, however, it might be better to make a distinction in cases such as the existence of things, and to speak there of "real being" instead (being in contrast with nothingness). In so doing, all real being would be reality, but not all reality would necessarily be real being. When I use the terms "reality" and "real" here, I am thinking of this broader sense.

2. Fëdor Dostoevski, *The House of the Dead* (New York: Macmillan, 1915), p. 216.

3. Cf. Immanuel Kant, *Religion within the Limits of Reason Alone*, Book I, 2−4 (New York: Harper & Row, 1960), pp. 26−27, 34.

4. *Notes Lamenting Differences* [歎異抄 *Tanni shō*], Epilogue III, (Kyoto: Ryukoku Translation Series, 1966, p. 79.

5. Jean-Paul Sartre, *Existentialism and Humanism*, trans. Philip Mairet (London: Methuen, 1966), pp. 32−33.

6. Ibid., p. 33.

7. Ibid., p. 30.

8. Ibid., pp. 44−45.

9. Ibid., pp. 41, 47.

10. Ibid., p. 47.

11. Ibid., p. 62.

12. *The Confessions of St. Augustine*, Book II, 4:6, trans. J. K. Ryan (Garden City, N.Y., Doubleday, 1960), p. 280.

2: The Personal and the Impersonal in Religion

1. T. S. Eliot, *The Waste Land*, I:60–63; cf. Dante's *Inferno*, III:55–57: " . . . sì lunga tratta / di gente, ch'io non averei creduto / che morte tanta n'avesse disfatta."

2. *Thus Spoke Zarathustra*, "Zarathustra's Prologue," trans. Walter Kaufmann (New York: Viking Press, 1966), sec. 3, p. 12.

3. I have spelled this out in further detail in my essay "Niichie ni okeru nihiri-zumu: jitsuzon" [ニイチェに於けるニヒリズム―実存 Nihilism in Nietzsche: the Existential], *Niichie kenkyū* [ニイチェ研究 Studies in Nietzsche], ed. H. Higami (Tokyo: Shakai-shisō kenkyūkai, 1952).

4. The similar concept of "emptiness" contained in Buddhism is what is called *śūnyatā*. Śūnyatā is the original nature of the Eternal Buddha, of Buddha as Buddha is, eternally, *in actu*. It is the unchanging state of perfection of the Eternal Buddha, present at all times and already fulfilled, always in the "present-perfect" mode, so to speak. In traditional Buddhist terminology, śūnyatā is the dharma-body of Buddha, the most original and authentic mode of Buddha-being. And as such, it represents at the same time the ground of the *sambhoga-kāya* (the "reward body"), that is, the ground of the mode of Buddha-being in its self-presentation as the Compassionate *Tathāgata* ("Thus-Come"). This Compassion is a compassion grounded in "emptiness." It is the so-called Great Compassion. Emptiness here takes on the quality and meaning of *anātman*, non-ego. Moreover, this emptiness that is identical with the Great Compassion is the ground of the *nirmāna-kāya* (the "transformation body") of the Buddha, that is, the ground of the mode of Buddha-being in its self-presentation in the Form of man as the Tathāgata Sakyamuni. Buddha, being originally "empty" and "without Form," takes the Form of the Thus-Come, whether as the simple Form of Buddha, as in *sambhoga-kāya*, or as the double Form of man-Buddha, and is revealed as such. Essentially this means an *ekkenōsis* ("making oneself empty"), even though at first glance it may appear to be just the opposite. The transition from being without Form to being in Form means non-ego and Compassion, like a schoolmaster playing with the children. In any case, throughout the basic thought of Buddhology, especially in the Mahāyāna tradition, the concepts of emptiness, Compassion, and non-ego are seen to be inseparably connected. The Buddhist way of life as well as its way of thought are permeated with *kenōsis* and *ekkenōsis*. Tathāgata is taken to mean both "Thus-Gone" as well as "Thus-Come." The reason is easy to understand, since disclosure is here inseparable from keeping hidden, being without Form from being in Form, emptiness from Compassion. That is, taking Form means a self-determination, and self-determination means negation (or self-negation). Compassion means a self-negation, a "making oneself empty," as a disclosure of the original emptiness. Thus-Come always means Thus-Gone.

5. See my *Kami to zettai mu* [神と絶対無 God and Absolute Nothingness] (Tokyo: Kōbunsha, 1949/1971).

6. "Alsô, als er mich durchbricht, alsô durchbriche ich in wider. Got leitet disen geist in die wüestunge und in die einekeit sin selbes, dâ er en lûter ein ist und in sich selber quellende ist." *Meister Eckhart*, ed. Franz Pfeiffer (Darmstadt: Scientia Verlag Aalen, 1962), p. 232, ll. 17–19.

7. Ibid., p. 66, ll. 2–3; XCVI:309–312.

8. Life and death are, by nature, contradictory opposites. Looked at fundamentally, from the ground where each of them presents itself in its own nature such as it is, they stand in absolute contradistinction to one another, as "eternal" or "absolute" life and death. Up to this point it is only a conceptual question of logical clarity. But then, along with that absolute opposition there appears the absolute inseparability of life and death. Although contradictory opposites in their natures and conceptually distinguishable as such, life and death make themselves present to us not as two separate things but rather as one inseparable unity in which there is full distinction without any separation whatsoever. The self-identity of this unity cannot be a self-identity in the objective sense, since nothing objective can be constituted out of contradictory elements. Were anything to be so constituted, it would be meaningless, a mere chimera or fantasy floating free of reality. The oneness in question here is absolutely nonobjective and absolutely nonobjectifiable. Were it taken into the field of the objective at any point, it would immediately cease to be absolute oneness, and would become an object of conceptual thought, thus falling into the duality of subject and object. The essential inseparability—the "absolute oneness"—of essentially contradictory elements, such as death and life, cannot be understood without giving heed to their nonobjective character. An understanding is only possible existentially, through immediate experience within human Existenz and principally through experience in the realm of religion. In order to express this sort of unity, the terms "life-*sive*-death," "affirmation-*sive*-negation," and so forth have been adopted here.

9. This is handled in greater detail in my *God and Absolute Nothingness* (see n. 5 above).

10. *Meister Eckhart*, p. 284, ll. 13–18.

11. Emil Brunner, *Wahrheit als Begegnung* (Zurich: Zwingli Verlag, 1938), pp. 92–93.

12. *Beyond Good and Evil*, trans. Walter Kaufmann (New York: Vintage, 1966), sec. 40, pp. 50–51.

13. The "Yellow Springs" refers here to the Underworld, or Hades.

14. Since for Eckhart the ground of God's being (*Gottesgrund*) is the ground of my being (*Selengrund*), and vice versa, the self referred to in the phrase "out of itself" is at the same time the true selfhood of the self.

3: Nihility and Śūnyatā

1. See Helmut Thielicke, *Nihilism* (New York: Harper & Row, 1961).

2. *Shōbōgenzō genjōkōan* [正法眼藏現成公案 The Treasury of Knowledge regarding the True Dharma: Absolute Manifest Reality], trans. N. Waddell and A. Masao, *The Eastern Buddhist*, N.S. 5, no. 2 (1972):133–134.

4: The Standpoint of Śūnyatā

1. This was Nangaku Ejō's answer to the question put by the Sixth Patriarch, "What is it that thus comes?"

2. Attributed to Ch'êng Hao, one of the founders of Sung Neo-Confucianism.

3. The phrase is taken from the saying of the Chinese Zen Master Chao-Chou (pronounced in Japanese Jōshū): "Do not remain where the Buddha is; run quickly across where the Buddha is not."

4. The allusion is to the Buddhist notion of attainment of the "yonder shore" of the sea of *samsāra* (life-and-death).

5. The story appears as the opening Case of the *Hekiganroku* [碧岩録 Blue Cliff Records]; see *Two Zen Classics*, trans. with commentaries by K. Sekida (New York and Tokyo: Weatherhill, 1977), p. 147.

6. See my *Gendai shakai no shomondai to shūkyō* [現代社会の諸問題と宗教 Religion and the Problems of Modern Society] (Kyoto: Hōzōkan, 1951), pp. 89–90.

7. This and the following quotations are taken from Book 10, sec. 27 of the *Avatamsaka Sutra* [華厳経 *Kegonkyō*].

5: ŚŪNYATĀ AND TIME

1. I have treated these questions in an earlier book, *Nihirizumu* [ニヒリズム Nihilism] (Tokyo, 1946/1973).

2. The six ways referred to are: the hells (*naraka*), the realms of animals (*tiryagyoni*), hungry ghosts (*preta*), fighting demons (*asura*), men, and devas.

3. This and other quotations from the *Shōji* [生死 Birth and Death] chapter of Dōgen's *Shōbōgenzō* have been taken from the translation of N. Waddell and A. Masao, *The Eastern Buddhist*, N.S. 5, no. 1 (1972):70–80. Their critical translation of the *Shōbōgenzō* has been appearing since 1971; plans are eventually to publish the whole. Another, popularized translation of the work is to be found in Rōshi Jiyu Kennett, *Zen is Eternal Life* (Emeryville, Calif.: Dharma Publishing, 1976), pp. 88–190.

4. To take another example, let us suppose you ask a friend to do something for you, explaining the matter and what it is you wish him to do. If he answers, *kokoro-eta* ("I understand"), he is expressing his consent ("You can rely on me"). Literally, the words signify that he has obtained your mind, the point of the matter requested, and also the meaning of the spoken words, all of which are implied in the one word *kokoro* ("mind-meaning").

5. These passages all appear in the *Hōkyō-ki* [宝慶記], a notebook kept by Dōgen during his study in China under Ju-ching which records his interviews with his master.

6. *Shōbōgenzō fukanzazengi* [普勧坐禅儀 Universal Promotion of the Principles of Zazen], trans. N. Waddell and A. Masao, *The Eastern Buddhist*, N.S. 6, no. 2 (1973): 121–126.

7. From the *Hōkyō-ki*.

8. Concerning this phrase, see my article, "Science and Zen," *The Eastern Buddhist*, N.S. 1, no. 1 (1965):79–108.

9. *Shōbōgenzō sammai ō zammai* [三昧王三昧 The King of Samādhis Samādhi], trans. N. Waddell and A. Masao, *The Eastern Buddhist*, N.S. 7, no. 1 (1974):119.

10. Ibid., pp. 121–122.

11. *Shōbōgenzō bendōwa* [辨道話 Discourse on Negotiating the Way], trans. N. Waddell and A. Masao, *The Eastern Buddhist*, N.S. 4, no. 1 (1971):128–129, 133.

12. The passage appears in Book V of Dōgen's comprehensive records, *Eihei kōroku* [永平広録].

13. *Hōkyō-ki.*

14. *Eihei kōroku*, Book I.

15. The "dust" [塵々 *jinjin*] signifies what is contrary to purity, clarity, and so forth: particle after particle of the trivial experiences and phenomena of everyday life. See the *Hekiganroku* [碧巌録 The Blue Cliff Records], Case 50 in *Two Zen Classics*, trans. K. Sekida New York and Tokyo: Weatherhill, 1977), pp. 284–287.

16. A well-known phrase associated with the Zen master Nansen (in Chinese, read Nan-ch'üan).

17. *Dokugokō* [独語稿 Notes of Monologues].

18. *Hekiganroku*, Case 82, trans. Sekida, p. 358. [The translation has been altered to preserve the sense of the passage as a whole.—Trans.]

19. D. T. Suzuki has formulated the logic of prajñā-intuition as "A is not A and therefore A is A. A is A because it is non-A." This he called the "logic of *soku-hi*" [即非 *sive/non*], *soku* (*sive*) here meaning the essential inseparability of two entities, and *hi* (*non*) expressing negativity. See his *Studies in Zen* (New York: Delta, 1955), pp. 119–120.

20. *Shōbōgenzō uji* [有時 Being-Time], trans. N. Waddell, *The Eastern Buddhist*, N.S. 12, no. 1 (1979):124.

21. *Fukanzazengi*, trans. Waddell and Masao, p. 126.

22. The original passage that this paraphrases appears in Hakuin's Zen commentary on the *Heart Sutra, Dokugo shingyō* [毒語心経 Poison Words on the *Heart Sutra*]. It is what is called an "attached comment," a pithy comment, attached to the utterances of Zen masters or to passages from sutras, meant to express in a free manner one's own appreciative interpretation.

23. Arnold Toynbee, *An Historian's Approach to Religion* (London: Oxford University Press, 1956).

24. Hubert Butterfield, *Christianity and History* (New York: Scribner, 1949).

25. I have dealt with this problem from a slightly different angle in an essay entitled "Religion, History, and Culture," contained in an earlier book, *Kongenteki shutaisei no tetsugaku* [根源的主体性の哲学 The Philosophy of Elemental Subjectivity] (Tokyo, 1940). I returned to the theme later in "Religion and Culture," *Gendai shakai no shomondai to shūkyō* [現代社会の諸問題と宗教 Religion and the Problems of Modern Society] (Kyoto: Hōzōkan, 1951).

26. From the *Dokugo Shingyō.*

6: Śūnyatā and History

1. The allusion is to the well-known verse in the final chapter of the *Diamond Sutra*.

2. See my *Nihirizumu* [ニヒリズムNihilism] (Tokyo, 1946/1973), p. 112.

3. Manshi Kiyozawa, "The Great Path of Absolute Other-Power," *The Eastern Buddhist*, N.S. 5, no. 2 (1972), 145. The translation has been changed somewhat here.

4. *Jōdo Wasan* [浄土和讃 The Hymns on the Pure Land], (Kyoto: Ryukoku Translation Center, 1965), 94:128.

5. *Notes Lamenting Differences* [歎異抄 Tanni shō], (Kyoto: Ryukoku Translation Center, 1966), 7, 30.

6. *Rinzairoku* [臨済録 The Records of Rinzai], no. 63.

7. *Shōbōgenzō bendōwa* [辨道話 Discourse on Negotiating the Way], trans. N. Waddell and A. Masao, *The Eastern Buddhist*, N.S. 4, no. 1 (1971):129.

8. "Von der Freiheit eines Christenmenschen," *Luthers Werke*, Weimarer Ausgabe, 7:20.

9. *Two Zen Classics*, ed. K. Sekida (New York and Tokyo: Weatherhill, 1977), p. 291; this is Case 52 of the *Hekiganroku* [碧岩録 The Blue Cliff Records].

10. This passage appears in the Hebiichigo [辺鄙以知吾 Snake (wild) Strawberries] of Hakuin.

11. Cited in *The Mirror of Perfection*, (London: Everyman's Library, 1950), CXV:291.

GLOSSARY

ACTION OF NON-ACTION [無作の作 *musa no sa*]

ACTUALIZE [実現する *jitsugen suru*] → **realization**

AGGREGATE → **skandha**

APPREHENSION [会得 *etoku*] After the opening chapter, regularly adopted as a synonym for **appropriation**. The Chinese characters that make it up connote respectively **comprehending** and **obtaining**, combining to yield the sense of the actualization of understanding in the **subject**. → **realization**

APPROPRIATION [体認 *tainin*] The literal sense of the Japanese is something like an "incarnate understanding," and points to a *real* understanding as opposed to a merely *notional* one, namely, an understanding grounded in experience. The same English word has been used to translate another term that Nishitani uses to introduce this one in order further to stress the element of "incarnate **obtaining**" implied in the actualization of understanding in the **subject**: *taitoku* [体得]. → **apprehension**.

ATTACHED COMMENT [著語 *jakugo*]

ATTACHMENT [執着 *shūjaku*]

AUTONOMY → **independence**

AVIDYĀ [無明 *mumyō*] Translated both as "the darkness of ignorance" and "fundamental darkness," the Chinese characters literally signify a "non-clarity."

BECOMING [生成 *shōjō*] Unlike the English word, the Chinese characters imply both "becoming" and "coming to be" or "generation." → **coming to be and passing away, extinction**

BEIFICATION [有化 *uka*] → **nullification**

BEING The Chinese character 有 is pronounced in Japanese in accord with its conceptual content. For the purposes of this book, it is sufficient to distinguish between the reading *yū*, which is used when "being" is placed within the framework of Western philosophical thought, and *u*, which is appropriate to its use in the framework of the Buddhist tradition. The text, as a rule, understands "being" as the correlative of **nothingness** and, in addition, ordinarily includes the connotation of holding, grasping, or being conditioned by **attachment**. It is to be identified with "true reality" only when it is finally subsumed in ultimate nothingness (see chap. 1, n. 1). Since however, both Western and Buddhist usages are found throughout the text with no direct indication of which is which, the meaning in each case has to be determined from the context. Its verbal form [有る *aru*] is set off in Japanese from the normal word "to be" by the use of the Chinese character in place of the usual syllabary form [ある]. In such cases it has been underscored (*is*), set in inverted commas ("is"), or paraphrased ("has its being"). The same holds true in the case of the frequent expression "mode of being" where the use of the Chinese character has been indicated by underscoring the word *being* or setting it in inverted commas (mode of of "being"). → **existence**

BEING-AT-DOING → **samskrta**

BODY-AND-MIND DROPPING OFF, DROPPED OFF BODY-AND-MIND [身心脱落、脱落身心 *shinshin datsuraku, datsuraku shinshin*] → **mind**

BOTTOM(LESS) → **ground**

CAUSAL KINSHIP [因縁 *innen*] I have translated the characters literally here as an English equivalent for *hetu-pratyaya*.

CIRCUMINSESSIONAL [回互的 *egoteki*] I have chosen the term "circuminsession" to translate this notion because the relationship it refers to seems to me to imply such a thorough reciprocity that nothing in Western thought can approximate it except this term used to describe the relationship between the divine persons of the

Trinity. I do not suggest that the Japanese word and the English word are exact equivalents.

CIRCUMINSESSIONAL INTERPENETRATION [回互的相入 *egoteki sōnyū*]

COMING TO BE AND PASSING AWAY [生滅 *shōmetsu*] → **extinction**

COMPASSION [慈悲 *jihi*]

COMPREHEND [会する *esuru*] The character adds the nuance of a "coming together" to create the sense of "understanding-through-encounter." → **apprehension**

CONVERSION [転換 *tenkan*] Literally signifying a "turnabout" or "switch-around," this term has been rendered by "conversion" not to convey any religious meaning, but in order to preserve the play in Japanese on the related terms "inversion" [逆転 *gyakuten*] and "perversion" [逆倒 *gyakutō*]. Note that the character 転 is also used to portray the "turning" of the wheel of **incessant becoming**.

COVETOUSNESS [貪愛 *don'ai* or *tonnai*]

DASEIN [現存在 *gensonzai*] In much the same way that Heidegger used the term *Dasein* to stress the here-and-nowness implied in the ordinary word *Da-sein*, Nishitani speaks of *gensonzai* in distinction to *genson* [現存], which has been rendered here as "actual presence." This latter term is used very rarely and should be kept distinct, in turn, from **self-presentation**. → **Existenz**

DHĀRANĪ [総持 *sōji*] Used here in the sense of "maintaining a collective hold on," the term is also used in Buddhism to denote a short, mantra-like invocation.

DHARMA [法 *hō*] This term is rich in meanings and admits of no one translation in English, even though Japanese uses a single character meaning "law" or "order" to render them all. In the present work it can refer to "things" (in which cases it is so indicated); to the universal truth proclaimed by the Buddha (where it is frequently capitalized in the translations cited); and as "order." Note that the same character appears in the term *rihō* [理法], which has been rendered here as "rational order," though without any specifically Buddhist meaning.

DHARMA-LIKE [如法 *nyohō*] Related to this is the term *nyohōshō* [如法性], translated here as "dharma-like nature."

DHARMIC NATURALNESS [法爾自然 *hōni jinen*] A term commonly used in the philosophic systems of Buddhism in China and Japan, denoting the ultimate form of "naturalness" that makes its appearance where assimilation with dharma comes to take on the character of "naturalness." It is also occasionally given in reverse order as *jinen hōni* [自然法爾] (as, for example, in Shinran).

DISCERNMENT OF NON-DISCERNMENT [無分別の分別 *mufunbetsu no funbetsu*] The sense of the Japanese word *funbetsu* implies an understanding by means of discriminating or distinguishing, for which "discernment" seems the best English equivalent.→ **indifference**

ECSTASY, EKSTASIS The same translation has been used for ecstasy referring to man [脱自 *datsuji*] and that referring to things [脱体] *dattai*].

ELEMENTAL SOURCE [根源 *kongen*] In adjectival form, translated simply as "elemental." The Chinese characters combine the image of "roots" and "wellspring." Although the context is different, the intention behind K. L. Reinhold's attempted grounding of Kant's notions of sensation and understanding in a common source (which he called *Elementarphilosophie*) seems to suggest a suitable translation for this important notion. → **ground**

EMERGE INTO THE NATURE OF [性起 *shōki suru*] The sense here is of the origination or emergence [生起 *shōki*] of a thing or individual into its nature [本性 *honjō*]. → **selfness**

EMPTINESS [空 *kū*] śūnyatā. In accord with the image suggested by the Chinese character, it is said to be "skylike" and is compared in the text to an all-encompassing cosmic sky. The same character can be read in adjectival form as *munashii* [空しい], thus creating a phonetic resemblance to *mu* or **nothingness**.

EXISTENCE [存在 *sonzai*] → **being, Existenz, Dasein, self-existence**

EXISTENTIAL [実存的 *jitsuzonteki*, 実存論的 *jitsuzonronteki*] Similar to the German distinction between *existenziell* and *existenzial*, the text uses two words for the same English equivalent, reserving the latter for allusions to Heidegger's idea of "existential (*existenzial*) interpretation."

EXISTENZ [実存 *jitsuzon*] The substantive of "existential," it is clear that Nishitani restricts the use of this notion to man, whereas **Dasein** can apply equally well to man and to things.

EXTINCTION [滅 *metsu*] The opposite of generation. → **coming to be and passing away, becoming**

FAR SIDE [彼岸 *higan*] The opposite of **near side**, this notion is intended to play on the Buddhist idea of the "yonder shore" of the sea of **samsāric** suffering, which uses the same characters. When this allusion is absent we have translated the literal Japanese equivalent for "far side" and "near side" as "yonder side" [彼方 *kanata*] and "hither side" [此方 *konata*].

FIVE HINDRANCES [五蓋 *gogai*] Literally the "five covers," these refer to the mental and moral hindrances of desire, anger, drowsiness, excitability, and doubt. It can also be written 五障 [*goshō*], thus recalling the word we have translated elsewhere as **hindrance**.

FORM [相 *sō*] A translation of the Sanskrit *laksana*, this notion is rich in meanings in Buddhism, among them: external appearance, phenomenon (as opposed to inner nature), mark, sign, characteristic, and mutuality. (In this latter meaning, it generally appears compounded with another Chinese character and has, accordingly, been translated any number of ways.) The upper case has been used to distinguish this Buddhist term from the ordinary and philosophical meanings of "form," for example, as *eidos* [形相 *keisō*], visible form or image [見相 *kensō*] and Kant's forms of intuition [形式 *keishiki*]. Thus we have been able to maintain Nishitani's distinction between such things as the form of non-form [無形相の形相 *mukeisō no keisō*] and the Form of non-Form [無相の相 *musō no sō*], and to draw attention to his use of the Buddhist term in such expressions as "real Form" [実相 *jissō*] and **original** Form [本来相 *honraisō*]. → **form is emptiness, emptiness is form**

FORM IS EMPTINESS, EMPTINESS IS FORM [色即是空、空即是色 *shikisokuzekū, kūsokuzeshiki*] "Form" here has the meaning of "thing." → **Form**

FREEDOM → **independence**

GRASP → **obtain**

GREAT DEATH [大死 *taishi*]

GREAT DOUBT [大疑 *taigi*]

GROUND [根柢 *kontei*] The text adopts a variety of terms to qualify this general sense of the "ground" of an existing thing. As the ground that is the source or birthplace, it is called a "home-ground" [もと *moto*]. A reduplication of the same term [もともと *motomoto*] refers to how a thing is "at bottom," that is, originally and by nature. As the base of **being** or **existence**, it is called simply a "bottom" [底 *soko*], and as deprived of that base as "bottomless" [無底 *mutei*]. As the place where it "takes hold" of its "ground," it is spoken of as a "roothold" [根拠 *konkyo*]. Finally, all of these terms, used more or less technically, should be distinguished from the wide range of synonyms used to carry the general meaning of a "basis" or "base." **elemental source**

HINDRANCE [障碍 *shōge*] Contrast with "non-hindrance" [無障碍 *mu-shōge*], the abbreviated form of which [無碍 *muge*] has been rendered here as "unhindered."→ **five hindrances**

ILLUMINATING INSIGHT [照見 *shōken*]

ILLUSION [仮 *ke*] The character carries with it the sense of the temporal, the provisional, and the ephemeral, in addition to the sense of "illusion", or more fully, "illusory appearance" [仮象 *keshō*].

IMPERMANENCE [無常 *mujō*]

IMPERSONAL → **personally impersonal**

INCESSANT BECOMING [生成転化 *shōjō tenke*] Although the Chinese characters convey the sense of the rolling of the wheel of **samsāra** and the migration of existing things through life, we have used the familiar English expression to avoid encumbering the text unnecessarily.

INDEPENDENCE [自立 *jiritsu*] The Japanese word lacks the negativity of "independence," connoting simply "self-standing," as does the word for "freedom" [自由 *jiyū*], which signifies literally a "self-stemming." The English word "autonomy" comes closest, etymologically, to both of these terms, but has been reserved to translate *jishu* [自主], literally "master of oneself."

INDIFFERENCE [無差別 *musabetsu*] The translation is Nishitani's own, but where the English word is not indicated, we have preferred its literal meaning of "non-differentiation," which does not carry the psychological overtones of "indifference." → **discernment of non-discernment**

INFINITE DRIVE [無限衝動 *mugen shōdō*] The sense of "drive" implied here is comparable to the German *Trieb*, which carries the connotation of an innate or instinctual dynamic of nature.

INFINITE FINITUDE [無限な有限性 *mugen na yūgensei*]. The contrast between **being** and **nothingness** is lost in the English.

JUST SITTING [打坐 *taza*]

KALPA [劫 *kō*] Aion

KARMA [業 *gō*] The text also mentions "karma from previous existences" [宿業 *shukugō*], literally, a karma that has "taken up lodgings."

KNOWING OF NON-KNOWING [無知の知 *muchi no chi*]

KNOWING OF NOT-KNOWING [不知の知 *fuchi no chi*]

LOCUS [場所 *basho*] Here Nishitani is clearly hearkening back to his teacher Kitarō Nishida (1870–1945), among whose last works is a well-known essay entitled "The Logic of Locus and the World-view of Religion."

MANIFEST ACTION [現行 *gengyō*] ⟶ **manifestation**

MANIFESTATION [現成 *genjō*] The word recalls the title of one of the chapters of Dōgen's *Shōbōgenzō* (see Ch. 3, note 2). The sense is that of the **self-presentation** of things as they are in themselves, without the interference of human reflection, in the completeness of the nature that was theirs from the start. I have chosen the English word "manifestation" (and the verbal form "to become manifest") because its etymology and history seem to suggest that immediate hitting up against (as Nishitani says, "in hand") that is beyond all doubt.

MIDDLE [中 *chū*]

MIND [心 *shin / kokoro*] Similar to the problem that the German *Geist* presents to translation in English, the Japanese word for "heart" or "mind" has no precise equivalent. It has been uniformly translated here as "mind," except for a single reference to the Buddhist expression "straight heart" [直心 *jikishin*]. Accordingly, we also speak here of "non-mind" [無心 *mushin*].

MIND-MASTER [主心 *shushin*]

MODE OF BEING ⟶ **being**

NEAR SIDE [此岸 *shigan*] ⟶ **far side**

NIHILITY [虚無 *kyomu*] Literally, a "hollow nothingness."

NIRVĀNA [涅槃 *nehan*]

NON-DOING [無為 *mui*]

NON-DUALITY OF SELF AND OTHER [自他不二 *jitafuni*]

NON-EGO [無我 *muga*] The reason this translation has been chosen instead of the more common "non-self" is that Nishitani himself makes a distinction between the word used for "ego" (for example, in his treatment of Descartes) and that for "self," and opts for the former to translate the Sanskrit word "anātman."

NOTHINGNESS [無 *mu*] The word is used here in two main senses: as a translation of such things as Sartre's *néant* and Heidegger's *Nichts* (its "Western sense"); and in an "Eastern sense" where its meaning varies according to its qualification as *relative* (or negative) nothingness (usually referred to in the present work as **nihility**) or *absolute* nothingness (usually referred to as **emptiness** or **śūnyatā**). When Nishitani speaks of *non*-doing, *non*-knowing, and the like, the added connotation that these are activities taking place within "nothingness" is implied through the use of the same Chinese character, instead of *fu* [不] or *hi* [非], which are simple privatives or negatives, here translated as "un-" or "not-" or "a-".

NULLIFICATION [無化 *muka*] This somewhat inelegant English word (and its verbal form, "to nullify") should be understood in the sense suggested by its etymology, as a "transformation into nothingness." The alternative expression *mu ni suru* [無にする] has been rendered literally as "to make into a nothingness." The related expression *nakunaru* [無くなる] meant to contrast with these two has been given as "to be annihilated" in the normal meaning of the word. The opposite of "nullification" is referred to as **beification**. ⟶ **being, nothingness**

OBSERVANCE [行 *gyō*] The sense here is of a "religious observance." The term "practice" has been employed in translating *san* as in *sanzen* [参禅], the "practice of Zen," and *shu suru* [修する]. All of this should, however, be kept distinct from the word "praxis" [実践 *jissen*] and its cognates.

OBTAIN [得(る) *toku/eru*] The Chinese character connotes a figurative sense of "holding" and hence comes to mean also "having within one's power" or "being able to." It is used in the composition of the words for **understanding**, **apprehension**, **appropriation**, and the term *jitoku* [自得], which I have translated as "keeping a hold on itself." More concrete words for "holding" are used in the text describing the act of "prehension" [把捉 *hasoku*] and the related intellectual "grasping" [捉える *toraeru*], which leads to "getting caught in the grasp of" [捉えられる *toraerareru*].

ONENESS [一つ *hitotsu*] Nishitani is careful to avoid associating this "oneness" with any of the metaphysical overtones or logical obligations that it has in Western philosophy when he speaks of something "becoming one" with something else. To preserve this difference, we have alternated translation of these phrases with "at one with" and "in unison with," and occasionally "in unity with." It is the **circuminsessional** oneness that is intended here, a oneness that admits of opposites coming together in a relationship of **sive** (see chap. 2, n. 8).

ORIGINAL [本来 *honrai*] This term is used in the text not only for such technical phrases as "original self" [本来の自己 *honrai no jiko*], "original countenance" [本来の面目 *honrai no menmoku*], and "original mode of being" [本来のありかた *honrai no arikata*], but also in its more ordinary sense of "coming from the origin."—►**original part**

ORIGINAL PART [本分 *honbun*]

PARAVRITTI-VIJÑĀNA [転識 *tenshiki*] The Chinese characters portray the sense of a "turn of thought," similar to what Greek speaks of as a *metanoia*.

PERSONALLY IMPERSONAL [人格的な非人格性 *jinkakuteki na hijinkakusei*] The text also speaks of the related concept of "transpersonal" [超人格的 *chōjinkakuteki*].

POSITION [自己定立 *jiko teiritsu*] Literally a "self-establishment," Nishitani pulls the Chinese characters apart and reassembles them to create the meaning of a "self-standing in **samādhi**."

PRACTICE —► **observance**

PRAJÑĀ-PĀRAMITĀ [般若波羅蜜多] The Chinese characters represent a transliteration of the Sanskrit word, which is composed of "wisdom" (prajñā) and perfection (pāramitā), combining to give the sense of a "wisdom that has gone beyond."

PREHEND ⟶ **obtain**

PRIMAL FACT [原事実 *genjijitsu*]

PROJECT The single word *utsuru*, when written without Chinese characters, is meant to carry the double sense of "to reflect" [映る] and "to transfer" [移る]. In these cases we have rendered the double entendre as "to project." The same pronunciation can be rendered by a third character, which gives it the sense of "to mirror" or depict [写る]. Unrelated to these is the use of the substantive "project" to translate the German *Entwurf* or the French *projet* in the sense that continental existentialism has used the word to speak of human life as an ongoing commitment of the self into the future [企投 *kitō*]. Finally, the English word is used to refer to the process of psychological "projection" [投影 *tōei*] in one context (chap. 5, sec. VI).

QUA ⟶ **sive**

REALIZATION Nishitani uses one of the Japanese syllabaries to transliterate the English word in which he finds a double meaning: on the one hand the sense of **actualization** or **manifestation**, and on the other that of **appropriation** or **apprehension**.

SAMĀDHI [三昧 *sammai*] The Japanese equivalent (the former is merely a transliteration) has been translated as "settling" [定 *jō*] and appears also in the phrase "samādhi-being" [定在 *jōzai*]. ⟶ **position, self-joyous samādhi**

SAMSARA [生死 *shōji*] birth-and-death. The same word appears in the term rendered here as "the sea of samsāric suffering" [生死の苦海 *shōji no kukai*].

SAMSKRTA [有為 *ui*] being-at-doing.

SELF-ENCLOSURE [自己－内－閉鎖性 *jiko-nai-heisasei*]

SELF-EXISTENCE [自己存在 *jiko sonzai*]

SELF-JOYOUS SAMĀDHI [自受用三昧 *jijuyū sammai*]

SELF-NATURE [自性 *jijō*] And its correlative, "*non*-self-nature" [無自性 *mujijō*].

SELFNESS [自体 *jitai*] Literally, the Japanese takes a reflexive pronoun and turns it into a substantive to yield "the oneself" or "the itself" or "the themselves." To avoid the duplication of terms, the one term "selfness" has been employed here. It should be understood, how-ever, that there is no implication of the **subjective**; the "self" has the same neutral quality that it takes, for instance, in **self-nature**, and merely points to the *per-seitas* of the thing or person in question.

SELF-PRESENTATION [現前 *genzen*] The verbal form, "to make oneself/ itself present" or "to become present," makes it clear that the term "self" is being used here simply as a reflexive. Roughly synony-mous with **manifestation**, this term should not be simply identi-fied with "actual presence," (→ **Dasein**) or with the temporal sense of "the present."

SENTIENT BEINGS [衆生 *shujō*] *sattva*

SETTLE → **samādhi**

SINCE TIME PAST WITHOUT BEGINNING [無始爾来 *mushi jirai*] → **time without beginning or end**

SIVE [即 *soku*] See chap. 1, n. 8. Nishitani frequently repeats the terms connected with *sive* in reverse order to stress their reciprocity; for example, "being-*sive*-nothingness, nothingness-*sive*-being." The same Chinese character can be inflected to yield the Japanese word *sunawachi* [即ち] (meaning "i.e."), although this tends to be written in modern Japanese by means of a syllabary, as indeed is the case throughout most of the text. Where the Chinese character is used, it has been rendered as "*qua*," to establish the proximity intended to the *soku* relationship.

SIVE/NON [即非 *sokuhi*] See chap. 5, n. 19.

SIX WAYS [六道 *rokudō*] See chap. 5, n. 2.

SKANDHA [蘊 *un*] Generally referred to as the "five skandhas" (or "five aggregates") that go into the composition of an intelligent being, in particular, man.

STRAIGHT HEART → **mind**

SUBJECTIVE The English word is ambiguous and includes at least two senses: (1) having to do with the private, emotional, and arbitrary reactions of the human psyche—hence, in opposition to scientific or "real" objectivity; and (2) having to do with the originator and carrier of cultural reality, with the historically creative human individual—hence, in opposition to the abstract and objective observance of cultural reality. Japanese has two terms, *shukanteki* [主観的] and *shutaiteki* [主体的], which more or less point in these two directions respectively. Although the context should generally make it clear which is meant, wherever possible the effort has been made to paraphrase the latter sense in such a way as to avoid the adjectival form "subjective."

SUCHNESS [如実 *nyojitsu*] The key element here is the character 如, which can be variously inflected and qualified to render the various cognates of "like," "such," or "thus." Nishitani plays on this fact in order to convey the connections between *tathatā* or "true suchness" [真如 *shinnyo*], the *Tathāgata* or "Thus Come" [如来 *nyorai*], and the "suchness" of all things. Note that this same character appears in the term **dharma-like**.

ŚŪNYATĀ → **emptiness**

SUPPLE MIND [柔軟心 *jūnanshin*]

TATHĀGATA → **suchness**

TATHATĀ → **suchness**

THREE WORLDS [三界 *sangai*] The three realms of sense desire [欲 *yoku*], form ("things") [色 *shiki*], and nothingness [無 *mu*].

TIME WITHOUT BEGINNING OR END [無始無終なる時 *mushi mushū naru toki*]

TRANSCEND [超越する *chōetsu suru*] Since the English word seems to convey the image of "rising above" whereas Nishitani wants to stress movement "to the ground," in one section he amended the English to read "trans-descend" at times. The first of the two characters in the compound, it should be noted, is used to express "going beyond," or simply "beyond" [超える *koeru*], to express the "trans-" of the following expressions: transhistorical, transtemporal, transteleological, transpersonal, transconsciousness, trans-form, transnihilism, and over- (that is, "trans-") man. The word we have translated here as "surpassing" [超絶 *chōzetsu*] also carries this sense of lying "beyond a breach."

TRANS-DESCENDENCE ⟶ **transcendence**

TRANSITORY [流転 *ruten*] *pravrtti* The double sense of "drifting" and the "rolling" of the wheel of samsāra is difficult to capture in a single English word.

TRUE EMPTINESS, WONDROUS BEING [真空妙有 *shinkū myōu*]

UNBIRTH [不生 *fushō*]

UNDERSTANDING [心得る *kokoroeru*]⟶ **obtain, mind**

UNHINDERED ⟶ **hindrance**

VERSE OF REPENTANCE [懺悔文 *sangebun*]

VIKALPA ⟶ **discernment of non-discernment**

VIRTUS [徳 *toku*] The Japanese carries the double meaning of the Latin, potential and moral strength, though it is only in the former sense that Nishitani employs it in those passages where we have rendered it as *virtus*.

VOID [空虚 *kūkyo*] The "hollow" of **nihility** and the "sky" of **emptiness** combine here.

WITNESS The writing of the word *akasu* in syllabary form is intended to convey the double sense of "to clarify" [明す] and "to confirm" [証す], both of which share that pronunciation.

WORLDLY PASSIONS [煩悩 *bonnō*] *klesa*. The number of these morally defiling "worldly passions" differs widely from one Buddhist school to the next, although the same basic meaning of the collective noun is maintained.

INDEX

Designer:	UC Press Staff
Compositor:	Trend Western
Printer:	Braun Brumfield
Binder:	Braun Brumfield
Text:	11 pt. Janson
Display:	Janson